KEEPING ARCHIVES

KEEPING ARCHIVES

Editor–in–Chief
ANN PEDERSON

Editorial Board
Sigrid McCausland, Paul Brunton, Tim Robinson, Kathleen Oakes

AUSTRALIAN SOCIETY OF ARCHIVISTS INCORPORATED
Sydney, 1987

With the support of the Museums Association of
Australia (NSW Branch) and the financial
assistance of the NSW Government.

First published 1987
Second Printing 1988

National Library of Australia
Cataloguing–in–Publication data

Keeping archives.

  Bibliography.
  Includes index.
  ISBN 0 9595565 9 1.

  1. Archives — Administration. I. Pederson, Ann E., 1943-
II. Brunton, Paul, 1950-   . III. Australian Society of
Archivists. IV. Museums Association of Australia. NSW
Branch.

025.17'1

Cover: Diane Quick; box graphics Sheryl Stephens
Design and Printing Liaison: Diane Quick
Typesetting: Set in English in 10/11pt Cheltenham
               by Dovatype, Melbourne VIC
Printing: Printed on 100gsm Glopaque by Australian
            Print Group, Maryborough, VIC
Binding: Soft, sewn, drawn–on cover by Advance
           Bookbinders, Adelaide, SA
Published by: Australian Society of Archivists Incorporated, P.O. Box 83,
               O'Connor ACT 2601 Australia. Telephone enquiries (02) 660-2611.

CONTENTS

ACKNOWLEDGEMENTS

Editors
Editor-in-Chief: Ann Pederson
Editorial Board: Sigrid McCausland, Paul Brunton, Tim Robinson, Kathleen Oakes

Authors
Gunnel Bellviken, Paul Brunton, Averil Condren, Sandra Hinchey, Sigrid McCausland, Kathleen Oakes, Ann Pederson, Michael Piggott, Barbara Reed, David Roberts, Tim Robinson, Anne-Marie Schwirtlich, Clive Smith

Drawings
Marion Sully, Diane Quick

Indexing
Averil Condren

Photography:
Ann Pederson. *Additional photographs* — Archives of Business and Labour, Australian National University; Archives Office of New South Wales; Council of the City of Sydney Archives; Tim Robinson; State Library of New South Wales; University of New South Wales

Contributors
Baiba Berzins, Neville Corbett, Ken Smith for their early work on the project and many other colleagues who assisted with suggestions and proofreading.

Special Thanks to Dr. Ann M. Mitchell, Christine McBrearty, Joan Fisher, Ray Locke, Peach Feliciano, Angela McGing, Anne Wilson, and the Westpac Banking Corporation Archives staff.

PREFACE

This book has been written as an introductory manual for those who are interested in or have been given responsibility for the keeping of archives. We welcome you as potential archivists and offer the assurance that you have chosen a fascinating area of involvement.

Keeping Archives is the result of collaboration on the part of many Australian archivists and represents a very considerable achievement. Not only is it the first comprehensive Australian book in the field of archives administration, it is the first book in the English language which reflects a consensus of experience and practice among archivists working in many different environments.

Each chapter has been examined by the editors, revised by the authors and examined again by the editors. The result is a true collaboration representing many types of archives, large and small, public and private.

The purpose of this manual is to provide practical guidelines based on sound archival principles and wide experience for the management of archival and manuscripts collections, however small. It is our hope that your reading of this book will be the beginning of a continuing involvement which will increase your confidence and skill in the keeping of archives. The best way to ensure this is to make personal contact with those practising the profession in Australia through membership in the Australian Society of Archivists Incorporated (ASA). Information about the Society can be obtained from the Secretary, P.O. Box 83, O'Connor, ACT 2601.

The authors and editors have freely given their time and knowledge to this project and any profits of this printing will be used by the ASA to continue its work on behalf of all who care for archival collections in Australia. We should like to record our deep appreciation to the Museums Association of Australia (NSW Branch) for their inspiration and assistance in applying to the New South Wales government for a grant which contributed substantially to meeting the costs of book production.

CHAPTER ONE

INTRODUCING ARCHIVES AND THE ARCHIVAL PROFESSION

Anne-Marie Schwirtlich

INTRODUCTION

What do archivists say when asked 'What do you do?' I am tempted to say that I build bridges.

Why? Because as archivists we are responsible for making sure:

- people today can reconstruct yesterday
- people tomorrow can reconstruct today
- archives are physically preserved and made available

We build bridges for people to move between time and place. How the bridges are built are what this book is about.

This introductory chapter concentrates on the context in which archival work is performed. It describes the environment in which the profession and the institutions operate and the principles underpinning our approach.

We hope that we can convey the strength of our purpose, our enthusiasm, our practices and our sense of community so that you will join us.

WHAT ARE ARCHIVES?

Someone mentions the word 'archives'. What does it mean to you? Table One provides a quick illustration of the three meanings of the word. It can mean the archival programme, the building housing the archival material or the archival material itself.

Archives: The Programme

The archives programme is a shorthand way of referring to:

- what we do
- how we go about doing it
- why we do it

So an archives programme is about the technical work completed — its standards, form, purpose, methods — and about
managing an organisational unit that requires funds, staff, equipment and accommodation to function.

With this manual we hope to share our knowledge about our
technical work. Not only what the objectives and responsibilities
of each area are but also the principles involved, the processes
used, the decisions that need to be made and the possible problems that will be encountered. The technical areas of our work
are those such as accessioning, appraisal, arrangement and
description — all of which are dealt with in later chapters. So the
archives programme is about the efficient and professional conduct of these functions.

The archival programme is also about managing. To run the
programme successfully you need to seek, acquire and manage
money, people, accommodation and equipment. Regardless of
the calibre of its technical work, no archives can perform
effectively if it does not have the direction and vision to proceed
purposefully and the wherewithal to do so.

Archives programmes are also people orientated. The success
of a programme depends on decisions that a variety of people —
records creators, depositors, users, advisers, financiers — make.
If they are dealt with considerately and are inspired and con-
vinced by the programme's purpose and administration they can
be instrumental in securing its success.

The programme needs to be sensitive to the professional,
administrative and financial environments in which it functions,
and to changes in those environments. An archival programme
needs to be based on sound reflection, principles and research.
This should ensure that it serves a purpose for its community, its
users, and its administrators.

Archives: The Building

The second sense in which archives is used is to denote the building, part of the building, or storage area in which the archival
materials are housed.

The prime objective of archival accommodation is the physical protection of the material it houses. However, it must also provide for the people working on, and with, the records and should
be designed to maximise the use of the available space and facilitate the flow of work.

Archival material does need protection. It needs to be protected from the elements, from the environment (particularly if it
is polluted) and any erratic changes in it, from insects and ani-
mals and from careless or malicious people.

Consequently archival buildings do have special requirements. The quality of material requiring protection and the
money available will determine the size and level of sophistication of the fabric and fittings of your building. The showpieces

Table One   Archives Are

1) The non-current records
    of an organisation,
    institution or individual
    which are selected for pres-
    ervation because of their
    continuing value.

2) The repository or building
    (or part thereof) where
    archival material is stored.

3) An agency responsible for
    the selection, preservation,
    documentation and mak-
    ing available of archival
    material.

The Archives Office of New South Wales. Courtesy — Archives Office of NSW.

of archival architecture tend to be those buildings commissioned by the national and state archival agencies. However, it is essential to remember that with planning and thought (as demonstrated in Chapter Two) many areas of existing buildings can be suitably adapted to provide for those of us who neither need nor can afford special buildings.

Archives: The Records

Some years ago a researcher approached several government archives trying to trace the records of one of the National Australasian Conventions. The researcher was working on the development of the Australian constitution which had resulted from the deliberations of several Conventions at which eminent representatives of each of the Colonies gathered. Initial enquiries established that the records were not in archival custody. Contact was made with the responsible government office to ascertain why records of such importance and value had not been transferred to archival custody.

Officers from the government agency, which had stored the material in a basement, advised 'Yes, of course we've got them.' It was pointed out that after almost one hundred years the records could not possibly still be used to transact business. The officers replied 'No, but as a special treat we go to look at them.'

The characteristics that the Convention records share with all other archives are:

- that they merit permanent preservation because of certain intrinsic factors — they are significant for administrative and historical reasons
- that they were created in the course of the normal business of an organisation but are no longer required for the effective conduct of that business

Sir Hilary Jenkinson succinctly identified the properties of archives:

> Archives are the documents accumulated by a natural process in the course of the conduct of affairs of any kind, public or private, at any date; and preserved thereafter for reference, in their own custody, by the persons responsible for the affairs in question or their successors.[1]

Organisations and individuals create and maintain records. For example, we document our lives and interests by writing letters and diaries, recording our thoughts on cassette; we save

Audio tapes, testimonials, videos, computer printouts and diaries differ in form but may all be archives. Courtesy — State Library of NSW.

---

[1] Hilary Jenkinson, *The English Archivist: A New Profession.* London:' H.K. Lewis, 1948.

menus, bus tickets and postcards; we keep cheque books, bank books and income tax statements; we hoard school reports, birth and marriage certificates; and we record important moments by taking photographs or making films and videos.

Similarly, governments, businesses and organisations have legal, financial, personnel, and administrative records which may also be in varied formats, such as registers, cards, microforms and computer files.

Whether created by persons or organisations, these documents, cassettes, films, photographs, plans and printouts are not all worthy of permanent preservation as archives. It has been estimated by archivists that 90%–95% of the records generated should be destroyed once they have outlived their usefulness for the conduct of business and have satisfied any other values, for example, government, legal and financial requirements.

The remaining 5%–10% of records are those identified as archives. Based on these points, we can say that all archives are records, but not all records are archives.

Archives are not usually transferred to archival care or custody until they are no longer needed for everyday business. Nonetheless it is important to identify these records or items as archives. Care should be shown in the way they are created, for example, using archival quality paper or film. They should be afforded good storage and it should be impressed on the people handling them that they are handling archives.

Records are created in all shapes, sizes and formats. Because archives are those records that are selected for permanent preservation it follows that archives too will be in all shapes, sizes and formats. For example, drawings, pamphlets, posters, files, charts, volumes, bundles of papers, photographs, invoices, magnetic tapes, film.

The diversity of formats in which information is recorded or conveyed can lead one to wonder 'Should archivists accept anything worthy of permanent preservation?' What happens to Edmund Barton's desk when his archives are transferred to the National Library? Where do Rod Laver's trophies and racquets go if his archives go to the John Oxley Library?

Our response should be to consider the interests of the object or artefact. These items are frequently rare, delicate and complex. They need specialised care and storage environments and they require expertise in their interpretation and control. It is in their best interest to be placed in the custody of professionals, in this case museum curators, who can accord them this care. When making arrangements to place this material in the custody of another institution it is vital to document the links between the archival material and artefacts and to negotiate an agreement that would allow the artefacts to be borrowed for the purposes of exhibition.

ARCHIVES — WHY DO WE KEEP THEM?

The fundamental reason for keeping archives is that they serve as a memory.

Just as individuals dysfunction without a memory so do organisations. Without archival recall they would have no perspective on which to base planning, nothing to prevent them repeating mistakes, no expertise or knowledge except what people remembered, perhaps inaccurately, no way of proving entitlements or ownership or of accounting for their actions. The extra research and energy required to reconstruct missing information can be very expensive, if it can be done at all — that is why we keep archives.

We also keep archives for broader reasons that can be called 'historical' or 'cultural' in addition to financial and administrative reasons. For example, the archives of the Westpac Banking Corporation (formerly the Bank of New South Wales) are vital to the Corporation. But Westpac's archives also form part of the rich memory of the nation as the Bank is our oldest financial institution and has played a very significant role in the development of Australia. All archives share this dual function; they are an essential resource to their creators and provide evidence of their important work over time to the wider community.

ARCHIVAL PRINCIPLES

An acute consciousness that unique materials with evidential value were being handled led early archival theorists to establish the two principles upon which archival work is founded.

The principles and their application are fully addressed in Chapter Five Arrangement and Description. However, by foreshadowing them here we can appreciate the forces guiding archival work, the responsibilities of archivists, and the basis for the difference in approach of archivists and other custodial professionals, for example, museum curators and librarians.

The principles are those of provenance and respect for original order. The principle of provenance requires that the archives of an organisation or person not be mixed or combined with the archives of another. Therefore, an archivist holding the records of the Waterside Workers Federation and the Foremen and Stevedores Association would not consolidate the records from the two organisations even though both are unions, both operate in the same sphere and both create similiar records, for example, membership records, dispute and arbitration records, financial records and minutes.

The principle of original order requires that the order in which an organisation or person created, maintained and used records be respected and preserved. Therefore, if you receive into custody files that are arranged numerically by postcode it is essential to retain them in that order. It does not matter if you believe that

Students learn principles of archival conservation in a workshop.

arranging them alphabetically by suburb name would make them easier to use. The fact that they were organised numerically and used numerically by their creators requires them to be maintained that way in archival custody. Discerning the original order and interpreting the context and use of the records pose the archival challenge and require the exercise of professional skills.

Why is it important to adhere to these principles? Archives are unique, organic materials with evidential and informational properties. These principles are designed to preserve these essential qualities. This means that archives in custody can still be used by their creators because their system of control is intact. It also enables successive generations of researchers to refer to the archives in their original state. It enables them to analyse, deduce and interpret for themselves.

ARCHIVES AND RELATED PROFESSIONS: RECORDS MANAGERS, LIBRARIANS AND MUSEUM CURATORS

Curators, records managers, librarians and archivists are guided by different technical principles, and they deal with materials that differ in terms of their origins and characteristics.

If the life of a record were plotted on a continuum it would be apparent how allied the work of records managers and archivists are. Records managers design programmes to provide economic, efficient and systematic control over the creation, distribution, organisation, maintenance, retrieval, use, protection and disposal of the active records of an organisation. Archivists are the custodians of those portions of their records systems — regardless of their format — that are judged worthy of permanent preservation.

Librarians usually acquire, by purchase, published material which, by its nature, is not unique and can be replaced. The material may be in many formats and is usually consciously acquired to serve the library's community. Therefore, a local library, a hospital library and a university library would each have different collecting policies.

Librarians also seek to arrange and control the material in their collections. This is accomplished by referring to a predetermined classification, such as the Dewey Decimal System, which provides a classification by subject for all information, and applying the appropriate classification. The number which is allocated to the item designates its 'address' on the shelf and denotes something about its content.

Usually librarians work with materials that are fully identified, for example, they have authors, publishers and titles and they require no examination to determine their internal arrangement. Two other important features of their work relate to access and use of their collections. Users may examine catalogues to determine items of interest but they may also browse unrestricted through the collection. Having selected items of interest they may be borrowed and removed from the library's premises.

Museum curators seek to acquire objects and artefacts, and any associated documentation that may shed light on their characteristics, uses and importance. These objects or artefacts may be unique, for example, the prototype of the orbital engine, or may be representative of something extremely common but significant to daily life of the time, for example, a telephone. They seek to acquire material that is relevant to, and will reflect, their institution's role and objectives. For example, a mining museum, a museum of performing arts and a social history museum would each have different objectives, roles, clients and therefore collecting policies. Curators also seek to control the material in their collections. This is done by systematically allocating a permanent, unique number to each item in the collection. The number need not reflect anything about the location or characteristics of the item — it is purely a mechanism to link the item to the paperwork about it.

Table Two 'What's the Difference? Registries; Archives; Libraries; Museums' summarises the differences and similarities of the work of the four professions. The skills, the experience and the principles that a practitioner of each brings to his/her work vary. Where they do not differ is that each is a protector of material in custody, a controller of the material in custody and the intermediary between the collection and the user.

Unlike library materials, archival records cannot be borrowed or browsed and must be used in a supervised reading area. Courtesy — Archives of Business and Labour, ANU.

Table Two   What's the Difference?

	Registries	Archives	Libraries	Museums
What do they keep?	Create and control the active records needed for conduct of business.	Inactive records that have been selected for permanent preservation. Usually unpublished (can be in any format) and unique.	Published material (can be in many formats, e.g. film, microfiche, cassettes) that is not unique.	Objects and artefacts (& associated documentation) which may or may not be unique.
How is the material arranged?	System of arrangement and control chosen/devised and imposed by records managers.	In the order determined and used by the creator(s).	According to a predetermined classification system (e.g. Library of Congress).	Arrangement is not significant. Control is.
Who can consult the material?	Employees of the organisation requiring the records to undertake their work.	Depends on archives policy (e.g. serious scholars only, anyone over 18) and on conditions imposed by depositor/donor.	Any member of their community (e.g. at a school library any student or teacher).	Any member of the public.
How do you find what you want?	Records managers maintain and consult indexes, registers etc. to determine appropriate items.	Through consultation of guides, inventories and other documentation made available to researchers.	By consulting name and subject catalogues or by browsing through the shelves.	You may only examine what is on exhibition or display.
Where do you consult the material?	Items may be removed from registry once assigned to you.	In the search room on the archives' premises and under supervision.	On the premises or, if you borrow, anywhere you wish.	In the display galleries or exhibition areas.
What is their objective?	Efficient, economic and systematic control and retrieval of records needed for conduct of business.	Protection of archives and their evidential and informational values.	Building appropriate and comprehensive collections that are properly housed, controlled and effectively used.	Collection and protection of selected objects for the community.
Why do you visit?	To undertake your duties.	For proof of transactions and actions, to study, undertake research, for enjoyment.	For educational and recreational purposes.	For educational, aesthetic or recreational reasons.
Who looks after the material?	Records Managers.	Archivists.	Librarians.	Museum Curators.

THE ARCHIVAL PROFESSION

Institutions and people have cared for archives in Australia for over a century. However, the archival profession is a relatively young one. Three of the most significant events for the profession have occurred only in the last thirteen years.

The first was the offering of the Diploma in Archives Administration, by the University of New South Wales, in 1973, as the only accredited and professional qualification for people wishing to work as archivists. The second was the founding of the Australian Society of Archivists, in 1975, as the independent professional body representing archivists. The third was the formation of the Australian Council of Archives (initially known as the National Archival Forum), in July 1985, a consultative body of archival institutions.

The archival community is a small one. Our challenges are enormous. There is an escalation in the quantity of material being generated. Archival principles and ethics are being subjected to greater scrutiny. There are rapid and complex changes occurring in the way society records information. There is a greater awareness of archives in the community and consequently an increase in their use.

Each of these factors intensifies the pressure on archival services, time, principles and procedures. As with any profession, its resilience and ability to surmount pressures is largely dependent on its members. Individuals must be prepared to contribute and sustain the profession and to expand their skills, knowledge and experience. A willingness to learn is vital personally and professionally — it is also crucial to the effectiveness of Australia's many archival institutions.

Postgraduate training in archives administration aids professional growth and career development.

Table Three   Where Can I Learn?

Where	How	Why
Professional literature	Books Journals Conference proceedings Leaflets	To learn about theory, practice and history To get ideas To read case histories and see examples To maintain awareness
Professional associations	Meetings Seminars and workshops Conferences	To meet colleagues To learn techniques To discuss problems To take concerted action on professional issues
Colleagues in other institutions	Visits Discussions	To discuss problems in common To develop a network of support To exchange ideas
Related institutions	Visits Meetings Training Publications (e.g. forms, guides, pamphlets, manuals)	To examine facilities and systems To discuss methods To learn procedures
Tertiary institutions	Formal study	To gain comprehensive training To earn professional accreditation

TYPES OF ARCHIVAL AGENCIES IN AUSTRALIA

Having discussed archives, the records, let us now look at archives, the organisations that care for those records.

There is a wide range of institutions in Australia which maintain archives. These range from the archival authorities of federal, state and local government, to manuscript repositories, university, school and church archives and the archives of businesses and other private sector organisations. Most of these archival agencies have been listed and their holdings categorised in a publication, issued by the Australian Society of Archivists Incorporated, *Our Heritage: A Directory to Archives and Manuscript Repositories in Australia*.

Despite the diversity of archival institutions in Australia their holdings or collections are of three types:

- natural or in-house (that is, the archives only collects the records of its parent organisation)
- collecting (that is, the archives collects records from a number of sources relating to a specific region/location, subject, activity, or of a specific format, such as film)
- a combination of the above

An instance of the first type of institution is the Archives of the Broken Hill Proprietary Company Limited (BHP). The Archives is a unit of the Company and accepts into its custody only the records of the Company and its subsidiaries.

The Archives of Business and Labour is an example of an institution which collects the archives of other bodies, that is, its holdings are not records of the Australian National University, the Archives' parent organisation. The Archives of Business and Labour acquires the records of businesses, of trade, employer and professional associations and of unions.

The last category of institution identified, that is, an archives with holdings combining both natural and collected material is exemplified by the J.S.Battye Library of West Australian History. The Library is an agency of the State Government of Western Australia and is designated as the repository for the State's official archives, but it also collects the archives of businesses, schools, churches and individuals. Table Four briefly lists the types of holdings of some institutions around Australia. Appendix One is a limited listing of the main institutions with full contact information.

Archival materials must be analysed for their provenance, arranged in their original order and described before they can be used by researchers. Courtesy — Archives of Business and Labour, ANU.

Archivists from other institutions are excellent and willing sources of experience and expertise.

Table Four   A Selected List of Who Keeps Our Archives

Responsible Authority	Example
Commonwealth Government	
In-house	Australian Archives (regional offices in all States and Territories). Some Commonwealth institutions maintain their own archives, for example, the Reserve Bank, the Australian Broadcasting Corporation
Collecting	Australian War Memorial (records of the 'fighting forces'), National Library of Australia, National Film and Sound Archive
State Governments	
In-house	Archives Office of New South Wales. Some state government institutions maintain their own archives, for example, the State Bank in Victoria
Collecting	Mortlock, Mitchell, John Oxley Libraries
Combined	Battye Library of West Australian History, Northern Territory Archives Service
Local Governments	
In-house	Melbourne City Council Archives, Corporation of the City of Adelaide Archives
Collecting	Many local governments deposit their archives in local libraries
Universities and Colleges	
In-house	University of Queensland Archives, Sydney College of Advanced Education
Collecting	Archives of Business and Labour — ANU
Combined	University of Wollongong Archives, Riverina–Murray Institute of Higher Education
Companies, Associations and Organisations	
In-house	Westpac Banking Corporation Archives, Royal Australasian College of Surgeons and Anaesthetists Archives
Collecting	Australian Jewish Historical Society, Dennis Wolanski Library and Archives of the Performing Arts
Churches	
In-house	Lutheran Church of Australia Archives and Research Centre
Combined	Sisters of Charity Archives and Information Centre
Schools	
In-house	Methodist Ladies College, Kew
Combined	The Kings School, Parramatta

[handwritten annotation: Part of government agencies in the U.S.]

A more comprehensive listing is available in: Olga White, *et al*, *Our Heritage: A Directory to Archives and Manuscript Repositories in Australia.* Canberra: ASA, 1983.

If you, or your organisation, are considering establishing an archives, or if you have recently assumed responsibility for one, it is important to understand and co-operate with the existing institutions that collect and care for archives.

Government, or official archives, are maintained by each of the three tiers of government — federal, state and local. Companies, organisations and individuals may either maintain their own archives or arrange for their deposit in an appropriate collecting institution.

Getting to know the goals, frames of reference and strengths of institutions at four levels:
- nationally
- in your state
- in your capital city
- in your locality

enables you to position your archives programme in relation to others and to clearly assess the unique contribution it can make.

Resources for archives are too scarce to either duplicate work already being done or to compete. There is more than enough work to be shared by all institutions.

This storage area features static shelving, generous aisles and a sprinkler system. Courtesy — Archives of Business and Labour, ANU.

THE ARCHIVAL PARTNERSHIP

Archivists are responsible for negotiating the deposit of material, for documenting the deposit, for providing access and reference services to deposits and for guaranteeing the physical protection of the deposits.

An archivist therefore enters a relationship with:

- donors/depositors
- users
- the archival materials
- his or her employing institution
- other archival institutions and colleagues

Practitioners must be aware of individuals' rights to privacy which often conflict with individuals' rights to know. They must be sensitive to the needs of the collection which frequently conflict with their institutions' charter to make archives available.

These professional tensions and responsibilities are recognised by every archivist. Archivists have an obligation to each of the five groups mentioned above and to their profession. It is for these reasons that archivists formulate and adhere to codes of ethics. The need for an Australian code was recognised by the Council of the Australian Society of Archivists in 1984 and work on its drafting is underway.

Table Five   Archival Ethics — Some Matters for Consideration

---

Note: The following points do not constitute a formal code of ethics. They are presented as illustrations of the ethical standards archivists should apply in discharging their various responsibilities, whatever the nature and size of the organisation for which they work.

Responsibility	Example
to the archival material	• to ensure the permanent preservation of those records in their care designated as archival
	• to work for the 'moral and physical defence' of the archives
to the employer	• to abide by the organisation's rules and not to disclose information from records to which he/she has had privileged access
	• to disclose any private interest in collecting or trade in archives
to donors/depositors	• to respect the confidentiality of negotiations
	• to accept material only if it can be properly stored and processed and falls within the collecting interest of your archives
to users	• to treat all users fairly and courteously
	• to make archival material available equally within the constraints of the access policy and privacy requirements
to other archival organisations and colleagues	• to co-operate in matters of relating to the acquisition, preservation and disposal of records
	• to exchange information on archival techniques and methods which will benefit archives and their users

The purpose of these codes is to specify the partnerships into which an archivist enters and to stipulate the obligations and responsibilities that must be honoured. This serves to protect each of the relationships and to harness them for the benefit of our national heritage.

The Australian Society of Archivists biennial conference draws participants from across Australia and the Pacific.

THE AUSTRALIAN SOCIETY OF ARCHIVISTS INCORPORATED

Because many archivists work alone or in small archives, most of us believe that the vigour and efficiency of our work is enhanced by communication and co–operation with other practitioners. All of us are anxious to promote the better care of archives and can do so by sharing solutions to problems and developing common codes of practice.

These motives impelled archivists to establish the Australian Society of Archivists, to sustain, participate in, and contribute to it. Between 1951 and 1975 the interests of archives and archivists were represented by the Archives Section of the Library Association of Australia.

The Society is a national body with a branch in each capital city (except Brisbane and Darwin). It is governed by a Council of eleven elected members each of whom serve for two years. A core of the Council, the Executive, manages the day to day affairs of the Society. Each branch elects a committee, on an annual basis, to organise branch activities. Recently the Society has allowed for the creation of Special Interest Groups which are designed to bring members with similar problems, affiliations or interests together, for example, school archivists or members interested in the archives of science and technology.

The Society has two main aims:

- as the professional organisation for Australian archivists it seeks to identify, analyse and address matters of concern to archivists
- to serve as a channel of communication and co-operation between archivists, between archival institutions, between archivists and users and between archivists and other professionals working in complementary spheres.

The goals of the Society are presented in full in Table Six.

Table Six   Objects of the Society

The basic objects of the Society are:
1) to promote by all available means the preservation and care of archives
2) to establish and maintain communication and co-operation amongst archivists, the institutions in which they work and the users of archives
3) to establish and maintain standards of archival practice and administration and of professional conduct amongst archivists
4) to establish standards of archival qualifications and professional training
5) to encourage research into any area of archival practice and administration and the care and use of archives
6) to publish a journal and other material relating to the objects of the Society
7) to provide a means of collecting, co-ordinating and disseminating information relevant to the practice, status and problems of the archival profession
8) to promote amongst the general public and special groups an understanding of the nature of archives and their value
9) to encourage the efficient and responsible use of archives
10) to promote a professional identity amongst archivists and to advance their professional standing and welfare
11) to co-operate with other organisations and groups having complementary objectives, particularly in the fields of conservation, research and records management
12) to provide an authoritative voice on matters of archival concern

Australian Society of Archivists, Incorporated, Rules and By-Laws June, 1985, Part I, Rule 3.

The Society has four categories of membership:

- associate membership, which is open to anyone supporting the Society's aims
- professional membership, which is open to any graduate employed as an archivist for two years or to any person holding a post-graduate professional qualification recognised by the Council who has been employed as an archivist for one year
- honorary membership which is conferred, by the Council, on any person in recognition of services to the profession or the Society
- institutional membership, which is open to archival and other institutions recognised by the Council

The Society's activities are designed to involve and attract members. Members receive the Society's journal, *Archives and Manuscripts,* twice a year and the Society's newsletter, *The ASA Bulletin,* every two months. Branches hold regular meetings (lectures, workshops, visits, discussions and social events) to discuss issues of concern or interest and to bring members together. The Society holds a biennial meeting at which Council reports to, and receives direction from, the membership. The Society's conference, which non–members are encouraged to attend, is held in conjunction with the general meeting.

The importance of the Society to individuals and institutions is generally recognised. It is our vehicle for communication, support, learning/teaching, socialising and campaigning.

CONCLUSION

Much of what has been said has concentrated on the daunting responsibilities of custodians. We cannot diminish the importance of these responsibilities, however, we hope that we can ease assuming them.

This book offers practical information about archival functions and it offers advice on their accomplishment. It can be the first link in the chain of your involvement with the profession.

Because the profession is small it is possible to develop strong personal, professional and institutional bonds. The ideas and enthusiasm of newcomers are welcome and invigorating. We urge you to embrace the challenge and to share your experiences.

FURTHER READING

Cook, Michael, *Archives Administration: A Manual for Intermediate and Smaller Organizations and for Local Government.* Folkestone, Kent: William Dawson, 1977.

Daniels, Maygene and Timothy Walch, editors, *A Modern Archives Reader: Basic Readings on Archives Theory and Practice.* Washington, DC: National Archives and Records Service, 1984.

Lytle, Richard, editor, *Management of Archives and Manuscript Collections for Librarians.* Chicago, IL: Society of American Archivists, 1980.

Schellenberg, Theodore R., *Management of Archives.* New York: Columbia University Press, 1965.

White, Olga, *et al., Our Heritage: A Directory to Archives and Manuscript Repositories in Australia.* Canberra: Australian Society of Archivists, Incorporated, 1983.

Appendix One   A Selected Listing of Archives Institutions in Australia

	State Archives	State Libraries–Special Collections	Australian Archives	
NEW SOUTH WALES	Principal Archivist Archives Office of NSW 2 Globe Street The Rocks Sydney NSW 2000 Telephone: (02) 237 0100	Manager Australian Research Collections & Mitchell Librarian State Library of NSW Macquarie Street Sydney NSW 2000 Telephone: (02) 230 1414	Regional Director Australian Archives NSW 24 Market Street Sydney NSW 2000 Telephone: (02) 296 352	PO Box C328 Clarence Street Sydney NSW 2000
NORTHERN TERRITORY	Principal Archivist N T Archives Service Cnr Carey & McMinn Streets Darwin NT 5790 GPO Box 1197 Darwin NT 5794 Telephone: (089) 821 261	Director N T Library Service Cavenagh Street Darwin NT 5790 PO Box 39771 Winnellie NT 5789 Telephone: (089) 897 177	Regional Director Australian Archives NT Kelsey Crescent Nightcliff NT 5792 Telephone: (089) 852 222	GPO 293 Darwin NT 5794
QUEENSLAND	Principal Archivist Queensland State Archives 162 Annerley Road Dutton Park QLD 4102 Telephone: (07) 443 215	Principal Librarian John Oxley Library State Library of Queensland William Street Brisbane QLD 4000 Telephone: (07) 221 8400	Regional Director Australian Archives Qld 294 Adelaide Street Brisbane QLD 4000 Telephone: (07) 229 5422	GPO Box 888 Brisbane QLD 4001
SOUTH AUSTRALIA	Manager Public Record Office of SA North Terrace Adelaide SA 5000 Telephone: (08) 223 8793 GPO Box 419 Adelaide SA 5001	Mortlock Librarian State Library of SA North Terrace Adelaide SA 5000 Telephone: (08) 223 8911 GPO Box 419 Adelaide SA 5001	Regional Director Australian Archives SA 11–13 Derlanger Avenue Collinswood SA 5081 Telephone: (08) 269 3977	PO Box 119 Walkerville SA 5081
TASMANIA	Principal Archivist Archives Office of Tasmania 91 Murray Street Hobart TAS 7000 Telephone: (002) 302 490	Director State Library of Tasmania 91 Murray Street Hobart TAS 7000 Telephone: (002) 308 033	Regional Director Australian Archives Tasmania 4 Rosny Hill Road Rosny Park TAS 7018 Telephone: (002) 440 111	
VICTORIA	Keeper of Public Records Public Record Office Nauru House, 19th floor 80 Little Collins Street Melbourne VIC 3000 Telephone: (03) 651 3695	Director La Trobe Library State Library of Victoria 382 Swanston Street Melbourne VIC 3000 Telephone: (03) 669 9888	Regional Director Australian Archives Victoria Outer Crescent Middle Brighton VIC 3186 Telephone: (03) 592 8388	PO Box 33 Brighton VIC 3186
WESTERN AUSTRALIA	State Archivist J S Battye Library of WA History Alexander Library Building Perth WA 6000 Telephone: (09) 427 3111	Principal Librarian J S Battye Library of WA History Alexander Library Building Perth WA 6000 Telephone: (09) 427 3111	Regional Director Australian Archives WA 384 Berwick Street East Victoria Park WA 6101 Telephone: (09) 361 8088	PO Box 114 East Victoria Park WA 6101

State Archives	State Libraries–Special Collections	Australian Archives	
ACT		Regional Director Australian Archives ACT Cnr Sandford Street & Flemington Road Mitchell ACT 2911 Telephone: (062) 421 411	PO Box 447 Belconnen ACT 2617

National Institutions

Librarian Adolph Basser Library Australian Academy of Science Gordon Street Acton ACT 2601 Telephone: (062) 473 966	GPO Box 783 Canberra ACT 2601		
Archives Officer Archives of Business & Labour Australian National University Acton Underhill Acton ACT 2601 Telephone: (062) 492 219	GPO Box 4 Canberra ACT 2601		
Director General Australian Archives Mining Industry House Northbourne Avenue Braddon ACT 2601 Telephone: (062) 433 633	PO Box 34 Dickson ACT 2602		
Principal Australian Institute of Aboriginal Studies Acton House Kendall Street Acton ACT 2601 Telephone: (062) 461 111	GPO Box 553 Canberra ACT 2601		
Director Australian War Memorial Limestone Avenue Campbell ACT 2601 Telephone: (062) 434 211	GPO Box 345 Canberra ACT 2601		
Director National Film & Sound Archive McCoy Circuit Acton ACT 2601 Telephone: (062) 671 711	GPO Box 2002 Canberra ACT 2601		
Director General National Library of Australia Parkes Place Canberra ACT 2600 Telephone: (062) 621 111			

CHAPTER TWO

GETTING ORGANISED

Anne-Marie Schwirtlich and *Gunnel Bellviken*

CARING FOR ARCHIVES

Archives are those records selected for permanent preservation. All programmes which care for records are therefore important and play a significant part in the national archival network. Therefore, it is important that each member of the archival community, large or small, independent or part of a museum, library, or historical society, be efficiently organised and managed.

Archives by their very nature have value and currency far beyond the lifetime of their custodians, creators and donors. In taking custody of archives we accept that we have long-term legal and moral obligations to our holdings, our donors, our parent organisation, and our researchers. It is not sufficient to initiate any archival programme on the basis of short term funding allocation and staffing provisions. Similarly, personal enthusiasm, although commendable, obviously cannot sustain an archival programme in perpetuity. The collection and care of archives need to be undertaken in a responsible, responsive, thoughtful, and committed way.

The key element of responsible custody is a clear acceptance of long-term obligations to the records, their creators and their users which includes providing:
- continuity of care and resources
- continuity of custody.

This chapter reflects these concerns. It outlines the practical considerations and decisions that are involved and discusses some of the tools that are useful in managing archives.

DEVELOPING POLICIES, PLANS AND PROCEDURES

Regardless of the project or the nature of the work for which you are responsible, you will be more effective and efficient if you plan, systematise, and document your work. Since archives deal with material that is unique, valuable and of public interest, it is particularly important for us to be orderly.

Archives work involves performing diverse functions in the context of competing priorities. Therefore, developing policies, plans and procedures to structure the archives and to ensure a consistent and steady approach is important. These tools provide a basis and checklist for work activities, ensuring that each time a certain task is undertaken, it is completed in a uniform and objective way. Aside from ensuring consistency, this is a way of codifying information and setting standards which serve as lucid and informative documents for the people who join or succeed us in our work.

The Archives Policy

The first and most basic of the organisational tools is the archives policy. It is very important that the archives has a clear role within the museum, library or other institution of which it is a part and that objectives should be clearly and concisely set out. The means of achieving this is to draft an archival policy document which is a broad written statement outlining the purpose, objectives, and conditions which define the scope of archival activities, the authority under which they operate, and the services offered to clients.

What is the Archives Policy Designed to Achieve?

The archival policy is designed to achieve several things:
- It creates a public statement of purpose and objectives for the archives programme.
- It defines the scope of the archives collections and establishes general conditions for access to them.
- It provides a legal and authoritative basis for the archivist to exercise all of the powers, and perform all of the duties, responsibilities and functions with which he/she is endowed by the governing body of the parent library, museum, historical society or other institution.
- It facilitates consistency, uniformity and impartiality in the procedures and conditions adopted for the management and use of the archives.

Drafting an Archives Policy

The formulation of an archives policy should be undertaken as soon as possible after the decision to establish an archives programme is made and should continue for some months after the actual archival work commences. During this formative period, it is desirable to perform all archival services, but at a minimal level, so that the archivist can develop and test new policies and forms and procedures without being swamped with work. The policy document must be developed in conjunction with, and have the approval of, the governing authority and other administrative units and officers of the parent organisation since all will have to support the policy if it is to fulfil its role as the touchstone of all archival activity.

Nature and Components of an Archival Policy

The archives policy, as previously mentioned, must be comprehensive and general, not particular, in its approach, rather like the overall constitution of an organisation as opposed to the more prescriptive by-laws. The archives policy sets out the broad philosophy and limits of the programme and establishes the administrative machinery to operate it. Using the policy as a base, the archivist can design specific services and develop procedures and forms for accomplishing the work. The archives policy gives authority and protection to the archives and the archivist and is a document that should be communicated widely within and outside the parent organisation.

A comprehensive archives policy will generally contain the following elements though not all will be relevant to every archival programme. It may, therefore, be necessary to modify this comprehensive model archives policy for the particular circumstances of your individual organisation.

1) **Authority of the Archives Policy Document.** State that the archives policy document establishes the framework within which the archives programme functions and that all practices and procedures must be in accordance with its provisions. State who should be involved and the general process for amending the archives policy document.

2) **Authority of the Archives.** State the proper name of the archives, and its host or parent organisation (if any) and set out the circumstances of the archives' establishment i.e. the Archives of the University of the Antipodes was established by Resolution 3 of the University Council on 2 September, 1980.

3) **Purpose of the Archives.** State the purposes which the archives serves within the parent organisation and in the wider community. In general these purposes fall into three categories: preservation of records, reference use of records, and promotion/appreciation of organisation and community heritage/history.

4) **Definitions.** Define selected terms so that all readers will understand the document fully. This section generally includes, but is not limited to, the following terms: records, archives, official and non-official records, current and non-current records, archivist, depositor, access, appraisal and disposal.

5) **Administrative Setting of the Archives Programme.**
Explain the following aspects of the administrative context
within which the archives operates:

- *Position within the present organisation.* Describe the
relationship between the archives and the organisational
units which supervise or co-operate/liaise with it.
- *Relationship with an Advisory Body (if any).* Describe
the composition of the Archives Advisory Body, the
method for selecting members of the body, and the
powers of any advisory group giving advice on the overall
direction of the archives programme and interpretation
of policy.
- *Position and Responsibilities of the Archivist.* State that
the archives shall be cared for by a professional archivist
and outline the method for selection of the archivist.
Describe the basis of authority delegated to the archivist
and outline his/her general responsibilities. State to
whom the archivist reports and liaises in carrying out his/
her work.
- *Obligations of Officers and Staff of the Parent Organisation to Co-operate with the Archives Programme.* State
that officers and staff shall co-operate with the archivist
to ensure the following —
  a) No officer or staff member shall alienate, relinquish
  control over, destroy or dispose of records of the
  organisation without proper authorisation.
  b) Officers and staff are to follow the guidelines and
  utilise the procedures, forms and supplies authorised by the archives in carrying out its work (see 6).
  c) Officers and staff of the organisation are to seek the
  advice of the archivist in any matter affecting the
  quality and quantity of records produced by the
  organisation (i.e. record media, types and numbers
  of copies, computer applications, microfilming,
  storage location and equipment).

6) **Scope and Nature of Archival Requirements.** Define the
scope and state the policy considerations for each of the following archival activities:

- *Acquisition.* This is an area that will be treated very generally in the overall policy as the details of what will be
acquired and the conditions of acceptance are usually
explained more fully in a separate acquisitions policy.
However, here it is necessary to state the responsibilities
the archives has *vis-a-vis* acquiring the records of its
parent organisation (by approved disposal schedules),
and the records of outside persons or bodies (subject to
archival appraisal and legal transfer of custody, title and
rights). State that agreements for acquisition oblige the

The archivist explains access policy to new researchers.

archives to care for records indefinitely and represent a major continuing commitment of resources. State that material acquired by the archives becomes its property to be administered as the archives sees fit, which includes the right of the archives to de–accession or dispose of material deemed non–archival. State that the process and conditions of acquisition must comply with guidelines and procedures devised by the archives (see Chapter Three Acquisition and Appraisal for discussion of more detailed acquisitions policy statement).

- *Arrangement and Description*. State that all records brought into archival custody shall be arranged and described according to archival principles to the extent necessary to make them available for research. State that in general,records that have not been processed cannot be used by researchers.

- *Preservation*. State that as the preservation of the archival materials is the basis for the archives pro-gramme, every effort shall be made to provide the proper facilities, environment and resources to prolong the life of the records in custody.

- *Access to Archives*. This function, like that of acquisition, usually has a separate statement explaining the conditions and processes for obtaining access to the archives and its records, so there need only be general policy expressed here. State whether the archives is available to the public or only to specific groups. State that because of the unique and irreplaceable nature of the

archives, all users must apply for an admitting document,
usually a reader's ticket, and register their use of records
from the collection. State that archival materials will be
available for research under conditions that ensure their
preservation and which comply with the requirements to
respect confidentiality, privacy, and legal agreements
with depositors. State that the archives' staff will administer access to the archives and its collections in accordance with sound archival principles, the available
resources, their legal and ethical obligations and the
physical integrity of the materials.
- *Community Education.* Many archives have a commitment to promote an awareness and appreciation of the
contribution the host institution (library, museum, business) has made, and makes, to the life of the wider community and a statement to that effect could be made here.
- *Management and Administration.* State that, in addition
to its responsibility to manage the records of depositors,
the archives also has an obligation to manage its own
resources effectively and to document its work carefully,
i.e. to measure and evaluate its effectiveness and to maintain and care for its own 'archives' documenting its work.

The creation of an archives policy document is a very demanding task but one which, when successfully completed, is all–
important. The archives policy document forms the foundation
of the archives programme and becomes the basis for all projects
and operations undertaken by, or in the name of the archives.
Within a strong and flexible framework, the archives programme
can evolve and develop, accommodating change and growth,
while maintaining a consistent philosophy and direction.

THE NATURE OF THE ARCHIVES PROGRAMME

An archives programme has several functional components:
- Acquisition and collection
- Appraisal and disposal
- Arrangement and description
- Preservation and storage
- Reference and access
- Outreach activities

Each of these functions will be discussed in detail in a later chapter where its particular activities and the context in which they are
undertaken can be explained. For our purposes here, we are concerned with the general organisation and balance among these
components.

What needs emphasis is that every archives has priorities. Few
archival programmes have their resources spread evenly across
their functions. Every archivist has to make decisions about the
order in which work is undertaken. The orientation of programmes is dictated either by policy or by demand.

The general direction of the archives programme should be set out in the archives policy. Consequently priorities should reflect this direction. For example, the archives of a company would have as its first priority the orderly transfer of the company's records and the comprehensive documentation of these transfers to enable quick retrieval of needed items. Arrangement, description and the preparation of extensive finding aids for the use of the public would not be of primary concern.

Compiling a list of priorities on the basis of the policy is a vital first step. Categorise functions as 'High', 'Medium' or 'Low' priorities. Within each category identify the tasks that are involved and rate them in order of priority. This provides a clear idea of how resources should be committed. Then it is possible to decide what particular projects will get done within the next year or six months.

Organising the workload:

- ensures that the most important projects get addressed first
- provides a sense of continuity rather than lurching from project to project
- provides a sense of accomplishment as projects are completed as planned.

Conflicts of priorities can arise. Take the instance of the company mentioned above. If there were a deluge of enquiries from the public it would cause some diversion of resources from meeting the company's needs to assisting the public. Decisions would have to be made about which was more important and how resources could best be apportioned to meet the demands. Making these decisions requires familiarity with the workload of the archives, with the state of current projects, with those outstanding, and with the likely consequences if any are neglected.

HOW DO YOU START?

Administering an archives involves managing five broad areas:

- Yourself
- The information needed to manage
- People
- Financial matters
- Facilities, equipment and stores

Organising Yourself

Successful administrators know that self–management is the first step. They realise that their personal resources such as time and energy, are non–renewable and must be scheduled and focused on priorities if they are to maximise productivity.

Structure your time and establish a pattern that enables you to be most efficient. The following ideas may be of assistance, particularly if you work alone, or with part–time assistance.

- Limit the hours that the archives is open to the public. This allows you uninterrupted time to:

a) process collections and answer research queries;
b) visit donors or potential donors;
c) schedule appointments and meetings.

- Arrange for the telephone to be answered. Telephone calls can be disruptive. Unanswered telephone calls can lead to disgruntled researchers and donors.
- Devise form letters for routine correspondence.
- Recognise that your metabolism affects your work. If you always feel sleepy after lunch either eat a light lunch or save repetitive and undemanding tasks for after lunch.
- Start each day with a clear idea of what you want to accomplish. Get the important things done first.
- Attack daunting projects by dividing them into stages. It is easier to start and sustain a large project if you have a picture of the steps involved and can gain satisfaction from completing each step.
- Say no to taking on jobs that are not part of, or of direct benefit to, the archival programme.

ORGANISING YOUR INFORMATION RESOURCES

Successful administrators also ensure that the information necessary to support their work and decision making processes is organised, up to date and readily accessible. This essential information will be both published and unpublished and falls into two broad categories:

- *administrative*, which helps to structure and co–ordinate work;
- *technical*, which prescribes concepts and techniques for accomplishing tasks.

Table One itemises the sources of information that should be kept at hand.

Maintaining your information in well identified folders, or well labelled shelves and cabinets, is advisable. Documents, particularly administrative ones, like procedures and instructions, should be current and comprehensive. Make sure that superseded and outdated documents are promptly removed from your master set and either transferred to the archives or destroyed. Keeping every version of every document will create storage problems in your office, will hamper your efforts to find the correct document and could lead to mistakenly using an outdated one.

Publications can be a problem. Browsing through journals will alert you to articles that could be of use, for example, on indexing photographs. Unless your memory is excellent the day you want that article is the day you spend thumbing through every journal in the library. It is possible to photocopy all potentially useful articles and file them. This takes time and can lead you to store

Table One   Information for Managing

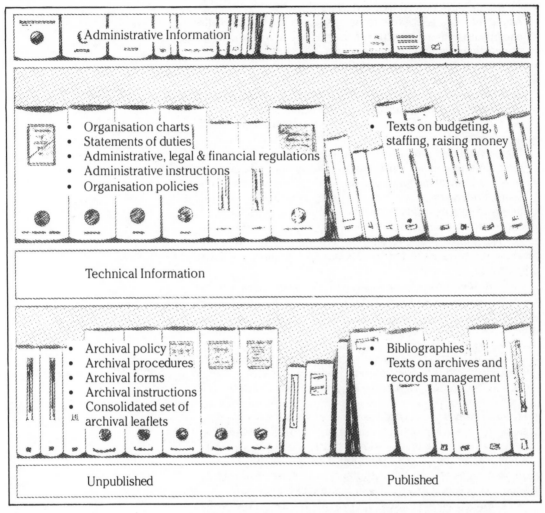

Administrative Information

- Organisation charts
- Statements of duties
- Administrative, legal & financial regulations
- Administrative instructions
- Organisation policies

- Texts on budgeting, staffing, raising money

Technical Information

- Archival policy
- Archival procedures
- Archival forms
- Archival instructions
- Consolidated set of archival leaflets

- Bibliographies
- Texts on archives and records management

Unpublished   Published

quantities of paper which you may never consult. It may be preferable to create a card index in which you nominate subject headings, for example, 'Photographs', 'Maps', and slot in a card with all citation details for each article of interest.

Information and documentation about your own operations is vital. You must have available to you accurate and complete data about your administrative and archival activities. Devoting time to your own record keeping is a gilt–edged investment. Whatever filing system you adopt or inherit, maintain it — make notes of developments, file them immediately, house your files safely and in order.

Developing Forms and Procedures

Developing a management system for an archives involves:

- clearly defining each function of the archives
- listing the work activities necessary to carry out the function
- identifying and creating the forms and procedures needed to structure the work
- devising ways of measuring performance
- formulating the information to be distributed to clients using your services
- documenting and reporting your achievements.

Table Two illustrates these steps in developing a management system for the function of arrangement and description.

The level of detail to which you develop your management scheme depends on the nature and complexity of your operation. Before you change anything, find out how things are done at the moment. Ideally the *status quo* will be documented by existing policies, procedures and forms. If there are none, then prepare a document that describes the current practices as they are understood by persons associated with the programme. Annotate it to show which systems or methods work and suggest improvements for those which do not.

You can then proceed further afield. For example, read the available professional literature; consult colleagues and ask for guidance. You can look at how similar organisations do things, and at their procedures, forms and systems. Most archival institutions are prepared to explain, and to provide you with examples of their procedures and forms. The Australian Society of Archivists, and other professional bodies with members who work in related areas, such as the Museums Association of Australia, can either give you direct assistance or guide you to sources that will. However you should not uncritically introduce another institution's archival practices. It is important to think about what you are seeking to do, and to know the characteristics, capabilities and limitations of your institution. This enables you to compare your organisation with another and to determine how compatible or useful its systems and practices may be.

For example, say you have responsibility for the archives of a small hospital and you are interested in organising your reference work. It would be advantageous to learn how the Mitchell Library organises its reference work. However, it would not necessarily be beneficial to use the Mitchell's forms and procedures. The Mitchell's systems are designed to cope with thousands of public enquiries which are dealt with by several staff, whereas your archives might serve specialist users i.e. medical personnel, and have records of a confidential nature. Thus the Mitchell's systems might be inappropriate for your reference needs.

The lesson is then to gather and analyse all available information, and select and adopt those features that are directly rel-

Table Two   Developing Documentation For Arrangement And Description

Define the function	• The arrangement and description of archival material in custody
List the activities necessary to carry out the function	• Examine new transfers/collections thoroughly • Determine priority for arrangement and description • Decide if any items need special storage • Recommend if culling of non–archival material is required • Determine the level of arrangement and description to be undertaken • Research the life of the person/organisation creating the records • Identify the record series • Arrange items — first on paper, then physically • Inventory and describe the records • Write the administrative history • Prepare the finished descriptive inventory/guide
Identify and create the tools for structuring the work	• Arrangement and description policy and priorities • Arrangement and description procedures • Worksheets to record progress/information • Series description sheets • Plan for contents of finished descriptive inventory/guide
Measures and statistics	• Number of series arranged • Number of series described • Number of descriptive inventories/guides prepared
Documenting and reporting	• Keep records in order • Prepare regular reports
Information for clients	• Introductory leaflet on the principles of arrangement and description of archives • Finding aids: finished descriptive inventories/guides

evant. Test the new form or procedure for a while. When you are confident it is workable, incorporate it in your system.

It is far more efficient to think long and hard before introducing a procedure or form than to adopt a succession of them, only to find them to be inappropriate.

Likewise, once you have introduced a form or procedure that is suitable, do not assume that it will work as intended. Evaluate its performance in use and be prepared to make modifications as required.

MANAGING STAFF

Archival work is labour intensive and detailed. These two factors shape all staffing considerations. Assessment of needs for personnel and of people's capabilities should be made in the light of these factors. Administering staffing involves:

- recruiting
- training and development
- allocating responsibilities and projects
- staff evaluation.

Before any decision can be made about augmenting staff it is necessary to know:
- Can your organisation acquire staff? If so, on what basis? (Can you afford to pay? Can you accept volunteers? Can you use people enrolled in work experience schemes?)
- Do you have the power to appoint people? If not, who does?
- What, if any, are the procedures for appointing people?

Equipped with this information you can identify whether you need more staff and of what type. To do this you need to assess:
- how many staff you have
- what hours or on what basis they work
- what skills/areas of expertise they have
- what the archives programme's priorities are
- how long/how many people it will take to accomplish various tasks.

A cautionary note: increasing staff is not the solution to all workload problems. An increase in staff entails more time spent on supervision and planning. It can strain accommodation and equipment and be counter–productive. In some situations, modification of procedures and priorities will achieve a satisfactory result.

People often think that only paid appointments need to be carefully planned. This is not so. Many small archives depend heavily on volunteer labour. There are two reasons for taking care with any appointment:
- Archives are unique — anybody who works with them must be selected with care.

Table Three   Duty Statement

Sunshine Press Limited

Position Title: Assistant Archivist   **Position Number:** 42

Branch: Administration   **Section:** Archives

Responsible to: Archivist   **Supervises:** Typist

Duties: Assist the Archivist in carrying out the archives and records programme. In the Archivist's absence assume responsibility for the Archives.
- Appraise records eligible for transfer to Archives. Make recommendations on their suitability and any necessary disposal activity (30%)
- Negotiate and document the transfer of records (10%)
- Arrange and describe the archives in accordance with procedures and priorities (25%)
- Prepare finding aids (15%)
- Provide reference assistance to researchers — both public and from within the Press (12%)
- Identify items requiring conservation treatment (3%)
- Assist with other archival and administrative work as required (5%)   **Approved:** 22 January 1987

Table Four   Selection Criteria

Sunshine Press Limited
Selection Criteria: Assistant Archivist (Position Number 42)
Knowledge
- Thorough grasp of archival principles and practices (Essential)
- Working knowledge of records management principles and practices (Essential)
- Familiarity with the principles and practices of conservation (Essential)
- Familiarity with the development and history of Australian printed news media (Desirable)

Attributes/Skills
- Good communication skills, both written and oral
- Ability to undertake and sustain complex research
- Eye for accuracy and detail
- Willingness to accept responsibility

Experience
- Two to three years archival experience — preferably working with business archives

Qualifications
- Postgraduate Diploma in Archives Administration (or equivalent)
- Professional membership of the Australian Society of Archivists, Incorporated

Approved: 22 January 1987

- Time spent on training is valuable — it should be invested wisely.

If you do recruit staff you will need to develop:
- a list of duties for the position/person
- a list of selection criteria
- an advertisement
- a list of questions you wish to ask applicants.

Formulating them will absorb some time and require close attention. They are important. They focus your requirements, streamline your search, and assist prospective applicants in deciding whether they are interested in, and suitable for, the vacancy. Moreover, they advertise your organising ability and your professional approach.

The list of duties is a schedule of the tasks the position undertakes and the responsibilities it carries. It can also indicate to whom the position is responsible and, in turn, who is responsible to the position. Every position, paid or volunteer, in the archives should have a list of duties. The lists should be accessible to ensure that all duties are distributed and that all staff are aware of the distribution. See Table Three for an example of a duty statement.

The selection criteria list is the basis on which you will make the choice for filling the vacancy. These criteria must relate to the duties on the list of duties (duty statement) and should be compiled before advertising the job. For example, say a list of duties includes 'Answer queries from members of the public'. An appropriate selection criterion would be 'Ability to deal with people' and/or 'Good communication skills'. An inappropriate selection criterion would be 'Blue eyes and red hair essential' as these attributes do not reflect on a person's competence to carry out the duty. Table Four is a sample list of selection criteria.

Once you have the list of duties and the selection criteria finalised, they can be made available to people enquiring about the vacancy. These documents indicate what the job entails and what you are looking for.

It is preferable to advertise the vacancy to give yourself the best chance of finding the most suitable person. Choose an appropriate vehicle for your advertisement. Would it be best placed in your own newsletter? In a local paper? In a national paper? In a specialist journal? In the window of a local shop?

Draft your advertisement carefully. The essential elements of an advertisement are illustrated in Table Five.

Take care over the advertisement's presentation and double check the final typed version with your original draft.

Table Five   Advertising A Vacancy

Sunshine Press Limited — Brisbane
Assistant Archivist — Permanent Appointment
(Position Number 42)
The Sunshine Press has been Queensland's largest printed news media organisation for 93 years. It is seeking to appoint, on a permanent basis, an Assistant Archivist.
Duties
• Appraise, accession, arrange and describe the archives . Provide reference services and identify items requiring conservation treatment.
Qualifications
• Postgraduate Diploma in Archives Administration (or equivalent)
• 2–3 years archival experience
• Professional membership of the Australian Society of Archivists Incorporated
Salary
$25,000 — $30,000 per annum
Benefits
• 20 days annual leave; 10 days annual sick leave; eligibility for Sunshine Press Superannuation Scheme; removal expenses
Apply by
19 June 1987
Contact
Barbara Winsome (07) 467 351 for further details, Selection Criteria and Statement of Duties.
Applications should be in duplicate and should nominate two referees. Envelopes should be addressed to:
Dr. Barbara Winsome
Archivist
Sunshine Press Ltd.
GPO Box 4444
Brisbane QLD 4001

Table Six   Framing Interview Questions and Running An interview

Framing Interview Questions
- Ask questions that are relevant to making the decision about the job. Questions should reflect the selection criteria.
- Keep questions concise.
- Make the questions open ended. That is, so that they require more than a one word response. For example, 'How would you try to persuade a notable local family to deposit its records?' Not 'Would you emphasise the benefits of tax deductibility when persuading a notable local family to deposit its records?'
- Vary the approach — ask a direct question, delineate a problem and ask for a solution, prepare a practical exercise.
- Graduate the questions so that the simplest are asked first. This helps everyone to settle down.
- Ask one question at a time.

Running an Interview
Before
- Get to know the statement of duties and selection criteria in detail.
- Frame the questions to be asked. Identify the answer to each question.
- Decide how response will be rated. For example, will each question carry a certain number of points?
- Select the other people who will sit on the panel. Provide them with the necessary documents (duty statement, applications, selection criteria, advertisement, questions). Decide how to run the interview.
- Schedule appointments.
- Organise interview room and ensure there will be no interruptions.
- Read applications thoroughly. Make necessary notes.

During
- Introduce every person on the panel.
- Be attentive.
- Be encouraging.
- Be prepared to direct any answers that go off the track.
- Be prepared to paraphrase questions and to provide prompts if people are struggling to answer.
- Give the applicant time to ask any questions he/she may have.
- Thank applicant for his/her interest and time.

After
- Tell all applicants of the interview results as soon as possible.
- Be available to provide advice on any of the applicants' performances.

Compiling a list of questions to ask applicants, either at a formal interview or over the telephone, enables you to satisfy yourself about a person's suitability. It also enables you to select the best person from a range of applicants because they have all answered the same questions.

Table Six lists some of the considerations to keep in mind when framing questions and conducting interviews. However you arrange to ask these questions it is important that you do make notes of the process and the results. This is for your own benefit and, if necessary, to show that the best possible decision was made.

Training New Staff

Having appointed someone who is interested and eager to contribute, it is essential to devote time and care to training. Effective training means that staff:

- can competently and independently undertake the projects assigned them
- will not inadvertently or unconsciously damage or destroy material
- will be able to learn and gain satisfaction.

Training can be either practical or theoretical. Remember that you train by example. Do not wonder why your colleagues treat the archives carelessly if you smoke, eat, and drink your coffee while working on them. *Table Three:* 'Where Can I Learn' in Chapter One may be of use when planning training.

If people are new to an organisation, training should encompass the technical aspects of the job, such as, the principles and procedures for doing the work. Training should also cover general or political aspects. For example, how the organisation functions, who are the decision makers, and who are the people with information.

Training needs to be carefully tailored and graduated to suit the needs and capabilities of the person. Nothing is more terrifying than being landed with a complex job in your first week just as nothing is more likely to kill enthusiasm than doing routine and repetitive tasks continuously.

When confident that staff can work independently, ensure that all projects and tasks are distributed. This enables people to take responsibility for their work and to vary it. When allocating work be clear in communicating your expectations. For example, when and how it should be completed and how complex or detailed the work should be. Attempt to roster or share the urgent, unpleasant or tedious work rather than expecting one person to do it all.

Most people want to find their work enjoyable and interesting. They would also like to derive some non-financial benefits such as increased skills or knowledge from it. If you work with volunteers this is particularly important as their only compensation is the self-satisfaction they gain from their work.

Being approachable, fair, encouraging, and appreciative is important for all supervisors — more so for those working in small organisations.

MANAGING FINANCE

The funding required to maintain your archives is dependent on your holdings, their condition, and your responsibilities.
Archives confront three recurring financial problems:

- Will there be funds?
- Will the funds be sufficient and continuing?

All job applicants should be interviewed using questions drawn from job-related criteria.

- How should the funding be allocated?

Because collecting and maintaining archives costs money, the enterprise should not be entered into lightly. If there are no sources of assured income the enterprise should not proceed. Neither the records nor the archival profession are well served by archives which are established on a flimsy financial basis. Almost inevitably they will close because financial support dwindles or is withdrawn, leaving their collections unusable and/or vulnerable to dismemberment or loss. None of these results is desirable.

At the same time, it is not always possible for a beginning archives programme to have its funding fully sorted out. What must be obtained is the commitment for start–up costs with the clear understanding that the amount requested will lead into an on going obligation for funding. This then becomes the first budget within which to plan your programme.

As you are developing your programme proposal for funding, consider engaging the services of an experienced archivist to advise you in a consultant capacity. This step, though it may require an initial investment in consultant fees, is time and money well spent. It is important to develop a clear programme proposal with a realistic assessment of required resources before seeking financial support.

Archives can receive funding in three ways:

- *from their parent organisation*. For example, the Archives of the Corporation of the City of Adelaide is funded entirely by the Corporation.
- *by donation/sponsorship/fees*.
- *by a combination of the above*. For example, the Mitchell Library's operations are covered by the State Government of New South Wales. However, the Library also has the income from the David Scott Mitchell bequest which it augments by seeking donations from individuals and businesses.

Anyone can see that an archives relying solely on the second method of funding is in a precarious situation. It is difficult to plan if one is unsure how much money will be available from year to year. Relying on donations involves the staff in planning and conducting fundraising activities. This means less time can be spent on caring for the archives.

Institutions soliciting money need to be mindful of the expectations of their patrons. People *will* give money for worthy causes but they *do* expect the money to be utilised and progress to be visible. A balance must be preserved between the archives programme and the fundraising programme. Patrons may need to be reminded that a donation does not automatically carry the right to influence the direction or priorities of the archives.

If your archives falls into the first category identified above, your strategy should be to define your financial environment. For example:

- Is there automatic provision in your organisation's budget for your operations?
- If yes, how much is allocated, on what basis and how can it be increased?
- Who drafts and approves the organisation's budget?
- What is the budgeting cycle?
- What is the procedure for seeking funds?

With this basic information it should be possible to target your requests most effectively.

Regardless of the source of funds, every archives should have a budget. A budget is a document in which calculations, for a specified period, of the amount of money to be expended and raised are presented. Budgets are usually done annually and are divided into categories so that they itemise expenditure and income.

The budget should be completed and submitted to dovetail with your organisation's financial cycle. There are three responses your budget can attract:

- it can be accepted and all funds sought provided.
- it can be pruned.
- it can be ignored.

Never be disheartened by the last two responses. The preparation and submission of a budget highlights the professional approach you have adopted to administering the archives. It also underlines the message that archives require funding. A first budget may have little success. However, it is an excellent public relations tool. People, whether allocating money personally or in an official capacity, are far more likely to give money to a unit with a clear purpose, well defined needs, and proposals which are properly justified. Prepare your budget with an eye to success:

- *Be realistic*. Do not seek money to buy 20,000 boxes if you will only use 200 within the budget period.
- *Be concise*. The budgeting review process is conducted under pressure. The people allocating money do not have time to read wads of paper.
- *Be precise*. Do your homework so that you can quote costs accurately and can show that you have chosen the most economical option.
- *Be lucid*. Do not use jargon. Explain what an item will be used for, especially if it is expensive.
- *Be frank*. Briefly explain what the consequences will be if funds are not provided for activities.

Budgeting and receiving funds are only the beginning of the cycle. Ensure that you use the money responsibly and in accordance with your predicted needs. If you have asked for a specified sum of money to last you for a specified period it is important to see that it does. Expenditure needs to be monitored and financial records (quotations received, invoices, receipts) properly main-

Box A   Characteristics of Accommodation for Archives

	Desirable	Avoid
Sites	Near major user community or good transport, room for expansion	Proximity to strategic targets, dangerous industries or utilities, floodplains, unstable earth zones, direct sun or wind
Building	Fire and vermin resistant materials, large open spaces, good load bearing capacity, limited points of access, mostly above ground, few windows, good loading/unloading facilities, air conditioning	Several separate buildings, totally below ground, extensive internal partitioning
Position within building	As above	Attics or basements, widely separated rooms, potential hazards such as water pipes, chemical stores, heating/air conditioning plants, kitchens

tained so that a financial report can be compiled at the end of the budgeting period.

The process of securing finance is often seen as a very dry and tedious one. In fact, the success of this vital process can be contingent on two aspects of your operation that are well within your control — the image of the archives and your capability for lobbying the appropriate people.

MANAGING FACILITIES, EQUIPMENT AND STORES

The proper housing of records is one of the most important issues the archivist will ever face. Give archives accommodation in poor facilities and their volume and useability will be drastically reduced in a relatively short time. Enemies such as heat, light, moisture, mildew and vermin are constantly at work; and once they have had an open go at the records, the cost to repair the damage will be enormous, if it can be accomplished at all.

Unsuitable equipment will, apart from increasing the wear and tear on records, also prolong retrieval time, possibly cause accidents to staff and will, in the end, be a bad investment. Money, a rare commodity in many archives, is therefore best employed to secure proper storage facilities and equipment.

The archivist's first responsibility, then, is to ensure that the records in his/her custody are given the best possible environment and care. The archivist's 'know how' about storage is particularly vital and can be a matter of life and death for the records. Before attempting decisions in this area, do a bit of 'homework'.

Read basic books and articles about planning archival facilities, such as those listed at the end of this chapter, and contact other archivists for help and support. Visits to major archival institutions will provide useful hints and ideas. The Australian Society of Archivists (ASA) and the Institute for the Conservation of Cultural Materials (ICCM) can give advice and act as an intermediary for making contacts.

The criteria to use when selecting accommodation are discussed in the following section. Before you start the process be prepared to:

- know what your current needs are
- forecast your needs for the next five years
- identify the features you want and those you must avoid for conservation or security reasons
- familiarise yourself with what is available
- realise that you may need to be extremely patient and persistent

When looking for accommodation you must be well versed in your requirements, present and near future. Remember that you need space not just for storage — room must also be allocated for administrative work, to allow researchers to consult items, and to enable staff to undertake work on archives. Ask yourself:

- how much and what types of material are in custody now? In five years?
- does any of the material have special storage needs?
- how many staff are there now? In five years?
- how many researchers visit per week, month, year?

Next, look for areas you consider acceptable — in terms of size, location and suitability. Identify vacant or under–utilised areas on the premises of your organisation and inspect them. Assess their suitability. Box A indicates features of sites and buildings that you need to take into account. If yours is a community organisation, find out whether your local council has vacant buildings or areas which could be used. If your organisation is in a position to pay for accommodation, have a preliminary discussion with real estate agents and monitor advertisements in the papers.

Any decisions about where and how to house and service the records of a particular archives are ultimately dependent on the nature of the holdings, activities and resources available at the time and in the foreseeable future. Therefore, this chapter cannot give advice on specific accommodation or equipment as the individual choices and decisions will vary too much from institution to institution. However, it is possible and desirable to provide to persons planning their archives facility some general guidelines.

The size and complexity of holdings determines the amount

and the sophistication of equipment needed. Equipment used in archives falls into four categories:

- administrative
- storage/repository
- reference/outreach
- conservation

It may be more satisfying to obtain equipment new but for most equipment it is not imperative. Typewriters, shelves, filing cabinets, ladders, desks, tables and chairs, and trolleys, can be borrowed, begged or bought second–hand. As long as the item functions and is safe (particularly ladders and shelving), it is perfectly acceptable. If buying second–hand it is also preferable to buy the product of a well–known company which is still in the retail market. This means that spare parts and servicing can be obtained. It is also wise to buy a basic model rather than a highly accessorised model as there are fewer components that can go wrong.

If you are relying on gifts, loans and second–hand purchases your most valued asset will be an extensive network of contacts. For example, people who can be vigilant in finding items you need, who can be relied upon to lend you items and people who will devote their time and skills to repairing or modifying the items you acquire.

Written Specifications for Work, Equipment and Supplies

Great caution must be exercised when setting up an archives facility. The builders and tradesmen, from the shelf manufacturer to electricians installing the lights, will assert that they have done similar jobs before (meaning libraries or warehouses) and know exactly what is needed, no worries. But there is great cause for worry and no margin for errors when you are housing irreplaceable materials.

As the archivist, it is your responsibility to write out your requirements precisely, not only for the type and quality of the

---

Box B   Some points to include in a specification brief

1) **Dimensions** — Height, width, depth, length
2) **Material**
3) **Use**
4) **Performance** — Load, speed
5) **Description of the work to be undertaken**
6) **Special Conditions or Requirements**
7) **Drawings**
8) **Time limit**
9) **Supply and Installation**
10) **Service, Spare Parts**
11) **Schedule of payment**

---

work or equipment but also for its maintenance and support and the security of the archival holdings while the work or installation is underway. Without these you have no legal recourse for correcting faulty work or shoddy supplies. Do not pay the bills until you are satisfied.

The Archives Facility

Archives facilities fall into two categories — a purpose built building, planned specifically to fit the requirements of a particular collection, or an already existing building or part of one which is to be converted for the archival use. Designing and building an archives facility is a very specialised and challenging task and one that will usually only be undertaken by very large and well established archival institutions. Therefore, this chapter will not include any discussion of this task. Rather, it will focus upon selecting and adapting existing buildings and spaces for archival use.

Once you have identified your needs and assessed the suitability of the areas you are likely to be offered, you are then in a position to state your case. Decide whether it would be most appropriate to outline it in person or to prepare a submission. If you decide on the former, give the person a concise statement of your requirements and follow the meeting up with a letter confirming the substance of your discussion. If you prepare a submission ensure that it is concise and clear. In both instances be prepared to send reminders.

General Conditions For Archives

Irrespective of whether your archives is a cupboard, a basement, or an old court house, the priorities are:

- to provide a suitable and stable environment
- to make it secure and safe
- to ensure that there is adequate space
- to arrange or allocate the space so that it enhances the work flow.

As the charcteristics of suitable space and equipment for each work area will be discussed later in the chapter, let us turn our attention to the general environment which all archives facilities should try to achieve. Overall, archival facilities should be secure, clean, temperate and protected from violent swings in climate.

Security in an archives facility is a number one priority. Because archives are bodies of one–of–a–kind materials, they require more stringent protection than individual published items which may be replaced if they are lost or damaged. Thus the use of archival records must be confined to the archives itself. It is unwise to permit records to be 'checked out' for use elsewhere, except under very special and controlled circumstances. Areas where archives are stored should be locked and records in

Large volumes do not fit modern, standard shelving. Wide aisles facilitate access to cumbersome records.

Mobile shelving with adjustable shelves provides secure, flexible storage with minimal floor space.

use supervised to avoid loss or, equally bad, misfiling. Access to the stacks should be limited to staff only. A record should be made each time material is taken from the shelves for use by researchers or for processing or conservation work as it is easy for material to be mislaid without documentation. There should be a supervised place where all persons entering and leaving the archives, be they staff, researchers or tradespeople, register their presence. After hours patrols and alarm systems will help deter unauthorised intruders.

The general environment within the archives is also important. Records which must last 'forever' must be kept under the best possible conditions in a stable, cool and clean environment. Proper containers, storage equipment and handling procedures are vital and every care must be taken to control levels and changes in temperature and humidity. A number of hazards must be avoided and minimised throughout the archives, but particularly in storage areas where the archives spend most of their time.

An intercom helps regulate access.

Environmental Hazards

Temperature and Humidity. The control of temperature and humidity is a problem for all archivists seeking to provide a stable and temperate environment for their records. In rooms where the temperature and humidity fluctuate a lot, between day and night or from season to season, paper is put under considerable strain. The paper will absorb humidity at night when the temperature sinks and humidity rises and then release its moisture the next day when the temperature rises again. A climate with high humidity and high temperature is very dangerous as mould thrives in such conditions. Where humidity is too low, paper becomes crisp and brittle to the touch.

Several approaches are possible in meeting this challenge. The most comprehensive of these is to install a well–designed air-conditioning system which will control both the levels of temperature and humidity and moderate their rates of change.

Air-conditioning can:
* heat and cool the air
* humidify and dehumidify the air
* clean pollution from the air

Once air–conditioning is installed it should run 24 hours a day, seven days a week or its good effects will be undone. Do not forget that to function properly the air–conditioning unit will have to have regular service and that the water drawn from the humid air will have to be carefully disposed of.

If you cannot afford to air–condition the entire facility all at once, consider installing it in the storage areas. If even limited use of air–conditioning is beyond your resources, obtain some good quality fans to keep the air moving and if possible, purchase a humidifier/dehumidifier unit to regulate the humidity. With the latter, water will be involved, so plan your installation and maintenance carefully.

Vermin and Insects. It is almost impossible to keep vermin and insects out of a building, particularly in hot and humid climates. Some protection can be incorporated in a purpose–built archives building, but most archives must depend on other measures. Regular inspections of the storage areas and the records themselves, together with regular fumigation of the whole building, are the best safeguards against pests. Commercial pest control com-

A sensitive hygrothermograph records the temperature and relative humidity over a seven day period.

*Small brown spots known as fox-
ing form when metal impurities in
the paper oxidize under humid
conditions.*

panies can be utilised for fumigation, using the chemical
fumigants recommended by the Institute for Conservation of Cultural Materials (ICCM). Minor outbreaks of mould or mildew may
be treated with the advice of a conservator.

Dust should be vigorously fought wherever it appears as it carries
fungi, mould spores and bacteria that destroy paper. It is
unpleasant, even harmful to staff. If the room has a floor made of
concrete (which gives off a particularly nasty dust), it should be
coated. The coating can be brushed or sprayed on to the floor
(varnish types of polyvinyl) or appplied with a trowel (paste). Linoleum or vinyl carpets can also be used. Fabric carpeting is not
recommended because it traps dirt and dust in its fibres and produces a lint of its own.

Light should be carefully controlled because of the chemical
reactions it encourages in paper and ink; and the most dangerous
of them all, sunlight, should be cut out completely, both because
of its intense ultra violet rays and the heat it generates. West-
facing windows, in particular, should be avoided or blocked with
panels, shutters or blinds, preferably those with a reflective coating to deflect the heat towards the outside.

If for some reason it is impossible to block the windows entirely,
a light filter film can be used on the windows to provide some
protection from ultra violet light. There are however many pitfalls
facing the buyer of film. The market is big and the promises are
many. Few of the brands live up to the standards of the glossy
brochures. Museums have the same problems as archives in this
area, and their advice should be sought. The Museums Association of Australia have published information on this matter.

The positioning of the shelving in the room can help prevent
sunlight falling on the records if it proves impossible to eliminate
it completely. Remember, lighting in storage areas is only needed
for retrieving and refiling records and, therefore, should be
located to illuminate the aisles between the shelves. Some
archives have their storage lights on a timer switch so that they
cut off after a period of time. Some fluorescent lamps, such as
Philips Trucolour, 37 and Softone, give off very small amounts of
ultraviolet light. Tungsten incandescent lamps also have low UV
emissions but as they do produce an amount of heat, they are not
recommended for the storage area. To compensate for the lower
watt lamps recommended for archives, you may wish to use wall
paints with higher light–reflecting qualities.

Water Hazards. Water is a major hazard, particularly for
records storage areas. Dampness encourages deterioration and
the growth of damaging fungi and mould, not to mention insects.
If possible, records should not be stored below ground level as
basement areas are particularly vulnerable to water invasion.
Pipes may be located in the ceiling and trays should be fitted
underneath these to allow water from leaks to be drained away.

Cleanliness in all aspects of archives operations is important.

Hot water pipes are particularly dangerous to records, as drops of condensation can form on the pipes from contact with the cooler air. Rising damp in the walls can wet the backs of boxes if open shelving is located against walls. The rising damp should be eliminated and the walls coated to seal them against seeping moisture. Furthermore, records shelving should be set away from the walls to encourage air circulation. The archivists should also be aware of danger of water from the storeys above, from faulty plumbing, overflowing gutters or damaged roofs. Water can flow down walls, stairs or ramps, through ventilation shafts or holes and seep through the ceiling if the floors above experience a drainage problem. For this reason, it is a good idea not to use the tops of shelving to store boxes of records.

Even if all the above measures have been taken to prevent water from entering the archives, it is advisable to install a drain in the floor. Ensure that water flows out and not in from blocked drains outside the building. Regular drain maintenance is advisable.

A very simple early detection system for water invasion can be installed with the help of a humidity sensor pushed into a hard dry sponge on the floor. The device is connected with an alarm which, when the sponge gets wet, sounds the alarm.

Fire is dreaded Enemy Number One and must be kept at bay. While the Conservation Chapter will discuss the varieties of detection and extinguishment systems in detail, there are a few general points worthy of mention.

Firstly, the room or the whole building itself can be protected from fire from the outside. The safest area inside a building should be chosen for the storage area. Fire resistant materials for walls, floors and doors are capable of withstanding fire for set periods.

Secondly, preventative measures can be taken so fire doesn't break out inside. For example, restrict or prohibit smoking in the archives; have the electrical wires insulated from the main struc-

Staff should be familiar with fire extinguishment equipment.

ture and locate master switches outside the rooms; isolate areas where heating, cooking or chemicals are stored or used.

If all records are properly boxed and tightly packed on the shelves fire will not easily get a hold on them. If the end of the boxes turned towards the aisle burn away, (boxes that stick out slightly over the edge of the shelf will be an easier target) the files or papers in boxes of the kind recommended in this chapter will sit safely on the shelf and not fall off and feed the fire.

Fire detectors and extinguishers are costs that cannot be compromised. A detector attached to an alarm will alert staff before the fire has established itself. Smoke detectors are more suitable for archives than heat or flame sensors because boxes of paper do not burst out in flames easily, but rather smolder and slowly emit smoke. When acquiring fire extinguishers, preference should be given to those utilising carbon dioxide or a fine spray, rather than a jet of water. Chemical extinguishers may be necessary for some types of fires, i.e. electrical or oil, but may leave a residue on the records.

To sprinkle or not to sprinkle. Sprinklers have been viewed with ambivalence in the archival world. They come highly recommended from some countries that have suffered badly from fire. In others, the archives prefer to rely on gas extinguisher systems or early detection because of the damage the water does to records.

In a properly managed archives a sprinkler system going off need not be a catastrophe. All boxes will be well above ground, and the shelves will have dustcovers on the top shelf to prevent drops of water from falling down from shelf edge to shelf edge. Bound volumes of records will not fare as well; it is therefore essential that, if sprinklers are installed, all archival material including outsized volumes be either wrapped or boxed.

Extinguisher systems with a gas such as halon or carbon dioxide, rather than water, have proved efficient in combating fire in archives. The gases will not harm the records and choke the fire by depriving it of oxygen. Unfortunately, it does the same for humans so staff must instantly evacuate if the gas is triggered off. It must also be noted that halon is costly and is likely to be beyond the resources of the smaller archives.

Thirdly, develop and practise emergency procedures to minimise the damage once a fire has started or has been extinguished. The Conservation Chapter has more details about disaster preparedness and recovery, but a few points need to be raised here.

Properly trained staff can not only prevent fire hazards they can also fight an already existing seat of fire. If fire breaks out during the day, staff are most likely to be the first people to arrive on the scene. If properly trained for fire emergencies, staff can extinguish a limited blaze long before the fire brigade arrives on the scene and salvage operations can begin immediately.

Box C   Space Allocation and Requirements

---

a) *Allocation of Space Recommended for Archival Facilities.*
    Records storage/stacks   60–70%
    Archival Services and Administration   30–40%
- Processing areas (closed to the public)   15–22%
- Reference Areas/Exhibits and Public Conveniences   7–10%
- Administrative Offices (semi–closed to public)   8%

b) *Absolute Minimum Requirements for Facilities and Equipment*

Storage Area		**Administrative Areas**	
Environment	Clean	Environment	Around + 22ºC
	Cold	Space	3.3 square metres/member of staff
	Dry (no less than	Equipment	A desk and chair/member of staff
	40% relative		Bookcase
	humidity)		Typewriter or WP
	Dark	**Public Areas**	
Equipment	Shelves	*Reading Room*	
	Fire Detectors and	Environment	Around + 22ºC
	Extinguishers	Equipment	A table and chair/researcher
	Ladders/Step stools		Bookcases
	Trolleys		Copy machine (share with office)
Processing Area			Microfilm Readers
Environment	No direct sun	*Exhibits*	
	Free of dust	Environment	Low light level if original material exhibited
Equipment	Brush or Vacuum	Equipment	Fire Detectors and Extinguishers
	Cleaner		Display cabinets
	Workbench		Screens
	Shelves, Racks,		Chairs or lounge
	Cupboards	*Seminar/Training*	
Supplies	Boxes	Environment	Around + 22ºC
	Cotton tape	Equipment	A table and chair/researcher
	Wrapping paper		Black/white board
	Folders		Slide projector
	Envelopes		Screen
	Clips		Overhead projector
			Film projector
			Video equipment

ALLOCATING SPACE

Having acquired your accommodation and attended to the general environmental requirements, you must decide how to allocate the space. The accepted formula in archives is that 60%–70% of space is devoted to storage, 15%–20% to processing and the remaining area divided between administration and public areas. Depending on the holdings, the clientele, the funding and the archives' relationship within its parent organisation, some physical areas of the archives may be emphasised and others kept

A limit of seven shelves high permits comfortable, safe access to records. Courtesy — Council of the City of Sydney Archives.

more low key. For example, an historical society archives may stress the importance of the reference and exhibit facilities while an in-house business archives may be more concerned with the storage and administration areas.

The level of your archival activity will also affect how you allocate space. For example, say you have a staff of three, the largest single deposit you receive is five boxes and you rarely have researchers. In this situation you can afford to restrict your processing area (because you never work on large quantities of records) and have a larger administrative area where the occasional researcher may work (as there are three of you it is likely that there will always be someone to supervise).

Remember to plan ahead for growth. Suppose you are planning to alter your acquisiton policy or raise your profile. You may have realised there is a need for local business records to be collected and preserved. Business records can be extensive and will require an increase, not only in storage space, but also in your processing area.

How you allocate your space also affects the efficiency and speed of your work. For example, if your storage area is distant from your processing and reference areas, there will be a delay in retrieving items. Non-adjacent processing, office and reading areas create difficulties in communication between you and your staff or readers. Particularly if you work alone, you will need to plan ahead so that you have suitable desk work to do when supervising researchers.

It is advisable to categorise the records in your collection into 'Highly Used', 'Frequently Used' and 'Rarely Used'. The categories can then be located so that the most highly used are closest to you and the rarely used furthest away from you or on less accessible shelves. If you have several storage areas which are dispersed this system of ranking records and storing them accordingly can save you precious time.

However, all archives facilities must plan to accommodate four basic functions: storage, processing, administration and public service; and the discussion which follows will treat each in turn. Some examples of layouts for small archives with different physical space are provided in Appendix One: Plans for small archives facilities, at the end of this chapter.

The Storage Area

Space and Conditions The storage area, which should comprise 60–70% of total facility space, is the permanent home of the records and its quality and management has an enormous impact on their continued preservation. Traffic and work activities in this area should be kept to a minimum so that the environment is kept stable. Also, the persons authorised to have access to the stacks should be limited to minimise misfiling of their material. If possible only one person should handle retrieval and refiling to ensure accountability and the only other persons permitted in the stacks should be cleaners operating under stringent guidelines.

The room itself should be clean, cool and free from water hazards. The ideal environment for paper records storage is $+15^0-20^0C$ and 50% relative humidity. Some lights are needed to access the records but these should be turned off when not needed for retrieval. A big open space is preferred and it is recommended that unnecessary walls be demolished to utilise the area more efficiently and avoid the creation of microclimates. Contrary to the popular conviction that archives are dusty and cramped, modern archivists aim to have storage areas as spacious, clean and uncluttered as possible.

Some non–paper records are very sensitive to dust (paper gives off dust and gases) and should be stored separately. The same records also benefit from lower temperatures and humidity than paper records. Categories of original records that should be considered for special purpose storage are

- photographic negatives
- microfilm negatives
- master magnetic discs, tapes and diskettes

In an area separated from the rest of the archives or insulated from the rest of the storage area, these records can enjoy an environment with temperatures as low as $+10^0C$ and a relative humidity of 20–30%. Usually these special storage arrangements are beyond the resources of a small archives. However, it may be possible for the archivist to arrange for use of such storage facility at a large state or federal archives.

Equipment for Records Storage in the stack area is of two kinds: storage for records, and equipment to retrieve and transport records. For storage of records, boxes are universally accepted as the best and most economical protection for loose papers, files, cards, small volumes etc. Requirements of a good box are discussed in the segment on equipment of the processing area. To store boxes, bundles and volumes the archives will need shelving of a size and make suitable for the records they will carry. For retrieval of records from high shelves stepstools and ladders will be necessary; and, whenever a number of boxes needs to be moved, a trolley will ease and speed up the process.

Shelving for records is the top priority in equipment purchases. However, the choice and number of shelving units will depend upon your needs and the weight–bearing capacity of the storage area. Almost any shelving can fit the basic requirements of storage, protection from water (from underneath and above) and dust. Costs have to be balanced against factors of space, convenience, safety, ease and speed of access. Most archival shelving is manufactured of steel, treated with an anti–corrosive agent and an enamel coating to prevent rust and scratching. Wooden

shelves have to be specially treated and sealed to withstand fire
and wood–eating insects and are more expensive than standard
steel shelving. The one major problem facing the purchaser of
steel shelving is that condensation easily forms on items in a
room with excess humidity.

Shelving is made up from standard components of uprights,
shelves, cross bars, bases, backs, ends and sides.

Shelves are fixed by steel clips or by nuts and bolts which
should be zinc plated to resist rusting. Preference is often given
to using clips, as shelves can easily be adjusted to accommodate
various heights of records. The distance between each shelf
should be the height of the tallest item on the shelf plus an allow-
ance of 20mm to enable items to be placed on the shelf and
retrieved without being damaged. The bottom shelf should be at
least 10cm above floor level to make it easier to clean the floor
and as an extra precaution in case of flooding. As mentioned previously, no records should be stored on top of shelving, in case
of water damage from above (including sprinklers); and the top
of the shelf should be protected by a 'dust cover' for added
protection.

The standard length of shelves can be either 900 or 1200mm
long and the standard depth is 400mm. The choice of length can
depend on the size of the boxes to be stored, the disposition of
the room and the load each shelf is to carry. Shelves and boxes
should both be in metric measurement, although some second-
hand shelving will be imperial. In this case, ensure the boxes can
be easily accommodated on the shelves, and that the space is not
wasted.

Problems will inevitably result if the floors or the shelves are
not made for the loads they are required to take. Before ordering
shelving, an average shelf of records should be weighed and the
result compared both with the building specifications and those
supplied by the shelving manufacturer. To accommodate most
archival requirements the floors should support 1500–2000kg
per square metre per storey, rising to a maximum of 80 tonnes per
stanchion for certain compactus style systems. A shelf measuring
900mm in length often takes boxed files which weigh about 30kg,
with bound volumes being over twice that weight. A range of
steel shelving should have the capacity of carrying a 100kg
weight per shelf, the total weight being calculated by multiplying
the total number of shelves.

One of the main choices which exists is whether to purchase
static (or fixed) shelving or mobile (or compactus type)
shelving.

Static Shelving or fixed shelving is generally of two types. The
most popular consists of rows of free standing shelves erected
with aisle space between each row or double row of shelving.
Shelving is normally installed back to back, except along walls or

other natural boundaries, in which case a single row is installed. If it is a heavy gauge and suitably braced, it is particularly good to accommodate heavier than average records such as bound volumes. It also has the advantage of being able to be dismantled and moved or reconfigured. Some brands can even be converted to mobile shelving if the need arises. The second type of static shelving consists of installing fixed posts from floor to ceiling and attaching shelves between them. Because this type requires more or less permanent placement, it is not recommended for small archives.

Mobile Shelving or compactus style comprises back-to-back shelving that is mounted on tracks. The shelving moves along the track, generally with a fixed, one-sided bay at each extreme of the shelving. As a row of mobile shelving requires only one aisle, the saving of space is considerable and increases with longer rows and few aisles. Movement of the ranges is accomplished by using a manual wheel or handle and can be powered electrically. Because of maintenance expense and the dangers of faulty operation, power driven units are not recommended for small archives.

Adjustable shelves are needed to accommodate the variety of record forms.

Mobile shelving, properly selected and installed, can be an excellent solution for an archives with limited space for storage. However, the construction of the room designated for the stack may determine that mobile shelving is an impossibility. The load-bearing capacity of the floor requires investigation before any shelving is installed. Mobile shelving, fully laden with records, generally requires much more load-bearing capacity than does static shelving, even up to 80 tonnes per stanchion. Another consideration is the need for a level floor, and some areas fitted with mobile shelving experience air circulation problems. The air problem can be moderated by providing rubber 'doorstops' at the bottom of shelving to prevent the shelving from closing completely, or by allowing for additional aisle space when ordering the shelving, so that the shelving is never closed completely. In a room without air-conditioning, particularly in humid climates, mobile shelving is not recommended for these reasons.

If, in addition, the Archives room has vertical columns or is of an irregular shape, the advantages of mobile shelving are not great. A floor plan of the area using paper cutouts to represent the shelving according to scale, should be used to plan the storage area wisely. Extra-wide shelving can be used for larger items and extra space should be allowed for the area required to open and use horizontal plan cabinets. Aisles between shelving need to be at least 800mm and central aisles at least 900mm or as much as economy allows. (see Appendix One at end of chapter).

The central aisle should always lead on to the main door to allow maximum ease of access for loaded trolleys and people.

Box D   Vocabulary and Measures

---

a) *Shelf Vocabulary*

	Archival use of term	**Shelf manufacturers' use of term**
Stack	Room, floor or separate area of shelving	Row of bays
Bay	One unit/section of shelving, 2 sides, 1 top, 1 bottom, 1 back (or cross bracing)	One unit/section of shelving, 2 sides, 1 top, 1 bottom, 1 back (or cross bracing)
Shelf	900mm–1200mm in length 250mm–500mm in depth	900mm–1200mm in length 250mm–500mm in depth

b) *Standard measures for areas and equipment used in an archival context.*

	Length	**Height**	**Width/Depth**
Box	390mm	260mm	175mm
Shelf	900–1200mm	1900–2100mm	250mm
Bay or row length	max. 10m		
Aisle, between rows			min. 800mm
central			min. 900mm
Doors			900mm
where trolleys are used			double doors min. 500mm each

From the central aisle bays of shelving are positioned at right angles. Bays arranged alongside a wall should have an airspace of a couple of centimetres between the wall and the back of the shelf. Tall shelves might need bracing so as not to topple over when loaded. For shelving higher than 2.1 metres, ladders or stools are required, however the use of ladders considerably slows down retrieval operations and increases the risk of accidents.

Shelving Layout. Within the stack area, all rows and bays of shelving should be uniquely numbered and identified to enable easy retrieval and to maintain accurate shelf lists. Where there are significant holdings of small accessions or groups of records, it is also useful to number each shelf. A simple system is to give each row of shelving a number from 1 to whatever, to number each bay within each row from 1 (starting always at the left–hand end of the row) and to number each shelf within each bay from 1 (starting at the uppermost shelf but ignoring the top of the shelving, on which you are not going to put records anyway). This will be sufficient for most needs and will also allow shelves to be renumbered easily if additional shelves are added or some are removed when making space for smaller or larger items. Under this system, Location 10/3/5 would mean Row 10, Bay 3, Shelf 5. In some repositories, more refined space allocations can indicate the exact position on each shelf of each box. For example, Location 4/6/2/3 would mean Row 4, Bay 6, Shelf 2, Box 3.

Loading the shelves. Storing a single row of boxes on a shelf provides easy access to all records. If deep shelving is the only shelving available, two rows of boxes, one stored behind the other will improve space efficiency, but involves double handling. Boxes with minimum retrieval could be stored in the back row. It is undesirable to have boxes stored three deep as the third row could not be reached by a normal reach. To stabilise the range and particularly if the unit is very high, it is advisable to load an empty range from the bottom shelf up.

Bench or Table. The storage area should be provided with a table or bench of the same type as is used in the processing area, so that a number of boxes can be opened and examined as necessary and paperwork to document the files and retrievals can be completed.

Essential Accessories. A constant flow of records will be moving in and out of the stack area and the provision of some mechanical aid for their retrieval and transport might be necessary. To retrieve records from shelving higher than 2100mm most people will need something to step up on. While a sturdy chair may seem sufficient, specially designed *stepping stools* with a non–slip surface are preferable (these stools are extensively used in libraries and are not expensive). Only *step–ladders* should be used to retrieve records in archives. Ordinary ladders are difficult to secure on a smooth surface and in narrow aisles the angle of the steps will not be correct, making it dangerous and difficult to

Trolleys and mobile tables facilitate heavy work. Courtesy — Council of the City of Sydney Archives.

Kick stools and ladders may be required to reach upper shelves. Courtesy — Council of the City of Sydney Archives.

climb. Folding step ladders of aluminium with a flat top on which to place the box while checking the contents are commercially available. Heavier structures on lockable casters will be suitable for very high ranges.

The use of ladders always involves a possible risk of accidents. That risk can be minimised if staff are using sensible footwear and are working in pairs while using the ladder.

Carting records to and from the stack area will be greatly facilitated by the use of a *trolley*. The size and type chosen depends basically on the amount of records which have to be shifted at the one time and the layout of the building.

Handtrucks with two or six wheels depending on whether there are steps to negotiate or not, carry 4–10 boxes at one time. The six wheeled handtruck is the only trolley that can negotiate steps and high doorsteps. They don't take up much space in the storeroom, but staff will have to bend and lift while loading and unloading the boxes.

Platform trolleys can be made of steel or plastic and vary in length. Plastic platform trolleys are light but with only one turnable wheel pair they can be hard to manoeuvre in winding and narrow aisles.

With bin trolleys and platform trolleys with the load placed at waist level unnecessary bending and lifting is avoided. With a good sized load this kind of trolley will be a bit top heavy and can topple over on an uneven surface.

Processing Area

Space and Conditions. The processing area of an archives is where records are received, accessioned, cleaned, arranged and described for future reference use. This area usually occupies 15–22% of the total archives facility.

As processing activities require materials such as boxes, acid–free paper and folders, this area should include space to store such supplies. To minimise the logistics of moving records, the point where materials are delivered or unloaded should be adjacent to the processing area, as should the storage area. If possible there should be a loading dock which has weather protection so that loading and unloading of vehicles does not expose records to rain and wind.

Space planning should then accommodate the requirements of these separate but interrelated activities:
- receiving and checking incoming shipments of records
- cleaning of dirt and dust from records
- sorting, arranging and describing records
- temporary holding of records awaiting processing or transfer to storage
- temporary holding of records awaiting destruction
- storage of supplies and equipment needed for processing

The room should have wide doors to enable trolleys to be used to transport material. Because records are kept here for some months, often without protection whilst processing is undertaken, the area should be kept scrupulously clean and protected from excess light. Individual worklights are acceptable for close work as no document will be exposed for lengthy periods. Floors should be of material which is easy to clean, linoleum or cork tiles being suitable. Because of light restrictions, the room should be painted in light colours. Since the area will be used by staff the temperature can be adjusted for human comfort without damaging the records.

Equipment. Workbenches or tables represent the most important pieces of furniture in the processing area. *Workbenches* can be built with fully lockable casters to enable them to be moved to form long benches in a row or pushed together to form a wide surface, according to the records being processed. These can also double as trolleys if there is not a formal loading dock, and incoming records can be easily placed on top of the benches and wheeled to the area for processing. Care should be taken, however, not to overload them in this use. Workbenches should be about 900mm in height, to be used by staff sitting on stools or standing up. They should be about 800mm wide, with the length to be determined by the number of people using the bench, the type of records processed and the disposition of the processing area. Shelf space can be built in under the workbench. Workbenches are often made of steel crossbars and uprights,

Cabinets holding records undergoing processing divide an open work area into 'offices'.

with the top made of a hard surface such as pineboards covered in hard laminate for a smooth and clean surface. Shelving manufacturers can make workbenches according to the individual archives' specification and requirements.

When *tables* are used for processing the rule is generally the longer the better. Alternatively, use several small tables of the same height to create one long flat surface. One person can comfortably reach over a table area of 2000mm long x 900mm wide while sorting records sitting down.

The height of chairs is dependent on the height of tables and vice versa. Regardless of the height of the table the distance between the top of the seat and the top of the table should be approximately 30cm for maximum comfort. Benches and tables suitable to work at while standing up (approximately 900mm high) will need to be equipped with special high chairs.

Brush or vacuum cleaner. Cleaning surface dirt and dust off records is one of the first tasks the archivist undertakes after records are received. This work should be done in an area separate from the archives proper, as dust and mould spores can get into the air circulation system and cause conservation problems. A library brush or a vacuum cleaner can be used for this task. A tank vacuum cleaner with adjustable suction and changeable nozzles, with or without bristles, is preferred as too much force can damage the records. Nilfisk makes a special attachment for cleaning of records and other precious materials.

The processing area needs plenty of storage space, for the records themselves and for materials used in conjunction with these activities. *Shelves* are necessary for the storage of records before and during processing and records awaiting transfer or destruction. If the archives is receiving records from people and institutions packing records in non–archival boxes, several ranges should have wider than normal (300mm) shelves to accommodate oversized parcels and boxes. For the same reason ranges with movable shelves should be used in this area.

Materials needed while processing records should be stored in the processing area or adjacent to it. Large *cupboards* for different sized boxes, folders, wrapping material, rope or tape makes it easy to keep the area tidy and dustfree.

Wrapping and packing materials are often sold in massive rolls that are difficult to handle. If the rolls are put on racks, either attached to a wall or freestanding, they are much easier to work with and the material is protected from unnecessary wear and tear.

Fumigation and conservation. When consingments of records are arriving from very different sources at the archives some of them are bound to be afflicted with insects or mould or both. These records will have to be treated before they are allowed into the stack or the whole collection will be affected before long.

As fumigation involves the handling of toxic chemicals it is recommended that the services of commercial companies or some larger archives that employ a conservator be utilised.

Before undertaking any repair or conservation work a trained conservator should be consulted. The pitfalls in the conservation area are numerous for the unwary. Materials and techniques that were perfectly safe to use in one situation can prove a disaster in another. For the minor repairwork that the archivist attempts, there are some good 'how to' manuals listed in the Conservation Chapter of this publication.

Supplies. Records stored in archives should always be protected from the outside environment by being boxed or wrapped. Inside the box or parcel records are separated by folders, envelopes, jackets or clips.

Boxes of varying shapes and sizes have been tried for archives storage.

A suitable box is:
- cheap
- made of strong board so that the sides do not cave in flat while stored
- easy to assemble without tools
- able to accommodate records without force being used in packing
- able to be carried by the weakest member of staff and taken off the top shelf when fully loaded
- suitable to be gripped when taking off and putting on the shelf
- capable of fitting the shelves without wasted space (old imperial shelves may not store metric boxes with good economy)

In Australia, most archives have adopted the standard Australian Archives Type 1 box or versions of it. This box is cut in one piece with creases to facilitate folding. The external dimensions are 39 x 26 x 17.5cm and it easily accommodates pages and files of A4 or foolscap sizes. Full of paper it weighs around 5kg, a manageable weight for most people. It has a hole at both ends to facilitate gripping it. But it is not perfect, as the flap of the lid is a bit too short and it is not quite high enough to store folders of A4 size. A boxmaking company can make up 'the perfect box' according to specifications for anyone. It is wise to confer with other archives in the area to see if a good box is already available from a boxmaker or if a co-ordinated effort can produce one.

Outsized material should be wrapped in a sturdy paper and tied with cotton tape. If the quantity of outsize material is large and regularly received, it may be more economical to investigate having custom containers made. In the same way, quantities of records of smaller dimensions, such as cards, can justify boxes to accommodate them, particularly if retrieval and usage is high.

Wrappings, boxes and folders can be ordered in acid–free

Records are wrapped in acid-free paper and stored in standard archives cartons.

materials. Unlike ordinary cardboard boxes and papers these will not affect the general deterioration of records by adding the impurities of their paper to those of the records inside. Records that have been deacidified by a conservator should definitely be housed with and in acid-free materials; and, if budget allows, consider acid-free boxes, envelopes and folders for sensitive materials like photographs and films.

When ordering materials, plan to buy sufficient quantities to last for a year so that time is not wasted ordering and doing paperwork for small amounts. Maintain a list of all suppliers, put the archives on their mailing list for catalogues and keep these catalogues in an easily accessible folder (see Conservation Chapter for suppliers).

Administrative Areas

Space and Conditions. In a small archives the reading room and the administrative areas are best kept adjacent because of the many activities interacting. Staff will want to use the reference library or the technical equipment in the reading room and researchers might have to be supervised from the office if a special reading room attendant is not employed. The use of glass wall partitions between the two areas is often a satisfactory solution to the latter problem. For the privacy of the staff, 'one-way glass' is recommended.

Each member of staff will need approximately 3.3 square metres of floor space, but if the office is used for other activities such as interviews with researchers, staff conferences etc. the space will have to be increased accordingly.

Equipment. In the office are generally kept all the records controlling the archival holdings and an extensive collection of forms and lists in volumes, binders and folders. To accommodate these and perhaps a reference library the office will need a filing cabinet and a large bookcase or two, apart from the indispensable desk and chair. A typewriter or a wordprocessor will be needed if these services cannot be obtained from elsewhere.

Public Service Areas

With the increase in genealogical research and the awakened interest in historical buildings and sites many archival institutions have felt a pressure for additional services to the general public. To make records available to researchers in a wider sense of the word, archives have expanded into the realm of user education and public relations. Additional activities such as exhibitions, workshops and lectures will involve additional space requirements. Figure 4 in Appendix One at the end of the chapter shows a plan for the full range of reference and public services.

Reading Room

Space and Conditions. Of the total space allocated, the reading room in a small archival set-up occupies approximately 7–10%.

The organisation may already have an area set apart for servicing information seekers — a library etc. The facilities of this existing service may be utilised for using original records — but do not forget the need for continuous surveillance by reference staff.

In the reading room researchers should be registered, interviewed and instructed before being left to pursue the use of reference books, indexes and archival material. To minimise the disturbance to other researchers, these activities could be in an office, rather than in the open reading area.

The needs of the users must be incorporated into the planning of this area. Researchers may be elderly, handicapped, have difficulties in reading or in understanding the language. Researchers may want to use the archives as individuals or they may visit as groups. Whether they be staff or the general public, all users require convenient, but controlled, access to the reading room, a logical layout with good signs and an environment which facilitates research work.

Glass partitions give the archivist some privacy yet permit supervision of reading areas.

Sunlight should be restricted in the reading room as in all areas where original material is used. If the reading room faces due south, light from windows is less damaging; but it is desirable to use curtains or shades to filter or block direct sunlight. To compensate for the loss of daylight each table may require its own individual reading lamp. General lighting should be kept at a low level.

Equipment. *Tables*, not desks, are used in reading rooms as no original material should be left in the room after use. To view large–format material without risk of damage, the table has to be big enough for large items to be opened on the tabletop. Minimum table size for a researcher is 1m x 0.70m.

The use of several small lightweight tables that can easily be put together to accommodate different sized material is more economical spacewise than one table. To utilise equipment to a maximum degree, all the tables in the reading room can be of this lightweight type.

The tables used in the reading room should have a smooth, washable top that paper does not stick to, and care should be taken when using metal tables as their sharp corners can damage leather.

Shelves. The reading room often includes a small library of reference books. For these standard library shelving of 0.25m depth is suitable.

For the finding aids and indexes used by researchers, an area should be provided in the reading room with shelves for binders, books and card drawers for card indexes. Index and reference copies of maps in big binders can be housed on a table nearby.

Microfilm/fiche readers are now almost standard in any archives. Reference material acquired from other archives and libraries is often sold in fiche or film format and in-house archives are increasingly faced with records consignments in a micro-format. Many archives are initiating filming of records to ˙facilitate access or for preservation purposes (see Chapter Nine Computers and Micrographics).

Microfilm readers enlarge the micro-image to a readable size. The miniature images generally come on film (in a roll or individual frames on an aperture card) or as a fiche (a flat sheet with several rows of little frames) and microfilm readers can be purchased for either film or fiche format or adjustable to read both. To view the reduced image in original scale the microfilm reader will have to be equipped with a lens that magnifies it at a readable ratio. It is important to choose the appropriate readers for the film or fiche, taking the reduction ratio into consideration as well as purchasing cost and maintenance cost.

Microfilm reader/printers are bulkier than readers and are more expensive. Like microfilm readers, some reader-printers can be purchased with different lenses making it possible to 'blow up' an image. They can also be supplied with carriers to read several different microfilm formats and reduction ratios and also have the added benefit of producing an acceptable copy. Microfilm printers that can use ordinary paper keep the cost of copying down considerably. Second-hand readers and printers can sometimes be on the market. The same warning applies to purchasing these as to any machine with movable parts — cars, washing machines etc. Investigate the machine's history carefully, consider how often you will use it, test-drive . . . what seems like a bargain at the time could work out to be a drain on your pocket . . .

Copies of paper records are generally produced by *photocopying machines*. In comparison with all the steps necessary to make a photograph of a document the photocopy is a marvel of ease and speed. Old or fragile documents should not be exposed to the hazards of photocopying because the heat and light in the process will damage the document. A once-off negative taken in an ordinary photographic setting can provide a reference copy for damaged or fragile material.

Complicated machinery always involves maintenance (someone will have to be responsible for the constant supply of bulbs, papers, liquids) and service of the equipment. The latter will be offered by the manufacturer/distributor and as an on-going expense it must be allowed for in the annual budget.

Before investing in any expensive plant it is sensible to seek advice from other archives or organisations using the equipment and to visit several suppliers to look at the machines in action.

Exhibits
Space and conditions. A small *display area* exhibiting some aspects of the archival collection in the reading room or outside

it will attract attention. Exhibitions displaying original material will of necessity have to be in locked cabinets and under supervision. Special restrictions as to light levels and necessary fire protection measures make it very hard to find suitable areas for display of original material. Copies of archival material magnified to a suitable size with labels and text are often a more satisfactory solution.

Equipment. Because of the risk of theft, vandalism or accidents, archival material should be displayed in special *lockable cabinets* or not at all. As it is possible to make very good copies of records for a reasonable price (as opposed to copies of most museum items — replicas — which are extremely expensive) reproduced archival material makes perfect exhibition material. And because the copies are conveniently flat they can easily be displayed on *screens*.

Other public areas needed/appreciated by researchers are restrooms, an area with lockable boxes (for bags, books and coats not allowed in reading room) and somewhere to have a cup of coffee and a sandwich.

Seminars/Training

Space and Conditions. An in-house archives can often utilise the resources of its organisation for seminars or training activities even if the facilities are not adjacent to reading room or offices. For other archives a separate room for these activities may not be feasible, but the exhibition or even the reading room may double as a seminar/training room when closed for researchers.

Equipment. For each user a chair and a table should be provided. The lecturer will need a black/white board and often a slide projector and a screen is called for. Additional equipment — film projectors, overhead projectors and videos can, unless they are extensively used, be borrowed or hired for the occasion.

OTHER RESOURCES

Small archival institutions with limited resources have a lot to gain by co-operation. Useful equipment not used on a day to day basis can be shared, professional staff can be acquired, and manufacturers can be approached to supply plant and boxes at a discount. Sharing facilities opens up enormous possibilities for the small archives. Centralised storage for archival records in a limited geographical area, e.g. the 'Hunter Valley Archival Repository', low temperature storage for master film negatives or regional conservation and microfilming facilities are some areas where co-operation could be invaluable.

If the archives is a part of a larger organisation there can be valuable resources to be tapped within the organisation. For example it may be possible to use photocopiers, computers, photographic equipment and human resources (such as carpenters, labourers) from time to time or on a regular basis. If these facilities cannot be obtained from within, other 'sister' organisations or nearby archives may give aid or advice. Disaster planning is one area where the resources of other archives must be investigated. Every archives should have a plan of where to turn when disaster, natural or human, occurs. To have discussed matters such as assistance from a conservator, and to have identified the closest archives with resources to assist in drying soaked records will make a big difference when instant remedial action is required.

All archival institutions have the basic functions of storing, processing and making records available for users. Each of these functions requires specific space and equipment.

The archivist will need to work out the requirements for a satisfactory archival service within the means at his/her disposal and with an eye to future resources that could be made available. To stretch the archives' meagre resources, the possibility of joint usage of facilities, from within the organisation and out, should be investigated. Assistance, in the form of advice or loan of equipment, can be sought from other archives.

As circumstances differ from archives to archives, so do the solutions to problems concerning facilities and equipment.

The increasing use of archives and the subsequent demand on archival resources means that the records themselves and improvements to ease their wear and tear must take first place. If an archives provides poor storage and equipment for its holdings, it will not enjoy much of a future.

KEEPING THINGS GOING

It is never too early to analyse existing practices and subsequently to introduce plans and procedures to improve them. Unfortunately, most organisations only review their practices when compelled to by other circumstances. The most common circumstances are:

- when new staff are appointed or positions abolished
- when the organisation is undergoing structural or functional change
- when the organisation is facing scrutiny or
- when things are going wrong

Whatever the causes, we should all realise that change is a natural and continuous process which we should incorporate rather than try to exclude from our organising process. What we seek to do is to manage the impact of change by having a definite, but flexible, framework of policies and structures within which to operate. Thus we develop definite limits for our sphere of action within which we can move to adjust priorities and procedures for maximum results.

Measurement and Evaluation

All the preceding paragraphs have concentrated on developing the framework, tools and facilities for your operations. The remaining chapters deal with the technical aspects of archival work. We hope it will be possible to digest and apply the information and strategies discussed. If you do so, how will you know how you are going?

The only objective way of assessing your situation and performance is to set measures of effectiveness. That is, to measure activities. Activities can be measured quantitatively — how often they occurred. They can be measured qualitatively — how good or effective they were. For example, you can measure the number of reference enquiries you received. You can also measure how many you answered and how quickly you were able to answer them.

Why collect this information? To enable you to:

- assess and monitor progress and, if necessary, adjust priorities and resources
- predict trends and plan for them and other contingencies in the coming month, quarter, year
- justify requests, analyse and report objectively
- compare your organisation with others
- promote and publicise the programme with accuracy and confidence.

Reserve time for your own record keeping to avoid scenes like this.

Most archival work is susceptible to measurement. Appendix Two lists archival functions and some of the ways they can be measured. To be valid measures must be accurate, they should be representative and they should be taken for specified periods.

It may not be necessary or useful for you to measure all the activities mentioned in Appendix Two. Conversely, there may be additional statistics you wish to keep. Whatever your decision it is important to identify what data you need and to plan to capture it in the most efficient way. Attempt to build the collection of data into your daily activities, or to have it produced automatically. For example, if you require every researcher to sign the search room register it is very easy to calculate how many people used the search room during the week, month, year. However, if you had to reconstruct this information it would be time consuming and probably inaccurate.

If you do invest time and stationery in recording and collecting statistics do use them. Collate, compare and evaluate them. Having done so do not keep the findings to yourself. Incorporate them in your annual reports, use them in justifying your budget, and quote them when arguing for additional space or staff.

Advertising Your Achievements

Archives belong to an organisation or community, they rely on that organisation and community for resources and support, and their survival can depend on their visibility. Publicising your achievements is a way of maintaining a profile, attracting interest and support from a wider community and assuring existing sponsors of progress.

Regardless of how you are publicising your achievements do present the information clearly, concisely, truthfully and attractively. Tailor your presentation for your readers. Plan your publicity so that you will be able to cope with its effects. It is damaging to create a demand that cannot be fulfilled or expectations that are unrealistic.

Be positive about your programme. Use every opportunity to keep it visible — mention initiatives, highlight how the existence/use of archives achieved savings or averted disaster, identify fresh uses of archives and publicise significant deposits.

CONCLUSION

This chapter has focused on establishing the framework for the archives programme. Without this structure, professional work, despite its excellence, will founder. The planning, organisation and management of archival resources is a continuous and continuing responsibility. It is a task that requires sensitivity to your immediate surroundings, its staff and clientele, but it also requires an awareness and responsiveness to the wider forces which impact upon our society and its institutions.

FURTHER READING

British Standard 5454: 1977. *Recommendations for the Storage and Exhibitions of Archival Documents.*

Duchein, Michel, *Archives Building and Equipment.* ICA Handbook No. 1. Munich: Verlag Documentation, 1977.

Hunt, John, *Managing People at Work: A Manager's Guide to Behaviour in Organisations.* London: Pan, 1981.

Lakein, Alan, *How to Get Control of Your Time and Your Life.* New York: Signet, 1974.

Robek, Mary F., Gerald F. Brown and Wilmer O. Maedke, *Information and Records Management.* 3rd edition. Encino, CA: Glencoe Publishing Company, 1987.

Society of American Archivists, *Evaluation of Archival Institutions: Services, Principles and Guide to Self Study.* Chicago: SAA, 1982.

Society of American Archivists, *Guidelines for College and University Archives.* Chicago: SAA, 1980.

Victoria Public Record Office, *Guidelines for the Storage of Public Records.* PROS 82/4. Melbourne: Government Printer, 1982.

Wild, Ray, editor, *How to Manage.* London: Pan, 1982.

**Figure One.
2 Room Archives**
Scale: 10mm =
1000mm
(research, office
& processing) +
(storage)

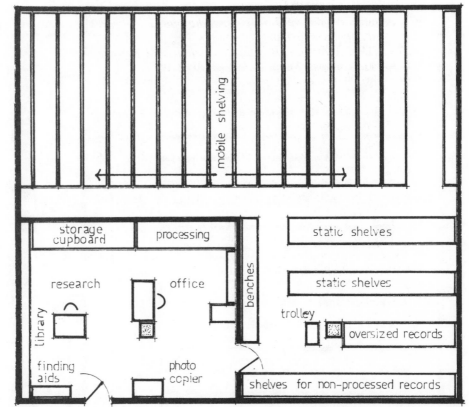

**Figure Two.
3 Room Archives**
Scale: 10mm =
1000mm
(research, office)
+ (processing)
+ (storage)

*Drawing by
Marion Sully.*

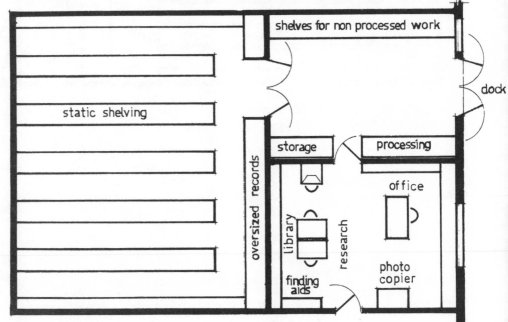

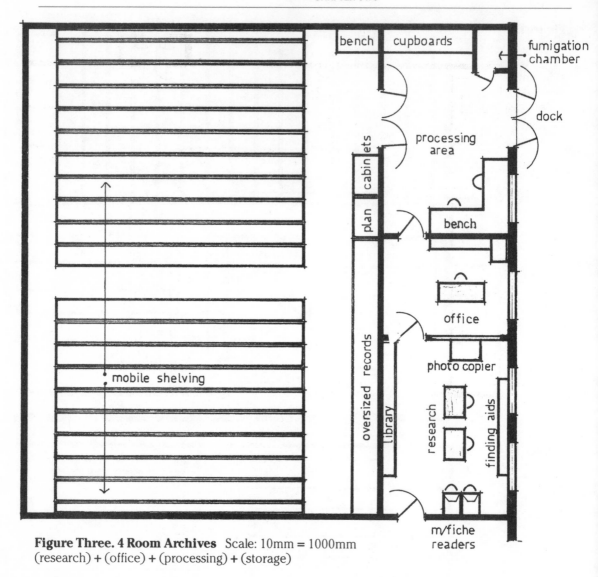

Figure Three. 4 Room Archives Scale: 10mm = 1000mm
(research) + (office) + (processing) + (storage)

Drawing by Marion Sully.

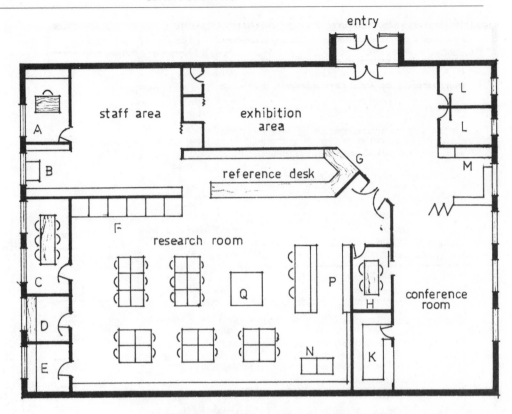

Figure Four. Archives Public Services Area

A   archivist in charge
B   staff photo copier
C   group room
D   soundproof room
E   research room
F   microfilm & microfiche readers
G   reception desk
H   multipurpose room
K   kitchen
L   toilets
M   lockers
N   photo copier
P   finding aids desk & catalogue
Q   returns table

Scale: 5mm = 1000mm

Drawing by Marion Sully.

Appendix Two   An Overview of the Archives System

Function	Work Activity	Tools for Structure/Control	Measures/Statistics
Total Programme	Purpose of programme Type holdings, clientele Facility location Administrative context Responsibilities of archivist Components of programme from acquisition through PR Facilities and services	Policy document Description of programme elements, goals, and functions Organisational chart Functional job descriptions Manual of policies and procedures Budget Long–range plan	Programme: short–term objectives for each element and work area
Basic Information for Clients: Information leaflets/brochures describing purpose/functions of the archives, how to obtain user privileges, hours and services available to clients, general types of holdings, location of facility; describing how to prepare to do particular types of research at the archives (family, graduate, historical); Also, a general guide to holdings which includes lists of publications and finding aids available for sale.				
Acquisition	Macro-surveying: for identification of potential archives, location, owners Contacts/negotiation Micro-surveying: for appraisal/disposal scheduling of particular collections and series Disposal scheduling Appraisal	Acquisitions policy and procedures Prospective acquisition log by donor and by item Survey forms: macro and micro Appraisal/disposal scheduling decision guidelines and criteria Disposal schedules Packing/Transfer Box lists Deed of gift Register of accessions Donor card file	No. of prospective donor contacts made No. of disposal schedules approved No. of surveys completed No. of appraisals made No. of accessions
Basic Information For Clients: Importance and process of retention scheduling; how to prepare shipments for transfer to the archives; types of materials sought/not sought by the archives, advantages of making donations, how to begin process of donation, general conditions of donations; reports of new accessions.				
Arrangement/ Description	Close examination of collections to set priorities, levels and recommend sorting, culling Arrangement: on paper and actual Description Preparation of finding aids	Arrangement/description policy and procedures Worksheet for A&D giving priority level, work to be accomplished, dates began/completed, by whom Separation sheets for non-textual or oversize items List of material recommended for cull Collection/series level forms for preparing descriptive inventories Finding aids 'linking' collections (i.e. chrono., subject/ function, creator/compiler)	No. of series arranged No. of series described Cost of A&D per series
Basic Information for Clients: non relevant				

Function	Work Activity	Tools for Structure/Control	Measures/Statistics
Conservation	Preventative: removing clips, refoldering, reboxing Managing storage areas Preservation services: conservation, restoration, preservation copying Environment/container stability monitoring Materials testing	Conservation policy and procedures Disaster plans Space allocation sheets Preservation services worksheets giving priorities, treatments recommended, work to be done Stability monitoring report sheets Test results sheets	No. of collections/ series shelved No. of sheets — deacidified — repaired — copied No. of stability tests carried out Savings from identifying faulty materials
Information for Clients: how to maintain your family papers and photographs; guidelines for scrapbooks			
Reference	On-site: Admission of users Reference interview Information/advice on holdings, use of finding aids General: Retrievals and refiles Copying services Remote: Research for mail inquiries Telephone inquiries Distribution of publications	Reference policies and procedures Reading room regulations Application for reader's card Reader/visitor register Record request forms Copy order forms Form/guide letters Checklists for research by staff Publications order forms/ inventory control sheets	No. of new cards issued No. of readers/ visitors No. of retrievals/ refiles No. of copies provided No. of letters sent No. of publications sent
Information for Clients: Leaflets described above under 'Total Programme' and Guide sheets for beginning researchers in various popular research specialties, scheduled 'mini–classes' for new researchers.			
User Education and Public Relations	Information and public relations Public seminars/ workshops Publications Exhibits Staff training Technical advisory services Documentation programme	Outreach policies and procedures Schedule of outreach acitivities Planning checklist for press releases, newsletters, seminars/workshops, publications, exhibits, etc. Activity evaluation form: staff and participants Participant agreements, deeds, access agreements, request forms	No. of events held No. of participants No. of hours training/ advice provided
Information for Clients: Newsletter, announcements of events, training, exhibits, technical leaflets as needed, media coverage of archives events, activities, accessions.			

An archival operation need not be large to be effective as this one room facility attests.

Selected reference works and literature on archival techniques and records management are essential.

CHAPTER THREE

ACQUISITION AND APPRAISAL

Barbara Reed

INTRODUCTION

Acquisition and appraisal are the initial functions of the archival process. Obviously, unless relevant material is identified and transferred to the archives, there is no archival collection. Once a collection has been established, however, acquisition and appraisal are equally important in ensuring that the collection develops in a controlled and organised manner. Otherwise, we face the kind of future envisaged by the character Koradubian in Kurt Vonnegut's novel *The Sirens of Titan*:

> 'In the year Ten Million . . . there would be a tremendous house-cleaning. All records relating to the period between the death of Christ and the year One Million A.D. would be hauled to dumps and burned. This would be done, said Koradubian, because museums and archives would be crowding the living right off the earth.'

The policies and procedures that archival agencies or collections use to select and manage their holdings are very similar to those used by well organised individuals to look after their own personal documents, but on a larger scale.

In the course of an ordinary day, most of us acquire or create a wide variety of personal documents: we purchase bus or train tickets; buy newspapers or books; compose letters, reports and memos; scribble notes; fill out forms; receive and send bills, invoices and receipts; take photographs; record sound and video tapes; receive computer-generated records of our financial transactions and so on. We acquire these documents, by choice or by chance, because they all have relevance to our lives: our habits, our likes and dislikes, our obligations, our work and leisure. But, in time, for one reason or another, we discard most of these documents — they may have outlived their usefulness or purpose; we may no longer have room to store them; the obligations to keep them may have expired; or we may wish to give or sell them to someone else. Altogether, we retain only a small percentage of the documentation that we create or acquire over time.

Regardless of how few documents we have in the end, we find that if we do not organise and maintain them in a systematic way, we soon lose track of them. More immediate records distract our attention from earlier ones, space becomes scarce, and the essential becomes hard to find amongst the ephemeral. In the face of chaos, the task of culling becomes progressively more daunting.

Personal muddle is, of course, our own problem, but it is one which archival programmes also face if they fail to develop and use policies, procedures and plans for ordering and controlling the records which come into their custody.

THE ACQUISITION POLICY

The acquisition policy is an important part of the general archival policies which will document the management and maintenance of the archives. The relationship of the acquisition policy to the overall archives policy is discussed in Chapter Two.

Defining and documenting acquisitions is of particular importance to every archives. An acquisition policy largely defines the nature of an archives. It defines what the archives will collect, what the limits of the collection will be and what types of material are of particular interest. The acquisition policy is the basic reference document for both archival staff and people interested in depositing their papers.

The purpose of an acquisition policy is to set down initial guidelines for assessing records offered for the collection. Without such a policy to define the intended scope and content of a collection, the temptation to acquire any material offered may be difficult to resist. Decisions on acquisition, made on the spur of the moment and without reference to a clearly stated policy, are often strongly affected by subjective considerations — for example, our knowledge, interest, or lack thereof, in the material being offered, or our personal impressions of the donor. One of the aims of an acquisition policy is to provide guidelines which will reduce the probability of personal biases affecting the collection of material. Similarly, an acquisition policy allows an archives a graceful means of refusing material unsuited to its collection.

The archivist explains archives policy on donations to a donor.

Decisions made under such a policy are also clearly understood by anyone who is subsequently in control of the archives. It is possible that, in the future, for reasons of space or expenditure, an archives may be required to justify its holdings. Material acquired within the scope of an acquisition policy, with documented criteria and reasons for its acceptance, will be less vulnerable than material acquired with no guiding principles. With proper documentation of decisions subsequent archivists will have no doubts as to why the particular material was acquired. Consistent acquisition policies provide the basis for the growth and continuation of the collection and also explain to future archivists the development of the collection.

The acquisition of any material commits the archives to continuing expense. The material must be accessioned, it must be arranged and documented, incorporated into finding aids, stored in the best accommodation available, treated by a conservator, if necessary, and made available for use. Thus collecting material that does not fall within the scope of the acquisition policy commits the archives to wasteful expense.

DEVELOPING AN ACQUISITION POLICY

Any acquisition policy derives from the purpose for which the archives exists. Most archives fulfill one of three purposes:

An *in-house archives* acquires and services the records of a parent organisation or inter-related organisations. For example, an in-house hospital archives houses the records relating to the hospital as a whole, including its clinical and administrative departments, and may also collect the papers relating to separate entities set up under the auspices of the hospital, such as fund raising foundations. Likewise a school archives cares for the official records of the school, but might also solicit the archives of closely associated bodies such as the Parents and Teachers or Citizens Associations and the organisations of ex–students.

A *collecting archives* collects records relating to a particular specialisation from the general community. For example the archives may collect within a geographic area, by type of institution or by research interest. A local history collection is a collecting archives in that it collects personal, organisational and business papers from a wide variety of sources within a specific locality. Other collecting archives may specialise in papers of individuals or occupational groups, others may acquire the papers of business, industry or labour organisations or single out particular media such as films or sound recordings.

Many archives combine in–house and collecting functions. Examples include the business archives which also collects the personal papers of senior staff associated with the business; local history collections which also care for local government archives; or a university archives which collects the materials reflecting the research specialities of academia, as well as servicing the archives of the university itself.

Acquisition policies will differ for each of the three categories of archives, as the needs of each will vary considerably.

The aim of an in–house archives is to document the history, functions and development of the parent body. The acquisition policy, therefore, needs to clarify the archives' responsibility for:

- Materials created or used directly in the work of the parent body
- Active and semi–current, as well as inactive and archival records
- Records which, over the life of the organisation, may have been lost or removed from official custody
- Records of preceding bodies or closely affiliated organisations
- Personal papers of individuals closely connected with the work of the parent body
- Various forms of recorded information, for example, will the archives acquire only paper or film based records; will it also accept objects and memorabilia?

The aim of a collecting archives is to document its particular specialisation. The collecting policy of such an archives must, firstly, identify that specialisation. For example, the local history society of any town or city should carefully designate what its geographic area will cover and focus its collecting activities within that area.

Acquisition policies, whether they are for in–house archives or collecting archives, will often undergo additional refinement. The archives may choose to limit its scope as to time span, type

Newly found archives may look a mess, but care should be taken not to disturb their order (or disorder)

of record, or categories of activity. For example, a sports archives may collect material about famous sports figures rather than the records of local sports activities and organisations; a film archives may only collect documentaries, but accept them in a number of formats i.e. 8mm, 16mm or 35mm film and video-tape.

The establishment of subject–related, theme–related or experience–related archives should be avoided. Problems about the definitions of the subject, theme or experience become inevitable. For example, an archives established to document the experiences of war will have a difficult problem in defining where the experience of war begins and ends. Will the collection include only records of the military services? Will it document the effect of war on the civilian population and if so, how far will this extend? Will records of rationing, transportation, and deportation be included? Will the experiences of those opposed to war be documented? Will it document peace movements? If a wide definition is taken, the records will overlap into many other subject areas, and will be useful for research into many subjects other than war.

The final determination of the acquisition policy for all archives will be dependent upon the following matters:

Resources
- How available is the material proposed for collection?
- Do other institutions or organisations already collect this or similar material?
- What are the estimated costs of acquiring the collection?
- What related resources (i.e. library materials) already exist, or are easily obtainable, to support the proposed collection?

Physical Formats
Which of the following physical formats are to be acquired and, more importantly, can be managed:
- Unpublished manuscripts and records?
- Printed and published material?
- Maps, plans and architectural drawings?
- Pictorial materials, including photographs?
- Audio–visual material such as cassettes, reel to reel tapes, video tapes?
- Computer–generated material, including computer tapes and printout?
- Artefacts and memorabilia, such as coins, costumes, stamps etc.?

Each record format has distinct requirements for preservation and storage. Computer records, for example, require access to a computer of the appropriate make and model to allow the recorded data to be read, and stringent environmental conditions for the storage of magnetic tape. Thus, while it is tempting to state that material in any physical format will be acceptable, available resources usually limit the kind of material which can be handled.

An archives collection should not attempt to cover too wide a range of material. Existing libraries and museums may already deal with publications, art works and objects; and co–operation, rather than competition, with them should be fostered. In many instances the most appropriate course of action is to recommend the deposit of such material with libraries and museums, with the understanding that the archives may borrow the items for exhibition, if required. Where such material complements an archival collection, a register of the final location of the object will satisfy information requirements. This solution allows an archives to avoid storing material which it is not equipped to care for and manage.

Users
It is important for the archivist to anticipate who will use the collection and how they will use it. Questions which will define potential users include:
- Is there a known demand for the proposed collection?
- Is the proposed collection serving more than a fad?
- Will it serve a variety of research interests?
- Are users likely to be interested in current as well as retrospective material?

Table One   Points to be Included in the Acquisition Policy

1) General statement of purpose of institution and/or archives programme.
2) Statement of authority to acquire material
   - Nature and basis of authority
   - person or body in whom authority to acquire is vested
3) Definition of terms:
   - records
   - official records
   - non-official records
   - reference library materials
   - non-current records
   - archives
   - archivist
   - depositor
   - archival value
   - de-accessioning
4) General description of acquisition responsibility:
   - official records
   - non-official records
   - reference library material
   - types of materials generally not acquired and why
5) General description of conditions which material must meet to be acquired
   Official • must be covered by disposal schedule
   Non-official • must fall under acquisition responsibility as outlined in 4)
   - depositor must be authorised to transfer title to material
   - material must undergo archival appraisal and be recommended for retention (unique, documented authenticity and integrity, demonstrated historical/archival value, reasonable condition, archives must be able to care for it properly)
   - material must be free of legal encumbrances or access restrictions which will diminish its research potential
   - material must become the property of the archives, to be administered as it sees fit
6) General description of review and de-accessioning of unwanted material
   - de-accessioning policy, including reasons for it
   - de-accessioning procedure — general
   - disposal options for de-accessioned material, including use of any proceeds from sale of such material
7) Information on whom to contact about material for potential acquisition

- Will users want copies of related material held elsewhere?
- Will users want copies of material from the collections for further study or publication?

Once formulated, the acquisition policy must be an authoritative document. It should have the approval of those to whom the archives is responsible, and it should be faithfully adhered to and widely communicated. It may be communicated via a brochure explaining the policy which can be distributed to all groups associated with the archives, be they researchers, current and potential donors, or other archival institutions.

The acquisition policy is a basic management tool for the growth of the archives, but it should not be allowed to fossilise. Periodic evaluation of the policy should be an integral part of management practice. Re–evaluation of the acquisition policy should involve all staff concerned in the implementation of the policy; and, wherever possible, donors' and users' views should be represented through an advisory body.

DEVELOPING AN ACQUISITION STRATEGY

Once an acquisition policy has been established and approved, it is necessary to assess the importance that acquisition will have within the archives programme. Such an assessment rests upon several key questions:

- What existing commitments must the archivist meet before accepting new material?
- Will priority be given to acquisition as opposed to arrangement and description, preservation and reference of material already in custody?
- What proportion of staff time and resources can be allocated to the collecting function?
- Will the archives seek material which extends or complements existing holdings or branch out into new areas?
- Will the archives actively pursue material which it wishes to collect or will it accept records only when they are offered?

Archivists must proceed responsibly in acquiring new material. Over zealous collecting contributes to one of the greatest archival bugbears — the backlog. Material collected in vast quantities and left unprocessed and unavailable serves neither the requirements of the archives nor its users.

AN OVERVIEW OF APPRAISAL

All archives must be selective in their acquisition of material, both to establish and to maintain a collection which is cohesive, compact and worthy of the resources required to support it.

The process of determining exactly which records fit within the boundaries established by the acquisition policy is known as 'appraisal'.

It is obvious that not all records can be kept indefinitely. Many creators and custodians of records have mechanisms, whether formal or informal, to reduce the bulk of their records during their active use in the offices. However, even with such mechanisms, the resulting bulk of records cannot be automatically considered as archives. Whether the creator is an institution or an individual, the proportion of records that are retained as archives will

3% – 7% retention ✓

usually be between 3% and 7% of the total records created. Thus only a very small fraction of records will become archives.

Decisions about what records to authorise for eventual destruction are difficult. There is a constant concern that many records are inherently unique, and that the information which they record is not recorded elsewhere. If an archivist does not designate such material as archives, they will be lost forever. On the other hand, many records exist in various formats and information is often recorded at many levels. A small quantity of records containing summarised information may be of much greater research interest than hundreds of metres of records containing diverse information. The process of appraisal is the process of balancing these types of concerns and arriving at decisions about the retention or destruction of records.

Appraisal, like acquisition, is an area where personal likes and dislikes can easily, and often unconsciously, dictate what is accepted into archives. For example, an archivist in an in-house archives who has worked in certain sections of an institution must not favour the records with which he/she is familiar over equally important records created by unfamiliar departments. Appraisal decisions based on personal likes and dislikes will lead to idiosyncratic, rather than representative, collection development.

Once this danger is recognised, steps must be taken to minimise the subjectivity of appraisal decisions. Specific criteria to establish value should be developed against which the worth of every record series is measured. Recording this information both for records which are accepted as archives and those which are rejected provides appraisal documentation which allows future generations of archivists to understand the basis of the decisions of the past.

Surveying records in storage areas is best done with one person recording information while the other examines the records.

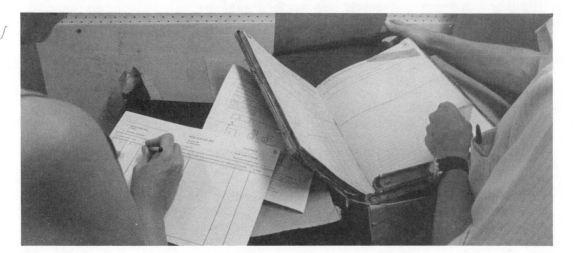

THE PRINCIPLES OF APPRAISAL

The principles of appraisal have been traditionally formulated with the needs of an in–house (and usually government) archives paramount. Despite the fact that these principles are couched in language most common to the in–house context, the basic principles are valid for the appraisal of all records.

Records have two basic characteristics which determine whether or not they are archives. These are often referred to as the *primary, evidential or documentary value* and the *secondary or informational value*. Table Two gives examples of records which fall within each category.

The *evidential value* of records is based upon the function the records had for the office or person which created and used them. Our interest as archivists lies in their value as evidence of how that office or individual conducted their business. The three major categories of records having evidential value are those that:

- Have continuing administrative, legal or financial use for the body or individual which created them, or for any subsequent bodies
- Record details which may serve to protect the civic, legal, property or other rights of individuals or the community at large
- Reflect the historical development of the creating body, its structures, functions, policies, decisions and significant operations; or which reflect the evolution of the individual's career, interest or activities

Records having *informational or secondary value* are defined as those records which contain information which is of interest not only to the creating person or organisation but also to researchers from a variety of fields of knowledge. Often such records contain information gathered originally for a purpose quite different from the uses to which the later researcher will put the records. Examples of records with informational value distinct from their original role include property insurance maps and records used subsequently by persons seeking to restore old buildings to their original appearance; census data which is used for family history; or property cards and rate books, originally used to collect taxes, and subsequently used to study changes in economic status or ethnicity in various neighbourhoods. The archivist, in consultation with experts from a variety of fields of research, must always be alert for such informational values which enhance or complement the value records may have as evidence of the work of their creators.

It should be stressed that these two basic categories are not mutually exclusive and that often the records of primary value are also those rich in information of research interest. The goal of the appraiser is to apply the values carefully and objectively so

Table Two   Examples of Records According to Appraisal Categories

Appraisal Criteria	Categories of Records	Specific Types of Records
Evidential	*Administrative records* Without a proportion of records which document the details of administration the creators of the records (or their successors) could not operate. It would not be possible to plan, organise, make decisions or to ensure consistency and continuity.	policy files statements of functions organisation charts procedures and instructions minutes of meetings reports on major projects regulations
Evidential	*Records of legal value* These records form proof of an event or agreement. Obligations, commitments, rights, and delegations of authority fall into this category. Without these records there is no security or foundation for decision making.	contracts leases original acts and regulations instruments of appointment treaties agreements wills
Evidential	*Records of financial accountability* These records document the honest and responsible conduct of financial affairs and financial standing and obligations. These records are essential to understand and transact business.	financial returns financial reports final budgets audit reports estimates of gross expenditure and income major reports on losses
Informational	*Records of historic interest for public relations and general interest purposes* Records of this type allow the context of the records creator to be understood. The social, political, economic, educational, and recreational activities and the relations to the wider community are documented through these records.	all of the above diaries letters photographs posters post cards souvenirs catalogues

that the archives contains only the best and most representative materials of the persons, organisations and events it seeks to document.

METHODS OF ACQUISITION FOR AN IN-HOUSE ARCHIVES

An in-house archives can be active or passive in its acquisition strategy. Passive collecting involves evaluating material when it is *offered* to the archives for retention. This approach to collecting implies that decisions about what records are of archival value are made before the material is offered to the archives. It also follows that the archivist may not be consulted on the weeding of material by office personnel. An active acquisition policy in an in-house archives provides a wider service to the parent institution. The archivist actively works with office personnel to assess all the records created by the institution for permanent retention or systematic destruction while the records are still in the offices of those who create or use them.

In many, particularly larger, organisations the major responsibility for the control and care of all records during their active administrative life, including the development of disposal schedules for them, rests with the records manager. The work of records managers complements that of archivists who are responsible for the protection and care of records of permanent value to the organisation. Traditionally, the line of demarcation at which records management ends and archival administration begins has been the point at which the records cease to be active. At that time the inactive records of permanent or archival value are transferred to the custody of the archivist for long term care and reference.

However, with the advent of high technology in the office, it has become vital for the archivist to become involved with records activity much earlier in the information life cycle. Computers, with their unprecedented ability to alter and eliminate information and the acknowledged impermanence of magnetic tape, some modern papers and some microforms, present real dangers to archivists charged with keeping selected documents for posterity. Information of potential archival value must be identified from the moment it is created and protected until its safe transfer to archival custody.

The archivist must work closely with management and other information professionals, such as information managers, systems analysts, data processing managers and records managers in the *design* of information systems to ensure that archival information is recorded on appropriate media and used with care throughout its active and semi-active life. In cases where there is no records manager on staff, the archivist should seek the advice of a qualified consultant records manager to assist with the design of active records systems and the development of an orderly disposal programme.

Assessing records while they are in the offices which created them allows the archivist to determine the nature and inter-

Table Three   Categories of Records

Types of Organisational Records Likely to be Archives

Please Note: This is not a comprehensive list. The general guidelines are based on the assumption that the organisation has a full range of records. If this is not the case, the value of the surviving records alters and should be assessed differently.

1) Minutes, agenda and business papers of the governing body or board and major administrative committees
2) Acts establishing the organisation and rules, by-laws or regulations governing the conduct of the organisation
3) Master sets of annual reports, newsletters and other publications issued by the organisation
4) Policy and procedure manuals
5) Contracts, leases or legal titles to property and major equipment
6) Official, often signed, copies of the annual accounts statements
7) Patents and correspondence relating to the issue of patents
8) Summary records of all staff appointments and details (Often known as 'staff cards')
9) Indexes, registers, file classification codes, subject thesauri and lists of files
10) Reports documenting or evaluating specific projects, or reports proposing the establishment of projects or departments

Types of Organisational Records Likely to be Important for a Short Time

Please Note: This is not a comprehensive list. The general guidelines are based on the assumption that the organisation has a full range of records. If this is not the case, the value of the surviving records alters and should be assessed differently. The records listed below are frequently updated and often summarised into records of archival value.

1) Material relating to the purchase of routine equipment and supplies
2) Routine equipment service contracts
3) Supply or equipment inventories
4) Documentation relating to the use and expenses of motor vehicles
5) Payslips and payroll records
6) Attendance records
7) Invoices, invoice listings, vouchers and receipts
8) Bank statements
9) Petty cash records
10) Unsuccessful applications for jobs

relationships among the various sets or series of records. This enables the archivist to select only those records of key importance while rejecting those which duplicate or contain fragments of the same information. For example, is the information recorded in one record summarised into another, or presented in a different form; is the information passed on to other departments which might also retain it; how many records are created each year; and how often are particular records used? The answers to these questions assist in determining where and for how long a particular series of records needs to be kept. The gathering of such information in a systematic way is referred to as a *records survey.*

The survey is a useful tool which allows the archives to identify records early in their existence and to determine which of the records should be protected and received as archives. Surveys also allow the archivist to collect information necessary to assess the future space requirements and resources needed to manage these 'potential' archives before they are transferred to archives custody.

The survey can, if required, also help the parent institution determine the length of time to keep non–archival material. Such periods are sometimes determined by law or financial regulation, but are most often dictated by the administrative need for the records in the conduct of business. After records cease to be administratively useful, they go through a stage where they are consulted less and less frequently. Once they have become inactive, records may be disposed of, provided they are not required for legal purposes. The process of determining the future of the records is called disposal, a term which embraces evaluation, transfer to archives, or any other final decision such as destruction.

Records Survey Sheet

Office responsible for records: Company Secretary's Department				*Office address:* 4th floor, 57 Young St, Sydney		*Contact Person:* N. White *Title:* Office Manager *Phone:* ext 4590
Location	*Creator*	*Records Series Title*	*Date Range*	*Description*	*Quantity*	*Retention Recommendation*
1. Filing Cabinet R.S.M.* 1	Company Secretary's Department	Minutes of the Board	1910–( )	a. Volumes, bound annually, containing agenda, business papers and minutes of meetings. Signed by the Chairman at the subsequent meeting. b. These records are microfilmed at the end of the calendar year onto 35mm film. Film stored in fire proof safe (R.S.M. 2)	1.2m	Retain permanently
2. Open shelves R.S.M. 1	Public Relations Department	Annual Reports	1910–( )	Leather bound set. Annotated by Company Secretary	0.6m	Retain Permanently
3. Filing Cabinet R.S.M. 1	Company Secretary's Department	Correspondence	1976–1980	Copies of official correspondence compiled when J. Lyons was Company Secretary	1.1m	Retain Permanently
4. Filing Cabinet R.S.M. 1	Employee Relations	Newsletter	1967–1975	Partial set of Newsletter Official set in Employee Relations	0.10m	Destroy

*R.S.M. = Records survey map

Sample Only
Records Survey Map (R.S.M.)

Office responsible for records: *Relates to Records Survey Sheet(s) No: 1   Map No. . 1. . of . 1. .*

Specific Location of records (Building, floor, room): 57 Young Street, 4th Floor, Room 43

Drawing of Room, Showing types and positions of storage equipment

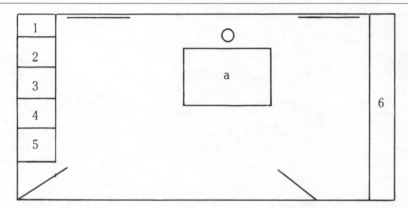

Legend: a) Company Sec.'s Desk
1)   Filing Cabinet
2)   Filing Cabinet
3)   Filing Cabinet
4)   Filing Cabinet
5)   Filing Cabinet
6)   Open Shelves

The systematic recording of disposal decisions affecting particular records is then compiled into a master list known as a disposal schedule. Disposal schedules identify not only those records which will be destroyed and the appropriate time period for their destruction, but also document which records are to be kept permanently and at what stage they will be transferred to archives.

DISPOSAL SCHEDULES

Disposal schedules are an important tool for identying potential archives during their active administrative life. They also ensure that appraisal decisions on specific material are consistent and that such decisions do not need to be made more than once. The task of preparing disposal schedules is one which requires careful preparation.

Prior to the preparation of a disposal schedule, background research on the body creating the records is necessary. To be able to determine what will be of continuing administrative value, or what will document the existence and policies of any body, it is necessary to know what the functions of the body are.

The archivist introduces the disposal survey team to creating office personnel.

Background research into the administrative history of a records creating body should be done before the records are themselves inspected. Investigations into the administrative history should provide the following types of information:

- When was the body created? What legal instrument documented its creation?
- What were the stated purposes of the body at the time of its creation and when and how have they altered?
- How do the various parts of the body relate together?
- What functions are unique to the body?
- What obligations does the body have to report on its activities? Where do such reports go? Are they preserved elsewhere?
- What records are required to be kept by law? What records are created by the body and not duplicated elsewhere?
- What parts of the body could be expected to have created records of a particular kind and over what period?

Reports and publications are excellent sources of information about creating organisations or offices.

From such information, and with regard to the acquisition policy of the archives, the importance of the creator or creating body can be assessed. How important are the types of records created to the archival collection? How representative of the activities of the body are the records?

The context in which the specific set of records requiring appraisal was created is essential. Any existing surveys of the creating body provide important information on what other records may be related to the records in question. A survey should be undertaken if such documentation is not already available.

The survey should aim to collect information about records in such a way that describes and identifies the records for a person who has not seen the records and is not familiar with the workings of the organisation which creates the records. Appraisal decisions will often need to be discussed widely both within the archives and with the creator. Not all parties to these discussions will necessarily have seen the records.

The creator or a person from the appropriate section of the creating body will often provide a great deal of information about the records. They can quickly summarise the reasons for which the records were created, how long they were in use, whether similar records are still in use, whether the activity documented by the records is still being undertaken, what the reference rate to the records is currently and give insights into the importance of the records within the administrative context. Some creators may not understand that records can be used for other reasons than those which dictated their creation. Other creators may feel that everything is of great value and everything must be kept. Neither view is necessarily wrong, but such opinions should only form one of the criteria on which the records are appraised.

Preparing a Disposal Schedule

Disposal schedules can only apply to the records created or substantially changed by an organisation. Records created by other institutions should be scheduled for retention as a part of the other institution's archives. Thus, for example, archivists should not become bogged down wondering if their own institution ought to retain the copies of newsletters issued by a relevant union. Such things should be retained in the context in which they were created, that is by the union, and unless they have particular significance for the subsequent actions of the receiving institution should not be scheduled, but routinely destroyed whenever they are no longer needed for administrative purposes.

Schedules work most effectively for records which are set up to document a particular transaction, for example, job applications, sales invoices etc. Such series of records can be easily classified into standard types of information which can then be assigned a disposal sentence. However, correspondence files and files organised by subject are not so easily classified and usually contain a multitude of subjects and a range of material from the ephemeral to the vitally important. A great variety of disposal sentences are therefore required, always assuming that every subject could be defined. Such material is not well suited to the disposal schedule technique.

Records must be identified according to the office or body which created them or which has custody of the series. This identification should be established during the records survey. Some examples of this identification are:

- **Board of Trustees** (Creator): *Minutes* (Series)
- **Company Secretary** (Creator): *Correspondence files* (Series)
- **Public Relations Department** (Creator): *Advance*, a weekly newsletter (Series)

Disposal schedules will only apply to material which is classified as non–current. That is, individual folders within the series must have ceased to be used for day–to–day administrative purposes. These inactive files may still be recalled at intervals for reference, but must no longer have new papers added to them.

Other information essential to successful scheduling of records must be collected. This information includes:

- *Description of the records series*. Data such as the title of the record series, its inclusive date range, the record types included in the series, the arrangement, and any information which could affect their preservation and storage.
- *Total Quantity* of the series, both in office accommodation and in any storage areas.
- *Accumulation Rate* is required to determine how fast the series is growing. This information is needed to plan storage accommodation.
- *Frequency of reference* by the creating office to the items within the series as they age. For example, during the first six months after the material is created as opposed to three years after it is created. This information is needed to determine what age items from the series should be when they are moved out of the current office storage.
- *Summary or published versions*. Does the information from the series exist in summary form? For example, many financial records are summarised and published in annual reports.
- *Are the records microfilmed or computerised*. Some series are regularly transferred into another medium for ease of storage or manipulation. It is important to gather information about all versions of the records and disposal recommendations for each of them should be included in the records schedule.
- *Requirements for retention*. Any known requirements, such as legal rulings or general regulations, which establish a minimum period of retention over a particular set of records should be noted. Such requirements are often not known by

Table Four   Summary of Steps to Preparing a Disposal Schedule for Official Records

1) Prepare, and receive top management approval of, plan and timeframe for the disposal scheduling programme.

2) Conduct background research on the organisation, structure and activities of the creating body or office to gain insight into the context in which the records are created and used. This phase involves gathering and studying sources such as organisation charts and annual reports and interviewing key administrators and records custodians.

2) Survey of existing records, beginning with the inactive ones in storage areas, moving to those in current use in offices. The object of the survey is to identify the various record series created or maintained by each office. The following information should be collected and summarised for each series:

- Details of the nature, organisation, content and condition of the records and their relation to any indexes or filing plans
- Details on numbers of copies and different formats (computer, microfilm etc) comprising the series
- Whether the information in the series is substantially duplicated in any other record series or is summarised or published regularly in reports
- Accumulation rates of the records per year and how often they are referred to and by whom
- Details of any existing legal, financial or administrative regulation requiring the series to be kept for a specified period

4) Using the information obtained via the survey, determine the length of time each series should be stored in current offices and when it should be moved into lower cost intermediate storage. This should be established for each version of the record, the original and all copies in whatever format they may occur.

5) Appraise each series for archival retention utilising the appraisal checklist. (Only 3 to 7% of the total of records created will usually be of archival value. The remainder can be destroyed appropriately according to the disposal sentences established at step 4.)

6) Draft a disposal sentence for each series. This should describe when the series is to be considered closed, how long it should remain in current office storage, where and when it should be transferred, and its ultimate fate — either as an archive or to be destroyed.

7) Review the draft sentence with the management and administrative personnel responsible for the care and use of the records and with appropriate legal and financial experts. Revise the sentences according to their advice and obtain their approval for the final recommendations.

8) Prepare finished disposal schedule and issue it formally bearing the signatures of the appropriate administrative, financial and legal authorities.

9) Assemble the appropriate office personnel to explain the disposal schedule and develop plans for its implementation. Training sessions for the implementation of the sentences may be necessary.

10) Assist and supervise the implementation of the disposal schedule.

the office creating the records, and the archivist must consult the financial, legal and audit sections to ensure appropriate minimum sentences are established.

- *Security requirements*. Any requirements for security handling or confidential access arrangements should be noted.

This disposal sentence transfers a non-archival series to the County Records Centre for eventual destruction.

Disposal Schedule

No.	DISPOSAL CLASS	DISPOSAL	ACTION
Agency: Zero Company Date Schedule Issued: 5.12.1986		Date Schedule Expires: 5.12.1996	
	Series Title/Description of Activity	Office of Record/Retention	All Other Offices/ Retention
1)	Minutes of the Board a. Official set of Board minutes detailing the administration and policy making of the Zero Company	Chief Secretary's Office: Retain in office for 10 years then transfer to archives	Retain for 5 years, then destroy
	b. 35mm security microfilm of minutes produced at the end of every calender year	Chief Secretary's Office: Transfer immediately to archives	—
2)	Correspondence of Mr J. Lyons	Chief Secretary's Office: Transfer to archives	—
3)	'The Nought' Company Newsletter	Employee Relations Department: Retain permanently in office. Send two copies of each newsletter to archives at the end of each calender year	Retain for 2 years then destroy
4)	Annual Reports	Public Relations Department: Retain permanently in office. Send two copies to archives when issued	Retain for five years then destroy

Writing the Disposal Schedule

A properly written disposal schedule must specify the following details:

- *The Office of record.* That is the office which is responsible for the record during its use for the conduct of business. Any other copies of the record can then be designated as not being the official record and can be destroyed whenever they are no longer required. Such designation of the official record allows institutions to destroy material routinely which otherwise creates great clutter.
- *Separate retention instructions for each copy and each format of the record series.* Records are often created in multiple copies or are transferred to microfilm or computer format. It is essential for a disposal schedule to specify the formats of the record and to assign a disposal decision to each of them.
- *When the items in the series are considered to be closed.* This is most often undertaken at the file folder level. Some of the means to determine when a folder should have no more papers attached are: when the folder reaches a specified number of folios or individual documents, at the end of a financial or calendar year or at the end of a term of office.
- *How long each component of the series is to be kept following closure and in what location.* A record series might be held in several locations before it is finally transferred to archives or destroyed. The disposal schedule should specify where the series is to be kept and for how long for each of these locations. For example, the disposal instruction might read 'Hold in current office for 2 years, then transfer to local storage for 5 years, then destroy.' Care should be taken not to specify disposal sentences such as 'Destroy when reference ceases' which are too vague to be useful. Such sentences encourage people to retain everything, just in case. A definite sentence should be established for all records, and if the office wishes to retain material for a longer period than that specified, it is at their discretion.

Issuing the Disposal Schedule

The schedule should be drafted with the co-operation of the principal creators and administrative users of the records. Once compiled the schedule should be considered to be an officially binding document. The signatures of the principal creators and administrative users, in addition to that of the head of the institution and the archivist, should appear on the official copy of the schedule.

Following approval of the disposal schedule, the next task is to explain its provisions to appropriate office staff and outline the steps for implementing the schedule. Once issued officially, the schedule can be used to destroy non-archival material from

An archival nightmare which occurred because there was no disposal programme.

Shredding non–archival records for paper recycling. Records destruction must be done responsibly.

Under approved disposal schedules, office personnel can weed temporary materials from their files at regular intervals.

office areas with no further reference to the archives and transfer of archival material to the archives can take place in an orderly manner.

Since organisations grow and change, disposal schedules must be regularly reviewed and revised to ensure that they are still relevant to the types of records being created in each office. To ensure this process of revision, many disposal schedules are issued with a limited life span, usually a period of five or ten years.

Before developing your own disposal schedules it is worth looking at the many disposal schedules which have been developed by records managers and archivists, some of which may cover records similar to those of your own organisation. Although schedules prepared by others are useful as models, no disposal schedule developed for one specific institution can be applied directly to another. Each organisation, even if performing the same overall function, will have distinct differences from its peers. Disposal schedules must be individually tailored for each institution.

From such a brief outline of the process of preparing disposal schedules, it is clear that it is a complex and time–consuming task. It is also one of great importance to any institution. A study conducted by the American Records Management Association established that a well organised disposal scheduling programme can yield great cost benefits to organisations which have not previously had such a programme. The study showed that, on average, only 43.6% of all records in offices are active and of the remaining 56.4%, 24% could be destroyed and 32.3% moved to inexpensive intermediate storage.

A great range of professional literature is available on disposal scheduling and records management as a whole. The publications of the Records Management Office of NSW, the Records Management Association of Australia (RMAA) and the Australian Society of Archivists (ASA) are recommended as starting points.

BENEFITS OF AN ACTIVE ACQUISITION STRATEGY

From the preceding discussion on active acquisition policies it is clear that this approach to archives is one which requires far greater involvement with the staff and policies of the organisation. This visibility for the archives is a desirable side–benefit to an active acquisition strategy.

Another benefit to an active strategy is the chance to influence the form of records which will become archives in the future. If, for example, it has been determined that a record produced as computer printout is of archival value, the archivist faces future conservation problems. Because of the poor quality of computer printout paper, it has been estimated that its lifespan is as little as ten to fifteen years — a far cry from the archival forever. If such a record is identified early in its administrative phase as being of permanent value, the archivist can recommend that the record be produced either in different format — such as archival quality microfilm or microfiche — or printed out initially on better quality paper. In this way the archives can prevent future conservation problems which are expensive, if not impossible, to correct.

The extent to which an in-house archives wishes or has the capacity to become involved in such activities will vary. The advantages of some level of involvement are active participation in determining what the future archival record will be, greater awareness and appreciation of the archives from the organisation, regular and planned transfers of material to archives, and an ordered programme for the destruction of unwanted material.

Regardless of whether an institution has a passive or active acquisition policy, every in-house archives must address the problem of recovering information which has passed outside the control of the institution. This can happen in a variety of ways — employees taking records with them when they leave, records being given to other bodies for some reason or records just disappearing to later reappear in the hands of a person or body not related to the institution. Such records are referred to as *estrays*. The archives will need to decide whether it will actively pursue those records known to have gone elsewhere or whether estrays will be accepted and be incorporated into their rightful places as the opportunity arises.

Where an estray comes to light in another archival institution which does not wish to part with it, the option of copying the material should be considered. In this way, although the original material is not recovered, the information contained in the record is not lost to the archives, and any potential ill-feeling is avoided.

THE APPRAISAL CHECKLIST

Having discussed how material of permanent value is acquired by in-house archives, the question of how to undertake the appraisal process to determine what is of permanent value must be addressed.

Because of the spectre of subjectivity in appraisal decisions, an appraisal checklist should be evolved against which all records are tested. An appraisal checklist is a list of criteria against which every series or collection should be measured. Commonly, such checklists either require specific questions to be answered, or require a relative weighting to be completed for each criteria. Of course, every archivist's interpretation of the extent to which a set of records will conform to specific criteria will still be subjective. However, such a document provides concrete categories against which to measure records and as such is infinitely better than an undocumented decision. Argument for or against retention or partial retention can then be based on the appraisal checklist and the survey documentation. A checklist also brings consistency of the appraisal decisions from collection to collection.

The elements comprising an appraisal checklist will vary from archives to archives. However, the following matters should be considered for inclusion:

- *Do the records conform to the acquisition policy?* All records must be measured against the archives' stated acquisition policy. The archivist should resist the temptation to accept material outside the scope of the policy or its logical extension.

- *Do the records detail the origins, structure, or policy of the creating body or the evolution of the interests of the individual?* Records falling within this broad category would be of evidential value.

- *Do the records document the rights of organisations or individuals?* Such records may include legal decisions, evidence of property ownership, records of service or records of individual attainment.

- *Do the records document the financial responsibilities of the creating body or financial planning?* Records which document financial responsibility may often be of continuing administrative use for the creator. Such records are often measured against external criteria, such as audit and legislative requirements.

The work area for detailed appraisal and the sorting of series by provenance should be spacious. Shelving holds material awaiting work. Courtesy — Archives of Business and Labour, ANU.

Table Five Summary of Questions for Inclusion on the Appraisal Checklist

Do/Are the records:
1) Conform to the acquisition policy?
2) Detail the origins, structure or policy of the creating institution or the evolution of the individual's interests?
3) Document the rights of individuals or organisations?
4) Detail the financial responsibilities or financial planning of the creating institution or individual?
5) Duplicated elsewhere or maintained in another form?
6) Relate to other records already in custody or held in another institution?
7) Contain classification schemes, filing codes or plans, registers or indexes?
8) Consist of transactional records or 'case files'?
9) Have a discernable arrangement?
10) Complete?
11) What is the quantity involved?
12) Require restrictions to maintain the privacy of business or individuals?
13) Have access restrictions placed on them by the donor?
14) What is the physical form?
15) What is the physical condition?

• *Are the records duplicated elsewhere or maintained in another form within the records of the individual or creating body?* Identical information may often appear in various documents at differing levels of the creating body. It is necessary to establish which records containing identical information should be kept. As a general rule, if information is reported at more than one level of an hierarchy, the information is kept from the higher administrative level.

  Records may be summarised into other records, for example, payroll slips usually contain information recorded in identical or greater detail, on a computer. The computer itself may hold the information as an active database in digital form and in individual configurations on computer printouts. A further example is the student record card maintained by many universities and colleges which provide a summarised form of individual student files. The two series of records, the comprehensive student records and the summary cards, should then be appraised in conjunction.

• *Are the records dependent upon filing codes or plans, indexes or registers?* Filing plans, classification schemes, indexes and registers are vital tools for the current and future use of the record series. They provide the key by which the records were originally organised and accessed. Without them the records can be used and understood only with great difficulty, if at all. For this reason, most registers and indexes to record series are regarded as permanent records. Record series accompanied by the original control records (that is, indexes, registers, file lists etc) prove much easier for both archives staff and future researchers to use.

- *Are the records 'case files'?* That is, are the records transactional records, recording the implementation of policy? In many instances such records contain material which is essentially the same, differing with each particular set of facts to be dealt with. Examples of case files would be student records, taxation files, medical records and social security files. Many such records have informational value for long-term statistical research. However, as such records are usually found in large quantities, they usually require more elaborate disposal decisions to be made which aim to preserve a representative sample of the records to demonstrate the processes of the operation, rather than to retain or discard the entire series.

- *What is the arrangement of the records?* The method of arrangement of the records can either facilitate the extraction of desired information or make such extraction difficult. For example, the records may be arranged chronologically for the purposes of the creator, but the researcher may find that an alphabetical arrangement would be easiest.

- *Are the records complete?* Fragmentary records need to be carefully evaluated. Such records often prove frustrating for the researcher because of the gaps they contain. In general the importance of offering only whole collections and complete series to the archives should be stressed to office personnel and donors. The opportunity to see the whole range of documentation is vital when the archivist selects which materials to keep.

- *What quantity of material is involved?* The archives should be characterised by records that are rich, concise and limited in quantity. Neither the archivist nor researchers will want to plough through hundreds of boxes if the same information can be obtained in a more compact form. Records series of large quantity need to be evaluated very carefully.

- *Do the records contain confidential information which would require protection for commercial viability or for the privacy of the individual?* Records which contain information which is potentially sensitive may need to be restricted from public access for a period agreed upon with the creator. The archives will need to determine whether the information recorded will be of sufficient importance to justify the administration of often complex access restrictions.

- *What are the restrictions required by the donor?* Are the access restrictions required by the donor unduly restrictive? Is the material of sufficient long term value to justify the costs of administration of unwieldy access restrictions?

- *What is the physical form of the records?* Do the records consist of paper files, computer printout, photographs, microfilm, volumes, or machine readable records? If the material exists in more than one format, which will be the most useable and durable?
- *What is the physical condition of the material?* Is the paper brittle? Has the ink faded? Are the bindings broken or rotten? Has the record been mounted on acidic cardboard? If the condition of the material is doubtful at the time of acquisition, the archives will be obliged to undertake costly conservation work to ensure the preservation of the material.

Once this process has been completed, the material needs to be evaluated within the context of the collection already in the archives. Will the material complete gaps or extend coverage in the documentation of an individual, organisation or event? Will the material substantially duplicate material already held? If so, is the new material a better representation than that already held?

Research trends and interests of the using public will also need to be assessed as they relate to the records. *Informational or secondary values* of records are often difficult to assess. Anything and everything could be kept on the pretext that someone will want to look at it at some time in the future. Such an argument does not aid the process of appraisal which, of necessity, is concerned with selecting material for preservation. No one individual, however well informed in a particular area of interest, can hope to predict research interests of the future. Research trends alter rapidly, particularly with the introduction of computers and techniques of evaluating masses of data. However, it is possible to select material based upon its importance to the organisation and society of *its own time*. The task of constructing a mirror of society is difficult, but possible, and it is this role which archivists should seek to fulfill.

The other major area to be considered is that of the resources of the archives. How much time will it take to process the material? What staff resources will be involved? How much space will the collection occupy? What are the existing commitments on staff time and resources? Where will this material fit into existing priorities for processing?

Once all this information has been gathered and placed into the context of the archives' general operations and collection, the archivist will usually have a good idea of the value of the material to the archives. The appraisal decision is one of weighing all the information collected. As a general rule, if, at the end of the process, the appraiser is still unsure of the value of the material, the material should not be accepted into custody. Much more material has to be destroyed than can be kept in any archives.

THE PROCESS OF ACQUISITION IN A COLLECTING ARCHIVES

In the same manner as an in-house archives, a collecting archives must also decide upon its level of collecting activity. Will it actively seek material which fits into its acquisition policy or take the more passive approach of only evaluating material as it is offered? Techniques of collecting involve an approved acquisition policy, a detailed knowledge of the collection as it currently exists to determine which aspects of the collection need development, and a good knowledge of the general research requirements of users.

The range of the archives' collecting interests must be made known to other archives and to potential donors. What will be accepted and what will not be accepted should be clearly stated. Without such statements the archives can become an eclectic 'dumping ground' for records, not a cohesive body of material suitable for research use.

Publicising the collecting interests of the archives may take a variety of forms, from notices in the professional journals of archives administration and of the major disciplines which the collection serves, or through indirect means such as appropriate methods of citation of the records as they are used. Many archivists also publicise their existence and their holdings by giving talks to gatherings of interested people. A short and simple

---

Table Six   Lead Card for Collection Acquisition

Main entry headings: Jones, Somewhere
Cross references: Diaries, Cattle Property Records

Date: 19.10.1986

Locality: Somewhere, NSW
Name of family: Jones
Possible owner: Mrs S. Short
Address/Telephone: 12 Blossom Avenue, Somewhere, NSW
Items: Family records relating to cattle property held in Somewhere district, 1856–1899. Diaries specifically mentioned.
Source: Mrs M. Jones. 14 High Street, Wherever. (Accession 86/29). Used records in local history research.
Contact Notes:
Date   *Nature of Contact*
11.11.86   Letter to Mrs. S. Short inquiring about papers (file no 86/456)

statement of what the archives does, what areas it documents and
what types of materials it collects should be available for general
distribution. (See Chapter Eleven User Education and Public
Relations for a discussion of useful approaches to publicity.)

However much it may try to communicate its needs, the
archives will inevitably be approached with the occasional
donation or bequest which does not conform to the acquisition
policy. Provided the publicity on holdings has been effective,
such an occurrence will be the exception rather than the rule;
and, in most cases, such offerings can be politely declined citing
the acquisition policy as the basis for doing so.

More frequently, publicity results in indications of where
material may be found rather than actual gifts. The archivist
should compile information files, often in card form as illustrated, documenting these leads with any details available on the
particular records and on the organisation or individuals who
possess them. These files form the basic resource files for organised collecting; and it is important that information about all contacts and potential donors is carefully recorded and
maintained.

The information in these files becomes the basis for fieldwork,
which includes the activities of locating and identifying the
material to be collected, negotiating for its deposit and finally
ensuring that the records reach the archives. Fieldwork usually
involves visiting the location of the material, which may not be in
the immediate vicinity, so budgeting for travelling expenses will
need to be considered. In fieldwork, one contact often leads to
other potential donations and time should be allotted to pursue
such unexpected opportunities. Even if a lead proves a dead end,
there are public relations advantages to making the existence of
the archives interests widely known.

Because many collecting archives have active field programmes to locate material, the process of appraising collected
materials begins early and continues on after the records have
been transferred to the archives. A field officer may hear of a
possible collection of papers in the possession of an individual.
In order to assess whether such material would be worth the time
and expense of pursuit, some preliminary work must be done to
determine the possible significance of the individual or organisation which created the records and the types of documents most
representative of their work. Often by the time the papers are
actually seen, the field officer will have a good idea of what
archival value the material is likely to have. Table Seven provides
an indication of the type of information needed to assess potential acquisitions.

All material must be assessed in relation to the acquisition policy.
To determine this, a quick survey of the material should be carried
out. This survey should describe the material accurately, noting

Table Seven   Background Information Required to Assess Potential Donations

1) What relation does the person possessing the papers have to the individual or organisation whose papers are being discussed? Are they his/hers? Were they inherited from a relative? Were they bought?

2) What position did the creator of the records have in relation to the particular field being documented?

3) How long was the person or business active and when did they cease to be active?

4) Are these records unique or are they likely to have been copies distributed to a number of parties?

5) Who has legal title to these papers?

6) Are the papers likely to contain much published material and is this published material readily available elsewhere?

7) Where are the records of other individuals or businesses relating to this collection held?

8) Are the records offered complete and representative evidence of the work of the creating organisation or individual?

the major types of records, the information they contain, their date range and quantity, the order or arrangement of the records, the possibility of future additions to the collection and any problems with the physical condition of the material. A useful companion to the survey is the drawing of a site plan, which documents the location and physical arrangement of the records as they were found at the time of the survey. This plan provides a valuable *aide-mémoire* of the records as they were first seen and may capture clues to their relationships that may be disturbed in packing the records for transfer to the archives (*Refer to the sample records survey sheet and map shown earlier*). As a result of the information recorded during the survey, sound decisions can be made as to the archival value of the material offered.

If the material is of sufficient importance to the archives, it is packed, listed and transported to the archives for more extensive appraisal. The detailed appraisal uses criteria very similar to those followed by in-house archives although they are more general since they rarely have the legal, fiscal and administrative concerns of the in-house archivist. The appendix at the end of this chapter has a sample form with instructions which is suitable for appraisal of material offered to a collecting archives.

Collections of personal papers often contain a greater proportion of ephemeral material than do the records of an institution. This material should be appraised with the remainder of the collection and measured against the dual criteria of the acquisition policy and the appraisal checklist. *Ephemera* can be of great interest if it has an integral link to the papers being appraised. For example, copies of all the company's advertisements placed in the national press will be of great value if they are complete and kept with documentation which explains the back-

ground of the advertisements. Random copies of unrelated advertising, with no logic, reason for collection or order, will be of little
value. Similarly, booklets, social tracts and pamphlets which
appear in personal papers have value if written by the creator or
consistently collected by him/her. However, random copies of
unrelated printed material may be best dealt with by a rare book
librarian after a record has been made of the material for the
archives.

DOCUMENTING THE ACQUISITION

If the material meets all the criteria for the acceptance by the
archives, it is necessary to negotiate for the acquisition of
material. The terms of deposit should provide for the transfer
both of legal title and of any literary property or copyrights vested
in the material. The questions of future copying or publication
and access for researchers should also be addressed at this time.
The most common methods of acquisition are donation of originals or copies of the material, bequests or purchase.

*A donor signs the official forms
transferring ownership of a collection.* Courtesy — State Library of
NSW.

A *donation* to the archives should be documented in a *deed of
gift*. It is best to have a standard deed of gift drawn up or approved
by a solicitor to cover the standard clauses. Some of the specific
matters a deed should contain are: the specific date when the
donation is made, a list or a description of the material in sufficient detail to allow future identification, and the signatures of
both the donor and a representative of the recipient institution.
Where an archives expects further donations from the one donor
organisation, a deed may be drafted so as to cover subsequent
donations. The agreement then becomes analagous to a disposal
schedule, with the organisation agreeing to transfer more
material from specific series after an agreed lapse of time. In such
cases the initial deed may state that subsequent donations will be
made in accordance with the provisions established in the initial
deed.

Any restricitions on use of the material required by the donor
should also be established in the deed of gift. Blanket or
unreasonable restrictions on the material, such as 'the papers
shall be closed to the public,' must be avoided whenever possible.
Such restrictions make the material useless for research. Conversely, donors should be advised by the archivist if restrictions
are needed for legal reasons or to protect privacy. In such cases,
advice from the archives' solicitor and from the Australian
Society of Archivists (ASA) should be sought.

Similarly an indefinite requirement that every person wishing
access to the material must be referred to the donor for permission should be avoided. Such a provision is often difficult to
administer and also raises the question of what happens when
the donor dies? Will the papers then be open? If not, who will give
permission for access? Donors should look to the archives for

Table Eight   Deed of Gift

(Please note: All deed forms should be legally approved)

Accession No. . . . .

File No. . . . .

I, *Joan Jenkinson,* of *43 Bligh Street, Sydney,* do hereby make a gift of the material specified below to the *Wherever Historical Society* and its successor organisations.

Being the sole owner of the material, I give this material (and any additions which I may make to it) unencumbered to the *Wherever Historical Society* and do declare that I made the gift of my own free will and without influence.

Any copyrights such as I may possess in this material or in any other property in the custody of the *Wherever Historical Society* are hereby assigned to the *Wherever Historical Society*.

The material specified below shall be available to members of public for use from *the date of this deed* with the exception of the items asterisked below which shall be restricted from public use until *1st January 2010*.

Items not retained by the *Wherever Historical Society* shall be returned to me.

Schedule of material donated:
Diaries of John T. Smith, 1932–1945 (5 volumes)
*Diaries of Jonathan Z. Jenkinson, 1940–1979 (16 volumes)
Account Books from the business of Jenkinson and Smith, 1930–1950 (20 annual volumes)

In full accord with the provisions of this deed of gift, I hereunto set my hand.

. . . .   Date . . . .
    (Donor)
Signed in the presence of *Jerome N. Wilson*:

. . . .

On behalf of the *Wherever Historical Society,* I, Jennifer Eccles, Archivist, accept this gift.

. . . .   Date . . . .

advice on the appropriate restrictions. In all cases, any restrictions should have a definite time limit and refer to specific documents rather than the entire collection.

The right to dispose of the material, or parts thereof, which fall outside the collecting interests of the archives should also be established in the deed of gift. Such a provision enables the archives to dispose of unwanted material. For example, multiple copies of reference publications such as *Hansard*, textbooks, or sets of encyclopaedia are not required by the archives. Such material takes up scarce space, exists in many other places and is inappropriate for a specialist archives collection. However, the archivist should consult the donor to see if s/he prefers that such material be returned or whether the archives may dispose of it in any appropriate way, including sale, gift and trade, as well as discard.

Donation of original does not involve the transfer of copyright unless this is specifically mentioned in the acquisition agreement. In negotiating the transfer of copyright it is important to remember that the donor can only convey copyright for material where he/she owns the copyright. For example, in a series of correspondence, a potential donor would own the copyright in the letters he/she wrote (both in the original and the copy kept for the record). The copyrights in letters received would similarly belong to their writers, not to the recipient. The issues of copyright can be complex, and it is recommended that the archivist approach the Australian Copyright Council to obtain up–to–date advice and copies of its publications.

A *bequest* is a gift of personal possessions, excluding real property and money, made in a will. For archival material to be bequeathed to an archives it must be specifically mentioned in a will. It is not sufficient to have a statement such as 'you may have the papers when I die', as it is too general to be legally enforceable. As with the deed of gift, the bequest should also detail the donor's wishes as to the disposal of unwanted material and the research use of the records. Copyright is always transferred by bequest unless it is specifically excluded by the will. Material may also be donated to an archives by beneficiaries to a will. In these cases the archives must ensure that all the beneficiaries agree to the donation and document the transaction with a deed of gift.

An occasional unwanted bequest may be made to the archives. Such bequests should always be refused by quoting the acquisition policy of the archives. However assistance in recommending a more appropriate repository will be a useful public relations exercise. Bequests can be encouraged within a local community by contacting local solicitors and suggesting that they encourage clients to consider the bequest of personal papers in their wills in addition to real property and money.

The Taxation Incentive for the Arts scheme established by the

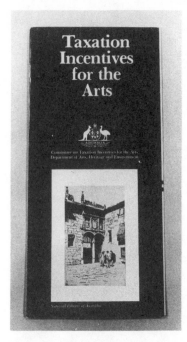

Gifts and donations to archival institutions may bring tax advantages to donors.

Australian Government provides a mechanism whereby material donated to an approved institution can be evaluated by accredited assessors and the value of the material taken as a tax deduction for the donor. The scheme is administered by the Committee on Taxation Incentives for the Arts within the Department of Arts, Heritage and Environment. Archivists should contact the Department for the latest guidelines, as they do alter from time to time.

Purchase is also a method of acquisition, but is not common and most often involves only large institutions with special funds to support such activity. In this case an agreement must be reached on the price to be paid for the material. Once agreed upon, a receipt for the cost of material acquired is mandatory. Such a receipt should record the vendor, the purchaser, the amount paid and describe the material in sufficient detail to enable future identification, if necessary.

Another method of acquiring material into a collecting archives is by *loan*; but it is an arrangement fraught with potential problems for the archivist. If material is accepted on loan, the archives will expend staff time and resources on processing and preserving the material in the best possible accommodation. Should the owner later decide to withdraw the material, the archives has no choice but to comply; and the time and effort spent on the documents will have been wasted. Similarly, should the owner die and the beneficiaries of the estate wish to reclaim the material, the position is identical. In cases where the beneficiaries are remote, unknown or take no action regarding the loan, the legal status of the ownership of the material can remain in doubt for many years. If the archives decides to accept records on loan, the archivist must draw up a loan agreement clearly describing the material on loan and the conditions under which it will be cared for and used. The agreement should set definite time limits on the loan period and make arrangements for the return of the material or conversion to a donation if the time limit is exceeded.

ACQUISITION ETHICS

The archives should be conscious at all times of the need to behave in accordance with archival ethics. In the sphere of collecting, this involves co-operation with other collecting institutions and confidentiality of conditions for deposit agreed with donors, including financial arrangements.

No responsible archives should deliberately attempt to collect material in an area where an existing archives has prior claim. Similarly, if a part of a collection is offered to one institution and the remainder to another, both archivists should advise the donor that it is unsound to split up bodies of archives. Such an action fragments the evidence and makes research use difficult. In every situation, archivists must consider the best interests of the records themselves and explain this position to all relevant parties. However, it is still the donor's perogative to decide the fate of the donation. When faced with the donor's decision to split a collection, it is possible to ameliorate the situation by having each archives copy the material for deposit in the other, provided the resources are available to finance the copying and both repositories have the right to reproduce their materials. The donor might be approached to bear some of the expenses associated with this solution.

An archives must he aware of the limitations of what it is possible to offer potential donors. Promises which cannot be realistically fulfilled should not be made. Similarly, collecting beyond the archives' capacity to house or process the records for research use should be avoided.

Table Nine   Container List

Diocesan Archives Box List
Donor/Transferring Agency: St Jude's Parish Church
Address: Hardy Vale, NSW   *Telephone:* (056) 245 6324
Contact Person: The Reverend Robert Spanish

Box No.	Contents (Series Title, inclusive dates or first and last folder titles/numbers)	Archives Only
1	Church Registers (5 volumes) 1859–1980 Volume 1: 1859–1889 Volume 2: 1889–1915 Volume 3: 1915–1939 Volume 4: 1939–1959 Volume 5: 1959–1980	(This area is often used for assigning shelf numbers once the records enter the archives)
2	Correspondence, 1957–1970	
3	Correspondence, 1970–1980	
4	Fund Raising Committee Minutes, 1945–1979 Ladies Auxiliary Minutes, 1950–1967 Youth Activities Committee Minutes, 1959–1975	

Note: An accurate box list for each donation accession is vital as it often serves as the basic documentation to control the new acquisition until it can be completely arranged and described. In many cases the box list contains sufficient information to be incorporated immediately into the archives' system of finding aids.

Box A   The Acquisition File

Types of documents appropriate for the file include:

- *Records Documenting Contacts with the Donor.* 'Lead' cards; correspondence; notes of telephone conversations, visits to inspect papers and negotiations of terms of acquisition.

- *Records Documenting the Evaluation of the Material.* Valuations for tax incentive schemes; disposal schedules; records appraisal sheets.

- *Records Documenting the Legal and Physical Transfer of Material.* Records Transfer receipt; Box lists; deed of gift.
  After the material is transferred and accessioned, further documents may be added to the file to reflect the work the archivist does to preserve the material and prepare it for research use.

- *Records Documenting the Archival Management of the Material.* Worksheets for arrangement and description and/or conservation; applications for access, photocopying or publication.

All archives have an implicit obligation to make the material accessible to the donor on request. This should not, however, include removal of the material from archives custody. In cases where appraisal decisions have recommended discarding some of the material from within a collection, the donor should be informed and given the opportunity to reclaim it. If a long absent donor or his/her heirs requests to see material which is no longer in custody, honesty about this fact explained with reference to the archives policy as a whole is advisable.

PHYSICAL TRANSFER OF THE MATERIAL

The archivist should be involved in the boxing of the collection following formal acceptance of the donation agreement. Whenever possible, the records should be placed into standard archives cartons to minimise the need for reboxing once the material is in custody. A rough list of the contents including date ranges of every box should be made. The boxes should be clearly numbered and labelled with the donor's name. A sample of the contents list is shown in Table Nine. At this stage it is essential that no attempt be made to sort or re-organise the material as valuable evidence inherent in the undisturbed order may be destroyed. A copy of the list should be placed in each box, and the original stored with the related accessioning documentation discussed in the next chapter.

In every case material received by the archives from each source should immediately be acknowledged with a receipt. The receipt should clearly state that the material will need to be examined and appraised in detail before any final decisions are made on whether all or part of the material will be accepted for permanent deposit.

SUMMARY

Acquisition and appraisal are keys to the orderly growth of an archival collection. Both are processes which should be carefully documented, not only to provide the archives with guidelines for present activity, but also to provide guidance for future generations of archivists to assess the development of the collection. The records documenting acquisition and appraisal are amongst the most important part of your own archives' archives.

The practice of acquisition and appraisal is not static but continuing. Review of acquisitions and reappraisal of collections accepted in the past is becoming more and more important in archival practice, especially as archives must justify their expenses and collections.

It is an important part of the archival service that acquisitions be reported as widely as possible. The professional archival journals and those of appropriate disciplines should be informed of new acquisitions on a regular basis, and the archives itself may feature them in a newsletter or issue acquisitions lists. Other archival institutions should be kept informed of the whereabouts of particular records, not only to reinforce collecting interests and areas, but, most importantly to enable reference staff to direct researchers to appropriate records held by other archives.

Sound acquisition and appraisal policies, well implemented, will form the basis for the continuing good management of any archival collection.

FURTHER READING

Robek, Mary F., Gerald F. Brown and Wilmer O. Maedke, *Information and Records Management*. 3rd edition. Encino, CA: Glencoe Publishing Company, 1987.

Peace, Nancy, editor, *Archival Choices*. Lexington, MA: Lexington Books, 1984.

Records Management Office of New South Wales (RMONSW), *Records Scheduling and Disposal*. Publications on Records Management Number 7. Sydney: RMONSW, January 1982.

Schellenberg, T.R., *Modern Archives: Principles and Techniques*. Chicago: University of Chicago Press, 1956.

Appendix One: Appraisal Sheets and Instructions

The appraisal sheets for collecting archives included here consist of two parts, the first to be compiled on site and will act as a receipt for the donor and the archives prior to more extensive evaluation. The second part of the form is the confidential appraisal document compiled in the archives. Both forms are accompanied by instructions.

Acknowledgement: The prototypes of these forms and instructions were developed by Louise Trott while enrolled as a student in the Diploma of Information Management–Archives Administration at the University of New South Wales, in 1986.

Instructions for Completing Records Appraisal Sheet One: Initial Appraisal

To be completed in *duplicate* by staff member at the time of the initial appraisal (i.e. either at the archives or at the location of the material prior to transfer). *Original* to archives. *Duplicate* as receipt to donor.

1) *Name, Address and Telephone Number of Donor.*
2) *Creator(s) of Material:* include name of person(s), society etc and details of life or work.
3) *Relationship of Donor to Creator(s):* Explain whether the donor is the creator or whether a relative, executive of society, heir, friend, executor of will, etc.

Appendix One: Appraisal Sheets and Instructions
Records Appraisal Sheet One: Initial Appraisal

1) *Name and Address of Donor:*
   Telephone Number: (w)   (h)
   Identification Number:

   Date material received:

2) *Creator(s) of Records:*

3) *Relationship of Donor to Creator(s):*

4) *Description of Material: Title:*

   a) Date range and period of concentration, if any:

   b) Quantity:

   c) Organisation, person(s) and/or events which material concerns:

   d) Types of documents and percentage of each:

   e) General condition

5) *Donor's Conditions:*

   I agree to leave the above material with the archives for further evaluation:

6) *Signature of Donor:*   *Date:*

7) *Signature of Archivist:*   *Date:*

4) *Description of Material:*
    Title: Allocate a working title to the collection which will
    reflect the creator, e.g. The Merlin Papers.
    a) *Date range:* Date range should be established as specifi-
        cally as possible, however an approximate date range
        should be included if exact dates cannot be easily
        ascertained.
    b) *Quantity:* Overall number of boxes, packets etc
        received.
    c) *Organisation/persons concerned:* Include names of
        person(s), organisations. This may differ from creator.
    d) *Types of documents and percentage:* Be as specific as
        possible e.g. inwards and outwards correspondence
        50%; diaries and journals 20%; financial records 3%;
        publications 10%; minutes 10%; photographs 6%; film,
        video and audio recording 1%.
    e) *General condition:* Is the material in good physical con-
        dition? Does it require immediate conservation work?
        What percentage of the material requires
        conservation?
5) *Donor's Conditions:* Use this space to record any specific
    wishes of the donor or any expectations of the donor.
6) *Signature of Donor* indicates assent to appraisal. Donor's
    copy of form signifies receipt for material handed to
    archives.
7) *Signature of Archivist* indicates completion of sheet and
    receipt of material from donor.

Instructions for Completing Records Appraisal Sheet
2. Detailed Appraisal
This is to be a confidential and detailed appraisal of material,
completed by an archivist subsequent to the initial appraisal
documented on form 1.
1) Reference Details: Obtain from Form 1 sections 1, 2, 3 and 4.
2) Detailed description/evaluation:
    Be sure to explain all relevant factors likely to affect the
    appraisal decision.
    a) Significance of creator: is the creator of the material sig-
        nificant in his/her own time; in an historical perspec-
        tive? To what extent?
    b) Quality of documentation of creator's work/life: Does
        the material reveal significant information concerning
        the activities of the creator? If yes, provide details. To
        what extent? Legal, historical, biographical, adminis-
        trative? Does all or only some of the material reveal
        such information? What proportion of the material?
    c) Uniqueness: Is the material original and unique? Are
        there other copies? Other formats? If so, where are they

located? Has the material been used for a publication concerning the creator? Do any persons or organisations hold supplementary material which would be of interest? Can it be obtained?

d) Research value: Is any known research being carried out in this field? Is the material in a format which would be accessable for research? If not, how much work would need to be done to make it accessable?

e) Is it likely that there will be any subsequent donations of material? Of what type? How often? What quantity? Are there/will there be the space and resources for the entire collection?

f) Appropriateness of material to the archives acquisition policy: Does the material offered conform to or provide a logical extension to the stated acquisition policy of the archives? Does all or only some of the material fit into the collection?

g) Related collections already held: Does the archives already hold material relating to the creator? Will this collection fill any known gaps in the collection? Is it compatable with the material already in custody? Does it duplicate material already held?

h) Related collections held by other archives: Do any other institutions hold such material? Would the material better suit their needs? Is there competition for these papers? Has the material been offered to any other institution at any time?

i) Factors which increase or diminish the value of the material to the archives: Will copyright be transferred to the archives? Is the material a gift, purchase or loan? Are there restrictive access conditions on the material? What proportion of the material will be available for use within the next ten years? Are privacy considerations necessary? For what percentage? What conservation work is required and on what proportion of the collection? Attempt to balance these factors against the research value of the collection.

j) Other comments: Be clear and frank. This is a confidential document.

3) Will the material be accepted for accessioning, conservation etc? In total or in part? Will the unwanted proportion be returned to the donor? Or should the material be offered to another archives? Which one? What conditions or terms of deposit should be recommended to the donor?

Records Appraisal Sheet Two: Detailed Appraisal
Detailed Appraisal of Records — Use in conjunction with Appraisal Sheet No 1.

1) *Reference Details*   *Identification number:*

   Donor:

   Title of material:

   Creator of records:

2) *Detailed Description/Explanation*

   a)   Significance of creator of material:

   b)   Quality of documentation of creator's work/life:

   c)   Uniqueness of records:

   d)   Research value:

   e)   Future donations which increase or diminish the value of the material to the archives:

   f)   Appropriateness of material to the archives acquisition policy:

   g)   Related collections or material already held:

   h)   Related collections or material held by other archives:

   i)   Factors which increase or diminish the value of the material to the archives:

   j)   Other comments:

3) *Appraisal Decision and Conditions of Deposit:*

Date Examination Completed: Name of Appraiser:

CHAPTER FOUR

ACCESSIONING

Tim Robinson and *Paul Brunton*

Having made sure that new material has been legally transferred
to your archives, the next, and vitally important, step is to gain
control over it. This initial process is called *accessioning* which
records information about origins, creator, contents, format and
extent in such a way that documents cannot become intermingled with other material held by the archives. Accessioning
provides the basic level of physical and intellectual control over
incoming material. It must be done as soon as possible after the
receipt of new records.

At the time of acquisition, dealt with in the preceding chapter
on Acquisition and Appraisal, you will have made a rough listing
of the material to be transferred and recorded some information
about the material's origins and creator. This documentation
must now be refined and extended as part of the accessioning
process.

Accessioning consists of a sequence of different activities.
These include preliminary sorting of the accession, recording the
essential identifying information about the material and its creator in the accession register and providing suitable storage for
the material. Some of these activities may be slightly different in
in-house and collecting archives. However, their purpose — to
gain basic control — is the same and the documentation produced is usually very similar.

Most records in an archives, unlike books in a library, will not
be in a physical state where they can be placed straight on to
shelves. The variety of formats found among archives may also
mean that the one accession cannot be stored on the same shelf.
Conservation requirements will also mean that different forms of
material such as photographic negatives, photographic prints,
magnetic tapes should be stored in special conditions (see
Chapter Eight Conservation).

ANALYSING MATERIAL TO DETERMINE PROVENANCE

The single most important step in accessioning material is the determination of provenance. The term provenance refers to the place of origin of the records, i.e. the organisation or person that created, received or accumulated and used the records in the conduct of business or life. This relationship to the records differs from that of other offices or persons which may have stored or owned the records at a later time. The latter refers to the sequence or chain of custody which is a part of the history of the material but does not determine its provenance in the archival sense. The central place of the principle of provenance in archival theory and practice is explained in more detail in Chapter Five Arrangement and Description.

As all archives are the products of work or life activities, they can only be fully understood through a knowledge of why and how they were created and used. This is why it is essential that the provenance of archival records is identified and recorded. The procedure for the determination of provenance will vary depending on whether the archives is an in-house archives or a collecting archives.

For in-house archives, it is not usually too difficult to work out the provenance of a body of records if the material has been received as part of a regular transfer programme. It is important, however, that the person or office transferring the records is not confused with the provenance. For example, a batch of student files may be received from the school caretaker. The provenance of these records is not the caretaker as he did not create or receive them in the course of business. The caretaker merely provided temporary storage for the student files, and their correct provenance is the Registrar's Office. The former location and provenance of records are both important information. Most often they will be the same person or office, but they need not be.

In a collecting archives, however, a single acquisition might contain material created by several different people and/or organisations. During the process of acquisition, it may have become clear that the material to be accessioned, although received from a single location or person, has in fact two or more provenances. If two or more parts of the material obviously have no relationship, and have only come together by accident, they may be separated. Each should then be accessioned separately according to its provenance.

Sometimes it will not be possible to identify easily the different provenances of various parts of the one acquisition. In such cases it is preferable not to attempt to separate the material until a very detailed investigation of the records can be carried out. How this is done will be explained in Chapter Five Arrangement and Description. Often the relationships between records are subtle.

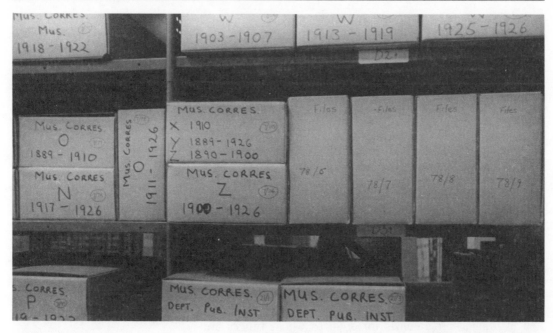

The label 'files' does not give sufficient information about the records in these boxes.

The temptation to sort new acquisitions too hurriedly must be resisted to prevent permanent damage being done to the integrity of the records through an inexact understanding of the relationship between various items.

Where there is reason to question the exact provenance of all the records in the one acquisition, it is best to accession it all as a single unit according to the provenance of the majority of the material. The aim of accessioning is to gain speedy basic control over all incoming material. If subsequent examination reveals more than one provenance in a single accession, it is a simple matter to accession the unrelated records again under their correct provenance.

ACCESSIONING IN AN IN-HOUSE ARCHIVES

An in-house archives provides a service to the various units of its parent organisation (whether they are called divisions, departments, branches, offices, or parishes etc.). In trying to make that service as efficient as possible, the archives requires the active co-operation of the units transferring material to its custody. When an office or other records-creating unit wants to transfer records to the archives, it should first contact the archivist to arrange a convenient time for the transfer and to ensure that the records are in fact eligible for transfer. (See Chapter Three Acquisition and Appraisal for information on the decisions to be made before records are accepted into the archives.) If the records are accepted, then the office should prepare them for transfer according to guidelines developed by the archives. This involves boxing the records in standard boxes and listing them so that they are securely housed and it is clear exactly which records are being sent.

Transfer Procedures

To assist the archives' clients, the archivist should produce procedures for the transfer of records which set out the steps to be followed when preparing the material for transfer. For example, the procedures should include instructions on how to complete the form used for the records transfer list and how to box the records correctly.

The importance of establishing and maintaining proper procedures for this activity cannot be overstated. The instructions should ensure that material received from different offices is identified and packed in a standard way. This helps the archivist manage his/her holdings more efficiently, both in terms of storage and of retrieval. For example, when an office requests records from the repository for further administrative use, the archivist should be able to locate them quickly and accurately using the records transfer list. The procedures are also useful in lieu of training programmes for archives whose offices are spread widely geographically, and/or who rely on the efforts of people who have many duties apart from transferring records (for example, a central church archives receiving records from many different parishes).

Having received the material, the archivist must carefully check the transfer list against the actual records received to make sure that everything is accounted for.

The archivist should then prepare an accession sheet for the records, one copy of which will be returned as a receipt to the office which sent them. After this, the archivist must arrange for the proper storage of the records in the repository, taking care to place any records which need special storage, such as films, in the correct storage environment. The archivist must record the location(s) of the records on the master copy of the accession sheet and on any other location controls he/she maintains. All the steps in accessioning for an in-house archives can be achieved in a fairly streamlined way when the organisation's records are covered by disposal schedules. This enables the archivist to work out a programme for the orderly transfer of records from the different offices, so that he/she can expect to receive transfers from a particular office at the same time each year.

ACCESSIONING IN A COLLECTING ARCHIVES

A collecting archives, sometimes called a manuscript library or repository, collects the records of a variety of organisations, individuals and families. In such institutions, records created, received or maintained by a single organisation, individual or family and received in one transfer by the archives, must be accessioned as a single unit as they share the same provenance.

However, collecting institutions, especially those that acquire organisational records, may receive several transfers of material of the same provenance over a period of time. To deal with these additions to the collection, the archivist will need to develop transfer guidelines for clients similar to those used in an in-house archives. The guidelines will help to ensure that the accessioning process is orderly and efficient. They should clearly outline the archives' requirements for the identification, labelling and listing of material to be transferred to its custody.

Often the archivist in a collecting archives will not have such a close relationship with the creators of the records as the archivist working in an in-house archives does with the various offices of the parent organisation. The work of accessioning will usually all be done by the archivist once the material has arrived in the archives, although if the archives has a field officer he/she may be able to list and box the records before they are sent to the archives.

Notes taken during accessioning enable the archivist to select material for more detailed analysis.

The following case studies illustrate some of the issues and questions involved with accessioning in a collecting archives.

Case Study One

The papers of a local identity contain the official minute books and financial records of the local Progress Association for the time that the person was secretary of the Association. If it is possible to separate these minute books and financial records from the rest of the material, without the loss of information gained through context, this should be done and then both groups of material should be accessioned separately as each group has a different provenance. It is most important that you refer to the other accession in your documentation for each of the groups of material, otherwise the information about the context in which they were received by the archives could be lost.

You may find that other records of the Progress Association have come to your archives from another former official. Accessioning by provenance will enable you to bring together all the records of the Association, even though they have been brought into the archives by different people at different times.

It is often thought that it would be easier for users if all material produced by the same person, or all material relating to the same subject, is brought together. Such an action violates the rule that only material which has the same provenance should be brought together. To remove an item from the context in which it was created, received or maintained (that is, its provenance) is to destroy much of the meaning of the item.

Case Study Two

A number of photographs by a particular photographer are received from the photographer. As these share the same provenance, because they were all created and retained by that photographer, they should be accessioned as one unit. Even though other examples of that photographer's work are already held by the archives, having been received from another source, say, from a client of the photographer, the new material should be accessioned separately because it has a different provenance. The difference is that the photographs were commissioned by the client and draw their meaning as part of the client's family records rather than as work of the photographer. Retrieval of all the photographs by a particular photographer can be achieved by the means of an index or other finding aid produced later. (See Chapter Six Finding Aids for more details.)

Although it may seem that observing the principle of provenance in accessioning is time consuming, it is time well spent. The determination and recording of provenance provides as much valuable information about the photographs as the recording of the photographer or subject alone.

Case Study Three

Your archives is presented with some family papers. Amongst the papers are found a number of unidentified and undated portrait

Examine photographs carefully for markings or other evidence of subject or photographer.

photographs. The knowledge of their provenance and their relationship with the other material may be used to deduce their approximate dates of creation. One of the letters sent to the family makes mention of enclosing a photograph. A diary, when examined in detail refers to the visit of an itinerant photographer to the town. These clues, when used in conjunction with further research, may eventually provide identification of the portraits.

If the photographs had been placed in a group of unidentified portraits, without the proper recording of their provenance, there would be little likelihood of any further information ever being discovered about them.

ACCESSIONING DOCUMENTATION

The recording of information about each new accession is vitally important to the running of the archives. Being the first level of control over new material it must be done in a standardised manner.

While the formats and media of records may determine how they will be stored, they will not have any influence on accessioning procedures. That is to say the archival theories behind accessioning apply equally to all types of material. Whether the records are photographs, magnetic tape or paper they will be accessioned in the same way, despite the later differences in storage and handling.

The Accession Register

The most important source of documentation for basic control information is the *accession register.* The register can come in several formats. The format outlined here consists of a loose-leaf folder of individual accession sheets, with one completed for each accession. This format has some flexibility as copies of the sheets can be made and filed in several different sequences, as explained below. Some archives use computers to capture accessioning details. (See Chapter Nine Using Computers and Micrographics for an example of accessioning documentation which can be produced using an automated system.) Whatever format the accession register is produced in, it is important to maintain a back-up copy in hard copy form. This is because the accession register is a vital record for the archives, that is, a record without which the archives cannot perform its basic functions. The accession register is the basic document for all subsequent control and processing of the collection.

Study the example of an archives accession sheet in Box A. This form is divided in two: the upper half records information which can be made available to the public, the lower half records details which should remain confidential. The original sheet, filed by accession number, will form your accessions register. It is one of the archives' most vital documents and must be kept in a secure place.

Box A   Archives Accession Sheet

Provenance: Accession Number:

Description:

Date Range:

Quantity: Location:

Access Conditions/Copyright:

Notes:

Confidential Details

Donor/Previous Custodian: Accession Number:

Address:

Telephone: (H)
            (W)

Intermediary/Contact Officer:

                                                               Telephone:

Acquisition File Number: Acknowledgement Date:

Compiled by: Date:

A computerised accession register allows the archivist instant access to basic information. Bright areas indicate where information is to be entered. Courtesy — Tim Robinson.

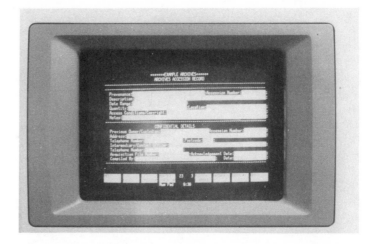

An explanation of what information to include under each heading on the form is given below.

Accession Number. It is easiest simply to make this an annual number, i.e. the first accession of 1985 would be 1985/1. This is the unique number which identifies each accession until further work is done during the arrangement and description stages.

Provenance. In most cases this will be the full name of the organisation or person, or agency within an organisation, that created, received or accumulated and used the records in the conduct of business or life. A standard format for the recording of these names should be adopted for ease of filing.

Description. This should briefly record the types of record, e.g. files, correspondence, ledgers, photographs, magnetic tapes and any unexpected material noticed during appraisal.

Date Range. The inclusive dates of the creation of the material, not the dates of its subject matter.

Quantity. The shelf metres occupied by the accession. The number and types of containers may also be useful.

Location. The location of every container forming the accession should be noted. The location information should be precise, giving shelf or drawer numbers, not just general storage area names such as map room or upstairs stack.

Access Conditions/Copyright. A summary of the conditions should be given here, with full details placed on the acquisitions file.

Notes. Information about the physical condition of the material, whether or not a Box List exists and any other information which may be of later use.

Donor/Previous Custodian. In the case of a collecting archives, the donor is the person, family or organisation who signed the donation form. If there was an intermediary, who brought the material to the archives, his/her name should be also recorded. For an in–house archives, the previous custodian will be the transferring office. Remember to record the name of a contact officer in the office.

Acquisition File Number. Record the number of the file which has all the information relating to the accession. A copy of the completed accession sheet should be placed on the file.

Acknowledgement Date. Record here the date on which formal written acknowledgement of receipt of the records was made.

Compiler. The archivist who accessioned the material.

Date. The date accessioning was completed.

Case Studies Four and Five present examples of completed accession sheets.

Accession sheets are kept handily in notebooks.

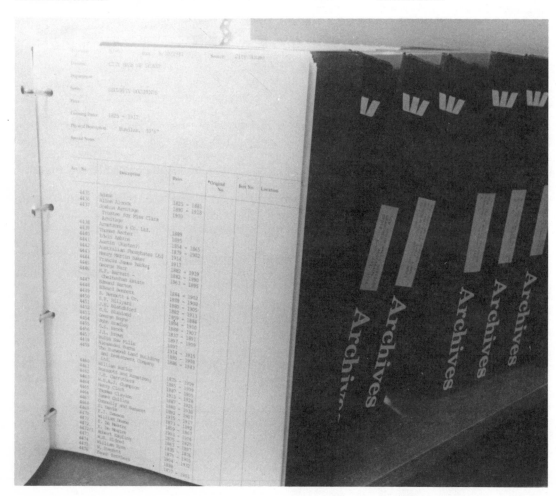

Case Study Four
In–house Archives

ARCHIVES ACCESSION SHEET

Provenance:	Accession Number:
Headmaster's Office	*1985/1*

Description:
Correspondence Files

Date Range:
1 Aug 1948 — 4 July 1960

Quantity:	Location:
4m (22 boxes)	*1985/1/1–10: Bay 20 Shelves 1&2*
	1985/1/11–22: Bay 40, Shelves 8–10

Access Conditions/Copyright:
Access only with written permission of Headmaster

Notes:
Arranged by annual single number system. See Index, Accession Number 1985/2. 1948–1949 files are water damaged. Box List available. Previous accession: 1979/4

Confidential Details

Donor/Previous Custodian:	Accession Number
Mr. Fraser, the Caretaker	*1985/1*

Address: *Room 22*
Telephone: (H)
(W) *x 95*

Intermediary/Contact Officer:	
Mr. Kerr, Assistant to the Caretaker	
	Telephone: *x 96*

Acquisition File Number:	Acknowledgement Date:
A.F. 103	*23 Feb 1985*

Compiled by:	Date:
Anne York	*25 Feb 1985*

Case Study Five
Collecting Archives

ARCHIVES ACCESSION SHEET

Provenance: Accession Number:
Benlith Potteries Pty. Ltd.   *1985/15*

Description:
Records, including minutes, financial records, building plans and photographs

Date Range:
1883–1958

Quantity: Location:
17m (100 boxes)   *Bay 10 Shelves 1–25*

Access Conditions/Copyright:
Open access. Copyright not held by Archives.

Notes:
Box list available. The donors are unrelated to Benlith, but purchased the building and offered the records they found.

Confidential Details

Donor/Previous Custodian: Accession Number
Development Inc.   *1985/15*
Address: *C/– Benlith House, George Street,*
         Benlith, N.S.W. 2999
Telephone: (H)
            (W) *93–762*

Intermediary/Contact Officer:
Mr. Andrew Howard — Manager, Human Resource Relations

                                                     Telephone: *93–762 x 88*

Acquisition File Number: Acknowledgement Date:
A. F. 401   *1 Apr. 1985*

Compiled by: Date:
L. Blunt   *10 Apr. 1985*

Other Documentation

The advantage of having the archives accession sheet divided in half is that copies can be made of either the top or bottom sections to create various finding aids to the records.

The top half of the accession sheet can be copied and the copies filed alphabetically by provenance. This provides one basic level of entry to the archives' holdings, that is, by name of the creating organisation or person.

Yet another copy of the top half of the accession sheet can be made and filed according to selected record types from information given under the *Description* heading in the form. This finding aid would provide a quick guide to all accessions of, for example, photographs or microfilms or magnetic tapes or maps held in the archives. Because the information on the top half of the sheet is not confidential, these copies in various configurations can be readily used by researchers.

In a collecting archives, it is very useful to have an alphabetical index to the donor of each accession. This is because people will invariably remember that one of their family or friends presented a collection to the archives, but they will not remember precisely what or when it was. An index to donors may be constructed quite easily by copying the lower half of the accession sheet and filing it alphabetically by the name of the person or group of people who presented the collection. However, because donors' names and addresses are confidential, these files should be accessible only to authorised archives staff.

To be able to retrieve material quickly from its shelf or shelves in the repository, it is necessary to create an index to holdings by location number. This could be done by copying the top half of the accession sheet, although it is more practical to extract the location and accession numbers and record them on cards if more sophisticated systems are not available. A separate location index has the advantage of being easily up-dated when further work is done on the records and locations of individual containers change. It is also the best way of keeping track of different formats of material from the one accession which may be stored in different locations.

Preparing a Box List

In the section on accessioning in an in-house archives, the importance of listing the records prior to transfer was stressed. For a collecting archives, this will often not be possible as the archivist may not have enough time to list the material adequately before it arrives at the archives. If this is the case, preparing a *box list* becomes one of the steps in the accessioning process.

The main point of the box list is to provide physical control of the records at a container level — that is, to indicate what material is in each box in a collection. Each separate item, be it folder, volume, album, map, plan or framed painting must have a distinguishing number that includes the accession number. Adding another number to the accession number will adequately identify the components of each accession. For example 1985/1/10 represents the tenth container of the first accession of 1985. Where the container holds a number of items, such as the contents of a small box, the accession number should be written in soft pencil on each item. The accession number, or any other annotation you make, should be always placed in square brackets to indicate that it is not a part of the original document. A standardised location should also be chosen for placing accession numbers, such as the top right hand corner, or bottom left corner.

CONCLUSION

The process of accessioning will provide a basic level of control over the records entrusted to your archives. It is a most important process in archival work. Accessioning needs to be completed as soon as possible after the receipt of records and is the foundation upon which all further archival work is based.

The completed accessions sheet, when copied, will provide several basic finding aids to the records. If time is limited, it is far better to have accessioned all your archives, and so have a basic level of control over them all, than to have completely processed only a small part of your holdings while the bulk of the records remain unaccessioned.

For further reading, consult the list of references at the end of Chapter Five Arrangement and Description.

Check new transfers of material to ensure that the list of material for each container is accurate.

ARRANGEMENT AND DESCRIPTION

Paul Brunton and *Tim Robinson*

An archives must have control over its holdings both for its own internal good management and so that the records will be available for use. Accessioning gives initial but limited control. It clearly defines the extent of a collection of records on the basis of its provenance, and ensures that the collection does not become intermingled with other holdings. However, before a collection of records can be used for research its various parts need to be identified and placed in context.

Researchers should not have access to records which have only been accessioned, as the archivist does not yet know enough about the collection to protect it or to describe its contents and arrangement accurately. Not only could physical damage be done to the collection, but the internal relationships of the material could be destroyed and the information revealed through this knowledge would be lost. After accessioning, the sequence of steps by which the necessary degree of control is effected and recorded is known as *arrangement and description*. It is the heart of the archivist's work and potentially one of the most stimulating of archival activities.

In some ways, arrangement and description are rather like doing a jigsaw puzzle, because the archivist is trying to fit all the different pieces together. He/she may have to return to the same place several times, each time gathering more clues as to how the different pieces fit into the overall pattern.

WHAT IS ARRANGEMENT AND DESCRIPTION?

Arrangement is the process of physically organising records in accordance with the accepted archival principles of provenance and original order. Examining the records to determine their original order is the first phase of arrangement. The second phase is the physical re-organisation of the records into that order, which may involve re-boxing, labelling and shelving the records.

Description is the process of recording standardised information about the arrangement, contents and formats of the records so that persons reading the descriptions will be able to determine whether or not the records are relevant to their research.

Arrangement and description are interdependent activities and are normally undertaken together. Arrangement is of great importance because archives, unlike published books, draw much of their meaning from their context. Books being discrete items, complete in themselves, can be catalogued and used and understood individually. However, archives, being the organic products of continuing work or life activities, can only be fully understood through a knowledge of why and how they were created and used over time. As one's life or business changes these new directions are reflected in the records and provide important evidence for the researcher. Each collection of records is different and the amount of arrangement that is necessary will vary. Some collections may still be in their original order, while others will need extensive re-organisation either to restore the order in which they were created and used, or to impose a new order if none previously existed.

A processing work bench should have sufficient overhead shelves to permit easy sorting of records into series. Courtesy — Archives of Business and Labour, ANU.

Arrangement involves sequential activities. First, the archivist surveys the whole collection to discern whether or not the material, during its active life, was kept in any particular way. If so, the archivist records the method of arrangement and if necessary restores to its original arrangement any material that might have been disturbed or disordered.

In the process of arrangement the archivist will discover much about the creation of the material and the relationships of its various parts which, if not fully explained, will soon be forgotten. Users cannot be expected to examine the whole collection in order to determine how and why individual parts were created, and what functions of the organisation or activities of the individual or family the constituent parts record. This information is vital if the records are to be fully understood. The description of a collection is, therefore, as important as its arrangement.

SETTING PRIORITIES FOR ARRANGEMENT AND DESCRIPTION

Arrangement and description, like all other archival functions, must be properly planned and made to fit in with an archives' other responsibilities. Whether the archives is in-house, or collects material from a variety of different people and organisations, the archivist will need to set priorities for arrangement and description.

The key questions to be answered in setting priorities are:
- Which collections to do first?
- What level of detail is required?
- How much time to spend on each collection?

Some collections will have high priority because there is a known research demand for them, while others will have lower priority because the basic control established during accessioning is sufficient for the time being. Often it will be difficult to forecast how long the arrangement and description of a collection is likely to take, especially if the archivist's time is divided between several archival tasks. However, targets should be set and progress reviewed at regular intervals. It is helpful to remember that arrangement and description are activities which reinforce archival control; they are not intended to provide an exhaustive interpretation of the records.

THE PRINCIPLES GOVERNING ARRANGEMENT

The arrangement of a collection involves the identification and organisation of its various parts according to accepted archival principles.

There are two basic principles of arrangement which are followed world-wide and have been developed over a long period.

These principles are the principle of *provenance* and the principle of the *sanctity of the original order.*

There have been many unsuccessful attempts to arrange archives in ways other than by following these principles. These other systems have generally tried to classify archives as if they were books in a library. On the surface, they may offer a useful system for retrieval purposes but they are actually a disservice to the material because they obscure much of its meaning.

For example, any attempt to place archives into arbitrary subject classifications would involve the archivist in a great deal of unnecessary work, which would actually make the material harder to use. Information on the context of the records and their relationships with each other would be lost forever. Difficulties would be encountered in trying to determine what category to place documents in, as very few documents have only one subject. It would also be extremely difficult to predict the uses to which the documents would be put in the future and therefore to which subject classifications they should be assigned.

The Principle of Provenance

The term *provenance* refers to the place of origin of the records, i.e. the organisation, office or person that created, received or accumulated and used the records in the conduct of business or personal life.

As has been mentioned earlier, in Chapter Four, Accessioning, archives that share the same provenance must be kept separate from those with different provenances. Material created and/or received by a single individual or organisation or office within that organisation must be treated as a single collection and not intermingled either physically or intellectually with material of a different provenance. The following are some examples illustrating the importance of observing the principle of provenance.

Case Study One

The widow of David Reid donates the papers and research material accumulated by her late husband to your archives. Included in the collection are letters addressed to David Reid, a number being from John Armstrong, a well known local history teacher. The other letters are from members of significant and long established families in the district. Before his death David Reid had been preparing for the centenary of the district's settlement and had been collecting information for use in celebration activities. Your archives already has a large volume of papers donated by John Armstrong and a great deal of other material relating to the families of the district.

It may be tempting to divide the letters from the David Reid collection on the basis of their authorship and to place them with other records by the same writers. However, to do this would be to ignore the principle of provenance. Even though the letters are

Annual reports are a major source for administrative history.

written by various people they were all sent to, and retained by, one person, David Reid. By separating them you would be destroying the evidence of Reid's activity in preparing for the centenary celebrations. The information contained in the letters is not lost because they are not being placed with other material on similar subjects or by the same authors. Good description and finding aids will clearly show where information on a particular subject may be found. What the finding aids cannot show is the information about David Reid's activity, work methods and the development of his research. These can only be gained by seeing his papers as he used them himself.

Case Study Two

The papers of Desmond Michael were deposited with an archives, however little was known at the time of the life or work of Michael. Included in the papers was a bundle of photographs of late nineteenth century buildings with cast iron decoration. It was only discovered years later that Michael was interested in architectural history and was researching the history of a particular architectural iron foundry. If the provenance of photographs had been ignored and they had been arranged on the basis of the building in each photograph on the assumption that this was the only information the photographs conveyed, important information would have been lost. Firstly, the results and methods of the collector's research would be destroyed. Secondly, the fact that the iron decoration on the buildings in the photographs was made by the foundry Michael was researching would be obscured. This was the reason the photographs were kept together originally, a fact, however, unknown at the time the photographs were received.

The Principle of the Sanctity of the Original Order

This principle states that records should be maintained in the order in which they were originally kept when in active use. It is not the order imposed on the material by someone who was not involved with the records while they were in active use.

This principle must be followed, i.e. the *original order* must be preserved, or re-constructed if it has been disordered, unless it is absolutely clear that there was no original order and the material has been assembled haphazardly.

The original order does not have to be neat, easily understandable or obviously meaningful to be retained. If an order has been imposed by the person or body whose papers they originally were this must be retained, for to do otherwise will destroy meaning in the material which may not be readily apparent or which needs special expertise to understand.

Re-assembling original order is much like the restoration of a vintage car where the aim is to restore the vehicle to its original condition and thereby ensure its maximum value. All later alterations or modifications are removed to reveal the car as it would have been when new. Just as one may be fortunate enough to find a completely original Rolls Royce untouched since its manufacture, so one may be lucky enough to find a collection still arranged in the way it was when it was created and used. This is why it is essential that the archivist supervises the initial packing of the records before their transfer to the archives. He/she may thus be able to ensure that the original order of the records is not disturbed.

Case Study Three

You have just been appointed the first archivist for a small company that has been in business for sixty years. Your first job is to clear out a basement storeroom where all the old correspondence files for the last fifty years have been stored. Initially the old files were stored on open shelving, then in boxes, and later it appears that staff just opened the door and threw old files into the room. To complicate matters further, the boxes have broken and many files have fallen onto the floor.

On closer examination, things are not as bad as they first appeared. Although the files are scattered, they are still individually intact and all have covers with numbers or other annotations on them. The earliest files were arranged by subject; then an annual single number system was introduced. The last system used was a classified number system, that is one where the number denotes the function of the file (policy, personnel, legal, etc.). Because of the filing system markings, putting the files back into order is quite straightforward, except for one portion. For the two years prior to a change in filing system, the old files have two sets of numbers: the old system and the one which replaced it. Renumbering files with new numbers is known as 'top numbering'. This is not a recommended practice because it leads to precisely the kind of confusion described here. However, it has been common. It would be incorrect to place these renumbered files with the older system. The top numbered files should be kept with the newer system as this represents a further stage in the active life of the records, and so constitutes the original order. The later system has been imposed by those responsible for the papers during their active life and the subsequent change does not represent a disturbance but rather a continuity that should be respected and retained.

A system or order imposed on the material by someone not concerned with the active life of the records need not be respected as it does not reveal anything meaningful about the original use or purpose of the records. Therefore, this alien arrangement will need to be examined to see if any clues to the original order remain. If so, material should be re–arranged to reflect the original scheme.

A particular case of the importance of original order can be found in Victorian family photograph albums. It is relatively easy

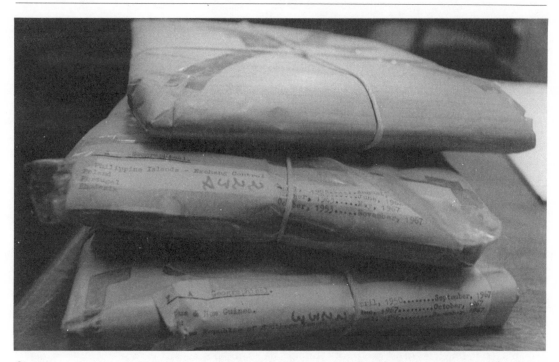

Outside wrappings may contain important information about their contents.

to remove the images from the pages, because they are usually slipped rather than glued into place. However, photograph albums usually have some pattern or plan. In family albums, the photographs were often arranged by family hierarchy, i.e. father and mother followed by children then other relatives and their families. Even if no other information is known about the people in the photographs, their relationships to each other may be tentatively deduced from their arrangement in the album. This information would be lost if the original order were not maintained or recorded.

PREPARING FOR ARRANGEMENT AND DESCRIPTION

At the time of accessioning the archivist will have given the collection an overall identifying Accession Number. This will serve to control the material intellectually and physically as the process of arrangement and description evolves.

Before attempting any work on an accession, the archivist should assemble source material which will reveal as much as possible about the organisation, individual or family who created, received or used the material. This will help the archivist to understand the background of the records, and will provide information useful later in the compilation of an administrative history or biographical note. The sort of information which it is desirable to record includes:

- For an organisation: the date of its establishment; its functions at that time and thereafter; the names of the various sub–units and their functions; names of principal officers, and any significant events or changes and their dates.
- For an individual: dates of birth, marriage and death; changes of address; names of employers and types of work; special interests and significant activities; membership in associations, and offices held, with relevant dates.

The archivist should then examine the whole accession without disturbing the order or disorder of individual items. This initial inspection should be carried out in a large work area where there is no possibility of the material under inspection being moved, disturbed or intermingled by accident with other material held by the archives. A large desk with shelving nearby is most suitable for this work. The archivist should have a pencil and notepad ready on which to record information about the types of material found and the rough dates.

Record survey documents identify provenance and series.

Archives by definition are unique, they are also often fragile and usually contain within them the seeds of their own physical destruction. For all these reasons, archivists must take great care when handling records during arrangement and description. *Always* clean your hands before beginning any work which requires you to touch records, keep work surfaces clean and do not handle the records more often than is necessary. Very simple conservation measures, such as removing pins, clips, staples and other fasteners can be undertaken. However, anything more complicated should not be attempted, and any damage to the records should be noted for the attention of a conservator.

This initial examination may also reveal desirable background information which has not been found elsewhere. For example, there may be an unpublished history of the organisation or biography of the person or there may be newspaper cuttings or other material which gives this information. Your notes should be kept in such a way that the collection can be re–organised and arranged on paper first before any physical re–arrangement takes place.

During the examination of the records you may discover confidential, sensitive or potentially embarrassing information. The archivist has privileged access to this information and should not reveal it to unauthorised persons. It is part of the ethics of the archival profession that the archivist respects the confidentiality of the records entrusted to his/her care.

When processing a large collection it might be found to be easier, and more productive of consistent results, if two people work on one entire collection together. One person can record the information while the other examines the records. If your archives does not have enough staff available to do this, there are several other ways of organising arrangement and description

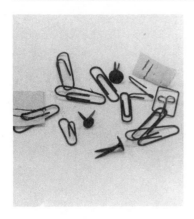

*Metal fasteners eventually corrode
and damage the records.*

work. One is to set aside a morning or afternoon when the archives is closed to researchers to work solely on sorting a large collection.

In examining a collection, the archivist should ask the following questions about the material and record the resulting information in a systematic fashion. The information thus gained and recorded will be further refined to provide the final description. As you become more expert, you will find that you do not need to be so detailed at this stage of the work to gain an understanding of the contents of the records.

• Who created, or received, or compiled and maintained the record during its active life? For an organisation, which department or office created it and for what purpose? For an individual, in what capacity and for what purpose did he or she create the record? In the case of letters received, it is not the writer (i.e. the creator) of the original letter who is important in this context but the recipient. Copies of letters sent, retained by the writer for his or her own record, remain part of the writer's records not part of those of the person who received the original letter.

• What is the type of record: diary, minute book, ledger, correspondence, publication, photograph, newscutting?

• What type of information does it record?

• What is the range of dates over which the material was created? These are the dates of the actual writing of the record, not the dates mentioned in the contents of the record.

• What is the arrangement of the material? Is it in some order? If so, what is the basis of the organisation? For example, is it alphabetical or chronological or arranged by some other system?

• In the case of volumes, is the whole volume used for the same purpose? For example, if it is a diary is all the volume used for that purpose, or does a section of it record financial transactions or the minutes of a meeting?

Archives, unlike books, do not set out to tell the user what they are. Therefore, do not automatically believe any title or description on a volume or bundle of papers. The archivist must look through the material to determine at first hand what it is. Before any physical re-arrangement is undertaken it may be necessary to examine the whole accession in this fashion a number of times. With each examination the archivist will become more familiar with the nature of the material and so will be in a better position to identify individual items and place them in their original relationship with other items. Arrangement and description are in fact one process. However, for ease of explanation, this chapter treats each process in turn.

ARRANGEMENT

Firstly, you should ensure that material of the same provenance has been brought together. You will have attempted to have done this at the time of accessioning, but now you have the opportunity to review the earlier work in the light of your research into the creator of the records. You must ensure that only items of the same provenance have been brought together, as the arrangement of individual items will now be determined.

In order to identify correctly the provenance of the records it is necessary to know which person or office created, received and/or used the material. For this purpose an organisational chart, or family tree, will be of great assistance. The archivist may need to compile this chart from the information obtained from the background research into the records. Information useful for this purpose may also be obtained during the initial inspection of the records themselves.

Identifying Series

Having brought together all the accessioned material with the same provenance, the next step is to identify the component series. A *series* consists of records which have been brought together in the course of their active life to form a discrete sequence. This sequence may be a discernible filing system (classified, alphabetical, numerical, chronological or a combination of these) or it may simply be a grouping of records on the basis of similar function, content or format. The important factor is that the grouping was made by those responsible for the records during the records' active life. This applies to both organisational and personal records.

In an in-house archives the identification of series will usually be quite simple as records transferred to the archives should normally still be in the same order as when they were created and used. In addition, most organisations arrange their records according to some identifiable system of filing so they can be easily retrieved and used. Each file or part of the series usually has an identifying number or symbol which clearly locates it within the series.

Particular attention should be paid to identifying those series which have begun their active life as the responsibility of one creator and have subsequently become the responsibility of another, or of a succession of further offices. The series should be recorded under the provenance of the last office, but each of the preceding offices (provenances) should be noted for the period of its responsibility.

Some examples of series are:
1) *Items arranged in accordance with a filing system.* For example, correspondence which has been organised using an annual single number system i.e. where each file has a

These building plans are a series because their form and their function required them to be maintained and used as a group.

distinguishing number consisting of the year and a sequential number; this would mean that the first file of 1956 would be number 56/1. Another example would be files which are arranged alphabetically by the title of the file.

2) *Items grouped together because of a similar function.* Most items grouped together because of a similar function, such as a run of cash books, will also come into the category of items arranged in accordance with a filing system, even if this is simply placing the books on the shelf in chronological order.

3) *Items grouped together because of similar content.* For example, a collection of papers kept together because they relate to a particular subject, such as a court case.

4) *Items grouped together because of similar format.* For example, photographs or sound recordings. It should be remembered, though, that it is not the form which determines whether a collection of items constitutes a series. In fact, the form of items within one series may change. A series is only determined by form when items of the same form have been kept together as a result of their creation, receipt or use.

In identifying series the principle of the sanctity of the original order must be applied. The archivist should determine what records have been brought together during their active life to form a single sequence.

A useful tool in identifying series and their original order is any contemporary finding aid to the records. For example, registers or indexes to correspondence can be of great assistance if a number of series have become confused. A register of letters received will provide the period of time the series was maintained, the order in which the letters were received, a summary of their content and details of how the letters were numbered on receipt. Indexes will not necessarily show the original order of the series they control, but they will give an indication of the filing system used and the scope of the records. The importance of these registers and indexes, and other similar records, is dealt with in Chapter Six, Finding Aids.

Often the archivist will be presented with donations of small quantities of material. These will have been accessioned on the basis of their provenance. When only a folder or small bundle of individual documents is involved the reconstruction of series may not be relevant.

In this case, a chronological arrangement, if feasible, based on the date of creation is probably the most advisable. However, this only applies to very small quantities of material and should be regarded as a last resort.

It will sometimes happen that an item is not related to any other item. In this case, it is correct to leave it as a single item series and

not attempt to force it into another series of which it is not naturally a part. There is no minimum or maximum size for a series.
Obvious examples of single item series are a diary, or a framed
portrait.

Artificial Series

Where there is no original order then artificial series will need to
be created. However, one must first be certain that there is in fact
no order and that material has been brought together
haphazardly. Order in this context is not the same as orderliness.
Just because a collection of papers looks messy does not mean
that the person who used the papers during their active life did
not have some order in the way individual documents were placed
with other documents. The significance of this positioning of
documents may not be immediately apparent to the archivist.
Also, before imposing an artificial order, one should be absolutely certain that the chaos is not the result of subsequent dis-
turbances of the collection in which case the archivist must try to
re–establish the order in which the papers were kept during their
active life. If order is imposed, it should be clearly noted that the
order of the collection is artificial and imposed subsequently by
the archivist.

In establishing artificial series from material which shares the
same provenance, items which record the same function should
be brought together. The form of these items may change over
time, but the form is not the criterion for the series. For example,
a series of ledgers may begin with bound volumes, change to
loose leaf volumes and then become computer printouts. Despite
the physical changes, the activity recorded remains unchanged,
and so all these items are a part of the one series.

Decisions concerning the formation of artificial series often
face the archivist when arranging collections of personal papers
that contain letters. Letters received, and copies of letters sent,
can be brought together to form series. Each of these series can
either be arranged chronologically or alphabetically by the name
of the writer or the addressee. The method chosen by the archivist
in establishing artificial series for letters will depend upon a number of factors. If the letters are undated, or inexact in dating, it
will be better to arrange them alphabetically than to try to establish dates. If it is clear from examining the letters that they are
more meaningful if grouped by writer or addressee, than if
arranged chronologically, this method should be adopted. It may
be found, on examination of the letters, that a chronological
arrangement will better reflect the 'flow of events' recorded by
the letters. If so, they should be ordered chronologically. Similarly, it might sometimes be possible to form one series comprising both letters received and copies of letters sent. Once again,
the determination as to whether this arrangement should be

chosen will depend on it being of value in making the letters more meaningful.

It is emphasised that this discussion is only concerned with letters for which there is no original order to be maintained. It is a situation which is more likely to occur with personal papers than with organisational records.

The format of records may be a useful key to establishing artificial series. Photographs are often kept together, and so may constitute a series. However, in the absence of any information about the original arrangement of material, function is a more important basis for creating artificial series. Photographs found included in files of correspondence would not be made a separate series just because they are photographs. Their function and meaning is dependent on their remaining a part of the correspondence series.

In the papers of a real estate agent, for example, where there were family photographs and photographs of sale properties in no order, it would be better to form two series. Family photographs would become one series and photographs of sale properties another. This would better reflect the function of the records.

Determining function should result from a thorough examination of the records. Do not accept at face value what is written on spines or labels. For example, a collection of volumes labelled 'Finance Minute Books' when examined could be found to contain also the minutes of the Security Committee of the same organisation. Each of these sets of minutes forms a separate series because it records separate functions. Each set of minutes would be described as a separate series, although, of course, physically the two sets co–exist within the same volumes.

The archivist will often find newscuttings clipped together or placed loosely in volumes. These should not be placed with other newscuttings to form a single series until a thorough examination has been undertaken to find out why particular newscuttings were kept together. Usually there is a reason, and separate series can be created on the basis of material that has been brought together to fulfil some function, or because it relates to a particular subject or activity. Examples could be newscuttings relating to a court case, or newscuttings written by or about a single individual which may have been kept together for these reasons.

In every archives there are always large numbers of photographs. Often photographs are wrongly thought of as museum objects, and not as archives. By now it should be clear that archival theory holds that the format of the record is not relevant in deciding how it should be treated. What is important is that the provenance of a record be determined and recorded, and that the original order of the records be respected and preserved. Photographs are therefore the same as any other record, and in order that their maximum informational value be preserved they must be accessioned, arranged and described like other records.

It might often seem the best solution to bring together all the photographs in a collection to form an artificial series. If there is no original order and photographs can be brought together by function this is to be preferred. In archival theory it is the function of a record which is more important than its form. For example, a series of photographs may have been taken by a local council

---

Box A   Some Terms to Describe Archival Materials†

Cartographic Records
Chart
Drawing
Elevation
Graph
Map
Plan

Correspondence
Correspondence
Letters (Sent or Received)
Letter Book

Diaries
Appointment Book
Daily Occurrence Book
Diary
Journal
Log Book

File Controls
Catalogue card
Classification Scheme
Index
Register
Subject Heading List
Thesaurus

Financial Records
Account Book
Balance Sheet
Bank Statement
Cash Book
Day Book
Invoice
Journal
Ledger
Purchase Order
Receipt
Requisition

Legal Records
Agreement
Certificate
Commission
Contract
Deed
Deposition
Estate Inventory
Indenture
Mortgage
Register of Shareholders
Will

Meeting Records
Agenda
Minute Books
Minutes and Related Papers
Proceedings

Photographic Records*
   (Colour, B&W)
Cine/Movie Film
Glass Plate
Microform
Print (positive & negative)
Transparency (positive &
   negative, including slides)

Private Papers
Family Tree
Manuscript, including drafts
Memoir
Recollection
Reminiscence
Report
Research Notes
Sermon
Speech
Typescript

Publications
Book
Broadsheet
Brochure
Catalogue
Circular
Flyer
Handbill
Handbook
Leaflet
Magazine
Manual
Newsclipping
Newsletter
Newspaper
Pamphlet
Poster
Programme
Proof

Sound Recordings
Cylinder (wax, wire)
Disc (acetate, compact,
   shellac)
Magnetic Tape (cassette,
   reel-to-reel)

Technological Media
Computer Output Microfilm
   (COM)
Disks
Diskettes (floppy discs)
Optical Disc
Printout
Videotape

---

†It is not uncommon for an archives to receive *copies* of these materials, rather than originals. You should state what type of copy each is (carbon, photostatic, electrostatic, etc.), as well as give the type of record (letter, plan, deed, etc.).

*For a list of types of nineteenth century photographic records, consult the references cited in the Further Reading at the end of this chapter.

specifically to document the demolition of buildings in its area. These photographs should be kept together and recorded as a series, just as other photographs produced for other purposes by the council should be kept as separate series reflecting the way they were created and used.

Often a series will not have a title of its own and the archivist will have to assign a title which accurately reflects the function and content of the records. In assigning titles it is of particular importance that terms are used consistently.

See Box A for a list of terms which will be useful when identifying and describing series. Often a series title will also include qualifying information, such as the system of arrangement or the function of the records.

DESCRIPTION

Description is defined as the process of establishing intellectual control over the holdings through the preparation of finding aids.

The basic description document used in most repositories is the *series description sheet.* The purpose of this is to record a detailed description of the nature, contents and format of each series and to relate it to its provenance. Examples of completed series description sheets follow. The layout of the sheet may be adapted for individual needs providing the essential information is included.

In arranging an accession a great deal of information about each item will have been discovered, such as why it was created, by whom, and its informational content. Each series must be described and an account given which places each series in its context in the whole accession. For records of organisations, this account is called an administrative history. For personal papers, a biographical note fulfils the same purpose.

Administrative History/Biographical Note

The organic nature of archives means that a description of each separate series alone will not adequately convey the full meaning and context of the records. Each collection needs to be seen as a whole with each of its constituent series placed in context. This is done by means of an administrative history or biographical note. In isolation, an individual series may not provide information on its links with the rest of the collection or on the reasons for its creation and demise. The reasons for changes (of form or function) within a series need to be explained because it will not be self-evident. The reason for the very existence of some series may not be apparent without an overall history of the organisation or person being given.

In writing an administrative history or a biographical note much information will be derived from the records themselves. However, it will be necessary to consult other sources in order to complete the details. See Box B.

Box B   Checklist of Sources

---

a) **For the Administrative History of Organisations**

The following is a guide to sources which should be consulted for background information about an organisation.
Some may be obtained in libraries prior to the examination
of the records, others will be found amongst the records of
the organisation itself, usually in files categorised as policy,
administration or history. The organisation may also have
produced procedure manuals, handbooks or organisational
charts which should also be consulted.

1)   Legal instruments of creation, e.g. letters of incorpor-
     ation, articles of association, registration of company.
2)   Constitutions, Rules or By–laws.
3)   Annual Reports, published or unpublished.
4)   Company records kept by various governmental auth-
     orities, e.g. bankruptcy records and those kept by the
     registrar of companies.
5)   Histories of the organisation, either published or
     unpublished.
6)   Published company and/or business directories.
7)   Newspaper or journal articles and notices.
8)   Interviews with present or past members of staff.

b) **For Biographical Notes on Individuals and Families**

As with organisations, the records of the individual or family
itself should not be overlooked as a source of biographical
information. Other sources are:

1)   Records kept by government authorities such as birth,
     death and marriage records, wills, bankruptcy records,
     immigration records, land records, musters and
     censuses, electoral rolls and cemetery records.
2)   Records of organisations with which the individual or
     family may have been associated, e.g. churches, banks,
     clubs and societies or employers.
3)   Biographies, autobiographies or family histories, either
     published or unpublished, and general histories which
     may include biographical detail.
4)   Biographical dictionaries both general and specific,
     e.g. those devoted to a particular trade or profession.
5)   Directories, telephone books and gazetteers.
6)   Newspapers and journals; articles and notices.
7)   Interviews with the individual or family.

Case Studies Four and Five are examples of an Administrative
History and a Biographical Note.

Case Study Four   Administrative History

1) *Name of Creator:*
Benlith Potteries Pty Ltd

2) *Date Range:*
1883 – 1958

3) *Administrative History:*

Benlith Potteries Pty Ltd was founded by Irving Smith in 1883. It began manufacturing earthenware pipes and sanitary fittings and by 1895 also produced domestic china ware following the discovery of a deposit of high quality clay. Irving Smith died in 1893 and his business was bought by Seymour Wheeler. In May 1901, Benlith Potteries became a public company. Seymour Wheeler became Managing Director and his son, Josiah, became General Manager. He remained General Manager until 14 August 1919 when he was succeeded by Cedric Ives. Ives was General Manager from 1919–31 Mar. 1930. He was succeeded by Colin Pitts who remained General Manager until the company's dissolution on 31 March 1958.

4) *References:*

Wells Industrial Gazetteer, 1885–1913

Peterson, A., *An Informative Treatise on the History and Development of Sanitary Ware in the Colonies.* Atlanta, 1899.

Boyd, R. (ed) *Biographical Dictionary of Plumbing.* Wagga, 1978.

5) *Name of Preparer:*
C. Conway

6) *Date of Completion:*
23 Dec 1986

Case Study Five   Biographical Note

1) *Name of Creator:*
Phillip Hall

2) *Date Range:*
1 Apr 1930–

3) *Biographical Note:*

Journalist. Born in Blackwell. He began work as a copy boy with the Blackwell Gazette after leaving Blackwell High in 1945. He became a journalist in 1950 and took special responsibility for the history of the Blackwell area. He was a founding member of the Blackwell Historical Society in 1949 and became its president in 1956, an office he has held continuously except from 1964 to 1969 when he was overseas. In 1955 he married Annabelle Roberts. He served on the Blackwell Council from 1960 to 1963, the final year as Mayor. He has published three books: *Blackwell Municipal Council: A Centennial History,* 1956; *The Roberts Family and their Circle,* 1970; *History of Blackwell,* 1976.

4) *References:*

Who's Who in Blackwell. Camford Press, Blackwell, 1974.

Hall, Emelia, *The Halls of Blackwell.* Oxbridge Press, Blackwell, 1972.

5) *Name of Preparer:*
C. Conway

6) *Date of Completion:*
8 Jun 1980

Series Description Sheet

A series description sheet should include the following information. The headings *Related Series* and *Notes* will not always be used, but entries should be made under the other headings. When abbreviations are used in the series description sheet, or in any other documentation, care must be taken to ensure that these abbreviations are standardised throughout the archives. An example of a series description sheet is shown in Box C.

1) **Provenance.** The organisation, agency of that organisation, person or family that created, received or accumulated and used the records in the conduct of business or personal life. This links the series with other series with the same provenance.

2) **Series Number.** A discrete number allocated to each series from the series register. This is discussed later.

3) **Series title.** This names the series. The series title should be succinct and incorporate the type of record and reflect the function it performs, e.g. *Applications for Registration of Motor Vehicle*. If the creator of the records has assigned a name to the series this must be used though it may sometimes need amplification. If there is no assigned title, the archivist will need to assign one. It should be noted if this is done.

4) **Date Range.** This should show the earliest and latest date of the material, any significant gaps or concentrations. For this purpose, the date is the date when an item was created not the date of its subject. For example, the date range of the correspondence of an historian of medieval times which discusses medieval history is the dates during which the correspondence was written not the dates of its subject. The date of a copy of an item, either a photocopy or a typescript copy, is the date when the original was created, not the date when the photocopy or typescript was made.

5) **Quantity.** Use a consistent standard of measurement. The accepted standard of measurement is to record the shelf space occupied by a series in metres. If the series has only a small quantity of material, the number and type of containers may also be recorded.

6) **Physical Characteristics/Condition.** A description of the physical characteristics of the items in the series. For example, are the items handwritten, typescript, a combination of both, reproduced in some way, newscuttings, or printed? Are they bound volumes, loose sheets, or files? Are they photographic prints, photographic negatives, or sound recordings?

7) **Content Description.** The important things to be mentioned in this section are: the relationship of the records to the work of the creating office or person, the types of records and the types of information contained therein,

and representative or exceptional matters or transactions conducted.

8) **Arrangement.** The manner in which the records are arranged, i.e. chronologically, alphabetically, according to a classified system. If the arrangement has been imposed by the archivist this must be recorded.

9) **Related Series.** Series which have a direct and significant connection to this series, e.g. file control records such as indexes or registers and, in the case of letters sent, letters received would be mentioned under this entry.

10) **Access conditions.** This documents the existence of any restrictions on access and the conditions affecting the supply of copies of the items or information from the records.

11) **Notes.** Anything the archivist feels should be recorded about the series that has not been recorded elsewhere and may be of use to persons using the records.

12) **Shelf List (including contents note).** A shelf list is a listing by identifying number of the contents of each container or free standing item, such as a volume. The contents note should clearly establish what is contained in each box so that researchers may choose appropriate records with precision. Usually, the information presented will identify the first and last unit of material in the box. Examples of brief contents notes are shown in Box D. This is basic for physical control of the holdings. The location of each container should be given. To simplify the location of containers each shelf in the repository should be numbered. For more precise location control, you may wish to assign a number to each 'space' on the shelf.

13) and 14) **Name of preparer and date completed.** For future reference it is important to know who prepared the description and the date it was completed.

Case Studies Six and Seven provide examples of completed series description sheets.

A well organised area for arrangement and description work.

Box C   Series Description Sheet

1) *Provenance:*   2) *Series Number:*

3) *Series Title:*

4) *Date Range:*   5) *Quantity:*

6) *Physical Characteristics/Condition:*

7) *Content Description:* (Relationship to work of office/creator, types of information contained therein, representative/exceptional matters mentioned):

8) *Arrangement:*

9) *Related Series:*

10) *Access Conditions:*

11) *Notes:*

12) *Shelf List:*

    Container No.: Brief Contents Note: *Location:*

13) *Prepared by:*   14) *Date Completed:*

Case Study Six   Series Description Sheet

1) *Provenance:* Phillip Hall

2) *Series Number:*
    41

3) *Series Title:* Research Papers for 'History of Blackwell'

4) *Date Range:*
    Mar 1959–Aug 1963,
    Jan 1970–Nov 1975.

5) *Quantity:*
    1m

6) *Physical Characteristics/Condition:*
    Manuscript, typescript, carbon typescript with manuscript corrections. Notebooks, loose sheets, correspondence, newscuttings. The notebooks show water damage.

7) *Content Description* (Relationship to work of office/creator, types of information contained therein, representative/exceptional matters mentioned):
    The material consists of notebooks kept by Hall during his reading of original sources, newscuttings from local papers, correspondence with various libraries and archives and local families. Includes three letters, 1962, from William Davis, novelist and former resident of Blackwell, concerning his childhood there. Some of the bundles include various drafts for Hall's *History of Blackwell*, published 1976. The records end in 1963 and begin again in 1970 because during the intervening period Hall was overseas.

8) *Arrangement:*
    Twenty bundles, each referring to a particular subject or person. Filed alphabetically by title.

9) *Related Series:*

10) *Access Conditions:*
    Available for consultation. Permission to copy must be obtained from Mr. Hall.

11) *Notes:*

12) *Shelf List:*

Container No.	Brief Contents Note	Location
41/1	Aborigines Blackwell Council Blackwell Family Blackwell Gazette Blackwell Lodge Court House Dairy Co-operative	Shelf 29/1
41/2	Davis Family First Settlement Gold Rush Hotels Land Scandal Majestic Picture Palace Moss Family	Shelf 29/2
41/3	Piper Family Roberts Family School Trade Transport War Memorial	Shelf 29/3

13) *Prepared by:* C. Conway

14) *Date completed:* 6 Aug 1980

Additions to Series

In an in-house archives, it will often occur that regular additions to series are transferred to the archives as material becomes non-current. Often, this can be planned for, as the material will be transferred under a current records disposal schedule. For example, correspondence files more than 10 years old may be transferred every 10 years. Similarly, in a collecting archives, additions to series may arrive as further material is unearthed or becomes non-current.

Once material has been assessed as truly part of a series already held by the archives, it will be necessary to revise the series description sheet to incorporate the additional material. The *Date Range* and *Quantity* will need to be changed and perhaps additional information will need to be supplied under *Physical Characteristics*, *Description* and *Notes*. The shelf list will need to be adjusted and the series register annotated to indicate the additional material.

A Note About the Description of Photographs

There are particular features of photographs that have to be borne in mind when describing them. Photography is a relatively recent phenomenon, 1839 usually being accepted as its begin-

Series description sheets record essential information in a consistent way.

An 1860's albumen print purports to show the tallest and the shortest men in the world.

ning date. During the nineteenth century photography went through a number of significant developments which people unfamiliar with the history of this record medium sometimes find intimidating.

The changes are quite simple to understand when set in their historical context, and the identification of the different processes becomes straight forward. All archivists have the responsibility to be knowledgeable about the records in their care. Just as an archivist who deals with early twentieth century paper records should know the difference between a press copy and a carbon copy, an archivist should be able to tell a daguerreotype from an ambrotype if he/she deals with early photographic records.

In describing photographs it is essential to be able to identify the process used to produce the record. This information is of great importance for the conservation of the records and is also of great value in determining their date range.

Some processes are also rare and so have their own intrinsic value as examples of the process which is important in the history of photography.

As with the creator of any record the photographer's name is a vital piece of information in the description of any photographic record, and it must be recorded on the series description sheet if it can be discovered.

No attempt will be made here to provide an account of the various processes or of the history of photography. It is recommended that any archives which includes photographs, and it would be an unusual collection that did not, should acquire some standard texts on the history of photography. The archivists should become familiar with the different processes. A selection

Box D   Examples of Brief Contents Notes Entries

Type of Series	Arrangement Item 12)	Shelf List:	Brief Contents Notes
Personnel Files	Alphabetical by name of employee	Box 1 Box 2	Files A–Ec Files Ed–G
Contracts	Numerical by number of contract	Box 1 Box 2	Contracts 1–19 Contracts 20–32
Correspondence	Numerical by annual single number	Box 1 Box 2	86/1–86/30 86/31–86/45
Subject File	Alphabetical by file title	Box 1 Box 2	Abbatoirs Aborigines Artists Bandicoots Buoys Cartoons Compost

of useful texts is included in the Further Reading at the end of the chapter.

For conservation and storage requirements it is often decided to remove photographic records from textual records and store them separately. This is acceptable, but where it is done the accession register, series description sheet and other finding aids must have the location annotated accordingly. It is also good practice to include a separation sheet (such as used for museum

---

Case Study Seven   Series Description Sheet

1) *Provenance:* Benlith Potteries Pty Ltd

2) *Series Number:*
    56

3) *Series Title:* General Manager
    — Copies of Letters Sent

4) *Date Range:*
    May 1901–Mar 1958

5) *Shelf Metres:*
    5m

6) *Physical Characteristics/Condition:*
    Press–copy letterbooks, carbon typescript volumes and loose bundles. From 20 May 1901 to 31 Dec. 1910 copies of letters were kept in press–copy books. Five volumes each with index at front. From 2 Jan. 1911–31 Dec. 1935 copies were kept on carbon typescripts which were pasted into volumes. 25 volumes, each with an index. From 2 Jan. 1936–13 Mar. 1958, copies were kept on carbon typescripts which were kept loose in bundles one bundle for each year. 23 bundles with one index kept on cards filed at 58/1.

7) *Content Description* (Relationship to work of office/creator, types of information contained therein, representative/exceptional matters mentioned):
    Series comprises copies of business letters sent to clients and suppliers of Benlith Potteries Pty Ltd. Major matters of business discussed include purchases of chemicals for glazes, additives for producing various grades of pottery, prospective orders for customers wishing unique items, marketing strategies and conditions. Also included are a few letters (20 August, 1915–1 February 1917) written by Mr. Josiah Wheeler in his capacity as secretary of the Patriotic Fund for the Benlith area.

8) *Arrangement:*
    Chronological. Each volume contains index, card index exists for loose bundles.

9) *Related Series:*
    Series 55, General Manager — Letters Received. Series 57, Register of Letters Received. Series 58, Index to Letters Sent.

10) *Access Conditions:* Open

11) *Notes:* Originals fragile. Issue microfilm (Microfilm 34).

12) *Shelf List:*

Container No.	Brief Contents Note	Location
56/1	May 1901–Dec 1902	Shelf 1
56/2	Jan 1903–Dec 1904	Shelf 1
56/3	Jan 1905–Dec 1906	Shelf 1
56/4	Jan 1907–Dec 1908	Shelf 2
56/5	Jan 1909–Dec 1910	Shelf 2

(series continues on additional sheets —)

13) *Prepared by:* P. Foster

14) *Date completed:* 19 Nov 1968

objects) when photographs are removed from a collection. An example of a separation sheet is given in Box E. Photographs, like any segment of a collection, have strong ties to the records surrounding them, and often only their context reveals their true significance. It is therefore important that a user of a particular collection be aware that photographs form an integral part of it, and that they have been stored apart from the papers. A particular example of the links between records of different media may be a photograph enclosed with a letter or a diary accompanied by travel photographs.

Case Study Eight provides an example of a completed series description sheet for photographic records.

Box E   Separation Sheet

Provenance: Control Number:

Item(s) removed by: Date:

Description of material separated   Action taken

(Give original container number and type of material   (Give details of recipient, new storage
e.g. photograph, map, drawing, printed material,   locations as appropriate).
medal).

Case Study Eight   Series Description Sheet

1) *Provenance:*   2) *Series Number:*
   Jonathan Williams   28
3) *Series Title:*
   Williams Family Portraits
4) *Date Range:* c. 1846–1956   5) *Shelf Metres:*
                                                         0.34 m
6) *Physical Characteristics/Condition:*
   1 sixth plate daguerreotype; 2 halfplate ambrotypes; 3 100x60mm tintypes; 25 cartes–de–visite in one album; 10 cabinet portraits; 1 framed black and white photograph with hand colouring 700x500mm; 1 octavo album with twenty silver gelatin photographs. The daguerroetype is tarnished.
7) *Content Description* (Relationship to work of office/creator, types of information contained therein, representative/exceptional matters mentioned):
   Portrait photographs of members of the Williams family. The photographs were collected by Jonathan Williams in the course of his family research. They cover three generations of the Williams family. Most are identified and dated except for some of the cartes–de–visite. The daguerreotype of Edward Williams c. 1846 is by Freeman Bros. of Sydney, NSW and the ambrotypes c. 1855 are by T.S. Glaister also of Sydney. The twentieth century photographs were all taken by members of the family.
8) *Arrangement:*
   Chronological. (Order imposed by archives)
9) *Related Series:*
   Series 29 Williams Family Research Papers
   Series 30 Williams Family Correspondence.
10) *Access Conditions:*
    Available for research use. 28/1–28/3 and 28/15 may only be viewed under supervision. Copying permitted by donor, subject to Copyright Act.
11) *Notes:*
12) *Shelf List:*

Container No.	Brief Contents Note	Location
28/1	Edward Williams, daguerreotype, c.1846	Security Storage
28/2, 3	Josephine Williams, ambrotype, c. 1860; Maybelle Williams, ambrotype, c. 1860	Security Storage
28/4	Williams family album, cartes–de–visite, c. 1865–1878	Shelf 18
28/5–14	Williams family members, cabinet portraits c. 1880–1890: Edward Williams, Jnr. Josie Williams Belle Williams Jones Fred Williams Thomas Williams Mary Williams Brown Frank Jones Bill Brown Frank Jones Jnr. unattributed infant	Shelf 18
28/15	Moses Williams family album, 20 silver gelatin prints, c. 1950–1956	Shelf 18
28/16	Josiah Williams framed portrait, c. 1915	Framed Storage

13) Prepared by: M. Griffith   14)   Date completed: 20 July 1962

SHELVING THE RECORDS

Once the intellectual arrangement of the records has been determined, the records themselves will have to be put into the correct order. The material should be physically arranged into the various series which have been determined so that individual items can be numbered to reflect this arrangement. This is especially important when some may need to be separated for conservation or storage reasons. Just as the intellectual control of a collection has been refined in the description process, its physical control is refined at this stage of the arrangement process.

The next step is the final boxing of the material for placement on the shelves. Boxing should be done by series, making an effort not to put more than one series in a container unless too much space would be wasted. Conservation is a major consideration here, as the records will remain in storage for most of their lives. Oversize materials and audio visual media may require special boxes or storage locations which should be noted on the series description sheet under Item 12).

As all material may not be able to be stored together the numbering system is the link between the individual items and the intellectual arrangement of the material which has been determined on paper. The numbering system is only a device for locating items and, unlike library classifications, does not have any intrinsic significance. It should be as simple as possible. The essential element of a numbering system is that each container or free standing item, such as a volume, must have a unique number. In Chapter Four Accessioning a container numbering system was outlined which was based on the accession number. The tenth container of the first accession of 1985 would be written as 1985/1/10. 1985/1 is the accession number, and 10 identifies the container. This system is used only to control the material to the point of arrangement and description. Following the determination of series, another numbering system is used.

Each series is given a number, beginning at one and having no upper limit. All series in the archives, no matter what their format, whether documents, photographs or magnetic tape, are numbered from the same sequence. For this purpose, a Series Register which records what numbers have been assigned to which series must be maintained. See the example below.

Box F   Series Register

Series Number	Provenance	Series Title	Accession Numbers
41	Phillip Hall	Research Papers for *History of Blackwell*	1980/13
42	Blackwell Sports Club	Minute Books	1980/14. 1984/29
43	Blackwell Sports Club	Correspondence Files	1980/14. 1984/29
44	Mavis McIntyre	Group Portraits	1980/15
45	Stephen Jones	Taped Interviews with C. Smith	1980/17. 1980/22. 1986/11

Not all the parts of a single series may be received in the one accession. Therefore a single series may be formed from two, three or more separate accessions as illustrated by Series 45 in Box F. A Series Register may also record other details such as cumulative date range, quantity and location of the records, particularly if it can be easily updated.

Each container, or free standing item such as a volume, within a series is identified with a second number. In an archives where series 42 is 18 free–standing minute books, each volume would be identified as 42/1, 42/2 and so on to 42/18. These numbers would be pencilled into each volume in a standard place, for example the top left–hand corner of the last page of the volume. It may also be desirable to number individual items within containers. For example, if one box contained four diaries, and the box number was 32/15, the diaries might be numbered 32/15/1, 32/15/2, 32/15/3, 32/15/4.

Each box should be given numbers to identify its series and its shelf location.

Having prepared the boxes and listed their numbers and contents under Item 12) *Shelf List* on the appropriate series description sheets, it now remains to assign them a shelf location within the storage area. Most archives have a numerical system for designating spaces on shelves. For a discussion of these see Chapter Two Getting Organised — The Basics: Managing Facilities, Equipment and Stores. A quick check of the master space allocation sheet should reveal available spaces for new material in the storage area. Do not worry about keeping all of the boxes of one series together. Archives systems are designed to allow random shelving. All that is important for future access is having a unique container number and a unique 'address' in the storage area. When the material is placed on the shelf, the shelf number should be recorded on the outside of the container or unboxed item, as well as entered on the appropriate series description sheet under Entry 12) *Shelf List: Location.*

THE FINAL STEPS

Now all the series description sheets and administrative histories or biographical notes for the one collection can be placed together in a folder. At this point, attention is paid to the sequence of the individual series description sheets, as their order should reflect the structure of the collection. For example, in the case of records of an organisation the folder would present the overall administrative history, then move through the individual creating offices as through an organisational chart. The individual series description sheets would be placed under each creating office in a sequence that reflected their importance for that office's work. An alternative approach would be an alphabetical one, giving the names of creating offices with the series listed alphabetically by title underneath each office. An approach which combines organisational hierarchy for offices and alphabetical for series titles is also acceptable. Whichever scheme you choose, the goal you are trying to achieve is to present the descriptions of the organisation's functions and record series so that the researcher can understand the structure of the collection and the relationships among the parts, as well as locate particular records of interest. Box G demonstrates the three approaches described above.

A title page might be added to the folder indicating the name of the collection of records, followed by a table of contents. Altogether, the folder with its label, the title/contents page, the administrative history/biographical note and the individual series description sheets, comprise the *descriptive inventory* or *collection guide,* which are described in more detail in Chapter Six Finding Aids.

The final step is to re-check all the documentation in the folder to ensure that the notes and numbers are all correct before sending the annotated drafts for final typing. When the polished description is returned, it can be photocopied and placed in the reading room as a preliminary descriptive inventory of the collection which is now fully ready for research use.

CONCLUSION

It is fair to state that of all the variety of interesting work associated with keeping archives none is more important or stimulating

---

Box G   Possible Presentations of the Benlith Potteries P/L Records

Approach	Creating Offices	Series
Hierarchical	Board of Directors	Minutes
		Chairman's Correspondence
		Annual Reports
	Managing Director's Office	Managing Director's Correspondence
		Production Planning Filers
		Plant Management Files
	Company Secretary's Office	Share Registers
		Minutes of Annual Meetings of Shareholders
		Shareholders' Correspondence
Alphabetical	Board of Directors	Annual Reports
		Chairman's Correspondence
		Minutes
	Company Secretary's Office	Minutes of Annual Meetings of Shareholders
		Shareholders' Correspondence
		Share Registers
	Managing Director's Office	Managing Director's Correspondence
		Plant Management Files
		Production Planning Files
Hierarchical/ Alphabetical	Board of Directors	Annual Reports
		Chairman's Correspondence
		Minutes
	Managing Director's Office	Managing Director's Correspondence
		Plant Management Files
		Production Planning Files
	Company Secretary's Office	Minutes of Annual Meetings of Shareholders
		Shareholders' Correspondence
		Share Registers

than the actual arrangement and description of the records themselves. Without a thorough arrangement and description programme there is no point in maintaining an archives. All the other aspects of archives work are of little consequence if the core activities of arrangement and description are not done well. Time devoted to arrangement and description will never be wasted, as once they are accomplished, the records will be easily accessible for ever more. Archives work is, in many ways, devoted to the future. The archivist's work in the present will be of inestimable value in the future.

FURTHER READING

Bearman, David A. and Richard H. Lytle, 'The power of the principle of provenance,' *Archivaria* 21 (Winter, 1985–86): 14–27.

Berner, Richard C., 'Arrangement and description of manuscripts,' in Lytle, Richard H., editor, *Management of Archives and Manuscript Collections for Librarians*. Chicago, IL: Society of American Archivists, 1980.

Collings, T.J., *Archival Care of Still Photographs*. Information Leaflet No. 2. Sheffield, UK: Society of Archivists, 1984.

Davies, Alan and Peter Stanbury, *The Mechanical Eye in Australia: Photography 1841–1900*. Melbourne: Oxford University Press, 1985.

Gracy II, David B., *Archives and Manuscripts: Arrangement and Description*. Chicago, IL: Society of American Archivists, 1977.

Hensen, Steven L., *Archives, Personal Papers and Manuscripts: A Cataloguing Manual for Archival Repositories, Historical Societies and Manuscript Libraries*. Washington, DC: Library of Congress, 1983.

Hill, Edward E., 'The preparation of inventories at the National Archives,' in Daniels, Maygene and Timothy Walch, editors, *A Modern Archives Reader: Basic Readings on Archival Theory and Practice*. Washington, DC: National Archives and Records Service, 1984. pp. 211–235.

Holmes, Oliver W., 'Archives arrangement: five different operations at five different levels,' *American Archivist* 27 (1964): 264–273.

Hurley, Christopher, 'Personal papers and the treatment of archival principles,' *Archives and Manuscripts* 6/8 (February, 1977): 351–365.

Ritzenthaler, Mary Lynn, Gerald J. Munoff and Margery S. Long, *Archives and Manuscripts: Administration of Photographic Collections*. Chicago, IL: Society of American Archivists, 1984.

Slotkin, Helen W. and Karen T. Lynch, 'An analysis of processing procedures: the adaptable approach,' *American Archivist* 45/2 (Spring, 1982): 155–163.

CHAPTER SIX

FINDING AIDS

Kathleen Oakes and *Sigrid McCausland*

WHAT ARE FINDING AIDS?

Finding aids are the signposts which lead the archivist and the researcher to the information they are seeking about or from archives. They come in many different formats, have diverse purposes and a variety of names. The purpose of this chapter is to outline the main types of finding aids and their characteristics and to highlight the main issues involved in producing them. In the preceding chapters we have explained the purpose and nature of *accession registers* and *series description sheets*. These are examples of important finding aids, and in this chapter we will show how they relate to other finding aids and how the whole network of finding aids fits together.

To define them more formally, *finding aids* encompass a range of descriptive media (such as registers, guides, inventories and indexes) that establish physical and intellectual control over the holdings of an archives and make it possible to retrieve particular records or information from these archives. Physical control means knowing how much material the archives contains, where it is and that it is safely housed. Intellectual control is knowing the provenance, form and informational content of the records.

This definition, with a few modifications, could also apply to that familiar library finding aid — the catalogue. It too establishes physical and intellectual control of the holdings through its points of access (by subject, author and title) and makes it possible to retrieve particular items or information from the holdings. However, whereas a library deals with single, discrete items, complete with distinctive title and author, the archivist deals with collections i.e. groupings of related items not necessarily created by the one person or organisation. The format of material in these archival collections can vary greatly and include correspon-

dence, diaries, photographs, maps, computer tapes, plans and
drawings. Furthermore, the size of a collection can range from
one item to thousands of metres of documents.

Trying to retrieve a particular book in a library without a catalogue would be impossible. Similarly items within an archives
cannot be retrieved without finding aids. A library catalogue,
complete with instructions on its use, is placed in the most central location in a library to allow users to locate material for themselves. So too, the finding aids for an archives are available for the
researchers themselves to use.

The consistency of library holdings everywhere means
libraries can adopt ready–made control systems such as Dewey
or Library of Congress. Archival material, however, is unique and
its formal arrangement and content varies from archives to
archives. Control of archival collections is imposed by first
studying the holdings and the history of the person or organisation which created them. Then, keeping in mind the principle of
provenance, a system of control is designed for the collection.
Finding aids therefore reflect the variety and complexity of the
holdings they control.

In–house archives are used by the creators as a basis for current administrative decision–making on anything from policy to
marketing. Those same records are used by researchers for quite
different purposes (biography, local history, architectural history
etc.). All of these uses may be for purposes for which the records
were not originally created. The demands for information which
are made on an archives are varied and the finding aids created
to meet these demands will reflect this variety.

Finding aids are produced by creators and archivists alike to
provide access to and information about the records. Their
coverage may range from a general overview of the archives'
entire holdings to descriptions of individual collections and to
specific material of interest within items.

Table One covers all contingencies. It is unlikely that any
archives will have all of these types of finding aids. Professional,
institutional and client requirements all influence the compilation of finding aids. How to decide what finding aids to prepare
is discussed later in this chapter.

Those finding aids marked 'essential' must be done. Those
marked 'desirable' are derived from essential finding aids and can
therefore only be done if the essential finding aids are already
prepared. Those finding aids marked 'if resources permit' are
compiled from the holdings themselves and/or finding aids
already prepared. It is these latter that need the most careful and
conscious planning. The considerations required for their planning are discussed later in the chapter.

Table One   The Network of Archival Finding Aids

Finding Aids Prepared by the Creating Institution or Person

Essential

- Registers
- Indexes
- Filing system descriptions
- Thesauri

Finding Aids Prepared by Archivists

Essential

- Accession Registers
- Descriptive Inventories
- Bridging Aids

Desirable

- Guides to Holdings
- Reports of Holdings
- Indexes to Descriptive Inventories

If Resources Permit

- Content Indexes

Compiled Sources

If Resources Permit

- Special Lists
- Subject Files
- Sources Analyses
- Reference Guides and Media Guides

FINDING AIDS PREPARED BY CREATING INSTITUTION

Finding aids are usually produced by the archivist, although there is an exception. An institution or business or person may compile indexes and registers, for example, to assist in the control and retrieval of their own records, such as correspondence, diaries or photographs.

When the records are transferred to the archives they are accompanied by their own 'finding aids', i.e. those indexes, registers and other material that enable the creators of the records to control and retrieve them more easily.

The finding aids produced by organisations with formal record–keeping systems are usually of the following types: registers, indexes, filing system descriptions and thesauri. These are sometimes referred to generally as *control records*.

These finding aids are considered essential and it is important for the archivist to ensure that they (or copies) are transferred with the material they control. They not only provide access to such material but also show how the creator used the records.

They may not be as perfect as the archivist would like but they do save valuable time for the archivist in retrieving items and information. Further finding aids may be required, but with these basic aids already in existence further work can be given a lower priority and the archivist can proceed to work on material which as yet has no finding aids. Even if the related material no longer exists, the registers, indexes, filing classifications, and other contemporaneous finding aids can still be useful as they summarise the information contained in that material.

It is unusual to receive finding aids of this kind with collections of personal and family papers. This is because most people have fairly simple systems for controlling their own private papers, for example, loosely–based alphabetical arrangement, and do not bother to record evidence of their systems. Occasionally, an individual or family might have produced and retained their own finding aids. Again, any such indexes and registers will help the archivist to understand the context in which the papers were created.

The creator's own finding aids, such as index cards, are essential for access to the records they control.

Registers are used to record information about each document or file that is received by, dispatched, or created in an office. If a register is being used to keep track of correspondence it records the date, author, a summary of contents and a file reference i.e. the file it will be placed on (if correspondence is coming into the office) or the file on which a copy of the letter can be found (if correspondence is going out of the office). Information in the register is arranged chronologically. If the register is being used to keep track of files created in an office it will record the date, file number and title. Information is arranged chronologically and numerically.

Indexes also control documents and files but do so by creating another point of access to the system. The file titles and contents of the documents are arranged alphabetically by name or topic.

Filing system descriptions, including filing classification lists and key codes, give outlines of filing systems, explaining the alphabetical, numerical or other codes and symbols used. These finding aids help you to understand how a filing system operated when it was in current use in a business or government office.

Thesauri list the authorised terms used to classify file titles in keyword filing systems.

FINDING AIDS PREPARED BY ARCHIVISTS FOR RECORDS RECEIVED BY THE ARCHIVES

The creation of finding aids flows naturally from other archival functions such as arrangement and description and reference. This work is very important to the efficient management of archives and should be approached in an organised manner. The different finding aids should always be considered as belonging to a system. The individual parts of the system may have different functions and different appearances, but they relate to each other and each one must work properly if the overall goals of control and retrieval are to be met.

The majority of finding aids are produced by archivists. They range from the '*essential*' to those where resource–intensiveness recommends against their production. The most important and essential of these finding aids are:

- Accession Registers
- Descriptive Inventories (also called Collection Guides)
- Bridging Aids

The finding aids considered desirable are:

- Guides to Holdings (also called Concise Guides)
- Reports of Holdings
- Indexes to Descriptive Inventories and Concise Guides

The finding aids which can be compiled only if resources permit are:

- Indexes to Item Contents

Accession Registers

Basic control over the archives is established when the material first enters the archives in the accessioning process. This provides a general description of what it is and where it comes from and proper housing (boxing and labelling) of the material. Each accession is given an identifying number which, along with a description of the material, name of the donor or transferring source, the provenance and other relevant details, is entered in the accession register. This first and most basic finding aid prepared by the archivist gives the essential details of each body of records received into the archives and also provides a profile of all incoming material in the order in which it was received by the repository. Duplicate copies of the register can be arranged by the names of the donors and by the name of the creating organisation or person to provide additional ways (i.e. indexes) to find the information. Separate indexes to donors, agencies and location may also be set up. These finding aids are further described in the chapter on Accessioning.

Descriptive Inventories (also known as Collection Guides)

These finding aids, which are made up of several different types of finding aid, give information about the context in which a particular group of records was created and about the nature and extent of the records in the collection. Their preparation requires a more detailed inspection of the records themselves and research into the administrative history of the creator (for records of organisations) or the biographical details about the creator (for personal papers). Descriptive inventories usually consist of the following elements — introduction; table of con-

tents; administrative history or biographical note (as appropriate); series descriptions; lists of items; indexes to physical
location or shelf lists; and indexes to the main names, functions
and topics mentioned in the inventory. Box A lists them in more
detail.

When the archivist prepares a descriptive inventory for a collection, he/she is attempting to reconstruct the original context
of the records, that is, to present the material as it was when in
use by its creator(s). This is an important point to remember as
the archivist's main duty is to preserve the material intact for
others to use and interpret. An analogy can be drawn with a court-
room where material is presented as evidence of a person's or
organisation's actions. Archival material is also evidence of the
actions of a person or organisation and it is of greatest value
when it most truly reveals those actions. If the archivist can present the material in the manner in which it was originally created
and maintained and can guarantee that this is so then the validity
of the material as evidence is enhanced.

The registers and descriptive inventories which have been produced as a result of the processes of accessioning and arrangement and description are the most essential of finding aids
prepared by the archivist as they establish primary physical and
intellectual control of the archives.

Once these basic finding aids have been compiled, access to
the archives by researchers can be allowed. Archives must be
properly controlled before being made available to researchers,
otherwise there is a risk that items will be lost or damaged and
the internal arrangement of the collection confused.

Bridging Aids

Finding aids in this category are so called because they bridge the
gap between the researcher's need for information about a person, organisation or event within a span of time and the archives'
system of finding aids based upon provenance. Finding useful
records in an archives requires a number of steps. For example,
a researcher seeking information about coal exploration in the
early twentieth century will first need to know the names of the
government bodies, companies and individuals involved in that
work. The researcher can then use the archives' finding aids to
locate descriptive inventories of records from those entities. The
inventory descriptions will lead him/her to the record series
which best document the creator's coal exploration activities.
Finally, the researcher can select from these series those records
which cover the early twentieth century and get to work. These
steps, from the general area to the specific documents, are easily
followed provided the researcher knows the names of agencies
or persons involved in coal exploration. However, if the
researcher does *not* know the names, the research process is
stymied, as there is no point of entry into the provenance or
creator–based system of finding aids.

Box A   Components of a Descriptive Inventory

1) **Title Page:** This page sets out the title of the finding aid which should incorporate the proper name and citation of the collection or group of archives; name of individual or office responsible for producing the finding aid; name of the archival repository and date of completion of the aid.

2) **Table of Contents:** This page lists the main divisions and significant sub–divisions of the inventory.

3) **Preparer's Notes (Preface and Acknowledgements):** This section comprises a brief explanation of major decisions made in arranging and describing the material and/or in producing the finding aid. It includes how the aid is designed and the best way to use it, lists of symbols or abbreviations, the proper form for citations, and closes with acknowledgements, if any.

4) **Introduction:** This section introduces the records themselves, explains why they are important (in their own time and in retrospect) and describes how they came to the archives.

5) **Administrative History:** The administrative history gives brief (1500 words or less) highlights of the individual's career and life or the organisation's foundation, development and major programmes. It can be illustrated with helpful items such as organisation charts, timelines giving an overview of major events, changes.

6) **Descriptions of the Categories of Material and Their Record Series:** The aim of this section is to present the record segments as parts of a whole and to describe them succinctly, not exhaustively. The categories of records usually reflect provenance, i.e. the hierarchy of an organisation, the key divisions in an individual's work or life, or the functions the records supported (accounting, policy, teaching). Arrangement of categories usually follows a hierarchy of importance or date.
   Each category will have three sub-parts:
   a) An *introductory paragraph* which explains the nature of and the basis for the grouping and gives additional (not duplicated) information about the particular activities of the office or individual(s) that created the record series which follow.
   b) *Descriptions of each record series* within that category, in order of significance, comprise the official title of the series; its inclusive dates; its quantity; its arrangement; the types of records within the series and the kinds of information they record. The description should also note any gaps, concentrations, or significant matters of business. They should not attempt to give a list of subjects discussed in the individual documents.
   c) *Conditions of use:* Note any access restrictions or problems affecting use.

7) **Comprehensive Shelf List of the Records:** This section may be in two parts. The main part lists the records in container/box number order, giving sufficient information about the contents of each one so that the user can select material accurately. Contents descriptions here are a much abbreviated version of those in 6, usually featuring the series title and the dates/number/alphabetical name of the first and last documents within the box. The secondary part lists each series title alphabetically and gives the numbers of the boxes holding it.

8) **Appendices:** This section presents glossaries of special terms and helpful lists which were compiled as a by–product of arrangement and description. Names of office bearers and dates of service and an alphabetical list of series titles keyed to work activity or function are examples. Be selective.

9) **Bibliography:** This section should include full citations of works (published and unpublished) which the preparer used in preparing the inventory and which he/she feels will give the user important insights. Again, be selective, rather than encyclopaedic.

10) **Index:** This is optional and should be keyed to the pages of the descriptive inventory, not to boxes or folders of records. Items to be indexed may include: series titles, major personal/organisational names, functions/activities of work or life (education, employment, policy, administration), major types of records (diaries, letters, minutes). Do not attempt to index the subject matter of individual documents.

This frustration, however, need not happen. If the archives has prepared a bridging aid covering all of its holdings, the researcher will be directed to the relevant creators. One type of aid, the function list, presents basic categories of political, social, and economic activities or functions in alphabetical order, linking them to the agencies or persons involved in or responsible for them. Since many researchers limit their research to a particular timeframe, another helpful bridging aid is a list organised by date segments, identifying the names of creating bodies or individuals active within them.

The provision of such bridging aids should be the next task the archivist undertakes after he/she completes individual descriptive inventories to the records of each creator. These aids can later become the basis for an index to the next level of finding aids, the guide to holdings. Table Two explains the two types of basic bridging aids in more detail.

Table Two   Basic Bridging Aids for Archives

Type of Bridging Aid	Purpose	Form and Content
Functional	To link basic social, political and economic functions with those involved in or responsible for them. This gives an overview of the archives holdings which relate to particular aspects.	Alphabetical list of functions with names of appropriate creators arranged alphabetically under each entry. It is helpful to include after each name their inclusive dates of operations. A variation of this aid for an in–house archives would list the functions or types of business conducted by the host organisation with the names of the sub–units responsible under each.
Chronological	To tie names of creating bodies or individuals to the dates of their operation. This gives an overview of the holdings in the archives which related to a particular period of time.	Timeline of five or ten year segments listing alphabetically the names of creators active within each segment.

Note: An example of an entry reflecting the functional approach is taken from the index to the *Guide to the State Archives of New South Wales: Supplement Volume 5, Number 4.* Sydney: Archives Office of New South Wales, October, 1975. The abbreviation CG symbolises 'Concise Guide.' It clearly shows the close relationship between bridging aids and future indexes.

Finding aids should be placed together in a prominent location.

Railways

Colonial Secretary CG pp.77–78, 88(66), 121, 123, 125,127–128, 141–142

Crown Solicitor S5 p.116(12)

Executive Council S5 p.131(9)

Government Printing Office S5 p.138(53a)

Lands S5 pp.155(1), 156(2), 165(71), 185(165)

Metropolitan Water Sewerage and Drainage Board S5 p.241(4)

Premier CG pp.304–305; S5 pp.294(18), 295

Public Service Board CG pp.348–351

Public Transport Commission. Railways Division S5 pp.303–304

Public Works CG pp.356(17)(18), 357(21)(22), 365, 366; S5 pp.307–308

Railways CG p.368

State Planning Authority CG pp.378(2)(3), 379(4)(5)(11), 380(12)(13)(14)(15)

Supreme Court S5 p.380(779)

Surveyor General CG pp.410(20), 424(169)

Treasury CG pp.429(16)(17)(18), 430(29), 435(130)(131)(132) (140), 442, 443, 444

Guides to Holdings (also known as Concise Guides and Summary Guides)

Descriptive Inventories provide detailed descriptions of individual collections; but for quick ready reference to the complex holdings of the archives, it is usual to produce a 'Guide to Holdings'. This consists of an abstract or precis of the information presented in the descriptive inventory and gives an overview of each collection. For example, the *Concise Guide to the State Archives of New South Wales* includes a brief administrative history for each public office, followed by lists of the series created by that office, with brief series descriptions of the more important series, then dates and shelf locations for each series. Some item listings are also included. A comprehensive index to the names of creators, key functions, events and topics of known research interest listed in the guide entries should also be attempted.

Not all users arrive knowing exactly what collection they wish to see or, indeed, if any collection will be of relevance to them. If a guide to holdings is available, they can quickly ascertain those collections of value to their research and then refer to the descriptive inventories for more detailed descriptions of these collections. If the researcher contacts the archives by mail or telephone the archivist can use the guide to the holdings to inform the researcher of any relevant material in the collection which they should follow up during their visit to the archives. This guide is usually typed and placed in folders. If funds are available then it can be published and distributed more widely.

Reports of Holdings

These reports gather information from different repositories about their holdings. They can be assembled at an international, national, state or regional level. Their purpose is to publicise summary information about different archives and their holdings for use by both the archival and research communities. Reports of holdings usually consist of brief entries for individual collections, as in the *Guide to Collections of Manuscripts Relating to Australia* (produced on microfiche by the National Library of Australia) or give basic information about each archives and its services, as in *Our Heritage*, the directory to archival repositories in Australia published by the Australian Society of Archivists, Incorporated.

An important feature of this type of finding aid is that the information is presented in a standardised way, that is, the entry for each collection or institution (depending on the type of report) will give data in a set order on a number of specified areas. For a collection, these areas would usually include control number, name of creator, general title of the collection, date range, quantity, location, brief description of contents, access conditions and additional notes. This information is extracted from other finding aids already produced by each archives.

In Australia, so far, these reports have been produced using manual systems, but in future they may be produced using automated systems. In the United States, a special MARC (MAchine Readable Cataloguing) format, the Archival and Manuscript Control (AMC) format, has been developed by the Library of Congress for the automated control of information about archival material. This very flexible format can be used to record and manipulate information required for the various different types of finding aids. It is being used for the United States national system for reports of holdings, the National Union Catalog of Manuscript Collections (NUCMC).

Many U.S. archives are recording information about their collections on series description sheets using the MARC AMC descriptors so that they will have an easy time later when they report their holdings nationally. Since the libraries of many countries already use an adaptation of MARC, such as AUS MARC in Australia, to report their library materials, it may only be a matter of time before an Australian version of the AMC format is used here. A copy of the current MARC AMC data entry sheet is included as Appendix Two.

Indexes

Indexes can be very helpful to researchers using archives, but they can also be very time-consuming for the archivist to produce. The aim of this section of the chapter is to show how indexes can supplement the essential finding aids, and then to describe the types of index most appropriate for archives.

The microfiche edition of the Guide to Collections of Manuscripts Relating to Australia *occupies a fraction of the space of the original.* Courtesy — State Library of NSW.

Appendix One: Constructing an Index, covers the basic decisions and procedures involved in designing an index.

In many cases the finding aids which have been discussed so far (accession registers, descriptive inventories and guides to holdings) will be satisfactory for the retrieval of archives in answer to certain inquiries. Using the examples of series descriptions in Chapter Five Arrangement and Description, a researcher could ask the following questions:

1) I am writing my family history. Do you have any photographs of the family of Jonathan Williams my great–uncle which I might include?

2) I am researching the history of aborigines in the Blackwell area. A history was written by Phillip Hall which mentions aborigines. Do you have any further material?

Items relevant to these inquires may be easily located because material relating to Phillip Hall and Jonathan Williams had been transferred to the archives. As the material consisted of their own personal papers it had been arranged and described (according to its provenance) in the descriptive inventories under their own names even though it might not have been transferred by them personally. A check of the series lists under their names would reveal the appropriate series and a check of the shelflist (or item list) for that series would show the relevant item:

e.g. 1) Jonathan Williams, 'Williams Family Portraits', 1846–1956.

e.g. 2) Phillip Hall, 'Research Papers for "History of
         Blackwell" ', 1959–1963, 1970–1975, item 13/40 —
         Aborigines.

However, reference inquiries are not always that straightforward, and sometimes require information about the contents
of the records which finding aids based on provenance do not
easily provide, for example:

1) Do you have any information on aborigines in NSW in the
    1930s?

2) I am writing a history of photography in Australia. Do you
    have any examples of the early work of Freeman Bros?

Applying the principle of provenance, the archivist describes
the material under the name of the creator of the records. Therefore you would not find material listed under 'aborigines'. You
could possibly find 'Freeman Bros.', but for the sake of this
example we are assuming that they or their descendants have
never transferred any material to the archives. However, if there
was a subject index to the descriptive inventory of the Phillip Hall
collection, then the archivist could locate an item on aborigines,
and if there was a name index to the descriptive inventory of the
Jonathan Williams collection, then the archivist could locate a
relevant item on the Freeman Bros.

Indexes to descriptive inventories, guides to holdings and
reports of holdings are the preferred types of index for the archivist to prepare. This is because indexing finding aids is much less
resource–intensive than indexing the content of the archival
material itself. For example, it will be much easier to index the
guide to a collection, than to index the forty shelf metres of
records in that collection.

Indexes to descriptive inventories and guides refer to the precise place in the inventory or guide (usually a page reference)
where relevant entries can be found. The references are taken
from the creators of the records, the titles of collections, series
and items, the series descriptions, the administrative histories
and biographies.

Although the researcher may be looking for a particular item,
if they are referred to the page of a descriptive inventory rather
than directly to the item required, they will be able to find the item
within its context in the series or collection, which may enhance
interpretation of this item or lead to further relevant items.

Sometimes an archivist will decide that it is necessary to index
the content of a particular collection or series. This could be, for
example, when other finding aids do not provide sufficient
access to the information contained in a highly–used series. As
indexing the content of records has a low priority for the archivist, and because it can take a long time, it is the sort of project
which is suitable for volunteers to undertake. Advice on handling
volunteers is to be found in Chapter Eleven: User Education and
Public Relations.

Indexing Photographs

Photographs present particular problems for access and retrieval for research purposes. Often their original titles (if there are any) will not be relevant to the researcher's inquiry. Some suggestions for types of indexes to photographs are given below.

The simplest indexes to produce for photographic records are those which index existing finding aids, such as series description sheets and item lists. Names of people and places, as well as subjects can be indexed from these finding aids. These indexes usually rely on the terms used by the creators themselves and may therefore not use standard terms for subjects. However, they can be useful in reducing searching time and unnecessary handling of original records.

An alternative is to index only those parts of the photographic collection which are most in demand. The archivist would then only provide lists or indexes of photographs on a specific topic or format for which there is a demonstrated need.
For example:

- photographs showing details of dress of a certain period;
- photographs of aborigines;
- photographs taken by Max Dupain;
- glass negatives.

Another alternative is to photocopy the photographic images themselves and to place the copies on standard–sized cards filed by name and subject headings. These finding aids are sometimes called *self–indexing files*. It is important to control the index terms used. As multiple copies of the photograph will be required if the image is to be indexed under more than one term it may be more economical to use 'see' references to direct the user back to the main entry card with the photograph affixed. It is also important to note the identification and location of the original photograph otherwise the index will have limited usefulness for retrieval purposes. Only dry process photocopiers should be used when photocopying photographs. Some photocopiers can copy photographs quite accurately, although if a dot screen (available from photocopier suppliers) is used, the copied image is improved.

COMPILED SOURCES

Archivists will need to accumulate information on subjects which are vital to a knowledge of the institution or locality which the archives services, and for using the collection. These finding aids are usually designed to answer research topics that are popular or inquiries that involve retrieving obscure information which the archivist does not want to lose. They are also used to answer inquiries which do not require documents, just information, such as: What was the first bank in town? They may also

lead researchers to other relevant non–archival material in the collection (such as publications) or relevant material in other archival institutions.

Although these finding aids do not have the priority of accession registers and descriptive inventories, it is almost inevitable that they will be compiled. Time should be taken to assess their usefulness and to control their growth in a planned and orderly manner.

Compiled sources and information lists usually occur in the following forms:

A contact print on the main entry card allows researchers to browse the photo collection.

Moder
Photography
?

Special Lists

These lists contain information about an organisation, locality or individual that provides quickly retrievable summaries of important facts. Such lists are often prepared as an aid to writing administrative history and can be appendices to relevant descriptive inventories. Some examples include:
- Lists of chief executive officers (managing directors, mayors, school principals), committees, public buildings or churches and their relevant dates (of appointment, of office, of occupation).
- Chronological lists. It may be preferable to arrange the previous lists chronologically or to prepare a timetable of key

events. Care must be taken not to include too many items on a chronological list, and to restrict its subject area or compile several different lists on different subjects. If the topic area of the list is too broad and it contains too many items, more time will be spent searching the list for the relevant event than is worthwhile.

Subject Files

Often, quite a lot of information is accumulated on a topic in the course of answering reference inquiries and 'subject files' can be created under the name of the persons or organisations or events or other subjects and arranged alphabetically. These files usually reflect topics that are very popular, very obscure or very difficult to research. They may also contain material donated by researchers or other interested people, which would not belong in the archives itself (such as copies of journal articles or newsclippings). The main problem is ensuring the quality of the material included. It may be necessary to check all material for accuracy or to indicate if the information cannot be vouchsafed by the archivist. If it includes material from other archives the archivist must ensure that there are no special access conditions attached to its use. These sorts of information systems can grow rapidly out of control unless they are carefully monitored. It may be necessary to periodically review and weed files.

Source Analyses or Special Bibliographies

Archivists often prepare lists of archival material held in their collections which relate to particular topics such as convicts, World War I or transport. These lists can include other sources such as published documents, newspapers and authoritative or obscure histories held by the archives' own library. They are compiled as a service for researchers who have contacted the archives requesting information on the holdings of the archives on a particular topic. They not only provide a guide to researchers about relevant holdings, but if copies are kept, can provide a quick reference for future research inquiries. It is surprising how often the same or similar inquiries are made in an archives. If resources are not available for preparing such formal lists a similar finding aid can be prepared by ensuring that a note is kept of everything a researcher uses for his/her topic (usually on the form prepared when the researcher first visits the archives) and then indexing the forms.

The source analyses are usually only lists of series. If the archivist has the time or if an item is particularly relevant to the research topic then the archivist may also list items.

Reference (or Subject) Guides and Media Guides

These finding aids list records relating to a particular subject or records in a particular medium. They differ from essential finding aids such as descriptive inventories because their main purpose is not the control of the archives' holdings. Rather, they respond to a perceived need from researchers, and direct them to selected series and items of interest. The entries for reference guides are usually extracted from other finding aids, such as series descriptions. These guides bring together material from different creating organisations and persons which deal with the same subject, for example, aviation, a local historic building or World War II. Similarly, media guides list material from different collections within a repository which are in the same medium, such as film, gramophone recordings or oral history tapes. Both these types of finding aid are often produced as part of a publications programme for which the archives must plan and budget accordingly.

The Network of Finding Aids

Whatever the extent of your finding aid system, it is important that all of the components fit together and build on one another. Understanding the types and interrelationships among the finding aids is a first step to developing an effective network. Table Three summarises the various types of aids and identifies their purposes and characteristics.

Table Three   Summary of the Network of Finding Aids

Finding Aids prepared by creating institution or person at the time records were in current use
Essential
- *Registers*
  Purpose: to control and record the receipt, dispatch or creation of an item or document i.e. to provide a record of administrative action.
  Characteristics: information can include identifying code, date, summary of contents, decision, title and name of action officer; arranged by date of receipt, dispatch or creation of item or document, or by number of item, in order created.
- *Indexes*
  Purpose: as above but provides an alternative point of access to the information recorded.
  Characteristics: entries include the same information as above but arranged alphabetically by name or topic.
- *Filing system descriptions*
  Purpose: to record the system which controls the filing order in record keeping systems such as classified number systems.
  Characteristics: code sheets list the alphabetical, numerical or other symbols, codes and abbreviations used in filing systems and explain their meaning (e.g. 34 = cattle; 65 = sheep; 78 = wheat).
- *Thesauri*
  Purpose: to control the terms used in creating file titles in keyword systems.
  Characteristics: alphabetical list of the permitted terms in a keyword classification system.

Finding Aids prepared by archivists for records received by the archives
Essential
- *Accession Registers*
  Purpose: to provide basic control of material and a record of receipt.
  Characteristics: basic descriptions of material received by the archives; entries are recorded by date of receipt.

- *Descriptive Inventories (also called Collection Guides)*
  Purpose: to provide detailed descriptions of each collection.
  Characteristics: inventories include administrative histories or biographies, series descriptions and item lists.
- *Bridging Aids*
  Purpose: to provide a point of entry for the researcher into the archives' system of finding aids based on provenance.
  Characteristics: alphabetical lists of functions keyed to names of relevant operators or date spans with alphabetical lists of creators names within each.

Desirable

- *Guides to Holdings (also called Concise Guides)*
  Purpose: to provide a general overview of the contents of the holdings for quick and easy reference.
  Characteristics: entries are usually a precis or abstract of the descriptive inventory.
- *Reports of Holdings*
  Purpose: to publicise and provide information about the holdings to researchers and the archival community, nationally or internationally.
  Characteristics: entries can be either a brief description of the total holdings (i.e. a precis of the concise guide) or a brief description of a particular collection (i.e. a precis of a descriptive inventory).
- *Indexes to Descriptive Inventories and Guides to Holdings*
  Purpose: to provide an alternative point of access to information in the descriptive inventories and guides to holdings.
  Characteristics: entries indicate the precise place in the inventories and guides where information can be found on names, functions, topics or events.

If Resources Permit

- *Content Indexes*
  Purpose: to provide direct access to actual documents within the collection.
  Characteristics: a brief record of information in particular items or documents such as photographs, publications, minutes, diaries and correspondence.

Compiled Sources

If Resources Permit

- *Special Lists*
  Purpose: to provide summaries of relevant facts.
  Characteristics: lists of officials, office–bearers, time lines — often prepared as an aid to writing administrative history and can be appendices to relevant descriptive inventories.
- *Subject Files*
  Purpose: to bring together information from or about the holdings, information about locality or institution.served by the archives.
  Characteristics: a variety of materials arranged alphabetically by names of people or organisation, topics or events; they usually reflect topics that are very popular, very obscure or very difficult to research.
- *Source Analyses*
  Purpose: to inform users of material held by the archives on a particular topic.
  Characteristics: a listing of record series and sometimes items; may also include non–archival material such as publications.
- *Reference Guides and Media Guides*
  Purpose: as above but often more substantial and often produced for publication.
  Characteristics: information is arranged by subject in reference guides, and by physical record type in media guides.

PLANNING FINDING AIDS

This aspect of the management of archives is very important, for without proper planning, an archives could produce finding aids inappropriate to its holdings and its users, thus wasting precious resources. Of course, planning finding aids is not done in isolation from planning for other archival functions. The archives' overall priorities must be taken into account when goals for the finding aids programme are set. Resources for the production of 'essential' finding aids should be allocated before those for projects involving the production of finding aids ranked as 'desirable' or 'if resources permit'.

When planning finding aids you will have to consider what they will look like as well as which ones to produce. If you have a manual system, this means choosing the materials — e.g. binders, folders, cards and microfiche — as well as designing the forms for the different finding aids. If you have an automated system, forms design will still be part of the planning process. You will also have to decide whether you will produce paper copies (and how many) of your finding aids on a regular basis or only in response to requests.

An important document in the development of any system of finding aids is the procedure manual. This sets out the rules, standards and the 'house style' for finding aids produced in your archives. It is one of the sources of technical information referred to in the section on *Organising Your Information Resources* in Chapter Two: Getting Organised — The Basics. The procedure manual does not have to be long or complex, but it should contain instructions for the completion of documentation such as accession records and series description sheets, along with model completed examples. The manual must always be updated whenever there are any changes in forms or practices. It has two main benefits — it is an essential tool in training new staff and it helps to ensure consistency and standardisation in finding aids produced by different people at different times.

Apart from these general planning considerations, there are several key questions which must be asked when the archivist is planning finding aids. They are:

- **Who Are The Users?**

  Firstly the archivists themselves use the archives for internal research needs. If the archives is part of a government or private commercial institution, the administrators will use records from the archives for anything from policy decisions to advertising. However, if the archives or institution is a public one, it is likely that members of the public will take up a large part of the time spent on reference work. Once upon a time only academic historians made extensive use of archives, but now one of the largest groups of researchers is the genealogist or family historian. Researchers also include social and local

Finding aids and appropriate reference works should be easily accessible to researchers. Courtesy — Archives of Business and Labour, ANU.

historians, biographers, journalists, architects, geographers, scientists and students (from primary, secondary and tertiary institutions). No doubt each archives will have different users according to the type of collections they hold and the place they hold in the institution or community. It is important therefore, to reflect the educational level, research experience and interest of the major user groups in designing the finding aids to assist them.

- **What Do They Need?**

Most inquiries refer to the name of a person or organisation, to a particular date, to a geographical area, to a particular format (photograph, map, plan, diary), to a building, to an event, or to a combination of these. However, since researchers cannot always specify what they want, there will be a 'dialogue' between the researcher and the finding aids, perhaps with the help of the archivist, as the researcher searches, refines the question or topic and continues searching. As the finding aid must be responsive to the researcher's needs, the vocabulary of the researcher and a facility for browsing become important aspects of the design of a finding aid.

- **What Can The Resources Of The Archives Reasonably Provide?**

Finally the archivist must consider the resources of the archives: the nature of the material, the numbers and the skills of the staff, the time available, the cost of production and how compatible the finding aids to be produced will be with other finding aids already available. If you inherit a system of finding aids which needs overhauling, or if you are considering automating your finding aids, you will need to think about the implications of major changes. For example, you will have to decide whether to bring in the new system gradually or all at once and whether you wish to convert existing finding aids to the new system at a later date. These decisions, too, must be made in the context of the archives' resources.

Finding aid systems are much easier to update and expand with the help of a computer.

CONCLUSION

Once a system of finding aids has been set up and is being used, it should be reviewed periodically to ensure that it is achieving the goals of control and retrieval. It is possible that problems which arise in the provision of reference services, such as difficulties in locating material in the repository, or researchers relying on staff to answer simple questions instead of using the finding aids, might result from deficiencies in the finding aids. They might equally result from poor staff training or inadequate user education. So, finding aids should be reviewed when monitoring and evaluating the effectiveness of all the other functions carried out by the archives.

Very rarely does an archives achieve the perfect state for finding aids — complete coverage of its holdings presented in the most attractive and user–friendly format available. For most archives, the production of finding aids is ultimately a compromise between the needs of the users (both archives staff and researchers) and the resources of the archives. Understanding that finding aids should be approached in systems terms, knowing the purposes and uses of the different types of finding aids and their priorities, and planning and reviewing carefully the whole finding aids programme should make that compromise less difficult. A system of finding aids which is flexible and easy to use is an achievable goal. It will help to ensure that the intellectual and physical control of the holdings grows in line with the resources of the archives and the demands of its users.

FURTHER READING

Berner, Richard, and Uli Haller, 'Principles of archival inventory construction', *American Archivist* 47/2 (Spring, 1984) pp. 134–155.

Cook, Michael, *The Management of Information from Archives*. Aldershot, Hampshire, U.K.: Gower, 1986.

Flint, John and Anne Berry. *Local Studies Collections:Guidelines and Subject Headings for Organising and Indexing Resources*. Second Edition. Sydney: Library Association of Australia (NSW Branch), 1985.

Pugh, Mary Jo, 'The illusion of omniscience: subject access and the reference archivist', *American Archivist* 45/1 (Winter, 1982) pp. 33–44.

Salton, Gerald, *Introduction to Modern Information Retrieval*. New York: McGraw-Hill, 1983.

Scott, Peter J., 'Archives finding aids — towards an Australian consensus', *Australian Society of Archivists 1979 Conference Papers*. Supplementary volume. Canberra: ASA, 1979. pp. 20–32.

Townley, Helen M. and Ralph D. Gee, *Thesaurus-making: grow your own word-stock*. London: Andre Deutsch, 1980.

APPENDIX ONE: CONSTRUCTING AN INDEX
Averil Condren

Initial Considerations
The decision to provide an index, whether to inventories or to original material, should not be made lightly for indexing is both difficult and expensive. The initial question is whether or not the expenditure of often limited resources will be justified by the result. For while it is true that a good index is a valuable tool, it is also true that a poorly executed or conceptually muddled index is worse than useless. Any index, however well executed initially, will need updating, extension and revision. Therefore unless this ongoing commitment of time and money and especially space — the index will grow — can be made with confidence, it is

almost certainly better not to undertake the index in the first
place. An index which is not maintained is a waste of the original
investment. The decision to index anything should thus be made
in the context of the best use of the available resources now and
in the future.

The second consideration is which type of index should be
provided. This is largely contingent upon how large an investment of resources is possible. Some indexes are more expensive
than others. The cost and the nature of the materials held will dictate what kinds of indexes would be appropriate. A large holding
of correspondence for example would benefit from a name
index, while a large series of minutes or committee papers would
be better served by subject and date access.

As mentioned earlier in this chapter, some records come into
the archives with the indexes which were used to retrieve information at the time the records were in active use by the creator.
These records should not require further indexing, as it is simply
a waste of resources to index materials for which adequate
access has already been provided by the creator.

Automated Indexing

Probably the simplest and cheapest index to produce would be
an alphabetical ordering of the significant elements in the titles
of items, files or series. A mainframe computer can easily produce an automated index, either in KWIC (Keyword in context)
or KWOC (Keyword out of context) format. The advantages of
these automated indexes are that they are fast, relatively inexpensive and provide multiple access points from one data entry.
Their disadvantages are that there is very limited intellectual control and they cannot be easily updated. Because the elements are
dispersed over the whole index the addition of further titles means
that the whole index must be re–run.

There are also numerous software packages for micro and personal computers which provide indexing facilities, and an investigation of the capacities of the various packages available could
be worthwhile. The choice of program will depend on the computer available, its capacity to handle the material and the cost of
setting up the system.

One major point to remember with automated indexing, and
indeed with all computer assisted control systems is that they are
subject to the 'garbage in: garbage out' syndrome. The more
accurate and consistent the input, the better the result. If the
decision is made to go with automation then consideration
should be given to the format of the input, the possible standardisation of titles and the compilation of a list of stop words to
ensure that only meaningful terms are indexed.

Indexing Techniques

If the decision is made to go ahead with a manual or computer
assisted index (not an automated index) then various basic tech-

A KWOC index lists relevant entries sequentially under keyword terms.

niques and rules have to be taken into consideration. There are nearly as many sets of rules for compiling an index as there are indexes. These rules cover things like alphabetical order, word–by–word or letter–by–letter; the treatment of apostrophes and abbreviations; the order of dates and other numerical items; the format of personal and institutional names; the amount of additional information to be added to terms to avoid ambiguity (such as geographical names); and the structure and type of cross–references.

It is not the purpose of this section to discuss these rules in any detail. The bibliography lists several manuals which cover all these aspects of constructing an index. The important point is that the would–be indexer be aware of the necessity to:

- Choose a system which is appropriate to the kind of index required.
- Stick to the system chosen.
- Communicate to potential users what the system is and how it works.

Groundwork

Any index is only as good as the preparation which lies behind its rule–based structure. The preparation must cover what is to be indexed, in how much detail it is to be indexed and the terminology to be used. The index provides the conceptual link between the creator and the user. The indexer's task is to provide a bridge firmly rooted in the usage of the former, which reaches out to the needs and preoccupations of the latter. Careful preparation and forethought as to the kinds of problems which might be encountered are the only hope we have of achieving this challenging task.

As a simple example: suppose it has been decided to provide a name index to a large series of correspondence files. Quite apart from considerations as to the actual format of the names to be indexed, the indexer must decide whether nicknames and familiar names are to be included either as main entries or cross–references. This will depend on whether the writer used such names frequently. The indexer also has to decide which names to index: all of them, however brief the mention? only the 'important' ones? only those which attract substantial comment? What constitutes important or substantial? Furthermore, will the index distinguish between the names of those who have letters addressed to them, and those who are mentioned in the course of a letter, and if so, how? It is essential to decide these things in advance. Half–way through a set of files is no time to decide that you will include nicknames after all.

Another example, and one which causes considerable difficulty, is the indexing of photographs. Photographs quite frequently have titles which are singularly inadequate as guides to the complexities of the image. A photograph of a building may

show not just details of architecture, but of streetscape and buildings adjacent now demolished. It may also depict public and private transport in the street; people and their dress, social class
and occupation and leisure; even the weather. How to index
these aspects of the image, and which ones to index are basic
decisions. Are we simply going to note the presence of vehicles
and people or indicate number and type? and if so, how?

This discussion leads us to the most important and basic piece
of preparation for indexing, the choice and control of
terminology.

Indexing Languages and the Thesaurus

The language of everyday life is not static. It changes over time
and through space. It therefore follows that the language of the
creator of a document may well differ significantly from the
language of the archivist working with the document, and is
bound to differ from the language of the user approaching the
document at some future date. In addition the creator of the
document may have used some technical language or jargon, or
have used ordinary language in some specialised way.

We have said that the purpose of the index is to provide a bridge
across which user and creator can meet. To do this the indexer
must take control of the language used and limit both the number
of terms to be used and the descriptive area which each will
cover. Such a word list in a controlled vocabulary is called a
thesaurus; and, as with all other aspects of indexing, the major
consideration is appropriateness. The first step is to decide on
the subject area to be covered and the people or range of people
to be served. Students of architecture need different information
from family historians, but both may use the same photograph or
street plan or letter describing a house. The indexer must therefore construct thesauri which contain terms appropriate to serve
these needs. This does not necessarily mean the construction of
separate indexes, although sheer size may result in the splitting
of an index into subject areas. It does mean that the indexer must
ensure that terminology appropriate to all subject based
approaches is included in the index via the subject based thesauri.

A thesaurus can be a simple list of subject names, or a complex
network of terminology which controls all the relationships in
the indexing language. Decisions such as which terms can be
linked with which descriptors, and in which order; which terms
of a set of synonyms should be used, and which not; and which
terms may be taken automatically to include other terms — must
be made. The aim of the thesaurus is to eliminate ambiguity as far
as possible.

There are a variety of sources to which the potential indexer
can go to find suitable terms for a thesaurus, the obvious one is
the document itself. Other sources are:

- **Archivists working with the collection.** Archivists involved in arranging and describing a collection are familiar with the subject content and the range of topics covered. It may be useful to provide for the inclusion of suitable index terms on the series description worksheet. Archivists who are involved in reference service will also have lists of frequently asked questions and subjects on which information is often sought.
- **Archivists working with similar collections** or in similar institutions may have faced the same problems, or at least be aware of problems which may arise and errors which can be avoided.
- **Secondary source material** may often include indexes which can be culled for suitable terms. Local histories, biographies, text and technical books may all provide terms which can be adapted for archival use.
- **Administrative manuals and key word lists.** Most registries compile lists of key words to control the organisation's filing system. There may also be rules concerning the way file titles are constructed. These will be useful for indexing this material.

From these various sources a draft master list should be compiled. Not all terms will be retained in the final list. A choice must be made between potential synonyms, between words of greater and lesser scope and as to which terms are to be used for cross–reference only.

The thesaurus will also require maintenance. Most obviously the addition of material to the collection may require the addition of appropriate terms, and while the language of the documents will not change the language of the potential user will, and that end of the conceptual bridge will need extension into the user's language space. Research topics and the approach to them will also change, and while it is not the archivist's or the indexer's job to anticipate this, a perceived change in the pattern of reference inquiries may indicate the need to update the thesaurus and the index. It may also indicate that the chosen terms are not as appropriate or effective for retrieval as hoped and should be replaced with others.

Feedback of any kind will of course be dependent upon users knowing what the terms are and how the thesaurus is constructed. This information together with a synopsis of the indexing rules used as these relate to technicalities such as alphabetical order, abbreviations, and the like must be readily available to the user if the index is to be in any way effective as a retrieval tool.

Index Entries

Each entry in the index will consist of the following elements:

- The *keyword* or index term taken from the thesaurus OR proper name of person, place, corporation etc.
- One or more additional *descriptors* if required, also taken from thesaurus.
- *Explanatory notes* or additional references.
- *Location code* or 'address' where the information may be found.

As an example, consider an index entry for our street scene photograph. 'Vehicle' is the term we have selected for our thesaurus to cover all types of vehicles, and we have allowed for additional descriptors 'public' or 'private', and for a further set of descriptors 'bus', 'tram', 'car', 'bicycle'. The first two elements of our entry might read:

vehicle — private — bicycle or
vehicle — public — tram

We may not require any further notes, or we may have decided to add a note when other vehicles are also present in the photograph, so our next element might read:

(other types present)

The final element is the location code, in this case probably a series number and an item number, e.g.:

ser/56, ph/34

The full entry will then read:

vehicle — public — tram, (other types present), ser/56, ph/34.

Index Format

The index, and the thesaurus, can be presented either on cards or as typed lists. Cards are easier to update; lists are easier to copy and circulate. If the thesaurus has been compiled with due care it will need less frequent updating than the index, which is potentially in a constant state of growth. It may be most effective therefore to keep the index on cards — which will facilitate splitting into subject areas if the index gets too large — and the thesaurus as a list, which can be widely circulated to potential users. This approach has the additional benefit of allowing clients to become familiar with the index in advance and will cut down access time.

What to Index

The problems of constructing any index are more or less the same and the points we have discussed are relevant whether the index is to the descriptive inventories or to original materials. However consideration must be given as to what materials to index. While it is clear than an index to all of the archives' holdings and finding aids is desirable, it is equally clear that such an achievement is unlikely. The vast quantity of records and limited staff predicate against this ideal. Box B sets out basic categories of materials which are suitable for a modest indexing programme in an archives.

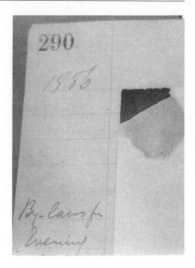

These unnumbered minute books were assigned page numbers by the archivist in preparation for indexing by volunteers.

Box B   Materials Suitable for Indexing Projects

Finding
Aids

- Individual finding aids, depending upon their complexity.
- All finding aids. A comprehensive index which links all finding aids is very desirable.

Archival
Materials

- Correspondence
- Diaries and personal journals
- Minutes of executive and governing bodies
- Photographs
- Publications
  - In–house
    - Annual reports
    - Journals, magazines, newsletters
    - Special commemorative publications
  - Community newspapers

Few researchers have time to read through *descriptive inventories* of all the holdings of an institution, and when in a hurry they will rely on file title or series names. It makes sense, therefore, especially if the holdings cover a wide range of subjects, to index these finding aids.

The minutes of committees and boards of management are the most central and vital records of an organisation, and hence are invaluable sources of information on all aspects of that organisation's functions. An index to the minutes is thus a way into all the records of the organisation, since other useful sources, correspondence, reports and the like will either be tabled in committee meetings or their contents briefly noted. Because minutes are usually complex it may be useful to start with a limited period of the available records, say ten years out of a run of forty. The experience of compiling a thesaurus and consistent index for this small section will be very useful as a basis for tackling the whole project.

Many organisations have an *in–house newsletter* or *magazine*, and there are also such things as *annual reports*, and *special commemorative publications*. These are frequently a mine of information which would be much more accessible if indexed. Even if a full subject index is not possible a guide to regular features or subjects covered would give initial purchase on the material.

Area based institutions — local history societies or local study libraries — may also have extensive holdings of *local newspapers*. These can provide a considerable problem in terms of both the space required to house them and the conservation of poor quality newsprint. One possibility, if it is known that a full set is housed elsewhere, or is perhaps available on microfilm, is

to index the papers in a fairly comprehensive fashion as an
alternative to keeping them. However the preparation of an index
to local newspapers involves the central questions as to what to
index and in how much detail and great care should be taken with
the ground work of such an index.

Who Does the Work?

It must be repeated that indexing is a time–consuming, professional task. If some of it can be passed on to the volunteers,
then so much the better. However what we have called the
'groundwork' should be done either by the archivist who
arranged and described the papers, or by someone with some
experience in indexing or familiarity with the materials. It is probably safest to regard indexing as two sets of tasks:

1)   setting the system up, designing the format and scope of the
     index and compiling the thesaurus; and
2)   the actual physical process of turning over the pages and
     making the entries.

The first task, which controls the quality of the index, should
be done by one person to ensure consistency and checked by
someone else, before the second task, which can be done by several people sequentially or simultaneously, goes ahead.

Whatever form and level of indexing you undertake, the effort
will bring benefits to the archives and researchers alike. Making
valuable records more accessible, a well–designed indexing programme is an undeniable asset for an archives.

Appendix Two   USMARC AMC Data Entry Form

Part A

(035)   LOCAL CONTROL # ƀƀ ($a) ....
(099)   STORAGE LOCATION ƀƀ ($a) ....
(100/110)   MAIN ENTRY (CREATOR) .... ƀ ($a) ....
        DATES ($d) ....
(245)   TITLE ....($a) ....
        DATES ($f) ....
(300)   EXTENT ƀƀ ($a) .... ($a) ....
(340)   MEDIUM ƀƀ ($a) ....
(351)   ARRANGEMENT ƀƀ ($a) ....
        ....
        ....
        ....

(506) RESTRICTIONS ♭♭($a) ....

(510) REFERENCES .... ♭($a) ....
       ($c)
(520) SUMMARY AND SCOPE NOTE .... ♭($a) ....
       ....
       ....
       ....
       ....

(524) PREFERRED CITATION .... ♭($a) ....

(540) USE/REPRODUCTION TERMS ♭♭($a) ....
       ....

(541) ACQUISITION SOURCE ♭♭
       RECEIVED FROM ($a) ....
       ADDRESS ($b)
       STATUS ($c)
       DATE RECEIVED ($d) ....
(544) ASSOCIATED MATERIALS ♭♭($d) ....
       ($a)
(545) BIOGRAPHICAL/HISTORICAL NOTE ♭♭($a) ....
       ....
       ....
       ....
       ....

(555) FINDING AIDS NOTE .... ♭($a) ....

(561) PROVENANCE ♭♭($3) ....
       ($b) .... ($a) ....
(583) ACTIONS ♭♭($) .... ($) ....
       ($) .... ($) ....
(584) FREQUENCY OF USE ♭♭($3) .... ($b) ....
(600) SUBJECT ADDED ENTRY — PERSONAL NAME 0
       ($a) .... ($a) ....
(610) SUBJECT ADDED ENTRY — CORPORATE NAME ....
       ($a) .... ($a) ....
(650) SUBJECT ADDED ENTRY — TOPICAL ....
       ($a) .... ($a) ....
(655) FORM/GENRE ♭7($a) .... ($a) ....
(700) ADDED ENTRY — PERSONAL NAME ....
       ($a) .... ($a) ....
(710) ADDED ENTRY — CORPORATE NAME ....
       ($a) .... ($a) ....
(851) LOCATION ♭♭($a) ....
       ($b) .... ($c) ....

Appendix Two   USMARC AMC Record for a Manuscript Collection   Part B

NOTE: This hypothetical example does not display Leader or Record Directory information. Such information, which is needed only in automated implementations, can be assumed to be generated and carried by the automated system being used. This sample also does not reflect the full range of possible options for the use of fields and subfields available to the AMC user. Its use of thesaurus codes and Library of Congress Name Authority references is conjectural. It is meant simply to show the type of record that *might* be created using the format.

001		NP000–85
010	∲∲	$ams∲61003623∲
035	∲∲	$a1939–0001
100	1∲	$aProvenance, William Fonds, $d1897–1938.
245	00	$kPapers,$f[ca. 1917–1937].
300	∲∲	$a15 cubic ft.
351	∲∲	$aOrganised into four series: I. War Participation, 1917–1919. II. College Years, 1920–1924. III. European Exile, 1925–1932. IV. Archival Career, 1933–1937. $bChronological arrangement.
506	∲∲	$aAccess subject to donor restrictions
510	4∲	$aHollinger, Abraham. 'W.F. Provenance and His Contribution to American Archives,' Archives Description Quarterly,$cvol. 7, 1985, p. 187
520	∲∲	$aIncludes cryptic diaries and illegible correspondence focusing on Provenance's unsuccessful literary endeavours and his development of the quark theory of archival description. Includes manuscript of his QUARKS: THE TAO OF ARCHIVES. Correspondents include Ernest Hemingway, Sigmund F. Groupie, and Ima Gusdorf.
524	∲∲	$aWilliam Fonds Provenance. Papers. Department of Manuscripts and University Archives, Freen College.
540	∲∲	$aLiterary rights of William Fonds Provenance have been dedicated to the public.
541	∲∲	$aProvenance, Gertrude Thruxton$b122 East Stack Street, Arlenville, CA 93706$cgift$d1939 September 18 $fWilliam Fonds Provenance Estate.
545	∲∲	$aArchivist and literary gadfly. Born at Last Chance, Nevada, 4 January, 1897. Served in World War I as ambulance driver. Following graduation from Freen College with a major in cryptogamic botany, he lived in Paris, where he tried, unsuccessfully, to attach himself to literary circles. To combat the depression caused by this rejection he began to develop his quark theory of archival description, published in his 1933 epic work QUARKS: THE TAO OF ARCHIVES. It was only after the development of the USMARC Archival and Manuscripts Control format that his ideas made any sense to the American archival profession.
555	∲∲	Box listing.
583	∲∲	$3Diaries$1microfilmed$cOctober 1985
583	∲∲	$3Hemingway letter 1927 May 3$aexhibit$c1985 December 1 through 1986 April 30$jMuseum of Literary Lights
600	10	$aProvenance, William Fonds, $d1897–1938.$tQuarks: the tao of archives.
650	∲0	$aQuarks.
650	∲0	$aArchival description$xQuark theory.
650	∲0	$aLiterary communities$zFrance.
650	∲0	$aTaoism$xUnorthodox interpretations.
655	∲7	$aDiaries$2uraful
655	∲7	$aLetters$2uraful
700	12	$aHemingway, Ernest.
700	12	$aGroupie, Sigmund Freud.
700	12	$aGusdorf, Ima.
851	∲∲	$aFreen College$bDepartment of Manuscripts and University Archives$cProvenance Memorial Building, 727 Prologue Boulevard, History City, MA$dUSA$eRange 1, Shelves 3–7

Parts A and B of Appendix Two are reproduced from Nancy Sahli, *MARC for Archives and Manuscripts: The AMC Format.* Chicago, IL: Society of American Archivists, 1985.

ACCESS AND REFERENCE SERVICES

Sandra Hinchey and *Sigrid McCausland*

INTRODUCTION

In earlier chapters we have looked at the activities which involve archivists in the acquisition and control of their holdings. However, archives are not kept merely for their own sake; they are also to be used. The purpose of this chapter is to explain the activities which involve the archivist in facilitating the research use of archives, namely access and reference services.

Access refers to the terms and conditions of availability of records or information maintained by an archives for examination and consultation by researchers. Access to an archival repository and thereafter to individual collections must be regulated in order to protect the documents, which are one-of-a-kind and irreplaceable. Archival collections are unique and therefore cannot be borrowed by researchers. Administering access to archives involves establishing procedures which will ensure that legislative requirements and donor agreements are upheld, and protect the records from theft, damage or rearrangement. *Reference Services* is the general name given to the facilities and services that enable the researcher to use the archives and its records once access to them is approved. Enabling that use involves the archivist not only in helping researchers to identify, select, and read records, but also in such activities as providing a suitable environment for research, answering mail and telephone enquiries, obtaining copies of records and acquiring appropriate books and journals to facilitate research. The types of access and kinds and extent of reference services will vary from archives to archives, depending upon the purpose of each operation and the nature of the records held.

ACCESS

Each archives should have a written access policy which takes
into account the nature of the information contained within the
collection and the purpose and resources of the archives programme. Policies establish the framework within which the archivist can administer access to records so that they can be used by
researchers. The access policy should be drafted to suit the
special requirements of each archives and the authorities
governing the archives should approve and issue the policy with
a full understanding of the resources required to administer it
properly.

DEVELOPING AN ACCESS POLICY

To design an access policy to suit the needs of the organisation
one must consider the following factors:

1) **Clientele.** The policy document should define the clientele
   or community of users that the archives programme will
   serve. This decision will largely be determined by the purpose of the archives, the composition of its holdings and the
   resources at its command. In the case of public archives, the
   clientele may be prescribed by legislation and will usually
   include government bodies and members of the public
   within an area of political authority. The State Archives of
   New South Wales, for example, serves the state government,
   the residents of New South Wales, and is authorised to assist
   local government agencies. In–house archives, such as
   those caring for the records of businesses or private
   institutions, may allow access only to their own employees
   or persons under contract to the parent organisation.
   Further limits based upon age, membership, affiliation or
   research interest may also be imposed. For example,
   readers' tickets may not be issued to children or to persons
   engaged in casual research. Persons living outside the area
   of service i.e. out–of–state or country may also be excluded
   from service or be required to pay a special fee.

2) **Sensitivity or Confidentiality of Records.** Organisations and individuals create records that contain information relating to their personal or business affairs which
   could cause embarrassment or financial loss if made available for examination by researchers. Records of this nature
   include agreements made by an organisation or individual
   with other bodies, information provided in confidence, personal and health records of staff or family members, and
   information relating to fraud or security procedures and systems that might hamper business operations if access to
   them were not restricted or monitored. Collecting archives
   may be required to restrict access to some records in their
   collections in accordance with the access provisions placed

upon records by depositors. They may also have to restrict access to records they have received which contain defamatory, libellous or personal information about a person other than the depositor.

3) **Protection of Individual Privacy.** Personal details about a living individual should not be released to researchers unless the individual's permission has been obtained. Information supplied by individuals, for the purposes of obtaining a particular benefit or to fulfil a requirement stipulated by law, should not be made available to researchers. However, information from these records may be able to be used for statistical purposes providing no specific names or identifiable information is recorded that would reveal the identities of particular individuals. Legislation relating to defamation and the right to privacy must be respected and archivists should restrict access to records accordingly.

4) **Restrictions Placed Upon Records by Depositors.** When an archivist is offered records by depositors access restrictions relating to them should be clarified. The archivist must consider the implications of restrictions placed upon records prior to accepting and accessioning them into the collection (See Chapter Three Acquisition and Appraisal and Chapter Four Accessioning.).

5) **Levels of Access.** As well as determining the clientele, the archivist must decide the level of access a researcher is to have to and within the archives. Access is usually granted in levels ranging from receiving general admission to the reading room to obtaining permission to reproduce or publish specific documents. The access policy statement must therefore cover conditions of access for:
- the reading room and finding aids
- inspection of particular collections or groups of archives
- examination of individual series or documents within a series
- copying of individual documents or photographs for private study
- quotation of portions of documents
- further reproduction or publication of documents, photographs or other archival materials.

6) **Degree of Control over Holdings.** Access to archival materials depends upon their being located and described so that appropriate documents may be requested and retrieved. Some types of records require more extensive controls than others. For example, a box of loose documents may require control numbers for each, while pages in a bound volume may not. Photographs may need more detailed descriptions since their subject matter can be com-

plex. Most archives control their records at the box or container level which means that the finding aids indicate what types of records are housed in a particular box, but not what specific documents or information might be present. Researchers unfamiliar with archival materials may be disappointed that the archivist cannot offer instant access to a particular document or piece of information and chagrined to learn that they must examine several boxes of material under supervision with no guarantee that they will find what they seek. It is useful, then, for the access policy to explain that researchers will be provided with finding aids and instructions for using them, but must select their own records and do their own research work. The policy should also state that records which have not been brought under control through arrangement and description will not be available for use.

A good orientation programme enables researchers to work confidently with a minimum of staff assistance.

7) **Physical Condition of the Records.** If the records are in a poor condition or have been physically damaged, the archivist should consider restricting access to them until they can be restored by a conservator. An alternative to denying access to badly damaged records is to provide a duplicate copy of the record to researchers (i.e. photocopy or microfilm copy). This alternative can be employed very effectively for highly used records, where closure would cause considerable inconvenience to a large number of researchers. If the majority of the records in a collection are in poor physical condition, access to the whole collection might be restricted until arrangements can be made for its repair or reproduction. Records should not be made available to researchers if continued handling will increase their deterioration.

8) **Security of Records.** Archival materials are unique and many records have importance as evidence of legal or fiscal responsibility. Access provisions, therefore, must protect them against loss, damage, misfile or tampering whilst they are in storage as well as during research use. Researchers, whether from the parent organisation or members of the public, should not have access to records storage areas. Retrieval and refile of material should be limited to one or a few authorised staff members. This practice minimises the risk of misfiles and pinpoints accountability for any loss or damage. Records required for research should be requested on a standard form and a copy of the request retained until the material has been returned, checked and refiled in its proper location. Staff must also be allocated to supervise records during use and security measures instituted to protect the materials, to detect breaches and to apprehend the persons responsible. See Table One: Security Measures for a checklist of recommended precautions.

Table One Security Measures

Security Requirement	Method of Implementation
Restrict Entry	Limit access of staff, visitors and tradesmen to the building or archives area and use specifically designated doors and entrance ways.
Identification	All visitors, including staff, should be required to show identification before being admitted to the archives and its reading room.
Registration	All visitors should be required to register their name, address, nature of business and the time of entry each day upon arrival. When visitors leave the archives, staff should record their time of departure in the same register.
Non-Public Areas	Issue all visitors, who will be frequenting non-public areas of the archives, with visitors' badges or identification cards which should be worn or carried conspicuously. Visitors should be accompanied by a staff member at all times while in restricted areas. The identification card or badge should be returned upon departure.
No Baggage	Do not permit researchers to take coats, brief cases, bags or enclosed containers into the reading room. Provide a cloak room or area where these items can be stored until researchers have completed their work for the day. As researchers leave the reading room their research materials should be inspected.
Requests	Record request forms should be completed for all original records. Users should not be permitted to order more than *three containers* or the equivalent in unboxed materials (volumes, folders, bundles) at any one time. Only *one volume or folder* should be examined by a researcher at a time. Original records must be used under direct supervision.
Reshelving/Refiling	Researchers should not be allowed to reshelve or refile records. Archives staff should be responsible for this function so as to reduce the dangers of mishandling and misfiling.
Copying	Copying should be done by staff members in order to ensure careful handling of the records.
Written Rules	Provide a concise but complete set of written regulations to each researcher and ensure that these are understood and respected by researchers.
Emergency Procedures	Develop clear, legally sound procedures for handling physically and emotionally ill or suspicious persons and be sure that all staff abide by them. Also establish procedures for the orderly evacuation of the building in case of disaster, emergency or threat and be sure all staff are aware of and abide by them.
Storage Areas	Limit access to storage areas to staff and keep the number of staff involved in the retrieval of original records to a minimum.

Box A   Points to Include in an Access Policy

1) **General Statement on the Purpose of the Archives and Use of its Holdings.**

2) **Clientele.** Make a general statement identifying who may use the archives, including any limits or conditions that users must meet (age, affiliation, type of research). Statement on services to clients outside the normal area of service. Statement that persons must apply for and receive authorisation to use the archives.

3) **General Statement on Right of Access to Holdings.** This statement usually says that author-ised readers may have access to holdings which are not restricted by law, regulation or deposi-tor agreement. The general right of access also includes the right to inspect the finding aids and to obtain copies of a reasonable amount of material for private study.

4) **Administration of Access.** Access to the archives and its collections must be monitored because of the archives' legal obligations to depositors and because its holdings are unique and irreplaceable. This section should describe the restrictions or conditions of use which serve to protect the records from loss or damage and ensure compliance with the laws, regulations and depositor agreements affecting the records. Points to be addressed are:

   a) *Non-circulation of Records.* State that original records and other archival materials must be used within the archives jurisdiction. In some situations loans or copies of records may be made for depositors or other archival institutions; costs associated with such loans or copies are met by the requestor.

   b) *Supervised Use of Records.* State that all archival materials are to be used under the super-vision of the archives staff.

   c) *Compliance with the Regulations of the Archives.* State that the archives may establish such regulations as needed to protect the institution and its holdings and that such regulations will apply equally to all persons, users, visitors or staff. Researchers must abide by the terms of access and the regulations governing the use of the archives facilities and collections. The archivist has the right to enforce these regulations and to refuse or revoke access to researchers who refuse or fail to comply with them.

   d) *Restriction of Access to Records.* State that the archivist has the right to refuse or restrict access to all or some archival materials when required to do so by law, regulation or deposi-tor agreement. The archivist may also restrict access to materials which invade the privacy of living persons, contain libellous or defamatory statements or allegations, are unpro-cessed or are in fragile or poor condition. Where material has been restricted, the archivist regularly reviews restrictions and undertakes measures such as preservation copying to make records available for use as soon as possible.

   e) *Equality of Access to Records.* State that the archives provides reference services without favour or prejudice and does not grant privileged or exclusive use of material unless required to do so by law, depositor or purchase conditions.

   f) *Quotation/Citation of Records.* State that the archives permits quotation of the text of records within fair dealing provisions of the Copyright Act 1968. All references to archival materials must carry an approved form of citation properly identifying the records and acknowledging the archives.

   g) *Copying of Records.* Copies of archival materials for private study only will be made under the fair use provisions of the Copyright Act. Copies of records are not to be sold or further reproduced or published without permission of the archives and of the copyright holder. In general the archives does not make copies from copies (microforms, photostats) of archival materials which have been obtained from other archives and libraries unless the other institution has given permission to do so. Copies of such materials should be ordered from the repositories which hold the originals.

h) *Permission of Copyright Holder and the Archives Required for Further Copying or Publication of Records.* State that the researcher must undertake to obtain prior permission from the archives *and* from the owners of copyright in any archival material that he/she wishes to publish or make additional copies for distribution or sale. Materials in copyright for which permission to publish has not been obtained cannot be copied for researchers. Permission to publish or further reproduce material is granted for a specific purpose or occasion and does not convey or transfer copyright in the original material to the requestor. Although it should not be a requirement for the granting of permission to publish, publishers and authors should be encouraged to deposit a copy of works based upon or using the archives' holdings in the archives' reference library.

i) *Fees.* State that the archives may set fees for the use of facilities or services and for the provision of copies as may be required by law or administrative regulation.

9) **Legislation.** Access to public archives and to government records may already be determined to some extent, by the provisions of acts of Parliament and statutory regulations. Organisations attached to federal, state or local government departments should be aware of all acts, ordinances and regulations applying to the records they create and maintain. Legislation can determine access to records and therefore can affect the services provided by archivists to researchers. Some government-funded archives may also be affected by Freedom of Information legislation.

Consideration of the above criteria will enable the archivist to plan and design an access policy specifically tailored to the needs and requirements of the parent or funding organisation. The archives should be aware of the repercussions of providing an access service to the public and the effect it will have on the parent or funding organisation and the allocation of archival resources especially as regards staff, time and money.

Statement of Policy

The statement of the archives' access policy should be approved by the governing authority of the archives or its parent organisation as appropriate. This approval will ensure that the archivist has definite guidelines for the administration and supervision of access to the archives for which they are responsible. Box A summarises the parts which should be included in the statement of the access policy.

Administering Access to Archives

Once the access policy has been set out and approved, the next step is to develop procedures for its administration. To assist with the monitoring of access, an application for access form should be designed. The design of an Access Application Form is vitally important because this form is a significant document in its own right. It is signed by both the researcher and the archivist to indicate that both parties are aware of their responsibilities in having archival material made available. The form must be clearly designed and not cluttered. It can be divided into three parts, namely, information provided to the applicant relating to the conditions of access, information supplied by the applicant concerning his/her research work and information supplied by the archivist concerning the outcome of the application.

The access form makes the applicant aware of conditions regarding the use and handling of archival records. See Table Two: Access Application Form.

The applicant should be asked to provide details including name, address and telephone number so that he/she can be contacted in the future. Acceptable proof of identity and address should be provided by the applicant. The applicant should be required to date and sign the access application form to signify his/her compliance with the conditions outlined.

In addition to setting out the general conditions of access on the Access Application Form, the archivist should spell out specific rules governing the behaviour of researchers in the reading room. See Table Three: Regulations for the Use of the Reading Room. For convenience, the rules can be printed on the reverse side of the Access Application Form.

The Access Application Form is a necessary document which should be used by every archives for without this form, applicants are not held accountable for what they do to the records, or publish from them. Formalising access to the archives means that the archives can take action against researchers if they violate the access conditions. The information provided by the researcher on the Access Application Form may also be used by the archivist as a source for defining trends concerning the use of the archives, and for planning other programmes such as the microfilming of potentially high usage records. The archives should decide whether access forms are to be completed by applicants on an annual basis or for a specific research project i.e. whether access is approved for a definite period of time or on a project–by–project basis.

The procedure for obtaining access to archival records may also include the issue of an annual reader's ticket or some other form of written permission to each approved applicant. The particulars regarding the applicant may be transferred onto cards and stored in alphabetical surname order as an index, so that the archivist can quickly refer to them if information concerning an applicant has to be checked.

Spacious tables allow researchers to work with records of all sizes. Materials not actually being examined should be kept boxed on a trolley or at the reference desk.

Table Two   Access Application Form

Conditions of Access to the Archival Collection

1) That all research conducted in the Archives be carried out under the direct control and supervision of the Archivist and his/her staff.

2) That records made available to the researchers will not be marked or interfered with in any way and will be returned upon completion of use in their original order and condition to the Archivist.

3) That no copies of records will be made without the specific permission of the Archivist. Any copying will be subject to the physical condition of the records and to copyright legislation.

4) That no publication of material from the archives will be undertaken without the written permission of the Archives. If publication of material from the archives is approved, then its source must be acknowledged.

Name of Applicant . . . .

Address . . . .

. . . . Tel. No. . . . .

Nature of Research . . . .

. . . .

I agree to comply in all respects with the above conditions.

Date . . . . Signature . . . .

OFFICE USE ONLY
Recommendation (Archivist)

. . . .

Date . . . . Signature . . . .

Approved by . . . .

Date . . . .

Table Three   Regulations for the Use of the Reading Room

1) Researchers may use the Reading Room only after they have completed the Access Application Form and the Archivist has authorised the form.

2) Access to records is governed by the Archives' access policy, and material is issued to researchers subject to any specific conditions relating to individual collections.

3) No bags, briefcases, coats or enclosed containers are to be taken into the Reading Room.

4) No smoking, eating or drinking are permitted in the Reading Room.

5) *Pencils only* are to be used for writing. Biros, fountain pens, felt tips and other pens, and correction fluid, are not permitted in the Reading Room, as they contain substances which can cause serious damage to records.

6) Researchers must handle all records carefully, and must not mark, fold, tear or otherwise harm the records in any way. Any damage found in material issued should be reported to staff immediately.

7) Researchers must not rearrange or interfere in any way with the order of archival material.

8) Usually only one volume or folder at a time will be issued to each researcher. Researchers must return materials to the issue desk as soon as they have finished using them.

9) No archival material is to be removed from the Reading Room by researchers.

10) Material from the Archives' collections will be copied if the conditions of the Archives' reproduction policy are met, and if the proposed copying does not breach the provisions of the Copyright Act 1968.

11) Researchers must respect Reading Room conventions of courtesy and, where possible, silence. Equipment such as typewriters and tape recorders may be used only with the express permission of the archivist.

Photocopy use must be controlled to meet copyright requirements and avoid damage to records. Courtesy — State Library of NSW.

COPYRIGHT

Copyright is the exclusive right, granted by law, to make and dispose of copies of and otherwise to control a literary, musical, dramatic or artistic work. Copyright belongs to the creator of a work and passes to his/her heirs, unless it is sold or transferred to another party. Copyright is a very complex area, and archivists are advised that virtually all of the holdings of an archives are subject to copyright under the provision of the Copyright Act 1968. If the material is a written record and is unpublished, as are most archives, copyright is perpetual. Once the record is published, the copyright has a fixed time limit, after which it may be copied without restriction. To make the matter more complicated, graphic materials such as photographs and maps are also subject to copyright, but for a stated period of time.

Determining whether or not material is out of copyright and, therefore, able to be copied without concern is time consuming, but necessary. Likewise, the effort to trace the owners of copyright for material created decades earlier can be demanding; but permissions are required if researchers contemplate further copying or publication of the material.

Since most archives consist of original unpublished works subject to copyright, the archivist's first step is to identify the copyright owner(s). Copyright is owned by the person who actually wrote the material unless the work was produced in a situation of employment. In the case of in–house archives, the host organisation would hold the copyright on records or publications produced in the course of its work. However, the institution does not hold copyright in documents sent to it by other persons or bodies. The ownership of copyright in material produced in the workplace or, under contract or commission, will depend upon copyright ownership or, under contract or commission, will depend upon copyright ownership being addressed in a specific agreement. If it is not then it is very likely that the employer or contractor will be the owner.

In collecting archives, since most of the records and publications are produced by outside persons or organisations, the copyrights belong to them, not the archives. Ownership of copyright does not pass with ownership or custody of the material. It must be transferred separately and in writing. The only exception to this is a bequest. Material bequested always includes transfer to the beneficiary of any copyrights held by the testator.

Under the fair dealing provisions of the copyright legislation, researchers may make their own copies (including handwritten or typed transcriptions, tape recordings or photocopies) of 'reasonable' portions of material for the purpose of research or study. Generally speaking, however, archives and libraries are not permitted to make copies of unpublished written material for researchers, unless the author has been dead for over 50 years

and more than 75 years have elapsed since the material was produced. Because of these copyright restrictions and the need to
protect original records from damage, archives do not permit
researchers to make their own photocopies.

For more information on copyright, consult the publications
listed at the end of this chapter, or contact the Australian Copyright Council at 22 Alfred Street, Milson's Point, NSW 2061.

REPRODUCTION OF RECORDS

An archival institution should consider very carefully the question of reproducing its records for the benefit of researchers. For
example, conservation problems can arise from the frequent
handling of original material for copying purposes. Also, the
clerical work associated with the receipt, checking, recording
and dispatch of requests for copying makes significant demands
on staff time. Reproductions cannot be provided to researchers
without first ensuring that the provisions of the Copyright Act
1968 have not been infringed.

An archives should require researchers to submit an application in writing for permission to make a reproduction of any
item from its holdings. The archivist should ensure that each
application includes sufficient detail about each item, so that it
can be identified and its copyright status determined prior to
copying. Specific information should also be supplied concerning the form in which the item is to be reproduced or published
e.g. photocopy or photographic print. A scale of fees must also
be fixed by each archives, depending upon the size and variety
of the copying services provided and the extent of their use. The
reproduction of records will be facilitated by a form requesting
information on the records to be copied and stating the conditions that must be complied with in order to obtain copies from
the archives. Examples of such conditions are as follows:

1)   The right of the archives to refuse permission to copy if any
     damage is likely to result to the record.
2)   A reminder to the researcher that sale of a copy does not
     involve sale of the copyright and no further reproduction of
     the work may take place without permission of the copyright
     owner.
3)   That any reproduction made cannot be sold or given away
     without the permission of the archives.

The applicant should be required to sign the reproduction
form, signifying his/her compliance with the conditions outlined.
For the archivist's use, a section might also be included at the
bottom of the form for recording information concerning the
copying of records such as the number of copies made, method
of reproduction (photocopy or photographic print), name of the
photographer (if applicable), fee to be charged, receipt number
(if one is issued) and the recommendation of the archivist. See
Table Four: Reproduction Application Form. This information

Table Four   Reproduction Application Form

Conditions of Reproduction of Archives

Conditions regarding the obtaining of photocopies, microforms and prints from the archives.

1) The Archives may refuse to approve any copying likely to damage the records.

2) Copies of records are provided under this agreement for the purpose of private research and study *only.* A separate application must be made for permission to reproduce further or publish material.

3) Where the Archives owns the copyright in any record reproduced, it shall not by reason of the delivery of such reproduction at the request of the applicant be deemed to have assigned or otherwise transferred the copyright thereto.

4) No copies of the archives are to be sold, or in any way further reproduced or published without prior written consent of the Archives.

Description of records to be copied: ....

....

....

....

....

....

I, ... of ....
do hereby apply for approval to obtain copies of the above records from the Archives. I have read the conditions set out above and agree to abide by them in full.

Date ....Signature ....

OFFICE USE ONLY

No. of copies: ....

Cost: ....Receipt No ....

Method of reproduction: ....

Name of photographer (if applicable) ....

Approved by: ....Date ....

could also be used to provide statistics for quarterly or annual reports, to record the utilisation of the reproduction service by researchers and to justify the appointment of extra personnel.

Copying can sometimes be a strain on the resources of the archives. It may be necessary in some cases to restrict the number of copies per week per researcher, so that the archives is able to maintain a balance in the services offered to all researchers. Also, copying of large items in full should be discouraged unless the archives or its parent organisation is able to include such material in its own copying programme. Copying of archives should not become a substitute for note taking by researchers.

Most archives charge for making copies. Fees levied for copies are of two types: those to recover the cost of producing the copy and 'royalty' charges for further reproduction or publication of the material supplied. Charges to recover the cost of producing copies should at least equal the expense of all materials and of the staff time expended in making them and in processing the orders. Fees which are 'royalties' for the use of archival material in media programmes or publications are less common, though some larger research institutions with rich collections of prints and photographs do have them. The main motivation behind publication fees is the need for extra funds for conservation, rather than the desire to make money. The problem with 'royalties' is that they usually cost more to collect than they bring in, and they do pose a hardship for many small or specialty publishers and documentary film makers. Government archives may find that fees for reproduction are regulated by legislation, and if so, the scale of fees should be incorporated into the reproduction policy statement of the archives concerned.

An archives with a large clientele, or a collection used and copied regularly, may consider designing a policy similar to that of the Mitchell Library in the State Library of New South Wales or the Council of the City of Sydney Archives. Both these organisations charge fees according to the use to which the reproduction is to be put e.g. motion picture film, commercial television programme, advertising, decoration, exhibition or for private research purposes. The fee is based on the monetary profit to be gained from the use of the material.

DESIGNING REFERENCE SERVICES

The provision of reference services can be one of the most rewarding aspects of archival work. The archivist can experience much satisfaction in giving direct assistance to people using archival material for research purposes, and the image of the archives may be enhanced by favourable reports of its service from grateful users. Careful planning is an essential ingredient for the success of any reference programme, for without it, chaos and frustration for both archivist and user can result.

The reference desk is the public face of the archives.

The design of the reference programme will depend upon the availability of funds; legal or administrative controls that could affect reference services; the clients the archives is servicing; the records held by the archives; the requirements for making them safely accessible to users; and the priority given by the organisation to reference services as opposed to other archival functions such as arrangement and description, and preservation. The implementation of the reference programme will depend on the available resources which include space, equipment, staff and funding, as well as that vital commodity for all archives — time.

Assistance to researchers should actually precede their arrival in the archives in the form of brochures or letters which explain the archives' access policies, services, general holdings, and regulations governing research use, as well as any logistical details such as location, hours of operation, public transport and parking. Researchers should be encouraged to contact the archives well in advance of their visit so that the documentation necessary to secure access to the reading room or to a particular collection can be prepared, eliminating delays which eat into all-too-valuable research time.

All researchers should be advised that archives, unlike libraries, are not self-service. Readers cannot be permitted in the stacks to browse and select material. Rather, they must use the finding aids provided and request records which will be retrieved by archives staff. In a large archives, this process can take half a day or longer, and researchers must understand this from the outset.

The reference desk should have a clear view of the reading room. Free-standing exhibition panels explain preservation microfilming to readers.

Microfilm readers must accommodate a range of image sizes and be comfortable to view.

Allow time at the end of each day to check and refile microfilms.

Reference assistance may be divided into four categories:
- providing a suitable environment for research
- providing information and advice
- providing support services to facilitate research
- administering and documenting reference services.

Providing a Suitable Environment for Research

A separate, purpose–designed reading room should be provided for researchers using archives. Even in the smallest archives, it is desirable to set aside a special area for research which involves original material, as opposed to books, other printed material and microfilm. Because these materials are unique and irreplaceable, they must be used under close supervision. If it is not possible to devote a whole room to this purpose, then perhaps part of a large room can be sectioned off. At the very least, a table or tables should be reserved exclusively for researchers using original material. The researcher must have enough space for the records he/she is consulting and for his/her own note–taking. The archivist, or other staff member, should be located nearby to answer questions, retrieve records and provide effective supervision.

The reading room should create an environment conducive to concentrated research work: it should be properly lit, away from noise and passers–by and it should have adequate heating, cooling and ventilation. (See the section on Managing Facilities, Equipment and Stores in Chapter Two Getting Organised for a list of the requirements for all public areas in the archives, including suggested reading room layouts.)

As well as facilities for the use of the archives themselves, enough space and appropriate shelving is needed for the archives' reference library . The archives own finding aids, generous supplies of all the forms to be completed by researchers and copies of any brochures and other publicity material should be kept as close as possible to the researchers' work area. Table Five: Reading Room Requirements sets out the factors to be considered in planning a reading room.

Providing Information and Advice

Assistance to Readers. Having persons come to the archives to use the records is desirable because it enables the archivist to give them direct assistance. However some archives may not be able to allow personal access due to legal or administrative regulations or lack of space. Consequently these archives may provide their reference services via mail or telephone.

Persons who have taken the time and trouble to come to the archives to use the records should be greeted and treated with courteous enthusiasm. Information should be provided to researchers on matters such as obtaining access to the archives and its records; hours of opening; types of records held and information they contain; types of finding aids and how to use them; qualified persons who can undertake research for a fee; and other repositories with similar or related holdings.

Archivists responsible for reference services are advised to plan the reading room hours and services to allow time for the staff on duty to prepare the room for each day's work, i.e. replenish forms, check microfilm readers and put finding aids back in order. Likewise, there should be time at the end of the day to check and refile materials. Below are some guidelines to follow in setting up hours of service.

- **Reading room hours** should be one hour shorter than the archives working hours, i.e. *Reading Room 9:30 am to 4:30 pm* when working hours are 9 am to 5 pm.
- **Reading room services:** In general,
  - New requests for records received less than 45 minutes before closing will be actioned *the following day*.
  - Photocopy orders will be processed *twice daily;* orders for same day delivery must be received by noon.

Another area for the archivist's advice is the citation of archival sources. It is most important for researchers to cite the material they use correctly, especially when their work is to be published and could lead to requests for the same material by other researchers. You should state the method the archives prefers researchers to use to identify records from which information has been extracted. The citation should include the name of the organisation holding the record, the creator of the record, information relating to the record's specific reference or archive

---

Table Five   Reading Room Requirements

For Researchers
- Separate supervised area for researchers using original materials
- Adequate tablespace for researchers i.e. a minimum of 1m x 0.7m per researcher
- Good lighting over research tables
- Effective ventilation, heating and cooling systems
- Provision for housing the finding aids — central location, appropriate shelving and generous space for staff and researchers to use the finding aids
- Shelving for specialist reference library and table space for people using this material
- Space for equipment such as microfilm readers and tape recorders, preferably away from areas where researchers are doing quiet research. Leave enough room for researchers to take notes when using this equipment

---

For Staff
- Desk/Counter
  - positioned to enable constant supervision of researchers by staff
  - equipped with supplies of record request and other relevant forms; telephone and emergency procedures manual
- Lockable area to store records overnight or for the duration of their use

---

number and title, date of the item and/or unique identification of the entry within the item.

The archives should produce a brochure containing basic information on its holdings and services. The brochure is useful for first–time researchers, and also as advance information for researchers who write before making a visit. You can exchange copies of information of this kind with other organisations as a further service to the researcher. The brochure can be used to promote the archives and its services. Larger archives with more complex holdings and a greater variety of services often produce a 'family' of related brochures for this purpose. See Table Six: Content of Archives Brochure.

Mail Enquiries. This method of providing access to archival information may be preferred by some archives more than others due to their large and geographically scattered clientele, or lack of space and resources to accommodate researchers. People requesting information must include basic facts concerning their requirements, for without specific information the archives may provide responses of limited value to the enquirer. All mail reference enquiries to the archives should clearly specify the topic and include:

- name of person/place/event
- approximate dates
- location of place/event/person
- type of transaction or document required eg. Will, rate assess ment valuation or notice.

In dealing with mail enquiries, the archivist will usually need to set some kind of limit on the time spent researching and composing responses. It is very easy to spend hours trying to answer one letter while other work mounts up. Alternatively, limits can be placed on the number and type of questions per letter, for example, no more than three requests per letter, all of which must relate to the same name or topic. Form letters, designed to suit the most frequently asked questions, are used successfully by many archives to reply to mail enquiries. You may develop a general list of sources to be checked; these should be developed for popular types of request, beginning with the general and moving to the more specific. These lists save time for the archivist and can be very useful to researchers.

Often researchers will want to order copies of documents you have found, so it may be advisable to send out a reproduction request form along with the response. All copies and postage charges should be paid for in advance to avoid the time consuming task of chasing bad debts.

Answering mail inquiries can be facilitated through the use of a Mail Enquiry Worksheet on which you record the request number, name of requestor, the sources consulted, results of the search, explanatory notes, copy order forms prepared, draft response, amount of time spent and names of staff member. Such a worksheet not only provides the information needed to respond to the request, it is invaluable for answering future requests on the same or closely related topics.

Telephone Enquiries. All archives should be prepared to give out basic information about their services, hours of operation, general holdings and finding aids over the phone.

The provision of detailed information by telephone is more difficult. In an in-house archives, answering telephone queries from users within the organisation will often be a feature of the archivist's day-to-day work. If these queries become fairly complex or require lengthy research, then it would be preferable for the enquirer to do the research him/herself (or to arrange for someone else to do it). Similarly, if a member of the public requests detailed information by telephone and that person is able to come in to use your research facilities, it is quite reasonable to suggest politely that they do so.

However, this is an area where it is difficult to make rules, as a friendly, efficient telephone service can be a very good advertisement for the archives. On the other hand, archival materials are often more complex and difficult to search than books and so are not suitable for quick reference services. A small archives in particular may not be able to cope with a steady flow of telephone enquiries while trying to maintain an adequate reading room service and carry out other archival functions at the same time. Careful monitoring of the volume and type of enquiries received, an awareness of the archives' overall priorities and resources, and common sense all need to be used when deciding on the standard of telephone service to be offered.

Researchers should be instructed to cite archival sources correctly.

Research Services

For members of the public. In most cases the archivist will need to set limits on the amount of research undertaken by staff on behalf of researchers. This is not because of any apathy towards clients and their needs, but rather because doing detailed, lengthy research is outside the archivist's usual role of supporting the research efforts of other people. The reference archivist's job is to guide researchers to the records, but not to interpret their contents. However, special circumstances, such as a major commemorative project for the parent organisation might require the limits to be lifted temporarily. In such cases it is essential that the work be well-defined and limited in time; and that extra funding be provided for its accomplishment.

One solution to the problem of providing research services, especially for distant users, is to refer the researcher to an individual who will do the work for a fee. Most archives maintain lists which include the names, addresses and specialities of contract researchers. The archives will supply the list to an enquirer, but further arrangements, including charges, are left to be agreed

A well-organised work area behind the reference desk provides space for staff to answer mail inquiries and keep records awaiting reshelving.

Reels of microfilm stored in drawers can be retrieved by researchers, but staff should check boxes before reshelving to minimise the danger of misfiles.

A simple display showing how to fill out a request for records saves time and reduces the need for staff instruction.

upon by the enquirer and the researcher. The list should carry an introductory sentence or two from the archives explaining that the list is provided as a convenience to persons unable to conduct their own research and should not be construed as a recommendation or endorsement by the archives of any of the contract researchers listed.

General guidelines for staff setting out the type and level of assistance to be provided to researchers should be compiled. Such guidelines should emphasise that the role of the archives staff is to support and assist rather than to do research. Giving tours of the archives; explaining how to use the finding aids; ensuring fair and equal treatment for all researchers; and referring people to other repositories with relevant holdings are examples of supporting work by staff.

For an in-house archives. The archivist may be required to provide detailed information to the organisation that the archives serves as a condition of its establishment and primary reason for existence. Some archives of an organisation may only be available to officers of a particular department for business or confidential reasons and therefore the archivist should ensure that strict security procedures are followed so that only those officers designated can obtain access to specific records, e.g. most organisations will only allow particular officers in the Personnel or Industrial Relations Department to view individual staff records. The problem of administrative change and recording the ownership of records and the creator or successor owners, will need to be addressed. Access to records by creators and owners can be very complex and requires written guidelines which should be determined at the time of accession and strictly followed.

The archivist should help researchers use the records, but not do their research for them.

Table Six   Content of Archives Brochure

Location	**The archives and its holdings**
Address with map showing location	History of the establishment of the archives
Mail Address	Scope of holdings/focus of collecting interests
Telephone Number	Records held by the organisation
	• main types
Opening Hours	• important collections

Access	**Services**
Access Policy	Finding aids
• summary	• types
	• availability
Procedures for obtaining access	Reproduction of archives
	• summary of policy and services
Special requirements	Equipment available
• e.g. reader's ticket	• e.g. microform readers, tape recorders
	Citation guidelines
	• include an example of a correct citation

*   This brochure can be designed as a four page pamphlet with the name and logo of the organisation recorded on the front cover and the above information contained on the centre double page.

*   The information contained in the brochure is intended as an introduction to the archives and its services, and does *not* replace the statements and forms associated with the different activities involved in providing access and reference services.

Employees of the organisation should be encouraged to examine records whenever possible in the archives reading room so as to ensure that they are handled correctly. The archivist may also be required to conduct searches on particular subjects for officers of the organisation. The archivist should not neglect this type of reference service as first and foremost the archives should be of service to the organisation funding and supporting its existence.

Providing Support Services to Facilitate Research

Finding Aids. Archival records are virtually useless to researchers unless finding aids or published guides are available or have been developed by the archives to lead researchers into the records. The more detailed and comprehensive the finding aids the easier researchers will find the task of locating the correct records for their research and the less time the archivist will need to allocate to assisting them with this task. This means that the researcher and archives staff are both aware of any limitations placed upon access to records by the organisation or depositors. For more details see Chapter Six Finding Aids.

Reference Library. A specialist reference library should be established to allow researchers to refer to general information on a specific subject from secondary source material. The reference library should be designed to supplement the archival collection and include finding aids from other archives with holdings of a

Table Seven   Record Request Form

Somewhere City Archives		**Record Request Form**

1) *Identifying Number*	2) *Requestor's Name*	3) *Date of Request*
	4) *Requestor's Signature*	5) *Reader's Ticket Number*
6) *Description of Material Requested*		7) *Date Range*

Archive Use Only

8)   *Authorised by and Date:*

9)   *Comments:*

10) *Issued by and Date:*	11) *Returned by and Date:*

Notes:
1)   *Identifying Number:* Record all numbers needed to retrieve series i.e. accession, series, box and shelf, as appropriate.
2)   *Requestor's Name:* Full name of person requesting records (in block letters).
3)   *Date of Request:* Enter day, month, year.
4)   *Requestor's Signature:* Requestor must sign all requests.
5)   *Reader's Ticket Number:* Enter Reader's Ticket or other appropriate number.
6)   *Description of Material Requested:* Give full and proper citation of material, i.e. collection or archive group, series, folders, document or volume.
7)   *Date Range:* Record date range of requested material.
8)   *Authorised by and Date:* Record the signature of the archivist responsible and the date to indicate approval of access.
9)   *Comments:* Enter any special provisions or conditions governing use or if records are unavailable due to conservation treatment, issue to another researcher or whatever reason.
10)   *Issued by and Date:* Initials of person retrieving the material and date of retrieval.
11)   *Returned by and Date:* Initials of person refiling the material and date of refile.

similar or related nature, copies of official or statistical information relating to the archives and historical information relating to the collection such as a history of the organisation or surrounding community or state. The reference library should not be a circulating library, rather it should be purely an in-house resource for the use of researchers and the archives' staff.

Retrieval/Replacement of Records. This is a basic reference service, but one which must be well organised, no matter what the size of the archives' holdings or the extent of its storage areas.

If records are stored in an off-site repository removed from the immediate vicinity of the reading room, a system of retrieval and replacement of records will need to be developed to ensure that this activity is carried out with as little disruption and harm occurring to the records as possible. Researchers will need to be informed of time delays that result from the retrieval of records from an off-site repository. Provision will also have to be made for the temporary storage of retrieved records in or near the reading room until they have been examined fully by researchers. Records should only be retrieved from and replaced in the repository by archives staff. An archives cannot afford to misplace or misfile records so the replacing of records should be supervised and monitored to make sure that records are returned to their correct locations in the repository.

A method of ensuring this is accomplished efficiently is to introduce a record request system which records not only the name of the person requiring the record, but also the location from which it was retrieved and to which it should be returned after use. A sample Record Request Form is shown in Table Seven. The record request system usually includes a triplicate record request form which is used to control the whereabouts of all records. The original part of the form is retained by the archivist, the duplicate copy can be used as a 'file out' marker and the triplicate copy is attached to the record and handed to the researcher requesting the record.

Upon retrieval of the record from the repository a copy of the duplicate record request form should be placed in the exact location of the record as an indication of its removal. The archivist can use a 'Record Out' card if preferred, but the same information concerning the researcher's name and the location of the record should be noted.

Reproduction. Most archives offer some kind of service for reproducing small quantities of material from their holdings. Photocopying is the cheapest and quickest method, but photographic prints and copies from microfilm reader/printers are also frequently supplied. Copies should be paid for in advance by researchers. The archivist should set scheduled times for researchers' copying to be done, so that this work is balanced with other reference tasks and so that researchers do not come to expect or demand service every time they want copies made.

Researchers may want to copy the records themselves for a specific purpose, such as for the production of a video or film clip on because the copying service they require is not supplied by the archives. In this case, you will have to provide someone, perhaps a volunteer, to supervise the researcher's photography session. It is a good idea to keep a special appointments book for this work if you have frequent requests from researchers to do their own photography.

Administering and Documenting Reference Services

These activities are important as they provide the archivist with the data to plan effectively, to allocate resources, and to report accurately to management on the work of the archives. Guidelines and procedures for the following activities are recommended in order to maintain a consistent and systematic approach which can be communicated to archival staff, researchers, and the parent organisation.

The Reference Interview. This is important for the efficient use of the archives' holdings. The reference interview basically provides the researcher with information relating to the archives i.e. access to the archives' facilities and collections, rules for the use of archives, the arrangement of finding aids, other archival collections that may be of assistance, and guidelines for citations and reproduction of records. Likewise, the interview provides the archivist with information about the researcher, i.e. his/her research topic; the purpose of the research (e.g. whether for publication or a thesis); the material he/she expects to see; any deadlines for the research; and possible copying requirements. (See Table Eight Guidelines for Reference Interview.)

Where possible the archivist should interview researchers who have completed their work in the archives. Discussion will produce feedback about the facilities provided, and information about related collections and sources that the researcher has used elsewhere. If the holding of an exit interview is not feasible, a simple questionnaire might be drawn up for researchers to complete and a suggestion box provided so that researchers are able to express their opinions more easily.

Documenting Research Use. The following procedures may assist the archivist in administering reference services and recording information concerning the archives' clientele.

- *Registration of Researchers and Topics.* As a security measure and to ensure that the volume and type of research use of the archives are properly documented, the archivist should record researchers' visits and may request researchers to sign a register of each visit, giving their names, reader's ticket numbers and times of entry and departure.

  Reader's ticket application forms are good sources of information about current clientele, research topics and types of

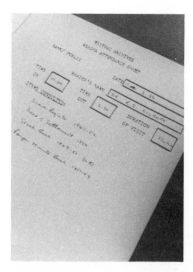

Reader attendance and use records identify client groups and heavily used materials for possible publication.

Table Eight   Conducting a Reference Interview

Topic	Explanation
The Archivist Provides	
1) Access to Archives	Policy relating to access, application for access; conditions and procedures relating to obtaining approval
2) Operation of Archives	Hours of opening, how access to the building or archives is obtained; identity requirements and reproduction policy
3) Use of Finding Aids	Arrangement and use of finding aids and other archival collections that might be of assistance to the researcher
4) Requesting Records	Procedures for obtaining records; how to complete a record request form and length of time generally required to retrieve records
5) Equipment	Equipment available to view records and its operation
6) Layout of Research Area	Floor plan of area with the location of facilities and equipment including rest rooms
The Researcher Provides	
7) Information Needs	Subject of research, scope of investigation i.e. a detailed research project or general information on a topic
8) Purpose of Research	Reason for wanting to obtain access i.e. for the purpose of a publication, educational requirement, personal history
9) Feedback	Completion of questionnaire; use of suggestion box or interview upon completion of research to obtain comments from researchers on services provided

research (thesis, publication, personal) underway. The archivist needs this information to set priorities for future acquisitions and for the processing of new material. Researchers should be assured that the information provided in both documents is used for statistical and planning purposes and is not for public use.

Researchers can also benefit if information about existing research work is shared. Persons working on the same families or on related topics may be brought in contact with each other by voluntarily registering their research topics or interests. The key work here is *voluntarily*, as not all researchers will wish to share their work with others. Those who are willing may complete a card, recording their topic and information on how they may be contacted by others. The card file can then be made available in the reading room.

• *Record Activity and Condition.* As part of the conservation programme, the archivist should review the record request forms to identify high use material which may require conservation or benefit from microfilming to reduce wear and tear. Records awaiting refile should also be checked to detect any conservation problems.

- *Responses to Mail/Telephone Enquiries.* Reference requests should be numbered and coded by type of request (family history, administrative) on receipt so that this information can be easily compiled for statistical purposes. Along with the original request the file should contain the research request worksheet which includes information invaluable for handling follow on or similar requests. Therefore, the archivist may wish to create a special file of cards arranged alphabetically by research topic and record on them the reference request and worksheet numbers so that these documents may be easily retrieved.

Research Aids. Special finding aids may be produced for highly used records on a given subject or in a particular media, such as sources relating to a particular geographical area or oral history tapes held by the organisation. These research aids could be developed by the organisation as part of its finding aids programme, or from the work of researchers using the records, or as part of a special project funded by the organisation. The production of supplementary finding aids is one area where the work of properly trained and supervised volunteers can make a valuable contribution to the archives operations (see Chapter Eleven User Education and Public Relations for further information on volunteer labour).

Researchers may use colour slides of large posters to prevent damage from overhandling of originals.

MINIMISING PROBLEMS

The archivist who assists researchers in using archives has a responsible and rewarding job. But, as in any service provider–client relationship, problems can arise simply because we are dealing with people. Some potential problems can be identified, while others require on–the–spot solutions involving the archivist's reserves of patience, tact and fairness.

You can start by putting yourself in the researcher's shoes: often he/she is in a new environment trying to cope with unfamiliar concepts when he/she starts research in the archives' reading room. This is why it is important that you have brochures and posters explaining your available services; and that the finding aids are logically arranged, well–signposted and physically easy to consult. This is also why the reference interview is such an important mechanism for breaking the ice and establishing rapport between the archivist and the researcher. In general, the more 'take away' information you have explaining your policies and services, the better you will be able to prepare researchers in advance of their visits.

There are some simple ways to reduce potential problems in the reading room. For example, your finding aids should clearly indicate when a copy rather than the original will be issued to the researcher. Always tell researchers how long they are likely to have to wait for their material to be retrieved, especially if it is stored off-site. Any changes to services, such as variations in opening hours, new scales of charges for copying, and especially relocation of the archives, should be publicised as widely as possible. Doing this is good sense and good business, but unfortunately, it will probably not quite eliminate the case of the researcher who travels 500km and arrives on the doorstep during the very week you are moving to another building!

Archivists usually find that the vast majority of researchers are very grateful for the assistance they receive, and that, in turn, they feel encouraged to continue to provide a fair and willing service. Occasionally disagreements or misunderstandings can occur in the reading room. In such cases, it is desirable to take the persons involved to a private setting where the matter can be sorted out without disturbing others. It is also a good idea to have a colleague, preferably a senior person, present during the discussion.

Health crises and other emergencies can also cause problems, and the archives should have effective, well-rehearsed procedures for handling them. Regular training of staff in first aid and emergency treatments is advisable.

During the last few years, there has been a great increase in the use of archives in Australia, particularly by genealogists and people interested in local history. This is a most welcome indication of Australians' growing interest in their own history. However, it has often been a problem for archives which have had to cope with increased demand without a corresponding increase in staff, facilities and equipment. There is no easy solution here, as resources invariably lag behind demand. However, you can anticipate some periods of peak interest. For example, you can note any centenaries and other anniversaries of local or general significance which are coming up, and remember these when you are working out priorities for finding aids.

For some archives, the only way to cope with a rising tide of enquiries and to maintain other archival services at a reasonable level will be to re-examine services to researchers. This decision should be based on a thorough study of the level and efficiency of your current services: for example, can more form letters be used? Can researchers be made more self sufficient using small group rather than individual orientation? Can the reading room hours be reduced based on a study of use patterns? Any reduction in services will usually be unpopular with your researchers. Once again, it is important to give people plenty of warning of the nature of any changes and the reason(s) for them.

Planning your reference services carefully and monitoring their effectiveness will help to minimise problems which arise in

218
CHAPTER SEVEN

providing those services. Add to this a welcoming and professional approach to dealing with people who need your assistance, and you will be well–equipped to deal with the demands of your clientele.

CONCLUSION

The fundamental reason for keeping archives is to enable them to be used. To this end, each archives must design policies and procedures which cater for research while at the same time ensuring the physical protection of the records it holds. The access policy should be clearly explained and properly regulated. Similarly, reference services which support the archives' overall goals must be designed, taking into account both the archives' resources and researchers' needs.

Reference is very much part of the public face of archives — the archivist should always strive to deliver appropriate assistance fairly and efficiently to all his/her researchers. Patterns in the use of archives vary over time, and the archivist has to be prepared to respond to changing types of enquiries and to changing levels of reading room demand. Documenting reference services well, evaluating them regularly, and adjusting them when necessary, will enable the archivist to carry out this important archival function in a truly professional way.

FURTHER READING

Australian Copyright Council, *Copyright Protection in Australia*. Milson's Point, NSW: Australian Copyright Council, 1985.

Australian Copyright Council, *Photocopying in Libraries and Archives*. Milson's Point, NSW : Australian Copyright Council, 1985.

Chalou, George. 'Reference' in Daniels, M.F., and T. Walch, editors, *A Modern Archives Reader : Basic Readings on Archival Theory and Practice*. Washington, DC: National Archives and Records Service, 1984. pp. 257–263.

Freeman, Elsie T., 'In the eye of the beholder : archives administration from the user's point of view', *American Archivist* 47/2 (Spring, 1984): 111–123.

Holbert, Sue, *Archives and Manuscripts : Reference and Access*. Chicago, IL: Society of American Archivists, 1977.

Howse, Janet, 'Access to local government records : the New South Wales situation', *Archives and Manuscripts* 10/2 (December, 1982): 141–148.

Smith, Clive, *An Introduction to Archives and Copyright*. Canberra : Australian Society of Archivists Inc., 1986.

Tissing, Robert W., Jnr., 'The orientation interview in archival research' *American Archivist* 47/2 (Spring, 1984): 173–178.

Walch, Tim, *Archives and Manuscripts : Security*. Chicago, IL: Society of American Archivists, 1977.

Yoxall, Helen, 'Privacy and personal papers', *Archives and Manuscripts*. 12/1 (May, 1984): 38–44.

CHAPTER EIGHT

CONSERVATION

Michael Piggott

INTRODUCTION

The belief of this volume's authors, and indeed of archivists throughout the world, is that a concern for conservation is central to the true responsibilities of the archivist. To ignore the matter is to be professionally negligent. There can be no compromise on this point, and not even a shortage of resources can excuse a lack of concern for conservation. As will be argued below, there are a large number of areas where the conscientious archivist can effect improvements and institute self–help programmes. Such hard–line sentiments must apply regardless of whether one administers single–handedly a small archival service within an historical society or one is among several hundred archivists in a huge organisation devoted solely to archival work.

The principle that the archivist must accept responsibility for conservation derives from a cause -and–effect logic which is difficult to dispute. Without properly preserved records, all other archival activities are negated. When the material in one's care is allowed to deteriorate unchecked or become damaged in any way, it is difficult and may be ultimately impossible to make it or the information it embodies available for use. Thus, the primary place of conservation is acknowledged in the classics of archival literature for the English speaking world, written by Sir Hilary Jenkinson and Dr. T.R. Schellenberg. Jenkinson in particular argued that the 'physical defence of archives' was one of the primary duties of the archivist. This view has never been superseded, and in recent archival manuals of equivalent general scope, such as that by the British archivist Michael Cook, conservation is presented as having central importance for the archivist. Practically every issue of the archival journal literature now includes articles on conservation and technical notes on new procedures, techniques and equipment.

Additional to stressing conservation as the archivist's responsibility, it is equally important to emphasise that virtually every archival function has a conservation aspect. Quite deliberately, other chapters have pointed to the conservation element in processes which can either endanger or contribute to the protection of one's records. Whether one is selecting shelving materials, formulating accessioning procedures, or enforcing reading room rules, the immediate and long term implications for conservation must be at the forefront of the mind. If readers retain only one point from this chapter, we hope it would be that the archivist's first responsibility is the archives and that, potentially, much of one's work has implications for their safety and longevity.

Archivists are not alone in their concern for the physical well-being of culturally important historical material. Other professions adopt a similiar stance. To varying degrees, librarians and curators in museums, libraries and galleries work for the protection and preservation of their holdings. What, then, is the role of the professional conservator and of the materials scientists, conservation technicians and craftsmen with whom the conservator may be grouped? In the archival context at least, the role of the conservator involves the more technical, scientific and manipulative aspects of both preventative and restorative conservation. The conservator's relationship with the archivist is a co-operative one in which the many challenges of conservation work are shared. In an organisation which employs both archivists and conservators, each specialist adopts separate, though complementary, duties. The degree of overlap becomes clear once the principal duties of each are elaborated.

RESPONSIBILITIES OF THE ARCHIVIST

1) **Resources/Storage.** Includes the difficult task of obtaining approval and funds to build secure housing for the archives which provides appropriate conditions. In conjunction with the conservator, the archivist contributes to the design and location of new buildings and the adaptation, renovation or extension of existing accommodation.

2) **Handling.** Involves tasks such as establishing procedures covering the handling and use of the archives, the aim being to ensure they are secure and their deterioration is minimised. The effort here is directed at archives staff (i.e. archivists, exhibition staff and conservation staff), public researchers and others such as contract workers and volunteers.

3) **Priorities.** Covers aspects like identifying the most important parts of the archival holdings for the purposes of disaster evacuation, for high security storage and for intensive restoration. Material warranting copying and exhibition must

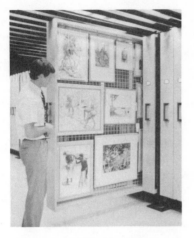

Sliding racks provide efficient, safe storage for framed materials.

also be identified, along with the priority ratings relevant to each item.

4) **Surveys.** The archivist knows the content of the archives not only in terms of its origin, historical and administrative value and subject coverage, but also its physical make–up and conservation needs. Towards this end, the archivist authorises surveys of storage environment, procedures and items within the survey. Surveys themselves, which often involve sampling techniques, are actually conducted by conservators.

RESPONSIBILITIES OF THE CONSERVATOR

1) **Technical advice.** Assist the archives management function by providing technical advice regarding design of buildings, equipment purchases, the environment of archival storage and exhibition areas, not to mention the conservation workshop and specifications for copying projects.

2) **Conservation workshop.** Establish a successfully operating workshop and allied facilities such as fumigation plant and bindery, including procedures, practices, equipment and supplies.

3) **Restoration.** Advise on the choices, including costs and advantages/disadvantages regarding intensive item by item conservation treatment; undertake research; assist with specifications covering restoration undertaken outside the archives by commercial conservators.

4) **Awareness training.** Foster a consciousness among both staff working directly with material and management personnel; provide training in handling and in basic techniques for processing, exhibition and records retrieval staff.

The size of archival services varies considerably and most programmes will have neither the staff numbers to employ trained conservators nor the means to provide them with a workshop, equipment and supplies. At times, this regrettable reality is compounded by the presence of a large and growing collection with many records in poor condition, housed in inadequate conditions, and subject to heavy user pressure. All too often when an archives service is first established by a company, association or school for example, the archivist may be expected to perform all archival functions with an inherited, decaying basement full of records. Here, conservation is only one among many problems to be faced. In such circumstances, funds must be sought to allow at least the use of an outside commercial service for major emergency work while proper plans and longer range solutions are devised. The happy, if less common, alternative picture is that of an archivist joining a long established organisation which has its own fully equipped conservation department. Yet, even here, the conservation challenge can be daunting once thorough surveys reveal the exact nature and full extent of the conservation problems. The most effective way in which to respond is to divide conservation into two major operations:

- planning/administration
- programmes.

The most important issues to be faced in each approach will be outlined and discussed in the remainder of the chapter.

CONSERVATION PLANNING AND ADMINISTRATION

The most sensible approach the archivist can adopt towards the conservation challenge is to calmly begin to prepare plans which will systematically identify and lessen the causes of deterioration. This gives focus to one's thinking, a structure to one's administration and a sound basis on which to establish conservation programmes. Plans covering surveys of conservation needs, disaster prevention and recovery, and the work area/ laboratory must be prepared. The provisions of each plan should outline procedures for monitoring and periodically updating the plan. Training, on the other hand, requires continuing rather than intermittent attention and administration. But before proceeding with any training scheme, the archivist should come to a decision about the overall scope of the conservation programme.

Determining the Scope and Focus of a Conservation Programme

To a certain extent, there will be aspects unique to the conservation problems facing each archives service. In determining how best to manage these problems, the archivist should consider the following factors:

1) **Type and size of holdings.** The scale and sophistication of your conservation programme will depend largely on the variety and amount of material held. In Australia, the typical archives is small — for example, a school archives, an historical society collection, or a regional college or library's local history collection. Such archives usually comprise paper–based records, and a conservation plan which concentrates on an environment appropriate for paper preservation is essential. Here a single room workshop would be adequate if combined with a policy of obtaining specialist help in dealing with non–paper items. The vast and varied holdings of state and national institutions will of course warrant large staffs and specialist conservation laboratories.

2) **Type of institution.** If the archives forms part of a public institution which includes large public galleries and which strongly emphasises the importance of displays, the archivist may decide to direct conservation priorities towards

A workshop on simple paper and binding repairs increases staff awareness of conservation.

ensuring that exhibition items and gallery environments are safe. It is important to be aware of any conservation references in the legislation, constitution, statement of purpose or similar document of the archives' parent authority. Some public institutions for example are governed by statutes which include specific directions concerning conservation.

3) **Type of use.** The type and nature of research use of an archives' holdings clearly have repercusssions for conservation. If genealogists form a large proportion of one's readers, the thrust of the conservation effort will be the protection of those record series in constant demand. Rules withholding originals, and programmes for copying them, are common responses to this type of use.

4) **Geographical location.** Archives sited in basements, in heavily industrialised areas, near rivers known to flood, on fault lines, or in cyclone zones, are areas obviously 'at risk'. Accordingly, the archivist might devote early attention to air filtration and disaster minimisation and recovery plans.

5) **Co-operation and outside assistance.** The archivist must investigate the possibility of obtaining assistance from regional conservation centres, conservation schools and freelance or expert consultants. Particularly in a small institution where funds are limited, it is more economical to hire conservation assistance as needed than to employ a full-time specialist. The possibility of sharing resources with other institutions (libraries, museums and other archives) should also be investigated; facilities such as fumigation chambers and nitrate film vaults, which require very large capital outlays to construct, naturally fall into this category.

Once the parameters of one's particular approach have been established, plans must be prepared to survey the holdings and existing procedures, to establish priorities for action, to train staff and to anticipate and recover from disasters. Each warrants some further attention.

Conducting the Conservation Survey

In addition to the broadly defined factors noted above which should be taken into account when determining the scope and focus of the archives' conservation programme, a detailed knowledge of the total conservation 'picture' is needed. Informed judgements about the appropriate conservation solutions can be made only after the details are known of the physical composition and condition of the records and their environment, of the conservation 'soundness' of existing procedures for holdings, storage and use, and of conservation plans already drafted.

The most popular method of obtaining this information is the conservation survey. Some are designed to obtain an overview of conservation needs, while others centre on a particular aspect such as shelving or aim at the gathering of detailed information on the physical stability of the records. When large collections are involved, sampling techniques or teams of volunteers or student conservators may be employed to conduct such surveys under the direction of a conservator. Archivists should be alert to the potential dangers of sampling error, of inconsistency and subjectivity, and of aimlessly amassing vast quantities of statistics about the records. An example of the headings under which survey information is gathered is listed in Table One:

Pigeon hole shelving causes damage to unsupported file folders.

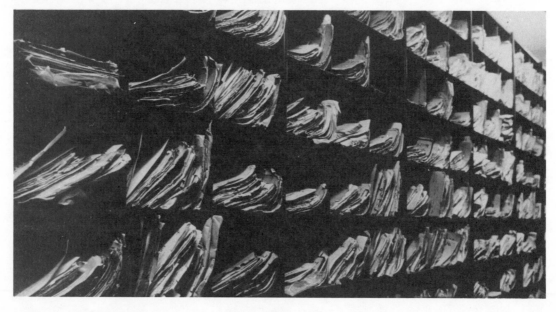

Basic supplies for cleaning and humidifying documents for flattening.

Table One   The Conservation Survey

Some Data Headings
1) Preliminary (date of survey, name of surveyor, etc.)
2) Type of item inspected (file, volume, map, etc.)
3) Shelf location of item inspected
4) Extraneous or interleaved material (staples, tissue paper, loose cuttings, photographs, etc.)
5) Primary protection (binding, folder/jacket, envelope)
6) Condition of primary protection (torn, spine split, warping, torn sewing, etc.)
7) Condition of paper (foxing, brittle, mould, etc.)
8) Suggested repair (phase box, rebind, withdraw from use, deacidify, etc.)
9) Priority (assessed in conjunction with archivist — eradicate mould urgently, prepare for exhibition, leave until additional staff, etc.)

Organising a Conservation Work Area

One of the many decisions which may flow from the survey and, indeed, from an overall assessment of the archives' conservation needs is that to establish a conservation work area. Obviously such a step assumes that space and resources are available to equip and staff a work area. In cases where the archivist is neither able to employ professional conservators nor likely to be contracting with specialists for extensive in-house work, the work area will be small, simply equipped and staffed part-time by archivists and/or volunteers. However, even a small conservation work area should be designed with further expansion in mind. The possibility of providing work experience for archives, library or conservation students should also be taken into account when assessing space needs. At the other end of the scale, one may expect to see a fully equipped conservation complex incorporating laboratories and work areas designed for the separate treatment of particular materials, a bindery, sound studio, dark room and fumigation plant. Timothy Walsh's article 'A typical archival conservation laboratory' (*Archives and Manuscripts*, 7(5), Nov. 1979: 268-275) provides an excellent description of the main features of the type of large conservation laboratory established during the 1970's by Australian Archives.

Irrespective of size and location, the conservation work area should be secure from forced entry, have facilities for plumbing and electricity and be lit in a manner which does not harm the items under treatment. Naturally, the precise features in a work area will vary depending on the type of work planned and the main types of material being treated. Even the smallest archives will include at least paper records, leather bound volumes, photographs of various types, and probably large flat items such as maps. Their elementary treatment in a work area would require workbenches, tables, light boxes, sinks and good lighting. A basically equipped work area can be set up in a single room, or even, if necessary, in one corner of a room. Equipment and supplies too will vary according to the type of materials being worked on and the nature of the treatments undertaken. Checklists of some basic items of equipment and supplies appear in much of the conservation literature. The Institute for the Conservation of Cultural Materials Inc. (ICCM), the Australian Society of Archivists Inc. (ASA), and the Museums Association of Australia (MAA) prepare up to date lists of suppliers of conservation materials in Australia. The addresses of their national offices appear at the end of this chapter.

The precise layout of a work area, including the location of equipment, stores and furniture, remains a joint decision for the archivist and the conservator. Efficient layout will usually be achieved when it reflects both the work flow and safety requirements. Those needing access to one or two suggested layouts for different sized work areas should consult the publications of, for example, John Davies, cited at the end of this chapter.

Strictly enforced rules should govern the operation of the work area. To minimise the chances of accidents and to discourage vermin, eating, drinking and smoking are prohibited and work benches, equipment and floors cleaned regularly. Emergencies and disasters should be anticipated by the preparation and prac-

Mobile rack keeps conservation supplies accessible and in good order. Courtesy — Council of the City of Sydney Archives.

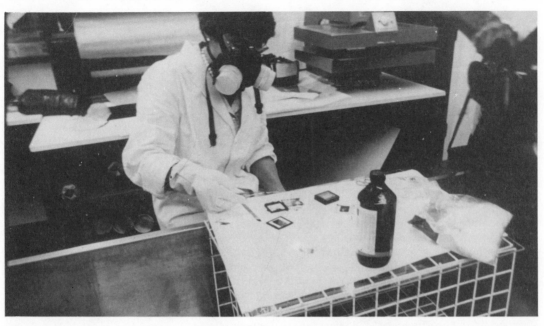

The solvents used in conservation work are hazardous and require protective clothing, equipment and special ventilation.

tice of disaster plans and first aid training. The presence in the work area not only of chemicals, water and extremely sharp instruments, but also of precious items from the archives underlines the serious need for this preparedness.

In parallel with the development of a conservation work area, no matter how small, the archivist should establish a basic conservation library. The number of manuals, texts and journal articles on conservation is vast; the bibliographies accompanying George and Dorothy Cunha's two books comprise over ten thousand entries and yet cover only English language works! In both titles, a list of recommended reading is provided. Several important conservation texts, in addition to the most recent by the Cunhas, which might form the beginnings of a work area library, appear at the end of this chapter.

Training

To undertake specialised repair restoration and preservation research, ideally one should employ professionally qualified conservators. The only general conservation course available in Australia is that offered by the Canberra College of Advanced Education School of Applied Science, where a Diploma and Masters degree course in materials conservation was established in 1978. To staff large conservation facilities, the ideal of a conservation staff with proven research and planning abilities and extensive experience should be pursued.

Small archives, where even the employment of a single professional conservator is sometimes impossible, may be forced to rely on their own staff or even volunteers to undertake basic repair work. Chapter Eleven, User Education and Public Relations deals in part with the issues surrounding the use of volunteers in archives. Here it need only be stressed again that volunteers should be carefully supervised or directed by a qualified conservator, one employed on contract if necessary. Archivists with the Diploma in Information Management — Archives Administration (University of New South Wales) will have received elementary training in simple and well–established techniques for the preservation and repair of textual records. Others will have acquired some knowledge through workshops and short courses run by the University of New South Wales School of Librarianship and by ICCM, the ASA and the Library Association of Australia.

If your archives is fortunate enough to be located near one of the tertiary institutions offering courses of study in museums, library, archives or conservation administration, there is the prospect of establishing a continuing relationship with these courses. Thus groups of students could work on your conservation problems, over time bringing continuity to the effort and enabling larger tasks to be undertaken. However, such outside help must supplement, not substitute for, your own conservation effort.

DISASTER CONTAINMENT

Irrespective of an archives' size, location and age, the materials it houses can, and almost certainly will, suffer from disasters. Fire and water are the common agents, the innumerable causes of which include faulty wiring, burst waterpipes, incorrectly stored flammable cleaning agents, blocked drains and guttering, leaky roofs, improperly done repairs or installations, carelessness of outside workers, cyclones, smoking, nitrate film in the holdings and water damage from sprinklers. Other categories of disasters are theft, vandalism, flooding and earthquakes.

Never think that a disaster won't happen in your archives — it is crucial in fact that you think the opposite. With a deliberately fatalistic mentality, one should approach the near certainty of disaster by:

- identifying as many hazards as possible which could endanger the archives
- adopting measures to reduce their likelihood
- preparing and periodically testing and updating a disaster recovery plan.

What does each involve?

1) **Identifying risk factors.** The potential sources of disasters can be subdivided into several categories. The archives building itself, its nature, age and foibles, is probably the most easily overlooked source of risk. Get to know the buildings' weaknesses, the vulnerable points, particularly if the archives is situated in a basement or on the top floor where

Magnetic media should be protected from metal and magnetism. Carbon dioxide extinguishers are preferred over water or chemical foam which can damage records.

the roof, guttering and air conditioning installations can cause problems. Externally located plumbing, for example, may freeze in winter and pipes located on the ceiling and along walls in stack areas are another source of danger. Electrical wiring and the heating system, especially if radiators are involved, are potential danger points of different kinds. Remember too that fire and water damage can easily occur during alterations or extensions to buildings. The site of the building may also put the records at risk, especially if it occupies part of a flood plain, earthquake zone or flight path or is located near substantial underground sewerage, water or gas distribution systems.

Having analysed the risks of the 'housing', look within at what it holds. Flammable supplies and materials have already been mentioned — detergents, chemicals and the like. But note too that some furnishings and drapery can be dangerously combustible, and within the archives' holdings there may lurk potential dangers, the most serious being nitrate film and/or photographic negatives which are inherently unstable and will ultimately decompose, sometimes by self combustion.

2) **Reducing the risks.** Once potential sources of danger have been identified, take steps to prevent each from developing and to minimise the damage if it does lead to disaster. At least four major areas of attention are involved. The most valuable parts of the records need to be identified and stored in the safest location. Electrical wiring and gas/plumbing pipes should have regular maintenance checks. Effective security procedures, covering inside and outside the archives, must be established. Moisture and heat detection systems should be installed to alert you of fire and flood. In the case of fire suppression, the choices are between none at all (relying on detection and the fire brigade and hand extinguishers), water sprinklers and gas based extinguishers. Remember that both the later options have the potential to initiate disasters of their own. Expert advice, particularly from local fire authorities, should be sought in deciding which system to adopt, although cost will probably be the final arbiter.

Reducing the chances of fire and water disasters goes well beyond detection. Each of the four aspects covered above will contribute, when spelt out as detailed measures. Effective security procedures, for instance, would include rules prohibiting staff smoking in work areas. Besides them, however, are many other steps which you should consider:
• choose storage boxes which are highly water absorbent
• install shelving which has a bottom shelf at least 10 centimetres off the floor in case of only slight flooding

- copy nitrate film and store the originals in properly designed vaults

3) **The disaster recovery plan.** Disasters may be inevitable, but a well–thought–out recovery plan will minimise their effects. Such plans include procedures for organising personnel, lists of key staff (including after hours telephone numbers), the location of building plans, keys, the stack areas, and the sources of emergency services, equipment and outside help. The immediate availability of cold storage and, ideally, freeze drying facilities are crucial for the recovery of records damaged by water, be it from sprinklers or firemen's hoses. Mould will begin to grow within 48 hours on wet or damp paper records, unless the temperature can be initially set at -7^0C. A successful recovery plan also covers staff training in emergency procedures, including first aid. The plan should also stress the necessity of keeping detailed records of recovery measures taken (not least for insurance purposes) and the importance of classifying the collection into categories of relative importance. To reduce the damage from a disaster, as we noted earlier, the most valuable items must be stored in the safest location; alloting an importance measure to the records also guides staff if the holdings have to be evacuated.

Table Two   Disasters : Prevention, Minimisation, Recovery

---

1) **Identify and Limit the Risks**
   Location
   - Keep the archives away from areas of potential danger
   Building and Grounds
   - Remove and/or minimise all sources of damage

2) **Develop and Maintain Information and Supplies**
   Identify key personnel
   - Get 24 hour phone numbers and addresses
   Compile and maintain up–to–date information about
   - Your own facility
   - Community emergency services
   - Resources, people, facilities you can use in emergencies
   Identifying holdings of differing 'values' for salvage
   Plan/Arrange for continuation of services
   - External personnel
   - External facilities and services
   Develop and Communicate Plans

3) **Maintain, update, communicate and test all parts of Section 2) at regular intervals**

A comprehensive list of points to cover in a recovery plan is included in the work by Upton and Pearson, cited at the end of this chapter. Waters' publication is also valuable, although it is confined to disasters resulting from water. The point to stress here is that you have a disaster plan, that you communicate it to all appropriate personnel, and that you rehearse it regularly.

> 'The frequency and variety of disasters is awesome. No one, even those in new buildings of modern construction, is completely safe from these unwanted natural or man–made misfortunes ... The requirement then is to benefit from the experiences of those who have had such calamities and plan accordingly.' George and Dorothy Cunha, *Library and Archives Conservation: 1980's and Beyond.* Volume 1. Metuchen, NJ: Scarecrow Press, 1983. p.79.

CONSERVATION PROGRAMME FUNCTIONS

Having established a work area and prepared for disasters and disaster recovery, the archivist will need to make decisions about his/her continuing conservation programme. Measures will fall into three functional areas, namely those designed:
- to prevent further deterioration of one's holdings
- to repair or restore broken or decayed items
- to preserve by copying the information content in the records

All three functions are most commonly found in continuous operation in the medium to large size archives, although all manner of archival services should consider establishing them. In the remainder of the chapter, the distinctive features of each sub–programme are outlined.

PREVENTATIVE CONSERVATION

The idea of taking steps to prevent an undesired future event is common to many spheres of life, from medicine to motor maintenance. In conservation, this approach seeks to combat the known causes of physical deterioration and to lessen or slow their effects. Disaster recovery planning is an excellent specific application of the preventative approach.

Two stages are always involved in the application of the preventative programme:
- the identification of the sources of the deterioration
- their frustration through appropriately designed environments, procedures and treatments

Identification of the sources of deterioration should be part and parcel of both one's conservation survey and the disaster recovery planning process. Disasters aside, what are some of the less obvious and less dramatic causes of deterioration?

1)   **Inherent weaknesses in the records**
     In even a small archives, records comprise many different
     types of material, either individual or in combination. An old
     minute book, for example, may be constructed of five or six
     different materials (paper, leather, adhesive, cloth, ink, gold
     leaf, etc.). Even correspondence files will include a good
     mix of different paper types, inks, and fasteners, while
     scrapbooks can contain postcards, newspaper cuttings,
     photographs, parchment certificates, drawings and even
     artefacts such as pressed flowers and metal hat badges.

     No material in an archives is completely stable or durable;
     in fact, all records have constituents which deteriorate or
     will combine with agents in the air to encourage deterio-
     ration. The archivist should be aware of each material held
     and should have a general idea of its inherent causes for
     weakening. Detailed information can be obtained in the
     literature and is, in any case, the forte of the specialist con-
     servator. The main points to remember about each medium's
     composition are provided in Swartzburg's book particularly,
     but also in the other recommended reading. It behoves all
     but the specialist audio–visual archivist to get to know one
     medium especially well, i.e. paper.

     The shorter fibres and inherent impurities in wood pulp,
     the material from which most paper since about 1850 has
     been derived, combined with the processes and chemicals
     used in paper manufacture, have resulted in papers prone to
     deterioration. Ingredients in inks and the presence of heat,
     light, moisture and atmospheric pollutants cause or aggra-
     vate a chemical acidity in the paper which eventually
     destroys it. The archivist's problem then becomes one of
     stopping or severely retarding this destruction, a problem
     which is worsened because most archives in Australia — the
     diaries, registers, correspondence, maps, photographs and
     scrapbooks etc. — are recorded on this unstable paper.
     Ironically, paper made hundreds of years ago from rags and
     bleached by natural processes is in much better condition
     than paper manufactured twenty years ago.

     Sample surveys for acidity should be made to gauge the
     extent of this problem, using one of the commercially avail-
     able acidity testing kits. As for remedying the problem, fil-
     tration systems should deal satisfactorily with air pollution,
     although the cost may be beyond the resources of small
     archives. Regarding deacidification of the archives, tech-
     niques to treat them en masse are also very expensive and
     still being developed. Aqueous and non–aqueous
     deacidification methods, on the other hand, focus on the
     individual item. More modest yet still effective alternative
     methods of retarding the spread of acidity are available. The

These letters were both written in 1864. The one on rag fibre paper is still in good condition; the other, on cheap ruled paper, is very brown from acid.

use of acid free storage folders, boxes and insert sheets are especially recommended because they discourage the tendency of acid to 'migrate'. Without chemically neutral or slightly alkaline buffers, highly acidic papers will rapidly worsen items filed next to them.

2) **The quality of the storage environment**

The environment in which records are stored is critical to their preservation. Temperature, relative humidity, lighting and air purity and circulation are the principal determinants. The recommended levels for the temperature and relative humidity for the main record types are listed in Table Three. If not maintained at the correct standard, each factor, singly or in combination, can cause considerable harm. Endeavours must be made to obtain the approved levels and to regularly monitor them using commercially available meters such as hydrothermographs. Concerning the main influences on storage environment, the following points should be remembered:

Temperature and relative humidity

- Incorrect levels speed up damaging chemical reactions in material, encouraging mould, acidity, shrinking and brittleness
- Short term fluctuations, called cycling, must be avoided at all costs, especially daily fluctuations

- Air conditioning plant can help control the temperature and humidity; install away from roofs, collections and any areas which may be damaged by flooding; ensure reliable maintenance

Air circulation

- Pockets of stagnant air must be avoided, as they can encourage mould growth
- Ventilation is critical depending on the material stored; nitrate film vaults for example must have excellent ventilation.

Dust

- Dust will abrade and thus damage material such as photographs in envelopes, volumes in slip cases, sound records played by styli, etc.
- A mechanical filtration system installed with air conditioning plant, and regular cleaning of floors, window sills, etc. will help reduce dust levels in storage areas
- Avoid electrostatic filters, because they produce ozone, which is harmful to records by encouraging embrittlement

Pollutants

- Air impurities, particularly those arising from industrial sources such as sulphur dioxide, will encourage paper to deteriorate
- An adsorption system attached to an air conditioning system should remove most gaseous pollutants; ensure reliable maintenance

Light

- Keep to a minimum in storage areas by avoiding natural light (i.e. no windows if possible) and the use of light timers and ultraviolet sleeves on fluorescent tubes
- Light damages particularly paper records, causing fading, discolouration, embrittlement through oxidation etc.

3) **Storage Equipment**

The choice of equipment on which to shelve and in which to store archives provides the archivist with an excellent opportunity to minimise further deterioration. Regardless of how good is the storage environment, badly shelved and housed archives can deteriorate if allowed to go unchecked. The archivist establishing an archives service from scratch is in the ideal position of being able to specify optimum equipment. More commonly, one inherits existing shelving, boxes and filing cabinets. The ideal to which all should aim is one which incorporates:

- Baked enamel metal shelving and cabinets with the lowest shelf or drawer at least 10 centimetres off the floor to avoid water damage in a small flood. If wooden shelves and cabinets are unavoidable, one should insist on wood which has been sealed with several coats of a varnish such as polyurethane

- ✓ • Boxes, folders, jackets, envelopes, spools and cans which are non–acidic and/or chemically inert. For some types of photographs, acid–free paper envelopes are to be preferred but these must not be excessively alkaline
- ✓ • Material which is neither too tightly nor too loosely packed in boxes; microfilm, magnetic tapes and cinefilm must be neither loosely nor too tightly wound
- ✓ • Material which is stored in a manner which best supports and places the least stress on individual items, i.e. either horizontally or vertically as appropriate.

There is a large literature devoted to the specific standards appropriate to the storage of many different types of materials found in archives. Particularly if faced with over–sized paper materials such as sheet maps and plans, or audio–visual or machine–readable archives, the archivist must become well acquainted with the specialised storage systems these materials require.

Table Three   Ideal Environment According to Type of Material

Material	Temperature	Relative Humidity	Storage
Paper	20°C	55%	Baked enamel steel shelves or cabinets; boxes, folders, etc., non–acidic
Animal skins	10–20°C	45–55%	Baked enamel steel shelves or cabinets; boxes, folders, etc., non–acidic
Photographs General	20°C	35–40%	Individually store in chemically neutral, seamless envelopes
Colour	− 18°C	25–35%	Refrigerate; individual storage in moisture proof plastic packets
Microfilm	20°C	<40%	Shelve vertically; boxes/reels, non–ferrous metal or inert
Nitrate	<10°C	30–40%	Purpose–built vaults; shelve horizontally
Discs, tapes	18°C	35–45%	Shelve vertically in dust proof envelopes

NB
- Details are summary figures/points which do not cover special types of materials (e.g. albumen photograph prints), and do not distinguish between staff and storage areas (except for colour photographs) or between conditions for preservation copies and working copies
- Avoid temperature and humidity extremes
- Avoid fluctuations in temperature and humidity, especially daily changes
- Compromise levels for combined media archives, for staff comfort and collection safety, are 18–20°C and 45–49% R.H.

A hand-made acid-free folder for manuscripts.

Use standard sized containers suited to the types of records held.

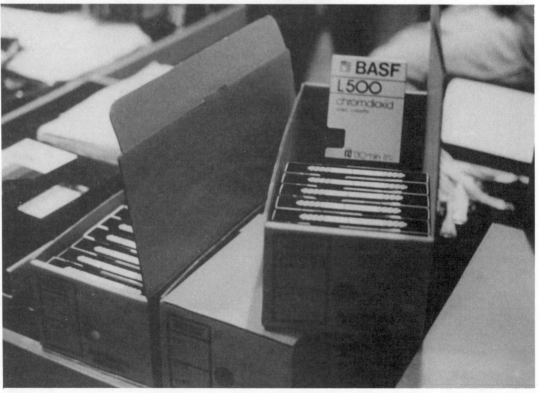

The acid in the cardboard cover (left) of this portrait has migrated through the protective tissue to etch a reverse image of the photograph.

In general, proper storage must be purchased and vendors should be presented with written specifications to guarantee quality and recompense if standards are not met. Accept that equipment will be expensive and budget accordingly; cheaper, poor quality items are a bad investment as they can cause damage which may be irreparable. In recent years, techniques have been developed permitting at least one type of storage method to be produced in-house, although they can be applied by vendors to your specifications. This approach involves such practices as the wrapping of volumes in stout acid-free paper, or the construction of a box using pliable acid-free board into which the volumes fit exactly. Known by such names as phase boxes, solander boxes, clam shells, wrap arounds, Kyle Wrappers and four flap portfolios, the boxes are basically holding measures which prevent deterioration from handling and provide good protection from light and water. There are many conservation texts which include instructions on their production, including those by Ritzenthaler, Morrow and Greenfield listed in the recommended reading at the end of the chapter.

4) **Biological Agents**

Mould spores, insects and pests are among the biological agents of deterioration in archives. Stagnant air and high temperatures and humidity levels are most conducive to the growth of mould and mildew. The component substances of records such as paper glue, leather, gelatin and cloth are not only the favourite foods of vegetable pests such as moulds, but they are highly edible to rats, mice, silverfish, woodlice, bookworms, termites and cockroaches. As in so many other instances, effective preventative measures must be predicated on regular monitoring of the archives' physical state. Of the common approaches to the problem of biological agents, the most passive is the strict enforcement of in-house rules banning food consumption to minimise the encouragement of cockroaches, rats and mice. Laying poisonous pellets should also be considered, once infestation is known to have occurred. Proper attention to temperature and humidity control and to the use of fungicides and insecticides should also help bring mould and smaller insects under control. The periodic fumigation of the physical facilities, especially storage areas, is also practised in archives, and varies in scale of operation and chemicals used.

As for the destruction of mould and other infestations in incoming records, the whole subject is one which should be treated with caution. Cost is one reason; only the very large institutions can afford vacuum fumigation chambers, and even they are rethinking the value of in-house treatments because of the health risks now understood to be associated with traditional fumigants such as ethylene oxide and thymol. The safest approach for small archives is to seek the co-operation of nearby larger libraries, archives and museums. Alternatively, commercial sterilisation organisations which serve the food and medical industries might be approached, but the archivist must be completely satisfied

A small, air-tight cabinet can be used for fumigation provided strict safety requirements are met.

with their reputation and skill in matching an infestation with the appropriate chemical. Be certain too that the records will not be harmed by the chemicals used; photographs, for instance, should never be fumigated. A final alternative approved by some conservators is to build your own small fumigation plant using thymol. There are serious potential health risks involved however, and this fumigation is useful primarily in inhibiting mould from appearing after papers have become water damaged.

5) **Human Factors**

The archivist should never overlook the fact that humans are potentially among the greatest enemies of archives. Harm can be caused directly through theft and vandalism, as was noted in our discussion of disaster management, but the incorrect handling of material whether by archives staff or public researchers, is the most common cause of human damage. No one, for example, should work on archival material while smoking, eating, or drinking. Accidents with cigarettes, food or drink can directly harm records, can attract vermin, and can present reading room rules in a hypocritical light. Fountain pens and biros too should be banned, as leaks, smears and blotches have the potential to permanently deface material. Hands should always be clean when working with records too, and when especially sensitive materials such as discs or photographs are being worked on, cotton gloves should be worn to minimise contamination by skin oils. For similar reasons, never lick your fingers when handling paper records.

6) **Exhibitions**

Well designed displays of record items can greatly improve the public's understanding of the archives. They may stimulate donations and they are excellent vehicles for explaining aspects of the history of a region, school, company, government or people. With preventative conservation in mind, it must also be said that nothing more stimulates the archivist to break, albeit unwittingly, all the tenets of conservation than the mounting of an exhibition.

Exhibition design and administration is a large subject, particularly in the museum studies field; there is a growing recognition in archives, too, of their complexities and potential hazards. In the introductory context of this chapter, it must suffice to emphasise that no items from the archives should be endangered in any way by their display. From the conservation viewpoint, it is preferred that the exhibition of originals be avoided and facsimile copies substituted, with each being clearly identified with captions. If originals must be displayed, the following requirements should be satisfied.

- *Lighting.* Exhibition illumination should be no stronger than 50 lux, be free of ultra–violet rays (definitely not sunlight) and be from a source which does not jeopardise the temperature levels of the display environment. If fluorescent tubes are used, they must be covered by ultra–violet filtering sleeves. Regularly monitor the light level in display cases and never leave an original item on display indefinitely. Fading and yellowing, it is worth remembering, are irreversible and incorrect lighting is the major cause of both.
- *Micro–Climate.* The display case, sealed securely from the potential thieves among the viewing public, has its own 'micro–climate' — in effect, a pocket of air quite different from the larger body of air surrounding it. The temperature and relative humidity of the micro–climate in which original record items are displayed, should be equivalent to that in the storage areas. Both the temperature and relative humidity of the display case's micro–climate should be regularly monitored.
- *Duration of Display.* Original record items should not be displayed for more than two or three months, regardless of the lighting used in displays. If permanent exhibitions are planned, prepare replacement items and captions, better still, display appropriately captioned facsimiles.
- *Security.* To guard against theft, the originals should be laid out in locked display cases and the gallery areas supervised by security attendants.

A conservator explains how to mount material for exhibition.

- *Item Support.* Individual documents, letters, etc. will usually be displayed lying flat or raised to enhance their comprehension by the public. It should hardly be necessary to add that if items are displayed vertically, this should not be done in a manner which is stressful. Pins, for example, should never be used on the item being displayed. Open volumes such as a diary or scrapbook should be supported by a cradle or incline and, alluding to our warning about lighting, their pages turned every two or three months. The manual by Casterline, cited in the recommended reading, covers simple methods of making display supports.

7) **A Little Knowledge is a Dangerous Thing**

Our final point about preventative conservation is a warning about an attitude of mind which really applies to the entire subject of conservation. The archivist's incomplete knowledge, inattention or eagerness to 'do something' can promote deterioration. To return to our medical analogy of preventative medicine, the cure must not be worse than the disease, and it must never endanger the 'patient's' life. In short, your attempts to better conserve your archives must not cause further harm. Thus, to house photographs in adhesive photo albums of the kind sold by stationers and chemists can result in badly damaged prints because the polyvinylchloride many incorporate degrades and emits harmful gases. The writing on a document may be ruined when soaked in a water-based rather than solvent-based deacidifying solution, unless the item has been first tested for ink solubility. Alternatively, the installation of an air-conditioning plant to control temperatures and humidity may be partially self-defeating. The archivist may fail to notice pockets of stagnant air due to poor circulation, or deliberately cause fluctuations in both temperature and humidity by turning off the plant at night and on weekends to save money. All actions must be thought through, in other words. The archivist/conservator is ultimately at risk too if one is not cautious; the ill-advised use of fumigants or solvents to remove mould or 'sticky' tape are two common dangers. The sensible archivist plans ahead, obtains proper advice, and sees that good ventilation, wash-up facilities and emergency procedures are in place.

RESTORATIVE CONSERVATION

Restorative conservation is the natural corollary to the preventative measures the archivist institutes to reduce further conservation problems. It has been described as 'the active, healing treatment' of an item's 'physical substance' and more succinctly as 'micro-conservation'. Restorative conservation often involves a highly technical mix of scientific and craft skills. In this area of conservation, the division of tasks between the conservator and the archivist is clear and permits few exceptions. Treatments such as the restoration of leather bound volumes, the mending of very brittle, very thin papers, the removal of stains and the repair of broken plate glass photographic negatives and broken shellac gramophone recordings must be left to the expert conservator. What may appear the easy or obvious solution to the archivist is almost always not the case. Ignorant eagerness can cause further harm to an item already in need of repair.

In addition to this 'surgery', it is the conservator who decides such issues as the urgency of repair, the nature and rate of deterioration of an item or series of records, the alternative treatments and the extent to which they are to be applied. The archivist nevertheless plays a most important role. Archives mainly comprise unique materials which in an earlier chapter we have argued is one of the key differences from library materials. We have also explained that to become archives, the archivist judges on the basis of specific criteria that their selection for indefinite retention is justified. Without vast resources for conservation, however, the separate items which make up archives can not all be individually treated by the conservator. Thus the archivist must decide, on the basis of historical value, research potential and available resources, which items should be urgently singled out for intensive, VIP treatment and of the alternative treatments established by the conservator, which can be justified financially. Specifying such priorities also involves a judgement that the remaining records, the vast majority, shall be left to slowly deteriorate on the shelves. But, we must quickly add, left to the protection of phase boxes, good environment and other measures of preventative conservation.

Surface cleaning of records requires a light touch and care to remove all fragments of both dirt and cleaner.

'National treasures' and their equivalents in companies, schools, State and other archives are some of the most common items accorded intensive restoration. The journal kept by Captain James Cook on his first voyage to Australia, the United States Declaration of Independence and Great Britain's Domesday Book are typical national examples. The original copies of constitutions, surrender documents, treaties and documents of foundation or award are others of lesser scale. The display of such items, so often prompted by their historical significance, adds another reason for their restoration.

The archivist is also closely involved in restoration when repair may necessitate a significant alteration to the damaged item. In these cases, the historical, legal and evidentiary importance of the item will carry much more importance than its appearance. Repairs should never be disguised, nor always withheld if they are the best means of ensuring an item's longevity even though some alteration is involved. Thus, the archivist might agree to the rebinding of a 'bolt' or 'post' bound ledger to prevent continued

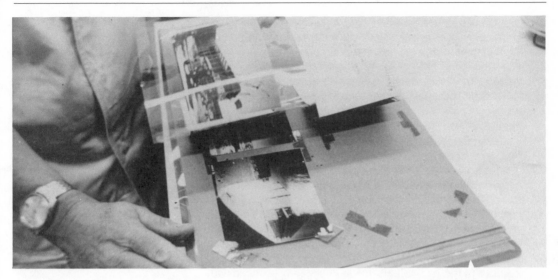

Never *mount photographs with sticky tape or use self-adhering albums. The adhesives stain, lose their grip and leave a gummy residue.*

damage to adjacent volumes, while at the same time insisting that photographs and descriptions of the original binding are kept.

When an archivist is unable to employ or even hire temporarily a conservator, some very basic in-house restoration work is justified. All such work should fulfil certain essential requirements, the key points of which are noted below, and reinforced in Table Four, which summarises the repair philosophy of Roger Ellis.

Table Four   The Repair Rules of Roger Ellis

- 'As far as possible . . . replace missing material with material of the same kind.'
- 'Leave the nature and extent of . . . (the) repair unmistakably evident.'
- 'Never do anything which cannot be undone without damage to the document.'
- 'Repair must never become tampering.'
- '. . . no process of repair may be allowed to remove, diminish, falsify, or obscure, in any way, the document's value as evidence . . .'
- '. . . no process of repair may be used which could in any way damage or weaken the material of which the document is made . . .'
- '. . . it is allowable... to alter a document's make-up for three reasons, viz., convenience of consultation; convenience of storage; and protection of the document itself.'
- '. . . before starting . . . ask . . . 'How little need I do to this document to make it fit for use again' . . .'

Cited in George and Dorothy Cunha's *Conservation of Library Materials*, Vol 1, Metuchen, NJ: Scarecrow Press, 1971.: 241–245.

Reversibility

Among the most important tenets are:
1) The treatment must be reversible, i.e. can be undone, should an improved technique become available
2) The treatment must not endanger the record item, for instance by leaving it permanently stained
3) New techniques of restoration must have been thoroughly tested by established conservation laboratories before being applied to original material. The literature is your best guide to legitimate techniques
4) The treatment must match the problem, for example, deacidification will not reduce a document's existing brittleness, even though acidity is one chief cause of brittleness. Deacidification will eliminate the acid as a catalyst for further deterioration, but the brittleness will need to be dealt with afterwards using a special strengthener
5) All treatment steps should be documented, including before and after photography.

Conscious of these essentials, the archivist may proceed with such treatments as document cleaning, flattening, simple mending, encapsulation, the removal of metal fasteners, humidification and even with non–aqueous deacidification and the removal of presssure sensitive tape, though it is vital that he/she read carefully before attempting such work. A worksheet to document treatments is set out in Box A.

A large number of books are available which explain the steps involved in these repairs and treatments. Clearly presented and well illustrated instructions are the hallmarks of the best 'how to' manuals; those by Morrow, Kyle and Ritzenthaler noted at the end of the chapter are all recommended. The references cited in Chapter 8 of the Cunhas' book are also worth pursuing.

Damaged records should be photographed before, during and after treatment.

Box A   Conservation Worksheet or Log

Collection Name: *Control Number:*

Contact Person: *Date Sent:*

Collection Date Range: *Quantity: (shelf metres)*

Container Type(s):

Type of Material: (Tick as appropriate and give amount or percentage of whole)

( ) Manuscript sheets	( ) Plain paper copies
( ) Typescript	( ) Carbon copies
( ) Computer paper	( ) Other copies (specify)
( ) Oversize	( ) Printed materials (loose)
( ) Woodpulp	*Bound Materials*
( ) Parchment	( ) Manuscript
( ) Seals or ribbons	( ) Printed
( ) Coloured inks	( ) Scrapbook

Condition Problems: (Tick as appropriate and give amount or percentage of whole)

( ) Mould damage*	( ) Staples, clips, pins
( ) Insect damage	( ) Elastic bands
( ) Mildew	( ) Sticky tape
( ) Surface dirt	( ) Fragile
( ) Folded/rolled	( ) Torn, broken
( ) Fire damage	( ) Stains
( ) Water damage	( ) Glues, adhesives
( ) Faded writing	( ) Red rot
*Evidence of active mould, insects,	( ) Other (specify)
mildew, dampness should be	
referred immediately to supervisor.	

Conservation Treatments (Tick those requested. Conservators only: Record completion date)

( ) Fumigate	( ) Copy (acid–free paper)
( ) Staple, clip, pin removal	( ) Support (acid–free paper
( ) Humidify, flatten	( ) Interleave (explain type)
( ) Dryclean	( ) Refolder (acid–free or other)
( ) Acidity test	( ) Re–attach fasteners (non–rusting)
( ) Ink solubility test	( ) Rebox
( ) Deacidify	( ) Rubber/tape removal
( ) Polyester protection	( ) Other (specify)

Conservation Work Documentation: The specific treatments undertaken by the conservator on all or parts of this collection are detailed in the following conservation work documents. These documents are permanent records maintained by the conservator.

Reference Numbers: *Treatment:*

Additional Comments/Instructions: (Use back for expected usage, donor obligations, items removed and where transferred, location of oversize and other explanations as needed.)
Authorised by: Date:

Workshops organised by groups such as ICCM and the MAA should not be missed either.

For the purposes of restorative conservation, having one's own conservator and a well equipped work area is a necessity, not a luxury, and one for which all archivists should lobby. Until these are obtained, there will be occasions when alternatives must be considered. Co-operation among small archives can provide partial solutions, particularly through agencies such as regional conservation centres. There will be times too when a consultant conservator is hired to undertake specific work or when items are sent out for treatment. The need to prepare material for exhibition would be one such occasion. Most State and large regional archives, libraries, museums and galleries have conservation departments where advice can be obtained when locating a suitable consultant. The ICCM can also provide lists of freelance conservators and reputable commercial services.

Perhaps the most challenging task in placing restoration work outside is the evaluation of completed work. Given the importance of one's archives, the approach should be cautious and conservative. Be wary, for example, about using conservation services which operate as a sideline to commercial bookbinders or photographic or art supply stores. The initial choice of an experienced conservator who is highly recommended should reduce the chances of receiving poor quality work. The insistence on pre-contract sample work and local references, and the use of specified standards of quality in commissioning particular tasks, will also help ensure high quality restoration.

CONTENT PRESERVATION

The copying of either single items or entire archival series is a time honoured practice popular with both archivists and librarians. Microcopying and microfilming in particular have been widely accepted methods of reproduction. Such copying fulfils many purposes such as:

- *Research use.* Copying allows unique materials in a particular archives to be made available through the loan or sale of copies to researchers in other cities or countries.
- *Storage.* Reduction copying such as microfilming allows originals to be removed from active use and stored under ideal conditions or destroyed, with the copies operating as substitutes. In the latter case especially, perhaps involving newspapers or voluminous administrative records, a great saving of space is achieved.
- *Collection Building.* The copying of material held privately or in distant institutions allows archives and libraries to add to their holdings, thereby complementing existing original material or filling gaps in the archives.

Perhaps the most convincing reason for copying is the conservation imperative, which aims to preserve the informational con-

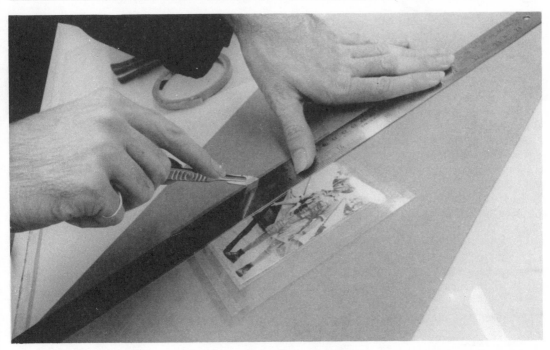

Encapsulating individual documents in a polyester envelope is a simple method of protection.

tent of the archives. Each of the other advantages accrue, and in addition, by producing a substitute for the original, its deterioration from handling by staff and readers is halted. Deterioration through exhibition, replay or screening is accommodated. Copying also means that the original and the copies can be stored in different locations, which greatly diminishes the dangers of disasters. Furthermore, because additional copies can be made from the first copy, wear and tear, degradation of original and damage caused by repeated copying to satisfy researchers' requests, are all avoided.

Photocopying is undoubtedly the best known form of copying. It has the great advantage that equipment is simple to use and is widely available and can be operated using acid-free paper. Photocopies are especially convenient in an archives when donors lend material for copying for a very limited period, and when microfilming is not possible. The drawbacks of photocopying should also be noted. Though some equipment includes reduction features, most does not, and there is a resultant doubling of the storage needed when the original is also saved. The act of copying may damage material, especially bound or large record items, unless great care is taken. Faded originals challenge all but the most expensive copiers. Lastly, the means of producing further photocopies when compared with microfilm and rapid tape copiers is limited. Nevertheless, for small quantities or very heavily used records in sizes up to B3, such as a nominal roll or passenger lists frequently consulted by genealogists, photocopying will undoubtedly foster their preservation.

For photographs, cinefilm and the many types of sound records, the production of duplicates is crucial to the preservation of the original. Where cellulose nitrate photograph negatives of cinefilm are involved, copying on to safety based stock is virtually mandatory once vault storage and correct environmental standards have been achieved (see Table Five).

Cinefilm, videotape, sound discs and magnetic tapes can also be damaged by constant screening and playing. Both their preservation and availability are achieved by the creation of high quality accurate copies from which further copies can be taken. The safety of many kinds of photographs, too, such as glass plate negatives, is best ensured by further photography to create modern copy negatives.

Microcopying produces a reduced image film copy which takes many different formats, including microfiche, micro cartridges and aperture cards (see Chapter Nine Using Computers and Micrographics). They are the most commonly preferred

---

Table Five   About Cellulose Nitrate

1) **What is it?**
   A film stock used very widely before 1952 which is an unstable compound and which decomposes from the moment it is made. The image in the emulsion is gradually destroyed. It is highly flammable. Some pre–1952 photograph negatives were also made of cellulose nitrate. Once alight it cannot be extinguished.

2) **How is it identified?**
   There are several tests, including edge marking, burning, ultraviolet fluorescence and floatation. Do not automatically accept the identification 'Safety' as an edge marking to mean safety base film. The best approach is to seek the advice of specialists if you have pre–1952 film or photograph negatives in the archives, and if you have the slightest reason to suspect they are nitrate.

3) **The five stages of nitrate film deterioration**
   - amber discolouration; image fading
   - emulsion becomes sticky; may be brittle
   - gas bubbles, noxious odour; may be brittle
   - film is soft and welds; viscous froth; very flammable
   - brownish, acrid powder; very flammable

4) **Storage and copying**
   Specialist vaults, incorporating strictly set temperature and humidity levels and design features, are used to segregate nitrate films and photograph negatives. The standard approach in combating their volatility is to copy them, another highly specialised and very costly process.

5) **Advice**
   The Australian Archives, and especially the National Film and Sound Archive, (both with headquarters in Canberra) have developed techniques for handling nitrate. The Preservation Commission of FIAF (Federation Internationale des Archives du Film) in Brussels is the most authoritative overseas source on nitrate.

Reel to reel tape is used for archival master tapes.

forms of copying in archives. They can be used for photographs and oversized items as well as the standard kinds of paper records, and when produced using silver halide stock and stored in the correct environmental conditions, they have excellent long term preservation quality.

Just as with choosing items for restoration, selecting what should be copied and with which medium this should be done, are matters the archivist should decide, but in consultation with technical specialists. Any archives in a fragile state which will be quickly damaged by use should be considered. The comparative advantage of copying items over methods of protecting the originals other than banning their use altogether should be assessed. The amount of material involved will be a consideration; microfilming, in particular, is geared to a mass approach compared with, for instance, treatment of originals. Microfilming also means that additional copies can be generated for sale to the public; yet this gain must be offset against the cost of physically preparing the records for filming and of compiling associated finding aids.

Finally, the archivist should clearly appreciate that copying can be fraught with complications. Some considerations, such as copyright and the legal status of the film copies, will only be mentioned in passing here, although the former subject is covered elsewhere in this book. There is a large body of writing on both aspects in archival literature. Bear in mind that unless the copied originals are destroyed, copying adds further to the list of archival media requiring conservation. With microcopying especially, it must be acknowledged that some researchers will not be happy with copies, for there is always some information which cannot be conveyed through copying. The archivist should anticipate user reluctance by strictly enforcing policy on the use of copied originals. For example, researchers with only partial sight, or undertaking projects to which the colours of symbols on a map or document are significant, may be allowed to inspect originals. Remember too that most researchers do not enjoy using microfilm readers, for several understandable reasons. It is worth repeating that the complexities of copying archives must be appreciated, regardless of whether this is undertaken in–house or by an outside contractor. Correct arrangement and identification of the original, standards to be achieved, the problem of variable size items within single volumes, precautions to ensure copying does not harm the originals and the question of reproducing colour are just some of the matters to be addressed. (Chapter Nine Computers and Micrographics provides more detailed information on these matters.)

A microfiche guide to major photographic series can be sold or loaned to distant libraries and archives.

SUMMARY

While acknowledging that the challenge of conservation is enormous, we have argued that it must be, nevertheless, of central concern to the archivist. No matter how small or poorly funded, any archives can do a great deal to meet this challenge. A systematic and planned approach is essential. The archivist must know what materials constitute the holdings, must learn to recognise the causes and signs of deterioration and must be familiar with the means to remedy them. Programmes should be adopted to stabilise and restore existing damage and prevent future decay. Plans need to be laid to anticipate disaster, train staff and establish work areas. In short, we have advocated a philosophy which is cautious and anticipatory, which ideally should pervade all archival work, and which urges planning over the piecemeal approach.

FURTHER READING
General Texts

The Abbey Newsletter: Bookbinding and Conservation. Ellen McCrady, Editor, School of Library Service, 516 Butler Library, Columbia University, New York, NY 10027 USA. 6 issues/year US$15.00 in 1983.

Casterline, Gail F., *Archives and Manuscripts: Exhibits.* Chicago, IL: Society of American Archivists, 1980.

Cunha, George and Dorothy Cunha, *Library and Archives Conservation: 1980's and Beyond.* 2 volumes. Metuchen, NJ: Scarecrow Press, 1983.

Davies, John, *A Study of the Basic Standards and Methods in Preservation and Restoration Workshops Applicable to Developing Countries.* Brussels: International Council on Archives, 1973.

Eastman Kodak Company, *Preservation of Photographs.* Kodak Publication No. F–30. Rochester, NY: Eastman Kodak Company, 1979. US$5.50 in 1983.

——. *Storage and Preservation of Microfilms.* Kodak Pamphlet D–31. Rochester, NY: Eastman Kodak Company, 1981. Free from Eastman Kodak Company, 343 State Street, Dept. 412–L, Rochester, NY 14650 USA.

Greenfield, J., *Books, Their Care and Repair.* New York, NY: H.W. Wilson, 1983.

Horton, Carolyn, *Cleaning and Preserving Bindings and Related Materials.* LTP Publications # 12. Chicago, IL: American Library Association, 1966.

Kyle, Hedi, *Library Materials Preservation Manual: Practical Methods for Preserving Books, Pamphlets and Other Printed Materials.* Bronxville, NY: T. Smith, 1983.

Morrow, Carolyn Clark, *Conservation Treatment Procedures.* Littleton, CO: Libraries Unlimited, Inc., 1982.

Ritzenthaler, Mary Lynn, Gerald Munoff and Margery S. Long, *Archives and Manuscripts: Administration of Photographic Collections.* Chicago, IL: Society of American Archivists, 1984.

Ritzenthaler, Mary Lynn, *Archives and Manuscripts: Conservation, A Manual on Practical Care and Management.* Chicago: Society of American Archivists, 1983.

Swartzburg, Susan G., Editor, *Conservation in the Library: A Handbook of Use and Care of Traditional and Non-traditional Materials.* Westport, CT: Greenwood Press, 1983.

Upton, Murray S. and Colin Pearson, *Disaster Planning and Emergency Treatments in Museums, Art Galleries, Libraries, Archives and Allied Institutions.* Canberra: Institute for the Conservation of Cultural Materials, 1978.

Waters, Peter, *Emergency Procedures for Salvaging Flood or Water Damaged Library Materials.* Second Edition. Washington, DC: Library of Congress, 1979.

The names and addresses of suppliers of conservation materials
can be obtained from:
*   The National Secretary
    Institute for the Conservation of Cultural Materials, Inc.
    G.P.O. Box 1638
    Canberra ACT 2601
*   The Secretary
    Australian Society of Archivists, Inc.
    P.O. Box 83
    O'Connor ACT 2601
*   The Hon. Secretary
    Museums Association of Australia, Inc.
    c/– Minister for the Arts
    186 Exhibition Street
    Melbourne VIC 3001

*Stacking unprotected rolls of maps
or plans in boxes or bins leads to
serious damage.*

CHAPTER NINE

USING COMPUTERS AND MICROGRAPHICS

David Roberts

The technologies of automated data processing, word processing and micrographics are useful tools which, as they develop, are becoming more accessible to small archival operations. They can permit economies in time and space — precious commodities in a small operation — and can make possible the accomplishment of tasks which may have seemed impossible. These technologies are not a panacea, and will not turn a poor system into a good one. They may even make it worse: chaotic records on microfilm are even less accessible than their chaotic originals. Carefully chosen to meet an institution's particular needs, however, like any other well–chosen tool, they will allow a better job to be done.

The purpose of this chapter is briefly to describe the new technologies and the ways in which they can be used for archives; to examine different ways in which they can be acquired or access to them can be gained; to identify the advantages and disadvantages which must be weighed in considering the use of these technologies; and to note a number of things which should be done or borne in mind when introducing or using one of the technologies.

This chapter is not intended to be an exhaustive examination of the subject and will be necessarily brief and practically oriented. For more background and detail, the reader is referred to suggestions for further reading at the end of the chapter. Nor is this chapter intended as a 'state of the art' guide to equipment. The range of equipment and related products, such as software, which are available for archival purposes is very large and is changing all the time. Rather, it is hoped that this chapter will show the reader what to look for or, more particularly, how to decide what to look for.

While such considerations will be dealt with in more detail for each of the technologies below, they can be summarised generally as follows:

1) The *cost* of the system or service in relation to the benefits it will bring; these must be expressed in measurable terms in order to be meaningful;

2) The *applicability* of the system or service, in terms of its size and level of sophistication, in relation to one's operation: there is no point in paying for functions for which you cannot foresee a need;

3) The *skills* which will be required to operate or make use of the system or service; this applies to clients as much as to staff;

4) The *compatibility* of the system or service with existing systems within your organisation or in allied institutions. This applies particularly to the choice of computer software;

5) The *capacity* of the system or service to cope with changes in one's operations or holdings and its scope for future development; where change has been part of the cause of one's problems, a capacity to change must be part of the solution, or it will become self-defeating;

6) Arrangements for *maintenance* and *repair* of equipment: where possible, this should be a part of the deal;

7) Whether a *less or a non-technological solution* might still be more cost-effective.

AUTOMATED DATA PROCESSING (ADP)

ADP may be defined as the use of an electronic device for processing information. The processing may simply take the form of storing information, albeit on a scale and with a speed of retrieval which were previously impossible, or it may involve the manipulation of the information towards a further end, such as producing an index.

Leaving aside the computing capacities of computers, that is, their ability to create new information from data already stored, the principal ADP process which is of use to archivists is the re-arrangement of information. The degree of flexibility with which information can be re-arranged for a variety of purposes will be an important consideration in determining the suitability of a system, in particular its software, for use in one's operation.

The software, or program, is the set of instructions which tells the computer what to do and how to do it. Some basic software is already built into the computer by the manufacturer, but this must be complemented by inserting programs which permit the computer to perform particular tasks. Programs may be bought as complete packages, adapted to one's particular needs, or developed from scratch. Additionally, software can include the

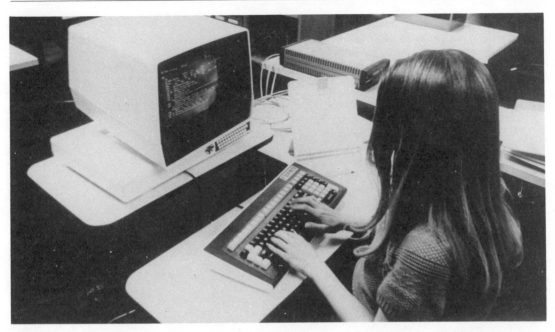

Microcomputers have many applications for archives, from word processing to the control of collections and the production of complex finding aids.

manufacturer's instructions or advice as to how to get the best out of the system.

Computer hardware, that is, the physical equipment, is generally regarded as falling within one of three categories, mainframe, mini and micro, according to the capacity of the system. In effect, mainframe and mini computers are beyond the needs of small archival institutions. Although micro computers have been designed principally for domestic and small business applications, their capacities are on a scale more suitable for the small archives.

In addition to the part of the equipment which does the actual processing, or the central processing unit (CPU), the hardware is likely to comprise the following:

1) Besides the *memory capacity* of the CPU, there are magnetic tape and disc drives which can be used for the storage and retrieval of data and for loading software to direct the activities of the CPU;

2) The *keyboard*, almost identical to that of a typewriter, remains the principal means of input of data, although such devices as light–pens and even voice–recognition are rapidly developing;

3) The *video display unit (VDU)*, similar to a television screen, displays information which has been retrieved or which is being keyed in;

4) A *printer* permits such information to be printed on paper, or hardcopy.

HOW CAN ADP BE USED

With the right combination of software and hardware, ADP can be an enormously useful tool for improving archival management. Its possible uses or applications fall into four main areas of archives work:

1) **Intellectual control of archives.** The term intellectual control means having a description of what the records are. Accessioning is the point when archivists establish the first level of intellectual control over their new holdings. Provided that appropriate details about the records are entered at the time of accessioning, the information can be presented in any order useful for one's purposes. For example, material can be listed in order of receipt for an accession register, or by provenance for a guide to holdings.

SAMPLE ACCESSION RECORD

01 ACCESSION NO.: AI983/47
02 DATE OF ACCESSION: 18.06.83
03 SERIES TITLE: Master set of minutes of meetings of Council
04 DATE RANGE: I953–1967
05 CREATING BODY: (To 1964) Honorary Secretary; (From 1964) Office of the Secretary
06 CONTROLLING BODY: Office of the Secretary
07 DESCRIPTION: This series consists of bound volumes containing the typed master set of minutes of Council meetings. Meetings were normally held quarterly. The minutes for each meeting are preceded by the Secretary's copy of the agenda and followed by a set of agenda papers. The minutes for each meeting are signed by the Secretary and the President
08 RANGE OF CONTROL SYMBOLS: 1/53–4/67
09 RELATED SERIES: 1983/48 President's annotated set of minutes of meetings of Council, 1964–1967
10 DIMENSIONS OF ITEMS: 34x22x3cm
11 QUANTITY (BOXES): 5 standard boxes
12 QUANTITY (LINEAR METRES): 0.901 m.
13 RETENTION/DESTRUCTION: Retain permanently
14 DISPOSAL AUTHORITY: DS 6, entry 1.1
15 STORAGE REQUIREMENTS: Air conditioned storage; acid–free boxes
16 LOCATION: N7.1.3
17 CONSERVATION STATUS: Good condition. No action currently required
18 ACCESS CONDITIONS: With the permission of the Secretary

RE-FORMATTED FOR A SUMMARY GUIDE ENTRY

CREATING BODY: (To 1964) Honorary Secretary; (From 1964)
Office of the Secretary
SERIES TITLE: Master set of minutes of meetings of Council
DATE RANGE: 1953–1967
CONTROL SYMBOLS: 1/53–4/67
ACCESSION NO.: A1983/47
QUANTITY: 0.901 m.
ACCESS CONDITIONS: With the permission of the Secretary

RE-FORMATTED FOR A SHELF LIST ENTRY

LOCATION: N7.1.3
ACCESSION NO.: A1983/47
SERIES TITLE: Master set of minutes of meetings of Council
CONTROL SYMBOLS: 1/53–4/67
DIMENSIONS OF ITEMS: 34x22x3cm
QUANTITY (BOXES): 5 standard boxes
QUANTITY (LINEAR METRES): 0.901 m.

A demonstration of the latest information technology — the laser-read optical digital disc. Courtesy — State Library of NSW.

Perhaps the greatest impact of ADP on the intellectual control of archives is in the area of indexing, which was once very time-consuming because of the sheer number of variations involved in manually setting out the same information under different index headings. Software packages are available which instruct the computer to arrange this information automatically.

2) **Physical control of archives.** The computer's ability to retrieve information and to alter it quickly and easily can be invaluable for keeping up with holdings as they are moved around during processing and use. Computers are often used to create a shelf location list, to update it with new accessions or changes of location, or to record and review the issue and return of individual archival items to the shelves.

3) **Control of archival processes.** An ADP system can be used to plan and monitor progress in continuing tasks such as conservation work. For example, one would enter the identifying number of a collection, its work priority rating, and the type of conservation work required. This would be followed by a log of conservation tasks and their date of completion. In this way, archivists could trace the material as it was conserved and gain valuable management information about productivity and resources invested.

SAMPLE CONSERVATION JOB RECORD

01   CONSERVATION JOB NUMBER: C1985/7
02   WORK PRIORITY: 3
03   ACCESSION NO./ITEM NOS. OF RECORDS: A1982/14, vol.6
04   JOB SIZE: Major
05   SUMMARY CONDITION REPORT: Evidence of insect activity. Foxing and dirt, particularly on early folios. Spine binding broken
06   TASK 1: Fumigation
07   COMPLETED: 10.06.85
08   TASK 2: Hand clean
09   COMPLETED: 21.06.85
10   TASK 3: Re-bind
11   COMPLETED:
12   TASK 4:
13   COMPLETED:
14   TASKS 5:
15   COMPLETED:
16   RETURNED TO STORAGE:
17   REMARKS:

Other archival activities such as appraisal of records and arrangement and description can also be monitored in this way.

Voluminous computer printouts are a major storage problem.

4) **As a general aid to archival management.** Such large-scale tasks as measuring available or future repository space, or stock control for consumables, become a great deal easier with the help of ADP.

Costs and Benefits

The decision to acquire or not to acquire an ADP system is essentially a weighing of costs and benefits. The major benefits include:
1) Speed
2) Accuracy
3) The elimination of many repetitious and boring tasks inherent in manual systems
4) The possibility of performing functions which are impossible or impractical with manual systems.

The major disadvantages include:
1) The cost of the equipment and related services
2) The cost and difficulty of finding or developing suitable software
3) Possible resistance by users, both staff and clients.

PLANNING FOR ADP

An ADP capability can be acquired in a number of ways.
1) *Use of in-house facilities of superior organisation:* Where the archives is part of an organisation which already possesses an ADP system, obvious economies of scale are possible if you 'plug in' to the larger operation. The problem may arise, however, that the system, especially the software, may not be suitable for the archives' needs.

2) *Sharing with other archival institutions with similar needs:*
    Some of the costs may well be able to be reduced in this way.
    While the sharing of hardware may not be a practical possi-
    bility, the sharing of development costs, such as the creation
    of suitable software or the selection of appropriate hard-
    ware, might be profitable.

3) *Use of a commercial bureau:* It may be convenient to use the
    services of a commercial system on a regular basis, rather
    than acquire or develop your own facility. Furthermore, a
    commercial bureau may be able to provide such skilled ser-
    vices as advice and development work for your application,
    preparation of information for input, and initial entry of
    data.

4) *Purchase of equipment:* With the comparatively low cost of
    micro computers, this option is now a possibility even for a
    very small operation.

The acquisition of an ADP capability must be preceded by
careful evaluation and planning, which should include the use of
expert advice, whether from one's own organisation or from
employing consultants.

The process of evaluation and planning might follow the following sequence:

1) **Analysis of needs.** That is, identify the particular problems
    to be solved by the use of ADP. By focusing on the problems
    as the first step, it is possible to decide what one wants the
    system to do. Thus one can identify the capabilities which
    are needed and incorporate them into a document known as
    a system design brief. It is at this stage, too, that other sol-
    utions to the problems, now isolated, may be identified and
    considered. Each 'solution' should be analysed in terms of
    costs, benefits, and additional problems that its adoption
    may create.

2) **Analysis of the effectiveness of the present manual sys-
    tem prior to automation.** — 'GIGO–garbage in, garbage out'
    is an important computer phrase to remember. Automating a
    system that isn't working well in manual form will only enhance
    its faults by making them more instantly obvious. Before, not
    after, is the time to look at how well your various processes are
    working and to clean them up for optimum efficiency. Areas
    that you should look at include:
    • Archival functions suitable for ADP
    • The activities that could be automated
    • What to look for to 'clean' them up prior to automation.
    Here the 'sins of the past' may need to be confronted. In
    areas such as finding aids, one may have inherited several
    different approaches. A choice would need to be made
    between starting afresh with an up–to–date system suitable

for automation — hoping to convert the earlier material at a later date — or bringing all the documentation up to a consistent standard first of all. Or indeed to leave the older systems alone, i.e. the problem, particularly where you may have several different approaches/types you inherited. Should you start afresh with a 'state of the art' system and hope to get funds later to convert all the existing aids to the new format...or simply leave them alone...or try to convert them simultaneously?

3) **Design of the system:**
   - *Software* must be chosen or developed. A number of commercial software packages have been written for the control of information sources, mostly in the library and records management context. Some programs deal with bibliographic access and control. Others are useful to manage collection movements and space allocation. It may therefore be possible to find a program or group of programs suitable for use, or capable of being adapted. If not, the software will have to be written, requiring the twin skills of systems analysis and computer programming.
   - *Equipment* will need to be chosen, including the type and number of terminals, if more than one is needed; memory capacity, with perhaps one or more disk drives for additional capacity; whether the printer will be able to produce hard copy of a quality suitable for use in finding aids.
   - *The location of the equipment* will have to be established. Because of the important role it will play, its location in the physical workflow is crucial. The most effective location will be indicated by the functions for which the equipment is to be used and by who will use it. If it is to be used for specialised functions or primarily for one person's area of responsibility, its location can reflect this. Where a number of people need access to it, a central location is required. If it is anticipated that users of the archives will be able to carry out searches with the equipment, it must be so placed as to permit supervision and ready assistance.
   - *Repair and maintenance* of the equipment should also be provided for at this stage, where possible; quotes for the supply of equipment should include a repair and maintenance plan.

Box A presents some questions you will want to answer as you select an ADP system for your archives.

Word Processing (WP)
Word processing is a limited and specialised type of program for

---

Box A   Selecting an ADP System

General Questions

Is the software and/or hardware I'm considering well supported and maintained in my locality?

Should I buy the most popular software?

How much storage does the system give me? Can I add more storage capacity later?

Is the software menu or command driven? In general, menu driven software is easier to use, at least at first, but can lack flexibility.

What security features are available, such as user codes and password checks?

Questions about Database Software

Should I use the same 'fields' or data elements as other institutions?

What are the limitations on the 'records' that can be created in the database? eg.
- upper limit on number?
- upper limit on size (ie. number of characters)?
- fixed record structure?

What are the limitations on the 'fields'? eg.
- upper limit on number? fixed or variable?
- upper limit on size?
- can fields be divided into sub-fields?

What kinds of 'reports' (selected information from the database in a given order and format) are available? eg.
- are they included in the package?
- can users design their own formats?

How easy is large-scale input or editing? eg.
- can information be loaded onto the database from another system?
- is global editing possible?

Does my purchase of the software include free or minimal cost upgrading if it is later enhanced or improved?

---

micro computers which is used to prepare, store, edit and retrieve written text.

This technology is in wide use in business, government and educational institutions, and is becoming as important an administrative tool as typewriters and telephones. An archival operation belonging to a larger organisation with existing WP services should first investigate the possibility of making use of them.

In addition to specialised word processing equipment, a range of word processing software is available to enable a micro computer to perform word processing functions. Thus, the acquisition of a small ADP facility will mean automatic access to a word processing capacity, for the price of a computer program.

Applications for word processing in the archival context can include:

1) **The production of finding aids and publicity material.** The capacity of the word processor to edit and insert new items into the text means that such publications can be kept up to date, as new accessions are received or as arrangement and description projects are completed.

2) **The preparation of reports and correspondence.** The word processor is a convenient tool for the composition of text, in that it eliminates the need for a series of written and typed drafts. The text can be fully prepared on the word processor and printed out for editing. In this way, there is no re-typing of the whole as only the corrections need to be inserted before the final hard copy is produced with the touch of a key.

3) **The preparation of standard letters.** Letters with a high proportion of standardised information represent a major part of an archivist's correspondence, and are used for such purposes as responding to frequently asked questions, acknowledging the receipt of records from depositors, and proposing arrangements for access to records. Where printed form letters have previously been used, the result of using WP is a letter with a more personal appearance. Where such letters have previously been typed individually, there is an obvious saving.

4) **The preparation of documentation for the control of holdings.** Word processing can eliminate the need to use printed forms for such archival activities as accessioning. The format for the information can be held in the word processor's memory, and displayed on the screen, the information required can be entered and the completed document printed out or stored for future reference.

If the acquisition of separate word processing equipment is being considered, similar considerations to those outlined for ADP will have to be weighed.

Occupational Health

Considerations relating to occupational health and ergonomics are also important in the choice of equipment, its location and the manner of its use. If possible, expert advice should be sought, but important rules to observe are:

1) The *VDU screen* should be of low reflectivity, and placed to avoid glare from windows and lights.

2) *Screen characters* should not be too small or too closely spaced.

3) The *table* on which the equipment is mounted, the operator's chair and holders for source documents should be easily adjusted to enable the most comfortable position to be found.

4) The *printer* should have a noise hood and may be best placed in a room away from people.
5) *Use of the equipment should be regulated* to minimise the risk of Occupational Overuse Syndrome (OOS), using regular rest periods (ten minutes every hour is a reasonable standard).

Care of Tapes and Disks

The magnetic media used with ADP equipment for the storage of information (tapes, disks, diskettes) are particularly susceptible to damage. They must be treated carefully, if the information recorded on them is to be protected.

By following a few rules, however, the risk of damage, and therefore of loss of information, can be greatly reduced:

1) Keep a back-up copy, in case of damage to the master. Update it regularly (preferably at the end of each session in which the master has been altered) and store it in a different location.
2) Avoid touching the surface of the disk or tape.
3) Avoid extremes of temperature and humidity in both the work area and storage locations.
4) Keep the equipment clean, especially following the manufacturer's instructions about maintaining the heads of the disk or tape drive.
5) Keep the work area clean. The presence of even minute particles of dirt on a tape or disk's surface can result in damage to the surface and significant 'drop-outs' of data.
6) Store disks and tapes away from sources of strong electromagnetic radiation, such as generators.

Computer tapes are best stored in protective cases shelved on edge.

An ergonomically sound computer desk allows the operator to adjust the heights and configuration of the equipment. Courtesy — Tim Robinson.

MICROGRAPHICS

Micrographics may be defined as the use of photographic processes to produce reduced size images of textual or graphic material on film. This definition requires some modification, since the development of computer–output microfilm means that images can be directly transferred to film from a computer without an intermediary paper or hard copy.

The most common micrographic formats are listed below:

1) **16 and 35mm roll film.** This remains the most common format.

2) **35mm aperture cards.** A single frame of 35mm microfilm is inserted into an aperture or 'window' in a card the size and shape of a traditional computer punch card. Information printed on the card permits the image to be identified without the use of special viewing equipment, and allows the item to be handled without touching the image.

3) **35mm slides.** Not commonly thought of as a microform, they have some applications in the micrographics industry, such as the reproduction of coloured pictures, maps, or works of art.

4) **Microfiche.** This consists of a sheet of film about 105mm x 149mm on which a large number of images have been exposed in a regular pattern of rows and columns.

   Microfiche has a number of advantages over roll microfilm: a microfiche sheet can be duplicated quickly for a few cents; a particular image can be found more efficiently with less effort; more images can be stored in the same space; microfiche readers are cheap and easy to maintain; the individual sheets can be stored in more convenient ways than roll film, for example, in holders resembling books. Unsurprisingly, most publications reproduced on microfilm appear in the microfiche format.

USE OF MICROGRAPHICS

Archivists are likely to use microfilming for one or more of the following purposes:

1) **To prolong the life of original records.** Even when the greatest care is taken, the repeated handling of original archival material results in damage and eventual destruction. Copying the material on microfilm permits the archivist to remove the originals from active use so that they may be conserved while still making the records available to researchers in microform.

2) **To make unique material more widely available.** Because archival records are one-of-a-kind, it can be difficult to make them available to everyone who wishes to use them. Microform copies make it possible for researchers in different locations to use copies of these records simultaneously. Also some original records may be unwieldy because of an awkward size, shape or mass, such as in the case of large maps, plans, or very heavy volumes. Microforms are compact, often reducing large or bulky items to a single roll of film which is easy to handle and transport.

Preparing materials for microfilming requires careful checking for complete issues in mint condition.

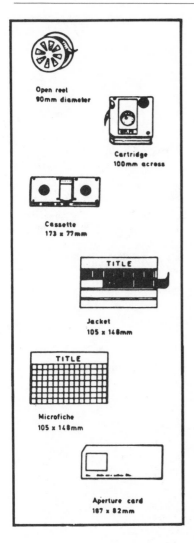

Open reel
90mm diameter

Cartridge
100mm across

Cassette
173 x 77mm

TITLE

Jacket
105 x 148mm

TITLE

Microfiche
105 x 148mm

Aperture card
187 x 82mm

3) **To reduce the use of high–cost storage.** Where the administrative and public areas of an archival operation are in a high–cost area and low–cost more secure storage is available in a different location, it may be more efficient to keep the original material in the latter area, and to provide access using microfilm copies.

4) **To protect security** of vital original records, such as finding aids or Board Minutes, which are essential to the ongoing work of your archives or its sponsoring organisation. The loss of these records by fire or vandalism could be disastrous, so copying them on microfilm and subsequently storing the film in a safe, physically separate location helps to reduce the danger.

LIMITATIONS OF MICROGRAPHICS

A microfilming project is an expensive undertaking and is likely to divert considerable resources from other important tasks. The benefits to the archives must be weighed to justify the cost.

Like ADP, microfilming is not a panacea to an archival operations problem. It will not improve access to poorly organised records, and, indeed, will make them even less accessible, since it is generally harder to browse or skim through microforms than through hard copy.

Some types of records are difficult or unsuitable for microfilming. Records in large formats, such as maps or architectural plans, can only be filmed properly on equipment designed to handle oversized materials. Such machines are not commonly available outside large metropolitan areas. There are often problems inherent in the records which make them unsuitable for copying onto microfilm. For example where the writing is faint or in inks of various colours, the film may not be legible.

There are also legal matters to consider. Microfilming is another form of copying and is, therefore, subject to the provisions of the Commonwealth Copyright Act of 1968 (as amended 1980). No item, either published or unpublished, can be copied without the permission of the copyright holder for a period of time following its creation. The Copyright Act is complex and the period of protection varies so it is wise to seek legal advice on the status of any material you plan to film early in the planning stages. Keep in mind that copyright ownership is quite separate from ownership of the physical item. The copyright protection belongs to the person who actually created the material or his heirs, and it is not uncommon for custody of material to be legally transferred without conveying the copyright to the new owner. For example, if you are planning to microfilm the letters written to Sir Robert Menzies by a number of different people, you would need to have permission from the copyright owner of each of the letter writers. Sometimes it requires considerable detective work to determine the current owner of the copyright.

If you plan to film your own administrative records or those of your 'parent' institution, such as Board Minutes or personal files, there are legal requirements that the filming must meet because these records provide evidence of how your organisation operated. The laws concerning the admissibility of microfilm copies of original documents as evidence in court proceedings differ from State to State, so you will need to have legal advice before filming these types of records.

Your decision as to the type of microform and the size of the image will be greatly affected by the equipment available to view it and whether or not you will want to make paper copies of individual documents from the film. Microform viewers or readers come in a variety of types with a range of features, conveniences, and prices to match. You will also want to consider the cost of supplies and maintenance when making your choice. Again, the rule of thumb is don't pay for capabilities you won't use regularly. If you anticipate making a number of photocopies from the microfilm, the lease or purchase of a reader–printer might be justified. For duplicate films or for few or infrequent copies, you can use the services of a commercial firm with copying facilities.

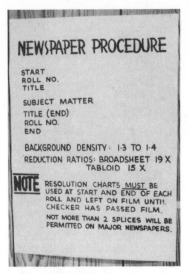

Identifying information must be filmed onto each reel of microfilm.

HOW TO HAVE MICROFILMING DONE

The small archival operation will be faced with three main options: a contract with a firm which microfilms records for a fee, the development of an in–house microfilming centre, or a mixture of both.

The use of a commercial microfilming bureau has the advantage in that equipment costs are limited to the acquisition of reading, and possibly printing, equipment and to the provision of storage facilities suitable for microfilm. Further, there is no need to acquire or hire the skilled personnel to operate microfilming equipment, which is essential to ensure a professional and legally recognised product. The commercial bureau is also a source of expert advice.

There are several precautions that one must take when using a commercial bureau for archival microfilming. Firstly, you must understand that the bulk of their filming is done for short–term business use and does not require archival standards of processing. Hence it is essential that the required archival standards are stated and understood when drawing up the contract for services. Since the records will leave the archives in order to be filmed on the premises of the commercial bureau, the archivist should have a detailed list of items sent and be sure that sufficient care is taken for their safety. Some archives send a member of their own staff along with the material to supervise and assist with the filming.

The acquisition of all the equipment and personnel required for a microfilming operation is an undertaking beyond the means

Box B Types of Micrographic Applications of Established Benefit for Archives

Archival Records/Materials

a) Registers, indexes to major series of proven research interest

b) Major series of significant organisations & agencies (minutes, correspondence, annual reports, newsletter or journal)

c) Papers of Significant Persons (Diaries/journals, correspondence)

Motivation

1) High research demand
2) Conservation/security of originals
3) Better service to users in remote areas

Cautions

1) Reference demand research potential is a major consideration
2) Legal issues must be resolved
3) Indexes and finding aids must also be filmed

Benefits

1) Research by mail is more efficient
2) Popular indexes can be conserved
3) Can be sold to other institutions

---

d) Extra large format records: Building plans, maps, posters, prints, works of art

Motivation

1) Conservation
2) Space
3) Ease of reference

Cautions

1) Coloured inks may require coloured films or colour separations
2) The reference activity, importance of records, and frequency of changes to originals influence filming decisions
3) Reader/printers are expensive for extra large format
4) Indexes must also be filmed

Benefits

1) Less wear and tear on originals that may be transferred to remote archival storage
2) Films formats are easier for researchers to handle and offer faster access
3) Aperture card mount can be coded for automated retrieval

Publications

a) Newspapers & Government *Gazettes*

b) Rare or 'brittle' publications

c) Guides, inventories and bibliographies

Motivation

1) Space reduction (gazettes & newspapers)
2) Conservation (rare and brittle)

Cautions

1) Bibliographic search to locate all & best extant copies (even from other archives and libraries) is essential
2) Legal issues must be resolved
3) Indexing desirable for large series

Benefits

1) Can be sold to other institutions
2) Originals may be transferred to remote archival storage for conservation or otherwise disposed of (newspapers)
3) Increased reference/research availability for better service to users in remote areas

of all but the largest institutions. While it is possible to purchase your own camera and related equipment, and have the film processed in a commercial laboratory, this is not recommended for the following reasons. The cameras, lights, tables, and related equipment and space needed for microfilming work are very expensive and too specialised. Whilst the actual photography may appear to be a simple matter of snapping a shutter, obtaining archival quality exposures requires great attention to technical procedures. For example, various colours of paper require light adjustments; the material must be absolutely flat and properly positioned; faded or damaged material may require special filters to render them legible; and the list of details goes on and on. Clearly the money you would invest would be better spent hiring professionals, as the large archival and research institutions will readily confirm.

As with the acquisition of ADP facilities, a microfilming program requires careful evaluation and planning which might follow the following sequence:

1) **Choosing the records to be copied.** Earlier we discussed conservation, wider access, and security as some of the reasons why archivists microfilm records. Whatever the purpose of establishing a microfilming program, there are likely to be more records which could usefully be copied than resources will allow. A priority listing of collections or record series which accomplish more than one of these purposes should be drawn up to ensure that the most important work is done. Box B lists some popular microfilming applications for archives. Detailed descriptions of the material should be included to help with estimating the size and cost of the program. Once the list is prepared, do contact other archives, particularly the larger ones, to see if any of the published materials, such as newspapers, might already have been preserved. Furthermore, your archival colleagues may have bits to add or better copies for filming. In fact, they may want to share the work of the project with you and help with the costs.

2) **Selecting the microform format.** The choice among roll film, microfiche, or aperture cards will depend on the purposes of the microfilming programme, the types of records being copied and the availability of viewing equipment. Microfiche and roll film for example, are particularly suitable for reference copies, because they are popular and easy to use. Fiche, in particular, are very inexpensive to duplicate. Aperture cards are most commonly used to copy large single items, such as maps and plans, because a one–to–one relationship can be maintained between the original items and the microform copies. When one chooses among the common formats, such as 35mm roll film or microfiche,

A planetary aperture card micro-film camera-processor is used to copy large building plans.

there is the additional advantage of having established standards of quality and a wide range of viewing equipment.

3) **Designating the film quality and the number of copies.** Because archival records and manuscripts are unique and often fragile, you may only have one opportunity to film them and it is essential that the microfilm product be of the highest quality. This standard of excellence is known as archival microfilming. When records are filmed to meet archival standards, it means that:

- The original records have been arranged and described as accurately and thoroughly as possible, and that any irregularities or flaws in them have been noted.
- The film used has a silver halide emulsion on a chemically inert polyester or triacetate base.
- The image of the original record reproduced on the film is a complete, true and faithful copy and has been produced to meet the highest technical standards.
- The exposed film has been properly processed and all residues of the processing chemicals have been removed by an especially thorough washing.
- The exposed film has been tested and has met the standards for archival quality both technically and as a true copy of the records it duplicates.

It is normal archival practice to produce a minimum of three microfilms of each original item, that is, a security or preservation negative on silver halide film, a negative copy for further duplication known as a duplicating master, and a reference copy. Use of microfilm, either for reference or for making a further copy, inevitably results in damage which can become quite extensive over time. For this reason, the security or preservation negative should only be used to produce the duplicating master and thereafter be kept undisturbed in the best conservation environment as security against loss of the original records or of the duplicating master. The duplicating master is used only for making further reference copies and is also stored carefully. However, the reference copies are for everyday use by researchers.

For the security or preservation negative, the only acceptable medium is black and white silver halide film. This is the only type of film for which archival quality standards exist and which is sufficiently stable, given proper processing and storage conditions, to last for long periods of time. For the duplicating master and for the reference copies, one may use the less expensive, easier to copy diazo or vesicular films which are also more scratch resistant than silver halide. Finally, a choice must be made between a positive or negative image for the copies. Duplicating masters are normally negative; reference copies can be either negative or positive. One advantage of having negative reference copies is that it is easier on the eyes to look at white lettering on a black background.

4) **Assessing the feasibility and cost of the microfilming project.** As with ADP applications, the costs of undertaking a microfilming project must be assessed and weighed against the proposed benefits of the filming. The expenses of equipment and materials should be included as well as the labour of preparing and checking the records before and after filming. An outline listing the types of expenses which must be anticipated in a microfilming project is helpful in estimating costs. (See Box C).

5) **Contracting with a commercial filming service.** Choosing a commercial service to do the photography, processing, and duplicating of microfilms should be done with great care. You must specify what work is to be done; the archival standards to be met, and seek written quotes from firms with proven skills. Ask the large, well–established archives which companies they use and request a copy of their work specifications sheet or contract form for microfilming. A sample of specifications used by the Australian Archives to film the Records of the National Australasian Convention, 1891, shown in Box D, is a good model. In addition to

stating the quality standards which must be met, it is vital to clarify how errors in the filming, processing, or duplication will be detected, what actions will be taken to correct them, and who will pay for them.

6) **Preparing the records for filming.** If it has been decided to employ the services of a commercial bureau to microfilm material in one's holdings, it is important that the material to be copied should be adequately prepared. This preparation involves paying very close attention to arranging and describing the material accurately and completely. There are three reasons for taking extreme care.

First, it is essential to realise that the microfilm camera operator is only responsible for producing a technically suitable microphotograph of the material. It is the archivist's responsibility to decide what is to be photographed, to communicate these decisions to the photographer, and to prepare the material for placement under the camera. This means that the archivist must see that all the material is present, in order, with pencilled page numbers and instructional notes on how to handle problems such as missing or blank pages, documents with envelopes or enclosures, folded or bound items.

Second, archivists preparing records for filming must remember that researchers using the microfilm copy will not have the originals to compare with the film; nor will they necessarily have an archivist with particular knowledge of those records at hand to explain any inconsistencies or legibility problems with the material. Therefore, the archivist has a responsibility to anticipate these needs and provide explanatory notes where necessary to make sure the researcher is fully informed of any factors which might have

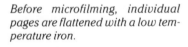

Before microfilming, individual pages are flattened with a low temperature iron.

affected the quality of the image on the film, such as missing pages, faint writing, or tight bindings.

The third reason for extra care is that use of a commercial filming service means that the records will be temporarily passing out of the custody of the archives which introduces the possibilities of externally caused disturbance, damage or loss of the records. Clearly the archivist responsible must take steps to prevent such occurrences and/or to facilitate full recovery should something happen to the material whether in transit or at the filming venue. A detailed inventory of the material should be made so that, if necessary, any lost item can be identified and the original order restored. The material should be carefully packaged so that the risk of damage in transit is minimised. As mentioned earlier, it may be considered worthwhile to accompany the material to the bureau and even to be present when the filming is done.

Equally, care must be taken during the return of the original material and the microfilm copies. In particular, extremes of heat and temperature must be avoided, since damage may be caused by the resultant changes in dimension and moisture in the film.

Examples of notes which are filmed along with the original records to explain any problems.

7) **Final checking of the microfilm and the original material.** Once returned, the original material and the microfilm copies should be checked carefully before paying the bill. To determine technical quality, it may be useful to have the microfilm tested independently by an institutional or commercial lab to ensure that the stipulated standards of processing have been adhered to. If necessary, re–washing or even re–filming should be insisted upon. Check the microfilm against the originals to ensure that it is complete and in order. Also check the order and condition of the originals before returning them to the shelves.

8) **Proper storage of microfilm.** It is not the purpose of this chapter to discuss in detail the storage environment that is required for the long–term preservation of microfilm. Indeed, the design of a controlled environment for the storage of microfilm is the province of engineers and architects. It is, however, useful to be aware of the most important factors which determine the suitability of a storage environment for master archival film:

- *Temperature in general.* A low temperature (10 degrees centigrade for black and white film, 0 degrees centigrade for colour) prolongs the life of the microfilm image by reducing the rate at which the chemical changes take place which result in deterioration; changes in temperature, such as the cyclical changes of office air-conditioning, should also be avoided.
- *Humidity.* A low (40% RH) prevents the growth of mould

or fungus which eats the emulsion of the film; but, if it is too low, the film base can dry out and become brittle; good air circulation is also important; and again, changes should be minimised.

- *Storage equipment.* Purpose-designed equipment, including shelving, drawers and boxes are available for storing microfilm. Alternatively, existing equipment may be adapted.
- *Hazards to avoid.* Microfilm should be kept away from such hazards as heat, light, and water, which could cause damage. For this reason, attics and below-ground storage should generally be avoided.

If it is not possible to provide your own storage which meets these conditions, a large archival institution could be approached to keep security or preservation negatives of your microfilm.

This strict environment is not required for reference copies. Here, emphasis should be placed on proper handling, care in loading and removing from readers, and keeping readers and printers clean and working well.

The microfilm camera operator photographs each page.

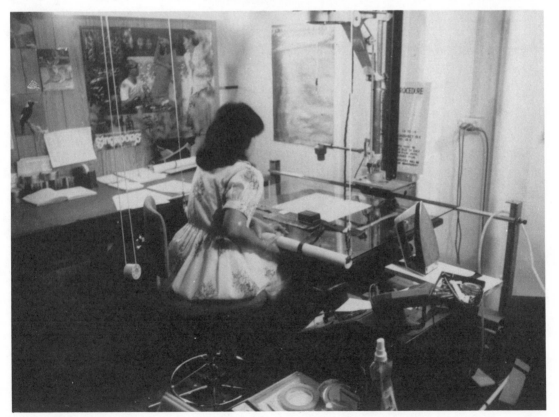

Box C   Estimating the Cost of a Microfilming Project

Area of Expense	Estimated Quantity/ Hours	Cost per Unit	Amount
1) **Quantity to be microfilmed**			
• shelf metres			
• number of frames (approx. 80–100 frames per cm of paper thickness)			
2) **Preparation of identification sheets**			
• archivist's time			
• typist's time			
• stationery costs			
• printing costs			
3) **Preparation of records**			
• conservation work required			
• removal of pins, staples, folds			
• final checking of page order			
4) **Filming**			
• supervisor's time			
• operator's time			
• equipment time			
• cost of ? x 100 feet of film at $ per 100 foot length			
• cost of 'permalife' protection			
5) **Examination of master**			
• checking time			
• cost of residual chemical testing			
6) **Filming of retakes/additions**			
• preparation of records			
• supervisor's time			
• operator's time			
• equipment time			
• cost of ? x 100 feet of film at $ per 100 foot length			
• cost of 'permalife' protection			
• checking time			
• cost of residual chemical testing			
7) **Reassembling of records**			
• replacement of pins, etc.			
• checking of order			
8) **Transportation**			
• of material			
• of staff			
9) **Copying**			
• cost of copy negative			
• cost of copy positive x copies required			
• cost of examining copies			
• cost of residual chemical testing			
Total:			

INTERNSHIP POSSIBILITIES

Maine
Vermont
New Hampshire
Massachusetts
_____ — N.
Montana

Cred.

3 — Interim Session

4 — 1st Far Weeks

3 — July 15 — Aug 20th
        Internship.

1. a. What were the conditions that encouraged early modern Europeans to undertake voyages of exploration and discovery? b. What factor do you believe was the most essential?

2. Compare and contrast Aztec society in the fifteenth century with that of early modern Europe.

3. Describe the empire that the Spanish established in America. Consider the character of the Spanish colonial economy, population, and institutional structures.

4. Discuss the developments that heightened interest in overseas exploration annd colonization among English political leaders, merchants, and gentry families during the 1570s.

Box D   Australian Archives Microfilming Specifications

1) **Documents to be microfilmed**
    a)   Commonwealth Record Series: Records of the National Australasian Convention, 1891 (CRS R1 — CRS R31)
    b)   Whether whole or part of the series: Whole series
    c)   Format: Mainly foolscap sheets and files, but includes six quarto volumes
    d)   Quantity of records to be microfilmed: 0.55 shelf metres
    e)   Approximate size of pages/folios: 335mm x 205mm (some larger, some smaller)
    f)   Approximate number of frames: 4000
    g)   Colour of documents: Blue, red, white (colour testing required)

2) **Camera**
    A planetary camera shall be used, under no circumstances will a rotary camera be acceptable.

3) **Film**
    To meet the American National Standard Specifications for Photographic Film for Archival Records, Silver-Gelation Type on Cellulose Ester Base, PHI.28–1973 or the latest revision thereof.
    Dimensions of film, processed and unprocessed, to meet the specifications set out in USA Standard Specifications for 16mm or 35mm Silver-Gelatin Microfilms for Reel Applications, PH5.3–1967, Section 4, or the latest revision thereof.
    To be 100 feet long, unperforated, and without splices, tears, cuts or holes.
    At least 50 cms must be left at each end of the film to permit insertion into microfilm reader reels.
    A space of 30cms is to be left between each series.
    A space of approximately three frames is to be left between each item.
    The film will be surrendered on spools and will be boxed and clearly labelled/identified.
    Before any copies are made the master negative will be surrendered for checking of image placement etc. and residual chemicals.

4) **Indicators**
    All title sheets and indicators will be provided by the Australian Archives.

5) **Image Placement**
    In Simplex fashion in position IB (Comic mode), or IIB for volumes, as recognised by the USA Standard Specifications for 16mm and 35mm Silver-Gelatin Microfilms for Reel Applications, PH5.3–1967, Section 5.

6) **Reduction Ratio**
    Approximately 11 times

7) **Archival Quality**
    The archival quality of the film must meet the requirements set by British Standard 1153.1975, Recommendations for the processing and storage of silver-gelatin-type microfilm; American National Standard PH4.8–1971, Methylene blue test for measuring thiosulphate and silver densitometric method for measuring residual chemicals in films, plates and papers, and Australian Defence Standards. The film will require additional perma-film protection.

8) **Conditions of Microfilming**
    The documents may be filmed on your premises in the presence of a member of the Australian Archives' staff. Transportation of the documents to and from your premises will be undertaken by this office. The documents must *at all times* remain in official custody.

9) **Microfilm Copies**
    Master negative: 35mm
    Copy negative: 1 copy (to be quoted for separately)
    Copy positives: 9 copies required (to be quoted for separately)

Microfilm Readers

A wide range of microfilm viewers or readers are available, new models are being introduced all the time and, given the cost of these machines, it is worthwhile to seek expert advice before making a choice. You may also want to consider leasing rather than purchasing your equipment at first in order to gauge user demand and satisfaction, prior to a major investment.

The following are some of the desirable features which should be sought:

1) Versatility in terms of the formats of microfilm which the equipment can accommodate
2) Capacity to adjust the screen's angle and brightness, with green and blue being the most restful screen colours
3) Quietness and economy of operation; easy maintenance and reliable, fast repairs.

If a reader/printer is to be chosen, the quality of the hard copy, the speed of the printing process and the ease or otherwise of routine maintenance should be investigated.

Having chosen a reader, consideration must be given as to where to locate it. Background glare should be avoided, as should light reflected from the screen. The intermittent noise caused by the operation of a microfilm reader may be distracting both to staff and to other researchers and, therefore, it is desirable to isolate it if possible.

TECHNOLOGY IN THE FUTURE

The two technologies which have been the principal subjects of this chapter, that is ADP and micrographics, have been treated quite separately. The evidence, however, would appear to indicate that these technologies are in the process of merging in two respects.

Computer Output Microfilm or Microfiche (COM)

Already larger archival institutions are receiving COM material into their custody as archives. The same may be said for records on magnetic media such as floppy discs and computer tapes. The magnetic formats also present peculiar problems of preservation: not only are they particularly susceptible to damage and deterioration through use and the passage of time, but the equipment required to read them will quickly be superseded, rendering their information inaccessible. One solution to this problem of technological change in computer–generated record formats may be to dump their information onto COM at an early stage. This action preserves the information in a more stable medium, and data on COM can be re–introduced into a computer system as needed in the future by being 'read' by a special scanner which converts the images once again to magnetic pulses. While micrographic technology and formats will also undoubtedly continue to develop, the rate of change should be much easier to accommodate.

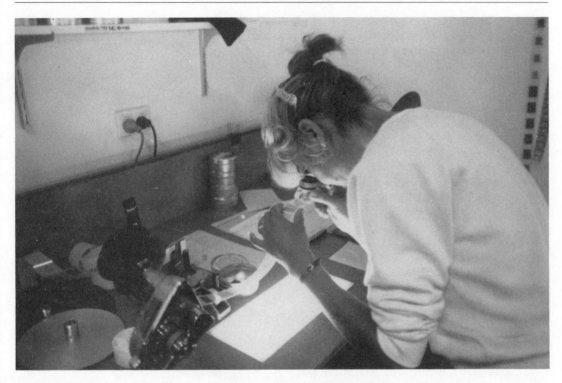

Master negatives must be inspected to meet archival requirements.

High Density Optical Disc Technology

It seems more likely, however, that the archival future of ADP, micrographics and, indeed, of audio–visual records, lies in the digital optical disc. The information is recorded in a digital form in pits embedded in the surface of the disc, and a laser beam reflected off the surface reads the digital information, which is decoded by a microprocessor. The audio compact disc (CD) is the best known form of laser disc at present. While developed originally for home video use, the potential of this format for high density data storage in ADP systems is already being recognised. With an adequate refinement of image sharpness, optical discs could replace microfilm as a means of recording images of paper records and photographs. Because all of the information present, including colours, is digitised, the previous problems with the stability of film colours is eliminated.

The optical disc presents the prospect of data, text, still and moving images, and sound all appearing on the same disc, thus blurring and almost eliminating the differences between these traditional record formats.

For the archivist, the optical disc has the advantage that, handled with care, it will not deteriorate through use, thus eliminating the need for master, working and reference copies — only an extra security copy need be kept in case of loss. While by no means indestructible, the optical disc would appear to be the most robust record format since the baked clay tablet. It may, therefore, be the answer to the archivist's prayers, both as the ideal original record format and as a means of preserving the information or image of original records having less permanent forms.

The use of computers and micrographics can be valuable for a small archival operation in a wide range of activities. The key to maximising their value is careful preparation: in assessing your needs; in selecting equipment, software and services; in preparing your holdings. While this preparation may be time–consuming, it should be seen as an investment, which will be well repaid by the better management of your archives which will result.

This reader printer accommodates reel–to–reel microfilms and microfiche.

FURTHER READING

Archives Authority of New South Wales (AONSW), *Guidelines on Establishing a Microfilming Program*.Technical Paper Number No. 3. Sydney: AONSW, 1983.

Archives Authority of New South Wales (AONSW), *Microfilming of Records*.Technical Paper Number No. 4. Sydney: AONSW, 1983.

Cook, Michael, *Archives and the Computer*.2nd edition.London: Butterworth's, 1986.

Evans, Max and Lisa B. Weber, *MARC for Archives and Manuscripts: a Compendium of Practice*. Madison, WI: State Historical Society of Wisconsin, 1985.

Hensen, Steven L., *Archives, Personal Papers, and Manuscripts: A Cataloging Manual for Archival Repositories, Historical Societies, and Manuscript Libraries*. Washington, DC: Library of Congress, 1983.

Kesner, Richard M., *Automation for Archivists and Records Managers: Planning and Implementation*. Chicago, IL: American Library Association, 1984.

Sahli, Nancy. *MARC for Archives and Manuscripts: The AMC Format*. Chicago, IL: Society of American Archivists, 1985.

Smith, Ken and Patricia Ward, editors, *Microfilming Local Government Records: Issues and Challenges*. Selected Papers from microfilm seminars held 29 April and 8 July, 1983. Occasional Paper No. 7. Sydney: Library Association of Australia (NSW Branch), 1983.

Sung, Carolyn Hoover, *Archives and Manuscripts: Reprography*. Chicago, IL: Society of American Archivists, 1982.

CHAPTER TEN

DOCUMENTATION PROGRAMMES FOR ARCHIVES

Ann Pederson

INTRODUCTION

Up to this point the chapters you have read have been quite specific in their discussion of the factors and steps involved in key archival processes such as acquisition or arrangement and description. This chapter on Documentation Programmes will be more general in its approach, focusing on how these activities may *complement and support* the major archival functions rather than on giving step–by–step instructions for carrying out each project. The reasons for having this general overview are threefold. First, there is an enormous variety of documentation activities which an archives can undertake and to treat even the major types in detail would require several books. Second, several of the projects highlighted, such as oral history or documentary photography, already have a considerable body of 'how to' literature available which can be perused. Third, because documentation programmes can be quite expensive, it is rather more important to see them as supplements to the existing core of archival functions, to be considered only after the essential archival work is progressing well.

WHAT ARE DOCUMENTATION PROGRAMMES?

Documentation programmes are efforts by archives to assemble documents or to record information of historical interest for future research. Not surprisingly it is often a wider community interest in culture or heritage that motivates projects which create, copy, or transcribe and organise previously inaccessible sources. Many of these research materials, such as oral or video history tapes, would not have existed naturally and so have been especially created to fill gaps in the written records. Other documentary sources, such as photographs in private hands, or gravestones, may already exist, but are so scattered and isolated that they are useless for research unless copied and organised.

The family of activities we are calling documentation programmes has three basic branches. The first and most controversial group, created documentation, includes projects which set out to make a special recording of unique information. While we have within this group the previously mentioned oral history and video recordings, we would also incorporate contemporary projects to photograph towns and institutions at regular or critical phases in their development.

The second major branch of documentation activity comprises efforts to re–record or make facsimiles of existing documents and records which are not available to the public. Examples of this work includes the copying of selected official or personal papers (particularly diaries, minutes and letters) and of photographs held privately in distant or scattered locations. The key characteristic of this category is that these projects seek to make facsimiles of existing private documents accessible to the public.

A third category, though closely related to the first two, is one comprising projects to transfer information recorded on gravestones, buildings, caves and other public, but inaccessible, structures to media more useable by researchers. Projects in this category often send out teams of people to transcribe information and/or photograph the structures bearing it for later compilation and subsequent use by researchers. These projects are generally more interested in transferring selected information to a more accessible medium than they are in facsimile reproduction, unless they are recording works of art.

Having enumerated these basic categories, we will proceed to examine each in turn with the goal of establishing some guidelines you might use to conduct them successfully. But first, a key piece of advice.

THE NEED FOR PLANNING AND COMMITMENT

The first questions an archivist or organisation considering documentation activities should ask are 'what resources are required for such programmes?' and 'how will they relate to the other commitments and priorities of the archives and of the organisation as a whole?' If your institution is currently struggling to find the staff, space, and equipment to manage its existing collections, perhaps it is not wise to rush into a new venture, particularly one that depends so heavily on having sufficient staff and money to ensure a quality product.

All successful documentation programmes require a certain standard of technical and historical excellence. Poor quality recorders, tapes, or photographic materials can result in totally wasted efforts because the resulting records are so inferior that

Oral history interviews are indexed using a counter on the tape recorder; always work from a cassette copy rather than the master tape.

they can have only limited use or will last a very short period of time. Over and above materials, it is equally important to have procedures to ensure that the process of selecting and recording the material fulfils the requirements of historical evidence.

Creating the best documentary products using proper materials and techniques is only the first step. Many archivists do these things well, yet end up with poor programmes because they did not plan carefully for the final and most important phase of the project — the facilities and staff to maintain and reference the collections. Of primary importance is the preservation of the original recording. This may be difficult, particularly in the case of audio and video magnetic tapes (see section on Video : The Pluses and Minuses, for more detailed explanation). Whatever the media, the original record must be secured and stored with no use, except to make a master duplicate which itself is used only to make additional copies for reference use. The expense of proper storage for original audio–visual media and of producing a minimum of three units (the original, the master duplicate, and a reference copy) per document is considerable, but essential. The preparation of indexes and other finding aids also tends to be expensive, since photographs and magnetic tapes cannot be easily scanned and summarised. Finally there is the need to provide and maintain equipment to enable researchers to safely and accurately re–experience the material. Again, this area involves considerable potential expense, especially as advancing technology can quickly render existing equipment obsolete. Over time then, the archives could face the costly prospect of maintaining a museum of machinery to play its media artefacts, if only for further reproduction or transfer to a more contemporary mode. Alternatively, it could form a co–operative with other repositories to ensure that, among the members, the full range of needed equipment and expertise would be available long term.

A final area that one must consider is the social side of documentation programmes. Perhaps more than other types of archival activities, documentary efforts bring you and your staff into very close contact with a variety of citizens of the community. Whether they be interview candidates, or volunteers conducting the project, people require considerable instruction, guidance, and support, if one hopes to produce materials of research quality. However, this direction and control must be flexible and applied with sensitivity. A major goal of the archives should be to generate community interest and involvement. People want to participate, enjoy themselves and feel appreciated; therefore those responsible for administering the archives must build a very strong component of training, encouragement and monitoring into the documentation programme if it is to be successful.

All of these factors — previous commitments, technical quality, good procedures, time, and a desire and willingness to be intimately involved with people — must be considered and accounted for in your decision to undertake a programme of documentation activities. Lest you think, at this point, that we are trying to send you on a 'downer', nothing could be further from the truth. Rather, we want to help you to be realistic and successful in your undertakings. The archives should be a source of clear thinking and advice on matters of documentation within the community.

Archives with sound records must also have the equipment to play them.

CREATED DOCUMENTATION PROGRAMMES

The search for a way to capture actual events, meetings, performances, and encounters so that they can be readily
re-experienced has been underway for many years. Always the
challenge has been how to replicate the sights, sounds, feelings,
and movements of life in process and incorporate them in a
long-lasting record. In recent times, many museums, archives,
libraries with local history materials, and historical societies
have become interested in the concept of *created documentation
programmes*. Since most institutions operate under a wide directive 'to collect and preserve the community's valuable historical
resources', a number of them have undertaken special activities
to *create* records reflecting the present and recent past. Whether
such activities are called oral history, modern heritage projects,
local history programmes, or historical photography, all created
documentation programmes select persons, places, and events
in their communities and attempt to capture them using the tape
recorder, the camera and, most recently, the video recorder. The
resulting products of such recording sessions are magnetic
tapes, both audio and video, and photographic negatives and
prints which the archivist takes into custody, preserves and
makes available for research.

Why Are Created Documentation Programmes Special and Controversial?

What makes these records different from the archival materials
we have described earlier is the way in which they are created. In
the case of created documentation programmes, the archivist is the
initiator, in some cases, the actual creator, rather than the custodian
of the material. He or she may even be said to be orchestrating the
quantity and quality of documentation and is thus intervening to
produce resources for future history which would not otherwise be
available. In short, the archivist is responsible for materials which
would never have existed at all without this conscious effort to create a record for posterity.

This type of intrusion into the natural course of events does not
harmonise well with traditional archival principles which advo-
cate a much more neutral and objective stance for the archivist.
While archivists are obliged to act to ensure that records created
in the normal course of an individual's or organisation's active
work are identified and preserved, they are cautioned not to interfere or distort this natural process. In contrast, because the archivist is seen as actually generating the records produced by
created documentation programmes, there is considerable
controversy about the appropriateness of such action and about
the validity or reliability of historical evidence created in such a
'self-conscious' way. By 'self-conscious' we mean that the
records have been produced with the idea that they are 'for

history'. Some critics feel that these types of documents may not
be as valid as those generated in the course of ongoing business,
political or social activity. The rule of thumb is then, whenever
possible, to make consciously created records such as oral history interviews, available in conjunction with a variety of other
documents which are more natural by–products of business or
personal life. Locating and acquiring letters, diaries, papers, and
photographs related to the events or persons under study provide the all important reference points from which to test the
authority and reliability of the interviews.

Perhaps it would be wise here to contrast the types of materials
we are discussing i.e. especially created documents, with audio
tapes, photos or videos which are the products of ongoing work
activity. Take as an example the regular audio taping of meetings
of the City Council. By virtue of the fact that these tapes are made
in the normal course of business and capture discussions in progress, they are primary documentation of those proceedings.
However, if the recordings are interviews with key Aldermen
asking their recollections and opinions about what happened in
the meeting, they have less authority as evidence. This diminished
status reflects the fact that the interviews were influenced by the
personal viewpoints of the Aldermen and of the interviewer, particularly if they were recorded much later or if they focus on a
specific issue which evolved over time. Such tapes are selected
and filtered accounts especially designed to capture definite
information and therefore must be used for research with those
factors in mind. While audio visual materials are especially vulnerable to subjective influences, the same filtering is present in
paper records. For example the tape recordings of meetings may
be summarised into written minutes which delete emotional
exchanges, the evolution of the discussion and other information
important to understanding how a particular problem might have
been solved.

Additionally, there are special aspects of sound, video and film
media which archivists must appreciate and plan to accommodate. The first is to recognise that these materials capture actual
events in progress, and therefore intrinsically convey two types
of information that written records do not — time and emotion.
Because of these additional dimensions, such records cannot be
summarised, edited or transcribed without distorting the experiences they were created to preserve. Thus special care must be
taken to maintain such records in their complete original form,
though copies, transcripts, and summaries of their informational
contents may also be made to facilitate reference use. The second fact to remember is that there is always more than one person involved in creating audio–visual records. With written
materials, the writer both creates the document and determines
its content. However, with audio–visual media, there may be sev-

eral persons involved — the subject, the interviewer who may or may not be operating the recording equipment, and perhaps others such as researchers, project directors, or technicians. Having multiple 'creators' means that the record can be influenced by several interpretations and viewpoints. It may present the subject or event as interviewed and/or photographed by another person, and this fact should always be recorded and noted when audio–visual materials are used as historical evidence.

Regardless of the issues or debate surrounding created documentation, one thing is certain. More and more institutions and people are becoming involved in created documentation programmes. They are tape recording oral reminiscences of the community, making videotapes of local events, drawing or photographing town landmarks, to name only a few such activities. Not only are people involved with creating records, they are also generating excitement and interest in community culture and history as a result of them. So we move now to discuss major types of created documentation programmes, both to identify good practices and those which are unwise or unsound, so that institutions may make the best use of their scarce resources.

Types of Created Documentation: Photography

Programmes centred around photography and historical photographs appeal to many audiences and afford excellent opportunities for involving the public in archival collecting efforts. Photographic documentation projects are of two major types: current and retrospective. The first we will take up here as it is a form of created documentation. The second, retrospective heritage photography or projects to re–photograph existing images from the past, we will discuss under *Compiling Documentary Sources*.

City landmarks should be photographed at regular intervals.

Modern heritage photography usually involves a regular programme of taking and obtaining high–quality photographs of events, persons, places, and activities occurring within the geographic area served by the archives. Such a programme offers a number of advantages. First, it generates a regular addition of significant images for the collections. Second, many professional and amateur photographers welcome an invitation to perform such a service in their communities. Third, there are good prospects for arranging joint sponsorships with other organisations such as art schools, camera clubs, or local press associations. Finally, most of the images can be accessioned and used without confusion about ownership, copyright, and personal privacy issues because they were taken under archival sponsorship or donated by the photographers.

In addition to receiving full information about the project, all persons taking or obtaining photographs for the archives should be asked to sign an agreement establishing the archives' ownership of the images donated to the institution. The ownership agreement should transfer custody of the image and related rights to the archives, as indicated in the sample in Box A. Copyright is specifically vested in the archives because the work was done for hire. When taking photographs that include recognisable persons, photographers should ask each subject to sign a release in which the individual consents to being photographed and grants unrestricted use of images in which he or she appears.

The success of these programmes depends heavily on the staff's ability to make the photographers aware of the kinds of images that are most useful for historical purposes. For example, the project could focus on local organisations in an effort to create a visual record of the various institutions — economic, social, political, and cultural — that shape the character of everyday life. Another approach is to document the buildings, streets, and neighbourhoods that form the physical fabric of the community. As part of this effort, photographers should be asked to submit logs containing all pertinent information about their subjects (i.e., date, name, address, and other details) so the prints can be properly labelled and catalogued. These records should be maintained on deposit at the archives as part of the project file.

Because such projects involve continuing photographic activity, the staff should work with the photographers in devising a plan for photographing sites, landmarks, and similar subjects at regular intervals, perhaps every three to five years. During the rest of the year, project personnel should try to document major events and gatherings by working with local print media personnel or arranging to dispatch a member of the project team to cover selected occasions.[1]

35mm negatives of private records copied by the archives are stored in polyester sleeves.

Types of Created Documentation: Oral History

Oral history is, perhaps, the best known and most widely practised type of documentation programme. A concept difficult to define concisely, oral history is essentially an information gathering technique whereby sound recording equipment is used systematically to capture '. . . verbatim accounts or opinions of persons who are or were witnesses to or participants in events likely to be of interest to future scholars.'[2] Aural or sound materials lend a colour and dimension that extends information beyond the written page into an involving experience. With sound we know not only what is said, but how. The nuance of the tone and timbre of voice, the urgency and cadence of speaking helps us tune in on the emotional wavelength of the speaker and thereby to come closer to his/her experience. Over the last twenty

[1]The material in the preceding section was taken from the author's work in *Archives and Manuscripts: Public Programs.* Chicago, IL: Society of American Archivists, 1982. pp. 24–25, 78–79.
[2]William W. Moss, *Oral History Program Manual.* New York: Praeger, 1974. p.7.

Box A   Photographic Documentation:
Photography Agreement Form

I, ..., in consideration of value
received, hereby agree to provide to ....
(sponsoring institution) the photographic services described below:

I understand that I will be working as a representative of ....
...............................(sponsoring institution), and I
agree that the ownership of the photographic images produced and all
rights thereto are vested in ....
(sponsoring institution). I understand that I will receive the following:

I hereby warrant that I have every right to contract in my own name in
the above regard.

....
(Date)   (Photographer's Name)

                                         ....
                                         (Name of Representative of
                                         Sponsoring Institution)

                                         ....
                                         (Name of Sponsoring
                                         Institution)

---

years, practitioners of oral history have fought for and achieved scholarly recognition at a number of levels. Professional researchers representing fields such as anthropology, sociology, history and literature, among others, regularly produce and consume oral documents in their work. Several Commonwealth research institutions such as the Australian War Memorial, the National Film and Sound Archive, the National Library of Australia, and the Australian Institute of Aboriginal Studies, to name only a few, and some major state libraries and archival agencies, have formal programmes in oral history which document the work of living Australians. They also accept cohesive collections of audio tapes representing the work of research professionals who have conducted their own scholarly investigations. Persons with an active interest in oral history have formed the Oral History Association of Australia, a branch of an international body; and those institutions and individuals who care for material in aural format, be it verbal, instrumental, or both, may be members of the International Association of Sound Archives (IASA). The reason for mentioning the various institutions and professional bodies is to underscore the fact that aural documentation is a well-established and important discipline which supplements

and fills in gaps in traditional paper records. Furthermore, the practice of it is professional and sufficiently widespread that most organisations considering undertaking an oral history programme can find qualified persons to advise them.

Oral history interviews should be conducted in quiet, comfortable surroundings.

Good oral history is seldom the child of spontaneity. A successful project requires careful research and preparation at many levels: 1) in selecting the focus of the effort; 2) in choosing the persons to be interviewed; 3) in designing the questions to be asked; 4) in mastering the art of being a good interviewer; and 5) in preparing the materials for long-term preservation and use. The following are some suggestions for achieving quality in all five areas.[3]

- Design the subject and scope of the project with a clear sense of what can be accomplished in terms of information, quality, and the potential value of the project for future research investigations.
- Be sure to consider the expense and technical problems involved in the preparation, use, and long-term maintenance of the tape products.
- Select and train personnel for the project so that all interviewers are skilled interpersonal communicators who are also well-versed in the subject matter to be covered.
- Select good-quality, reliable, and manageable recording

[3]The oral history points and tables were adapted from the author's work in *Archives and Manuscripts: Public Programs.* Chicago, IL: SAA, 1982. pp. 23–24, 71–77.

equipment and tapes. Even with the best equipment, you will also need backups in case of mechanical difficulties or tape snarls. Use a good–quality microphone and invest in special filters to block out extraneous noises. Local broadcasters may be willing to recommend, or even lend, equipment to suit your needs.

- Do your archival and legal homework so that your effort yields long–lasting results and produces taped interviews available for research and quotation. Carefully document the purpose and design of the project, the conditions under which the interviews were conducted, and any factors that might have affected the objectivity of the interviewee's comments.

- Have the interviewer (if not an employee of the archives) and interviewee sign a release in which they agree to participate in the project; to donate their interviews to the archives, together with all literary rights and copyrights; and to permit research use of the interview tapes, transcripts, or other copies. Examples of such agreements appear in Tables One, Two and Three.

- Keep the project moving with training, direction, regular progress reports, and encouragement. Appendix Four shows the text of a training leaflet covering many of the basic procedures that ought to be reviewed with all new project personnel.

- Ask interviewees to contribute photographs and written records to the archives. If possible, photograph or videotape subjects at the time they are interviewed. (See Box B for ideas).

- Publicise the project during the phases of its development: conception, planning, progress, and as the materials become available for research.

- Protect original tapes immediately through proper labelling and storage and do not play them except to produce a duplicating master from which additional copies will be made for indexing work or for later reference use.

- To transcribe or not to transcribe, that is the question. Because of the expense of transcription and the loss of information which can be conveyed only by sound, it is recommended that archivists not transcribe but rather prepare notes describing the contents of the tapes keyed to the numerical counter of the tape recorder/player. These notes then serve as a rough index to the tapes.

- Be sure to thank personnel connected with the taping and, if funding permits, enclose a duplicate tape of the interview as a memento of appreciation.

- Consider using copies of project tapes to create slide–tape presentations or public service announcements for radio and television stations. After all, there is no substitute for hearing the spoken word spoken.

Table One   Oral History: Participant Agreement Form

I, ..., hereby declare my
willingness to participate in the . . . . oral
history project, sponsored by . . . .
I understand that the audio tapes from this project will be deposited at
the . . . . (archival repository) as a
supplement to the written records of the . . . .
. . . .

   I hereby agree to an interview conducted by project personnel during
which I will discuss my involvement with . . . .
activities and share my opinions regarding these matters and related
issues. I understand and accept the need for forthright and candid discussion and also understand that I will approve, in advance, the subjects
to be discussed. It is agreed that I will be given an opportunity to hear
the complete interview and to correct or add material in a separate format prior to signing a formal document for archival deposit. Finally, I
pledge my cooperation in making the tapes created during the interview
available for research use within sound archival guidelines.

. . . .
Preferred Interview Date and   Signature
Time

Preferred Interview Location: . . . .
[   ] Home   Name
[   ] Archives Repository
[   ] Other . . . .

                                     . . . .
                                     Street

                                     . . . .
                                     City   State   P.code

                                     . . . .
                                     Date

                                     . . . .
                 Signature of representative of (project sponsor)

Table Two   Oral History: Donor Form

....
(Name of archival repository)
Gift of Personal Statement

By ....
(Name of Narrator/Interviewee)
(Official name of person/organisation/event being documented)
Oral History Collection

I, ... (narrator/interviewee), hereinafter referred to as the donor, hereby give, donate, and convey, to the .... (archival repository) .... (name of collection) Oral History Collection, and for administration therein by the authorities thereof, the audio tape recordings, hereinafter referred to as the material, containing my observations and statements and made on .... (date). This gift is made subject to the following terms and conditions: (tick those appropriate)

[ ] a) The donor transfers full title of the material and all literary rights, to .... (name of archival repository) as of the date of this agreement

[ ] b) As donor, I understand that I will have the opportunity to listen to the entire interview when completed and may, at that time and in a separate format, provide additional information, correct errors, and designate any portions as confidential for a specified period of time.

[ ] c) If, in the future, funding is available to prepare transcripts of the taped interviews, I, as the donor, understand that I will be given the opportunity to read and approve the transcription and may, at that time, provide additional information, correct errors, and designate any portions as confidential for a specified period of time.

[ ] d) As the donor, it is my wish that access to the material transferred hereunder be as follows:

[ ] 1) The material may be made available to anyone applying to use the collection.

[ ] 2) Persons wishing to use the material in the next .... years must have written approval from me or my representative .... (name of representative) before they may receive access to the material. I understand that I agree to respond to such applications promptly and that it is my or my representative responsibility to notify .... (name of archival repository) officials of current addresses. After .... years, the material will no longer be restricted.

DONOR FORM

Gift of Personal Statement of ....
(name of narrator/interviewee)
Oral History Collection

A written revision of any terms governing access to the material for research may be entered into by the donor or his representative and officials of the .... (name of archival repository), if either party wishes to do so.

.... Name of Narrator/Interviewee   .... Name of Interviewer

.... Signature of Narrator/Interviewee   .... Signature of Interviewer

.... Street   .... Signature of (Name of Archival Repository) Representative

.... City   State   Postcode   .... Date of Agreement

[ ] Interview Tape Approved   .... Signature of Narrator/Interviewee
.... Date

[ ] Transcript Approved   .... Signature of Narrator
.... Date

Table Three   Oral History: Donor Form

GLENELG REGIONAL LIBRARY SERVICE
A. Interviewee
I/we . . . . (names)
of, ... (address)
agree to the use of the tape–recorded interview between myself/
ourselves and . . . . (name of
interviewer) made on . . . . (date) in the
following ways.

1) The original tape–recorded interview, to be known as the MASTER TAPE will be held in the *State Library of Victoria*.

2) A copy or copies of the Master Tape will be made on duplicate tapes and held by the *Glenelg Regional Library Service*.

3) The *State Library of Victoria* or the *Glenelg Regional Library Service* may prepare or cause to be prepared a transcription of the Master Tape if they so desire.

4) The recording/s, duplicate/s and/or transcript/s may be made available in the *State Library of Victoria* to *bona fide* scholars.

5) The duplicate tapes and/or transcripts may be made available in any *Branch* of the *Glenelg Regional Library Service* to all persons who would normally be granted use of the *Library's* resources.

6) The *State Library of Victoria* may provide further copies of the tape/s and or transcript/s for purposes of historical record, research or private study to other libraries and institutions.

7) The recording/s and or transcript/s may be quoted in part in published works, broadcasts or public performances provided in each case, acknowledgement be made to *me/us*.

8) Permission to use the recording/s and or transcript/s in full, in publications, broadcasts, or public performances must be through an initial approach to the *Glenelg Regional Library Service*.

9) After 10 years rights in the tape/s are vested in the *Library Council of Victoria*.

10) Special conditions:

Signed by interviewee:

Witness (Interviewer):

Date:

B. Interviewer
I, ... (name)
of, ... (address)
agree that the tape of the interview referred to above may be used as itemised in Points one (1) to ten (10) of the previous consent form signed by the interviewee and witnessed by myself as the interviewer for and on behalf of the *Glenelg Regional Library Service*.

Signed: . . . .
Date: . . . .
Witnessed: . . . .
Regional Librarian, Glenelg Regional Library Service

Agreement for deposit of a tape–recorded interview for the Oral History Project (1979) conducted by the Glenelg Regional Library Service. Points underlined or in parentheses have been added to show places where you will need to put in the names of persons or organisations appropriate for your oral history programme.

Box B   Don't Forget the Photos!

The person whose recollections you are recording may also have other valuable documentary material in family albums, in suitcases, in boxes under the house and in other places. This material can assist during the interview by stirring memories. It is also a valuable asset for an archival collection, and in any presentation of an ethnic community's history and/or an individual's history.

The following list suggests some of the types of documents which may be found among private papers.

1) **Personal records:**
Scrapbooks
Photographs
Letters to and from the country of origin
Diaries
Memoirs
Documents (e.g. naturalisation certificates, passports, employment records, trade union and political party tickets, etc.)

2) **Government publications and documents:**
From country of origin:
School textbooks
Information about emigration (e.g. pamphlets, newsletters, etc.) Directories (e.g. of government agencies, regulations, etc.)
Tourist brochures
Posters

From Australia:
Publicity pamphlets and posters about Australia directed at migrants
Guides for new immigrants
Citizenship booklets
Letters (e.g. to and from Australian government authorities about the possibility of immigration; complaints/congratulations to government authorities).

3) **Newsletters, newspapers and journals (in English and other languages):**
Including *ad hoc* publications produced on board the ship on the way to Australia, or in holding centres; or by ethnic communities in Australia or elsewhere.

4) **Records of social clubs, welfare associations, political organisations, religious groups, etc.:**
Minutes of meetings
Notices of activities
Statement of objectives
Histories
Commemorative programmes or publications
Membership lists
Conference, seminar, workshop, etc., records, news releases
Photographs
Personal accounts of activities and involvement
Letters

Wilton, Janis and Angela Bollard, *Balancing The Books: Oral History For The Community.* Sydney: Ethnic Affairs Commission of NSW, 1983.p.24.

Table Four   Oral History: Guidelines for Interviews

GUIDELINES FOR ORAL HISTORY INTERVIEWS

1) **Select the subject** of the interview. Is it to be biographical, general, or topical?

2) **Select the interviewee.** You will get suggestions for possible interviewees (narrators) from family, friends, civic groups, teachers, etc. Try to set priorities for whom you interview so that your time is used as profitably as possible. If accuracy is important to your project, think about the reliability of the narrator you select. At the same time, don't be so selective that you ignore all but the leading citizens of your community and miss some of the most interesting and informative people.

3) **Make initial contact.** Initial contact should be made in person, if possible, by the individual who will actually be doing the interview. This is an opportunity to establish rapport with the narrator, but be careful to prevent this first meeting from turning into an interview session sans tape recorder. Keep the meeting brief and to the point.

    This is the time to tell the interviewee about your project and why you want to interview him/her. Make sure he/she understands how the tapes of his/her interview will be used. You might also take this opportunity to get the release form signed or at least to tell him/her that you will be asking him/her to sign one. Also, point out that you will give him/her the opportunity to review the tape or transcript of the tape to make separate changes or corrections as needed. You might use this time to show the person a list of the kinds of questions you will ask, but use your judgment on this. Don't make the narrator feel compelled to stick to the topics on that list.

4) **Pre-interview research.** You will be able to ask better questions if you know as much as possible about the person being interviewed and about the subject of the interview. Be careful to use this information only to open questions, not to tell the interviewee your opinion.

5) **Prepare a list of interview questions.** A list of possible questions will help you move through the interview easily. It will also inspire confidence in beginning interviewers. Keep this list brief and remember to be flexible enough to add other questions or delete prepared ones as you get a feel for the interview. Remember this list is only to help, not direct or dominate you. And don't read the questions off the sheet!

6) **Be sure of your equipment.** Practise with the recorder you will be using several times before going on the interview. Practise interviewing a friend or relative so that you will be comfortable in your new role. You might experiment with the pick-up of your microphone and the best place to position it for maximum effectiveness. Also, familiarise yourself with the recording time of the tapes you will be using. Check the recorder before *each* interview to make sure it is functioning properly, and carry spare tape (and batteries if an electrical outlet is not available) and an extension cord.

7) **Pre-interview points.** When you arrive at the interview, chat casually with the interviewee for a few minutes while you set up your equipment. Treat the machine casually and make it as unobtrusive as possible so that you don't overwhelm or frighten the narrator with all of your technology. Make sure the recorder is easily visible for you to check the tape occasionally. If possible, cushion the recorder and microphone with a pillow, sweater, etc. to reduce vibrations. Try to minimise outside noises since the recorder will pick up sounds you might not even notice. Be especially alert to air-conditioners, dishwashers, radios, TVs (even in the next room or back of the house).

    Try to interview only one person at a time and make sure you talk with him/her in surroundings that will make the narrator feel as comfortable as possible. Try to keep away from a lecture-type atmosphere.

    Before beginning the actual interview, record a brief introductory statement that states whom you are talking with, the date, location, and subject of the interview.

8) **During the interview.** Make notes as you go along so that you can follow up on ideas later. Try to pick up clues on what the interviewee would like to discuss next. You might jot down words or names you are not sure of so that you can clarify them at the end of the interview.

During the interview ask questions that will allow the narrator to talk freely and at length. Avoid questions that call for one-word answers ('What was it like to grow up in Athens in the 1920's?' rather than 'Where were you born?') Be attentive, courteous, and responsive as the interview progresses. Nod your head and let the narrator know you are following him closely. If something is not clear to you, restate it in your own words and ask if that is what was meant. Also remember to check the tape occasionally so that you can turn it over at a convenient break in the conversation. Better to waste a little tape than to interrupt in mid-sentence for a mechanical adjustment.

Watch the time as the interview progresses, particularly with older people. Don't overtire the narrator. Keep the interview within a comfortable length of time such as 1–1 1/2 hours. You can always come back for subsequent interviews so don't feel you have to get it all the first time. If another interview is necessary, make arrangements for it before you leave.

9) **After the interview.** Be sure to label the tape(s) carefully with the names of the narrator and the interviewer, date, place, topics, etc. Before you leave, make sure that the release form is signed and remind the narrator that you will give him/her a copy of the tape and/or transcript for review. Be sure to thank him/her for his/her time and co-operation.

Very soon after the interview record your own evaluation of how the interview went. i.e., name of interviewee, physical environment, reaction of interviewee, problems encountered.

Tips for Interviewers (condensed from Willa Baum's *Oral history for the Local Historical Society*, pp. 32–35.)
1) An interview is not a dialogue but a chance for the narrator to tell 'his/her' story.
2) Ask questions that require more of an answer than 'Yes' or 'No'. Start with 'Why, How, Where, What kind of . . .'
3) Ask one question at a time and keep the questions brief.
4) Start with non-controversial questions.
5) Don't let periods of silence fluster you. Give your narrator a chance to think of what he/she wants to say before you hustle along to the next question.
6) Don't worry if your questions are not beautifully phrased for posterity.
7) Don't interrupt a good story because you have thought of a question or because your narrator is straying from the planned questions. If the information is pertinent, let him/her go on.
8) If the narrator persists in talking about non-relevant things, get back on the track with a few leading questions.
9) Do not challenge accounts you think are inaccurate. This could make the narrator angry or defensive.
10) Try to avoid 'off the record' information. Try to get permission to record, then let them listen and restrict access.
11) Interviewing is one time when a negative approach can be effective. You might try, 'Despite the mayor's reputation for good works, I hear he was a difficult man to work with. Did you find him so?' The narrator is going to supply useful information whether he/she challenges or defends your statement.
12) Don't use the interview to show off your own knowledge, vocabulary, charm, or other abilities. Good interviewers do not shine, only their interviewees do.

Types of Created Documentation: Video

Television has been an integral and increasingly important part of life in industrialised societies for more than thirty years and serves as the major point of contact that most Australians have with events beyond their immediate experience. This powerful electronic window has been praised and criticised on many levels, but few can deny its unique capacity to capture and present events that years ago would never have been recorded, much less viewed in the intimacy of the lounge room. Rapid advances in technology, lower costs, and a growing interest in re–experiencing moments in one's own life have made home television recording even more popular than home movies were several decades ago. In fact, electronic equipment and expertise are becoming integrated into our business and personal lives so much so that the videotaping of events and experiences is rapidly overtaking audio recording as the major medium for created historical documentation; and this trend is expected to continue.

Video: The Pluses and Minuses

If we are then to consider undertaking video, as well as oral, history projects, what are the benefits and drawbacks of such an effort?

On the plus side, video recordings undeniably capture human activity far more completely than most other forms of records except for motion pictures. Colour, movement, sound, and perspective are a powerful sensory combination for documenting life in progress. Video technology is also becoming cheaper, more portable, and easier to use than its film equivalent. Video recording is an electronic rather than a photographic process; it also offers the benefit of instant replay, making it possible for users to view the quality of their record on the spot and re–record portions that are faulty. The quality of immediacy also creates in the beholder a greater sense of involvement with actions and events because he/she is watching them as they unfold. A final benefit of video is its popularity. It is literally a household fixture which reaches out to the world; and, since surveys have shown that most people utilise television as their major source of information and entertainment, it follows that people are potentially more receptive to events and messages presented through this medium.

The negative side of video documentation is also impressive, particularly its instability as a record medium for long–term retention i.e. for archives. Video, and audio for that matter, records are created through a process which transforms light and/or sound into electronic pulses which imprint their message magnetically onto a flexible metal oxide coated tape. The information is stored as tiny magnetic arrangements of metal particles which can later be 'read' and replayed. Because the process is

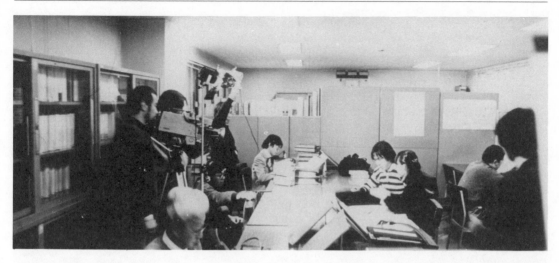

A video tape about the archives can promote wider understanding of its activities.

magnetic, it is also delicate and can be altered by exposure to other sources of magnetism. Furthermore, the metal particle coating can deteriorate and the flexible tape backing can stretch or grow brittle with age. All of these factors make current videotape an unsuitable medium for recording information which needs to be kept permanently.

A second feature of video technology which is undesirable for archival documentation is the ease with which it can be purposefully manipulated, edited or recorded without a trace. Archival records must have integrity as evidence of reality; and therefore, videotape cannot be used for recording information which must stand alone as legal evidence unless very stringent controls and conditions are met, such as those for building security systems.

However difficult these problems of stability and archival integrity are, there is hope that they may be solved in the near future. The new compact or laser digital disk technology which uses lasers to imprint digitised audio and visual information onto an archival quality medium is emerging as a solution. Already commercially available in the music world as pre-recorded compact disks or CDs, this technology is gaining popularity, though the recording process is still too expensive and complex for all but very large information distributors. As costs come down and portability increases, it is possible that smaller institutions like archives may transfer their video and audio magnetic tapes to this medium. Still further in the future laser digital disk technology may replace magnetic media altogether for the recording of archival information.

The third major area of disadvantage of video for archival documentation relates to the production of videotapes. Because we are regular consumers of professional television programmes, we tend to look for the same technical qualities in archival audio and video tapes, forgetting that most professional productions are just that — productions — with actors, scripts, direction, lights, cameras, and re-takes, when any of the above is not exactly right. Not at all like the real life which archival video attempts to capture. So archival footage may appear long, monotonous, rambling, with poor or uneven illumination and amateurish camerawork in comparison with its commercial cousins. The important thing to remember here is that the archives needs the complete footage, as well as the edited final programme.

Uses of Video for Archives

Having assessed the pluses and minuses of video technology as a medium for storing archival information, let us turn now to some of the uses it can have for archives. Most of these uses stem from the advantages video possesses i.e. its capacity to make a multi-sensory record of events in process and its suitability for reaching a wide audience.

Documentation

Despite its technical limitations, video is still a very effective and attractive way to record community personalities, activities or events. Video history interviews are replacing oral history as the popular choice for documenting local identities. Like audio recording, video is now highly portable and brings the additional dimensions of vision and colour to the project. Not only can the person be seen and heard, but so can his or her surroundings and companion photographs, letters and artworks. The video eye can move from the speaker's face to focus on items as they are read or discussed, adding much more information and variety to the interview.

Video is also useful to record community or institutional events or to do 'slice of life' documentation. Commemorative events such as centenaries offer such subjects as re-enactments and parades. Festivals present opportunities to document current public tastes and interests in art, music, food and entertainment. 'Slice of life' projects choose a person or occupation and record their activities over time. Examples might include 'A Day in the Life of a Coal Miner' or a video on woodchopping.

Documentary video is also useful for archival management. Video cameras and viewing sets are often important features of a building security system, particularly the reading rooms, though most often these are monitored 'live' by a security guard and only recorded when that person is away from his/her post.

Video can also be used for special problem-solving studies such as documenting the traffic or workflow patterns of visitors, researchers and staff for later analysis and use in the planning of facilities and services.

Interpretation/Outreach

One of the most important and effective uses of video for archives is education, both in teaching research skills and in acquainting users with archival resources and facilities. Since archival records are unique and must be carefully preserved, they do not circulate like library items. Since researchers must generally visit the archives to gain access to the materials, it is important that their time be spent as productively as possible, and video can be a great help in several ways. Firstly, a video explaining the purpose and services of the archives, the nature of its holdings, and how to prepare a research request can be made available to a number of local libraries and educational institutions. By viewing the video, potential researchers can prepare themselves for their visit to the archives so that, when they arrive, they can spend less time learning their way around, and more doing research. A second and related type of video is the 'How to' programme which provides instruction on research techniques for specialised interests such as family history or historic photographs. These videos make use of the archives holdings and reference staff to explain the use of archival sources and various approaches and methods which can be employed to solve research problems.

The third type of video is one primarily designed to inform and entertain, with the secondary purpose of raising the level of community interest and appreciation for the archives, its work and holdings. Such programmes are the video equivalents of tours, exhibits, and publications and enable the archives to contact and interest potential users where they live and work. This capability can be very important for archives, such as those of a State or the Commonwealth which must serve a large geographical area. Some sample titles of videos which might be undertaken include: 'Know your State Archives', 'Treasures of the Mitchell Library', 'Circular Quay, Then and Now' (comparing historic photographs of the area with shots of present day). Almost any topic that is suitable for an illustrated book or exhibition can be videoed. In fact it is a good idea to make a video as a companion to an exhibition or illustrated publication since the video can live on usefully carrying the information to a wide audience long after the exhibition has been dismantled or the book has gone out of print. The possibilities are only limited by the richness of the archives' holdings, the staff's imagination, and, of course, its resources.

Getting into Video

As with any other area dependent on technology, video programme development requires careful planning, substantial resources, and, most of all, expertise. While it is beyond the scope of this chapter to set out a detailed step-by-step list of what to buy and how to produce quality videotape recordings, it is useful to note the types of activities that you will have to plan and to point out the options available for incorporating video into your archives programme.

In developing a video production capability for the archives you will be planning and managing resources (staff, equipment, facilities) to support a number of distinct work activities, the most important of which are:

1) Planning/administering the video programme;
2) Selecting/designing video projects;
3) Making the video recordings;
   • Setting up for the recording session
     a) Booking/preparing the site/studio
     b) Obtaining/producing titles and other graphic illustrations
     c) Deploying/checking the recording and lighting equipment
     d) Writing/editing narrative
     e) Planning/rehearsing content and sequences
     f) Obtaining permissions to use any materials covered by copyrights
   • Recording the video
   • Editing the video
   • Inspecting the completed video
4) Preserving the video original;
   • Making a copy for reference use
   • Storing the video original and reference copy
5) Documenting/cataloguing the videos (master and reference copy) for future retrieval and use;
6) Using the reference video;
   • Viewing the reference video
   • Arranging for copies of all or portions of the reference video
     a) Obtaining agreements for further use
     b) Making copies
7) Evaluating/monitoring the video programme.

As you would imagine, many of these areas require technical expertise beyond that provided by archival training. Thus it is best to work in concert with one or more video professionals.

Participation in Created Documentation Programmes: The Options

Whether one is planning a video, oral history or photographic documentation programme or all three, the options available for incorporating such activities within the archives operation remain the same. The archives can set up its own facility, equipment and staff to undertake such work; however, this option is rarely economically feasible for most archives. An alternative is to contract these activities out to professional firms or consultants who will undertake the work on a project–by–project basis. This option is attractive since it avoids the heavy cost and ongoing commitment for facilities, equipment and staff.

A third choice is to participate in joint ventures involving other archives and historical agencies such as museums in specific documentation projects. Because such efforts are on a larger scale, they may attract the participation of professional photographers, radio and television companies, as well as outside funding from government or corporate sources.

If documentary production capability seems beyond the resources of your operation (and it is for most small archives), but you would like to include such materials in your holdings or use the occasional video as an educational tool, consider the fourth option: becoming a repository for recordings made by others. This role will limit your commitments to providing safe storage for audio–visual materials and facilities for reference viewing. There is no need to have in–house copying equipment as this service may be purchased as needed from commercial firms. However, the archives will need to be sure that the researcher has obtained written permission from those who control the rights for the specific recordings and images to be copied before any copies are made.

Whatever participation in documentary work your archives choose, full, some, or none, these major and powerful forms of human communication must be considered in any full–scale archival programme.

COMPILING DOCUMENTARY SOURCES

So far in this chapter we have concentrated upon programmes which aim to create information that would not otherwise exist, using audio, video and photographic technology. This section explores a different aspect of documentation: projects to compile widely scattered or obscure existing documents into more convenient and accessible forms. These projects can involve both images and written information.

Compiling or Re–photographing Historic Images

Programmes designed to solicit the donation of original photographs, or to copy privately–held images for research use, can prove fruitful, particularly when they are done in collaboration with newspapers, local photography studios, or organisations of professional photographers. Yet, regardless of whether you are seeking a large collection or a small one, the means of obtaining it will come through contacts with individuals who must somehow be persuaded to join your cause.

As in other forms of field work, success depends on the ability to inspire confidence in oneself and one's institution. The first step is to provide the public with accurate information about the types of images that the archives wants and does not want. Most people will understand a need to be selective; few will understand if you invite any and all donations only to reject half of them because they are 'not significant'.

The Great Film Search conducted by the National Film and Sound Archives successfully copied a number of early Australian films and saved them for posterity.

Box C Documentation Project Worksheet

. . . .
Location
. . . .
Dates of visit

Dates of Visit: . . . .   District: . . . .
Town/City: . . . .   Work Site: . . . .
Local Co–ordinators:
Name: . . . .   Name: . . . .
Address: . . . .   Address: . . . .
Telephone: . . . .   Telephone: . . . .
Affiliation: . . . .   Affiliation: . . . .
Name: . . . .   Name: . . . .
Address: . . . .   Address: . . . .
Telephone: . . . .   Telephone: . . . .
Affiliation: . . . .   Affiliation: . . . .

Schedule

. . . .   Contact President of leading local
6 months in advance   historical/cultural group and invite organ-
                                 isation to participate in the project and to
                                 co–ordinate the local activities.
        Confirmation letter sent . . . .
        Declined participation
Notes

. . . .   Contact leader of local effort to explain
8–10 weeks in advance   logistics of visit and archive for names of
                                 other groups/individuals who might like or
                                 need to be involved with the project. Sched-
                                 ule trip to location to meet with the local
                                 co–ordinating committee.
                                 Completed: . . . .
                                        date   initials
Notes

. . . .   Meet with local committee; explain project
5–7 weeks in advance   fully and show slides; suggest means to
                                 publicise and promote project, provide
                                 samples of newspaper articles and public
                                 service announcements, give local con-
                                 tacts a good supply of project posters and
                                 brochures.   Check   out   local
                                 accommodations.
                                 Completed: . . . .
                                        date   initials
        Visit Notes:

.... Maintain frequent contact by telephone and mail to answer questions and make sure publicity is reaching the general public. Line up workers from own staff and make arrangements for overnight stay.

Contact notes: Completed: ....
                         dates   initials

Staff Workers for Trip: ....
....
....
Hotel/Motel Arrangements:
Local phone number:

Field Report
No. of People Interviewed: ....
Names of Local Volunteers: ....
....
Subjects of Most Interesting Images/Papers: ....
....
Visit Notes: ....
....

Follow–up
Thank–yous written to: ....
(addressee, date, initials of writer)...........................
.... Film Processed   Papers Arranged/
date initials   Described
.... Contacts Mounted   Copies Sent to
date initials   date initials   Locals
.... Negatives Filed   Images Catalogued
date initials   date initials
Summary Remarks: ....
....

Frequently one donation leads to another. Encourage project participants to suggest the names of other area residents who may be willing to share their images with the archives. Be sure to ask donors if they have written records that could be contributed to the archives as companion pieces to the images.

Because the public becomes heavily involved with projects of this type, public relations and careful advance planning for copying project sites are essential. It is vital to document the names and addresses of local sponsors and volunteers and to ensure you have mailed or personally presented sufficient information in the locality to attract an enthusiastic response. Box C provides a Documentation Project Worksheet which is invaluable for keeping track of the innumerable details of the proposed visit.

A retrospective documentation project which copies images that will continue to be held by their owners, presents certain

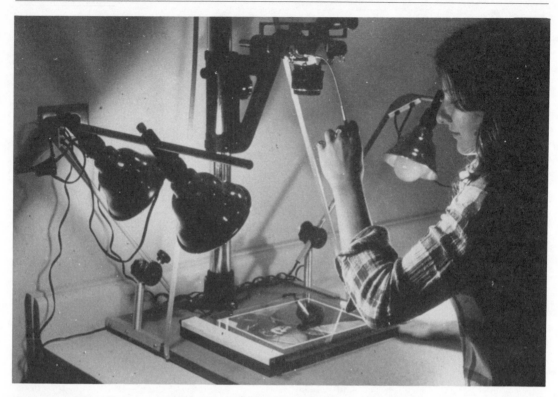

legal problems for the sponsoring archives. The institution is receiving not a gift, but rather an opportunity to make film copies (usually negatives) of unique materials for preservation and future research use. But what exactly can the archives do with its copies? The announced purpose of making these images accessible for research certainly implies an intent to make further reproductions of them, either as reference prints for the reading room or for sale to researchers. And there is a reasonable certainty that some of these images will be in demand for publication. Can the archives legally take such actions and charge fees for services without consulting the owner of the original, who may or may not also own the copyright to that image?

These are cloudy issues indeed, and they are, as yet, untested in the courts. The best protection available at present is an agreement between the archives and the owner of the original as to the use of the donated or copied images. Box D shows an example of such an agreement. It is important for image owners to indicate whether or not they wish their names and addresses to be confidential. Some people may not welcome the prospect of being contacted by researchers or photography collectors seeking the originals.

By the same token, it is vitally important for project field

A special stand with lights facilitates accurate copy photography.

Box D   Photographic Documentation:
Image or Reproduction Rights Donation Form

CONTROL No. . . . .
Heritage Photography Project Release
Terms of Accession:
(   ) 1) HISTORIC IMAGE RELEASE
I, ...
(name of owner of photographs) hereby authorise the . . . .
. . . . (name of archival repository
hereafter cited as 'the archives') to make a photographic copy nega-
tive(s) from my photograph(s) identified by number in the List of Items
below. I understand that once my photograph is rephotographed by the
archives, the photographic copy in the possession of the archives
becomes a part of its holdings and the use of the images will be governed
by the requirements that apply to the archives. I understand that I waive
all title and rights so far as I possess them to the negative(s) described
and to any future prints or copies produced from it/them.

Control No.   . . . .
. . . .
. . . .

(   ) 2) DONATION OF PHOTOGRAPH(S) OR PRINT(S)
I, ... , (name of
owner of photographs or prints) hereby convey to the . . . .
. . . . , (name of archival
repository) for deposit in the . . . .
(name of collection if appropriate) and for administration therein by the
authorities thereof, the photographic and/or print material herein identified in the list of items below. Title to the photographic and/or print
material listed, together with all rights so far as I possess them, shall pass
to the . . . . (name of archival
repository) as of the date of the execution of this Deed of Gift.

Control No. . . . .
. . . .
. . . .

Date: . . . .
. . . .   Signature of Donor
Signature of Representative for   Address: . . . .
the . . . .
. . . .
(name and address of   *Cross out as appropriate:*
Repository)   I *do/do not* wish my name and
                                         address to be made available to
                                         enquirers about the material
                                         above.

workers to elicit all pertinent details about the image at the time
it is offered for copying. While a contact person is available who
may be able to supply the information, ask him/her to date the
image and identify the subject or the occasion shown.

Documenting an historic site includes copying inscriptions.

Whether the photo project is current or retrospective, a schedule must be set up for processing the films and for describing
them for use by the public. Great care must be taken to ensure the
quality and longevity of the film negatives, for they are the
archival record. Some agencies double–shoot the photograph to
create two archival negatives, one for separate security storage
and one to use in making reference prints. Proper storage and
retrieval systems should be imposed in each case.

Making the collection of images accessible to researchers can
be a long and painstaking process. Each image should be
described and subject indexed. If possible, a contact print of
each image should be affixed to the main entry card so that
researchers may view the image without having to consult the
negative. Some projects provide a copy of their catalogue cards
and contact prints to the local historical societies or libraries
serving the areas in which the images were copied. The distribution of these materials does much to make the local heritage
available locally, and the resulting good will facilitates the work
of the projects.

Whether your images are donated or copied, do not neglect to
share them with the public. For example, the staff could prepare
a 'Historic Photograph of the Week' series in the local newspaper
(accompanied by a short caption and credit line mentioning the

archives and the name of the donor with his/her permission). A public exhibition of photographic prints drawn from the project files can also be very effective in arousing community interest.[4]

Compiling or Re–recording Textual Information

Projects which compile written information are also popular. An example of this type of undertaking is the copying of gravestone inscriptions in local cemeteries, thus providing access in written form to information that would be largely unavailable to researchers. Projects to re–record information may not utilise sophisticated technology or specialist skills, but they do require careful planning and management to yield optimum results. Some of the aspects which must be considered are:

1) Planning/administering the overall programme;
2) Selecting/designing the compilation projects;
3) Planning the specific project activities;
   - Designing the data recording sheets
     a) Selecting the information to be recorded: full text or specific portions
     b) Designing the format, sequence, and content of individual entries
   - Designing the format and content of the final compilation and its indexes
   - Choosing the site/sites to be included
   - Breaking the project up into manageable segments: half or full days in sequence
   - Recruiting/training the project personnel (usually volunteers)
   - Arranging for transport, supplies, and amenities for project personnel (soliciting donated goods and services from the community)
4) Conducting the project;
   - Transporting project personnel
   - Distributing supplies
   - Deploying/maintaining amenities
   - Monitoring/guiding progress
   - Collecting completed data sheets
   - Thanking project personnel and sponsors
5) Analysing and processing the data sheets into the final compiled product;
6) Distributing the product;
7) Monitoring/evaluating project, product and programme success.

[4]The discussion of re–photography projects is based upon the author's experience with the Vanishing Georgia Heritage Photography Project and was taken from *Archives and Manuscripts: Public Programs*. Chicago, IL: SAA, 1982. pp. 21–25, 80–83.

These projects have lasting value for the archives, both in terms of making remote or scattered information available to researchers in a compact form and as a way of involving the wider community in heritage activities. Well-organised compilation projects are rewarding and fun; they bring people together in a well-defined worthwhile activity that has been organised into manageable segments. Remember that, although the end product is the ultimate goal, the process of achieving it must always be through a well-organised sequence of small satisfying steps for the participants, whether staff or volunteers or both.

In closing, it is desirable to summarise the common benefits and cautions surrounding all types of documentation programmes for archives. Oral history, videotaping, and photographic surveys do supplement and render more human the records of our present and recent past. The sensory dimensions of such materials bring our lives back to life in ways ink or paper cannot. But it is precisely because these documents have such emotional power that the programmes to create them must be carefully planned and executed. Moreover, documents created 'for the record' raise legal, historical, and ethical issues which affect the relationships among the persons recorded, researchers, and the archives staff. Properly structured and funded, documentation programmes can become major assets which not only enrich the collections, but also raise community support for the archives as a whole.

FURTHER READING

Baum, Willa K., *Oral History for Local Historical Societies*. 2nd edition revised. Nashville, TN: American Association for State and Local History, 1974.

Charlton, Thomas L., 'Videotaped oral history: problems and prospects', *American Archivist* 47/3 (Summer, 1984) : 228-236.

Douglas, Louise and Peter Spearritt, *Australia 1983 Oral History Handbook*. Canberra: Australian National University, 1981, and 'Talking history: the use of oral sources' in Mandle, William F. and Graeme Osborne, editors, *New History: Studying Australia Today*. Sydney: Allen and Unwin, 1981.

Jolly, Brad, *Videotaping Local History*. Nashville. TN: American Association for State and Local History, 1982.

Lance, David, *An Archive Approach to Oral History*. London: Imperial War Museum, 1977.

Moss, William W., *Oral History Program Manual*. New York: Praeger, 1974.

Thompson, Paul, *The Voice of the Past: Oral History*. London, Oxford University Press, 1978.

Wilton, Janis and Angela Bollard, *Balancing the Books: Oral History for the Community*. Sydney: Ethnic Affairs Commission of N.S.W., 1983.

CHAPTER ELEVEN

USER EDUCATION AND PUBLIC RELATIONS

Ann Pederson

All of us who keep archives and other historical materials have two equally important responsibilities. The first is to identify, acquire, and preserve records of lasting value. The second is to make these materials, and the information they contain, available for use. It is in fulfilling this second mission that we undertake educational programmes — a planned sequence of projects and activities which inform the wider community about our holdings and services and involve its members directly with their documentary heritage.

This second task is especially challenging and important for archivists because, unlike libraries and museums, visits to archives are not a feature of one's early life or education. Most people do not come into contact with original records until university and, even then, not unless they are doing research degrees. The result is that few people know what an archives is, what sort of work goes on there, and why that work is invaluable. This lack of general knowledge and understanding about archives is sufficient reason for archivists to undertake active programmes aimed at the public. It is vital that archival work be understood and appreciated by the wider community, not just an educated few. Otherwise archivists will reap the fruits of their own indifference: inadequate facilities, diminished funding, reduced services, or, at worst, closure. History abounds with the losses of those who smugly catered to an elite. The treasures of the ancient world destroyed by uninformed hordes and the works of the Italian Renaissance burned by Savonarola come immediately to mind. While these are dramatic examples, we must all be reminded that neglect can destroy just as effectively as violence.

Given resources and imagination, there is a smorgasbord of

educational activities and projects which may be offered. Some of the better known include publications, workshops and seminars, exhibitions, and special events such as open days or commemorative celebrations. However, it is essential to select from this banquet with care, choosing projects which complement and strengthen the archives effort overall, rather than those which, though exciting, actually divert staff energies and resources for little lasting benefit.

THE BENEFITS OF WELL–PLANNED EDUCATIONAL PROGRAMMES

The key concept in describing the value of educational programmes is involvement. Educational activities attract and involve people with the archives and its work and, in so doing, transform those faceless members of the general public or of our own higher administration, into personal clients of our services — into researchers, donors, volunteers and active supporters of the archival enterprise. Educational programmes are engaging vehicles which bring people face–to–face with archival materials, generating an initial interest and enthusiasm which, properly nurtured, will develop into a continuing relationship of mutual appreciation.

Educational activities provide occasions for the public to view rare or unique works. Courtesy — State Library of NSW.

Take the partriarch of an influential family who was invited to lend some photographs to an exhibit for the town centenary. This man had never entered the doors of the Historical Society until the day he came in to discuss the loan, but became so interested that he not only came to the exhibit opening, but subsequently joined the Society and donated his family papers to its archives. Furthermore, through his influence, several leading businesses made donations of money and services to the Society. Examples of such conversions abound ranging from the workshop attendee who becomes a committed volunteer to philanthropists like David Scott Mitchell whose bequest established the superb research library of Australiana that bears his name.

Educational programmes, then, must be developed as tools which naturally extend from and enhance other archival work, such as research, preservation, and collecting. They can be very rewarding, both for planners and participants.

Many of the products of educational activities serve a dual purpose. Designed to inform and instruct the clients of the archives, they are equally useful for orienting and educating new members of staff and prospective volunteers. In addition, the research and analysis involved in developing educational aids often improves the overall standard of archival services. In a material sense, they foster appreciation for the value of historical records and help ensure support for those who care for them.

Perhaps, most important of all, they encourage greater communication between the keepers of archives and the various institutional, social, and professional communities to which they belong. Archivists who plan and take part in educational activities develop perceptions which help them to do a better job of serving the needs of their clients. Correspondingly, members of the community who are introduced to archival work through educational projects may come to appreciate the legal and financial, as well as cultural benefits of well-managed modern record services, and use these insights to economic advantage in their personal and business enterprises.

A PLANNING APPROACH TO EDUCATIONAL PROGRAMMES

Educational programmes come in such variety of type and scope that careful planning is needed to select those which best suit the purpose, resources and clientele of your institution as a whole. Most people underestimate the amount of work and coordination required in undertaking educational projects. Involving the wider community in activities at the archives or using archival materials requires special care. Public interest, enthusiasm and contact with original sources is to be encouraged, but not at the peril of the records. For example, you must ensure the safety of the archival items in the exhibit without making those who view them feel uncomfortable. All users and visitors should be courteously informed, preferably in advance, of the security measures which must be followed in the archives to eliminate the possibility of misunderstandings. Likewise, archivists must accept the fact that they will sometimes make mistakes with educational activities.

One cannot absolutely predict public response to a workshop or publication; they can love it or leave it for a dozen reasons that have little to do with the project's worthiness. One can only research the undertaking well, seek and accept professional advice, plan for reasonable contingencies, and go. Above all, keep good records (you are keeping your own archives too, remember!) and evaluate the project thoughtfully. Thorough documentation of all phases of work will be invaluable in planning future activities.

At this point the need to plan is clear, but what exactly should one consider in developing a programme of appropriate and beneficial educational projects? To create an effective education 'portfolio', archivists should follow four basic steps. First, define the goals of your institution. Second, determine the nature and needs of your audience. Third, locate and obtain the necessary resources. Fourth, select and plan an appropriate programme to suit them. All activities must harmonise with the purpose and responsibility of your institution. Study the documents which established your archives and any subsequent records modifying them. Acts of Parliament, corporate charters, and archives policy statements are records which determine the scope and focus of your work. These documents will also help you identify your audiences.

Finding out who your clients are and what they need to know and do in order to make the best use of the archives is a critical second step. Some of these clients may not be obvious, because you know them in another capacity and may not think of the importance of their active support for your operation. They may be the managers or advisory board of your own host organisation or they may be current users of your services, either researchers or donors. They may be *potential* users, i.e. people whom you are there to serve but who have never made contact with you.

Identifying client groups is a simple matter of knowing where to look. The most obvious user group is the archives' present researchers. There are records readily at hand which provide information about who they are and their interests. The most important of these records is the reader's ticket application form, but other documents, such as daily registrations of visitors/researchers and lists of participants in workshops, are also valuable. People, offices or organisations who deposit their records with the archives comprise another important client group, one that uses the archives' storage, conservation and reference facilities and services as extensions of their own information systems. Acquisition and accession records and record request forms (call slips) will reflect who they are and their patterns of use. The administrators, managers, and advisors of the host organisation are particularly important clients for an in-house archives, as the effectiveness of their work may depend upon the archives' care of vital organisational records. Furthermore, their decisions in allocating funds are so crucial to the archives operation that the needs and interests of this group should receive top priority. In-house correspondence, reports, and budget papers provide important sources of information about management concerns.

Another important group, often overlooked until their services are needed, is that comprised of information officers and media representatives. These professionals should be sent, at least selectively, special event invitations and externally focused communications, such as calendars and newsletters. Maintaining regular contact and encouraging involvement with archives activities is a long-term investment that will yield dividends, including that all-important media coverage when the archives really needs it.

Knowing the groups and the information sources about them enables the archives to establish a regular programme of user documentation. One of the first things you will want to do is create a mailing list which enables you to communicate easily with your clients and with other individuals and organisations of

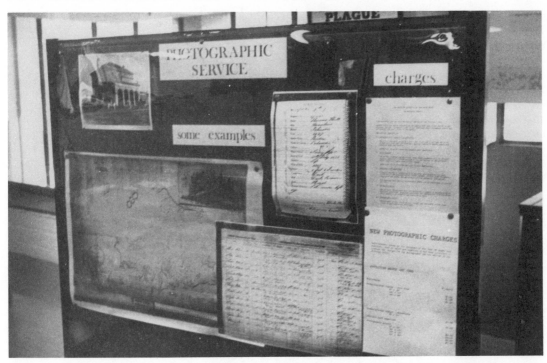

A panel display demonstrates the types of copies available and their cost.

importance to the archives. This aspect will be discussed in more detail later in the chapter. Abstracting information from the records provides a base of statistical data which will be invaluable in justifying expenditure and forward planning. Usage statistics may include:

- Number of contacts made with prospective depositors (individual and offices)
- Number of accessions
- Number of visitors/researchers
- Number of readers tickets issued
- List of research topics
- Number of records retrieved/refiled
- List of record services used and frequency of use
- Number of copies provided
- Number of letters sent
- Number of publications sent
- Number of events/workshops held
- Number of participants in events/workshops
- Number of hours of training and advice provided

Obviously, each archives must select the level and range of statistics it keeps on client use according to its own resources and needs. Over-documentation is almost as bad as no documentation, and statistics which are not used are a waste of valuable time.

In setting priorities for reaching client groups, a suggested rule of thumb is to begin your efforts by making the delivery of your existing services to established client groups more effective. For example, new researchers visit the archives daily. All first–timers, regardless of their previous experience with archives, will require orientation, and they usually ask the same basic questions as they try to learn their way around. What educational tools could be provided to facilitate this process? A leaflet about the archives, its location, its holdings, and services could be sent to inquirers in advance of their visit. Attractive, welcoming and easy–to–read signs can orientate newcomers quickly to the facilities. A simple plan of the public areas showing major features and explaining rules for using them could be distributed to visitors on arrival. A self–service library of brief video presentations on selected topics may ease researchers into their work with more confidence. Any or all of these suggestions could streamline the transformation of a new client into a productive researcher and make reference services more effective for all.

After you have improved the delivery of existing services to established clients, you can then begin efforts to attract or impress the groups that can help your institution most, with the aim of building up additional resources. The point is that you now have a base from which to extend your reach to new activities and/or to contact new groups of potential users.

No educational activity can function without a commitment of resources of various kinds. The category that comes most easily to mind is that of facilities, equipment, and supplies, but it need not be the first to be considered as often such items can be hired, borrowed, or donated. Your most important resource will be the time and talents of your staff members, their knowledge of the archives, and their continuing involvement and commitment, before, during and after the project.

Bring your staff together and ask what kinds of projects would interest them and find out as much as possible about their skills and hobbies. You may have a good photographer, writer, designer, or speaker among the crew. Others may have special subject knowledge that could be used in creating exhibits or publications. When considering a new idea, ask the staff from a variety of work areas for their views before things get too far along, and give all interested staff an opportunity to be involved in all stages of the project, especially in the evaluation of its success.

In deciding where to start with the planning of educational programmes, begin with what you know best. Choose projects that will enhance the services, collections, and audiences most important to your archives. Ask staff members for suggestions of educational aids that would make work in their areas of responsibility easier. For example, a one page handout could explain how to fill out a request for documents from the collections or how to

Table One   Overview of Education Aids for Archives Work

Archival Function	Individuals	Audiences Small Groups	Wider Community
Access and Reference	Orientation interview. Basic brochure on holdings, facilities and terms of access. Simple handouts (reading room rules, how to request records, obtain copies, special access).	Letter inviting use (universities, genealogical societies, teachers) Mini-classes for beginning researchers. Slide-tape show about using the archives or beginning research. Training for volunteer reading room assistants.	Slide-tape or video encouraging use of the archives. Loan/sales of microforms of selected records. Seminars on popular research topics.
Finding Aids	Leaflet guide to major holdings. In-house finding aids.	Comprehensive guide to holdings. Training for volunteer indexers.	Individual guides to records of particular creators (Colonial Secretary) or on special subjects (gold, convicts). Reports on national or international guides or databases. Sale of microfilms of finding aids or indexes.
Acquisition and Appraisal	Personal contacts with prospective depositors (persons, organisations) Leaflet on donating material to archives. Rotating exhibitions of new acquisitions.	Slide-tape show on identifying archival materials. Slide talks on donating material to archives. Workshop on identifying materials of historic value or disposal scheduling training for volunteer field workers.	Field projects to survey and record potential acquisitions or to copy records in private custody. Video or slide-tape about archives field work. Conference on appraisal.
Arrangement and Description		Slide-tape or video on arranging and describing a collection. Training for volunteer processors.	Work placements or intensive courses for students, volunteers or other professions.
Conservation	Leaflet on handling of various record media. Simple exhibitions (before and after, types of damage, particular problems).	Slide talks on damaging agents, preventative measures, disaster minimisation. Workshops on basic preventative and restorative techniques. Training for volunteers.	Slide-tape show or video on various aspects of conservation. Conferences on conservation issues.
User Education and Publications	Tours of the archives. Feature articles and news releases on major holdings, collecting efforts, new acquisitions, research projects. Simple exhibitions on facets of archives work or background of the archives programme.	Tours of the archives. Seminars on archival work or research methods for students. Slide talks about various aspects of archives work or research projects undertaken at the archives by staff or researchers.	Newsletter Open Days Conferences Major Exhibitions Friends of Archives events

order a copy. Frequently asked questions provide clues to areas where such aids or special small group training sessions could streamline reference service. Likewise, persons contacting the archives by mail often have similar questions, presenting the opportunity to design special information sheets or brochures to satisfy common types of requests.

While these ideas focus upon improving reference services, similar measures are helpful in other areas of archival work. Table One summarises ideas for educational aids which facilitate a number of archival functions.

Whatever types of educational aids you choose, whether designed for individual, group or community use, keep in mind that your aim is to have a coordinated and complementary programme, rather than a disparate array of bits and pieces pulling in different directions. One effort should lead or extend logically to another, either in content or scope or both.

Look into ways that the effort and expense of one project can be used to advantage in related or 'spin-off' activities. Design your basic slide talk with sections that can be tailored to different audiences or edit your basic brochure information into a script for a video about the archives. Similarly the visuals and text information for an exhibit might be turned into a slide show which can be shown to audiences long after the original exhibit has been dismantled.

There is also an advantage in clustering activities around a major event or point in time. A local centenary, holiday or festival presents a good opportunity for the archives to attract wider publicity and a larger audience than usual for tours, workshops or exhibits featuring the special theme. Some institutions which sponsor conferences plan exhibits to complement them or *vice versa* so that the interest generated by one activity encourages participation in the other. Such an approach is useful because it gives participants an opportunity to explore more facets of a subject once their interest has been captured.

Do not hesitate to take advantage of the experience and resources of other institutions. Many archives, libraries, museums, and historical societies will have undertaken similar projects and may be willing to share their experiences with you. Why invent the wheel when someone else already has it rolling? Collect copies of brochures, signs; solicit slide shows, workshop and exhibit ideas, and ask for planning reports and documentation. Consider joint ventures with neighbouring institutions. The benefits of shared projects are numerous. Pooled resources can lead to larger and more professional activities, as well as to improved relations with colleagues in related professions.

A distinguished speaker, such as Sir Ninian Stephen, the Governor-General of Australia, attracts public interest and media attention.

USER EDUCATION AND PUBLIC RELATIONS : SELECTED PROGRAMMES

Potential user education and public relations programmes are as numerous and varied as the archival institutions that sponsor them. However, all successful ones are characterised by the following qualities : *a clear purpose, well-defined scope and content and appealing presentation.* Materials and projects for clients, whether internal or public, must be attractive and evoke interest and participation.

The text which follows focuses upon selected types of activities, and is intended to provide general guidelines for development, rather than explicit how-to instructions. Readers needing more detailed information should consult the works cited under *Further Reading* or explore the extensive literature available on individual types of programmes. Educational activities will be discussed in the following sequence: Exhibitions, Public Relations Publications, Classes, Seminars and Workshops, and Community Support Systems.

EXHIBITIONS

Exhibitions for archives may be described as the use of archival material to present ideas which inform or educate the viewer. Exhibitions provide a vehicle for the archives to show off its collections and help fulfill the archives wider mission of encouraging public respect and appreciation for past achievements. Although difficult to measure, the effects of a well designed exhibition programme are undeniably beneficial. Exhibitions inspire interest and involvement which can result in donations of records, funds, services or personal time to the archives. An archives need not be large or wealthy to mount a good exhibition programme. Since most archives have very modest facilities and resources, archivists will be relieved to know that research on exhibition effectiveness affirms that viewers respond best to small, well presented exhibitions. It is the subject matter of the exhibition, its placement and its design, rather than its size or complexity, that determine its appeal.

Still, all exhibitions, however small, require commitments of money and of that even scarcer commodity – staff time and skill. They also present conservation and security problems and are, by nature, temporary in duration. For these reasons and in light of other priorities and commitments, archivists must not embark on a series of exhibitions simply because it is expected or because other institutions have done so. Rather the decision to exhibit should be a positive and considered one, made to achieve genuine benefits for the archives.

Planning an Exhibit

Once the archives has committed itself to an exhibition programme, the first step is to decide the focus the exhibition will

Receptions to open exhibits are popular 'friends' group events.

have. Below are some questions that will facilitate this process.
Will the aim be mainly:

• To show off materials from the collection?
• To inform viewers about the nature of archival materials, archival work, and/or your archives?
• To educate them on a point of history?
• To interest, intrigue or inspire them?

Ideally the exhibition programme will be structured to accomplish all four of these purposes, either simultaneously or sequentially.

After the exhibition goals have been identified, planners must then determine the location, structure and audience for the exhibition. Decisions here are more difficult because they must be reached by weighing many variables, such as resources, facilities, available equipment, and existing work commitments, to come up with a workable plan. Sometimes key factors such as conservation and security will limit possibilities for the location and presentation of the exhibition. Some venues, though popular, are not sufficiently secure. For example, it would be unwise to place an exhibit case of original archival treasures in the central railway station or a very busy shopping mall.

Many archives must mount their exhibitions in donated cases, often obtained from shops which have closed down. While these gifts are most welcome, they were not designed for the display of irreplaceable documents and impose limits on the kinds of records that may be displayed to maximum advantage. Exhibition planners then must determine which of the variables affecting the exhibition are most critical and adjust their choices accordingly to come up with a workable compromise.

If conservation and security considerations seem to be cramping your plans for exhibits, consider using skilful facsimiles or duplicates of printed items instead of unique originals. Reasonable facsimile reproductions can be made by photocopying the originals onto paper of the same age taken from the blank pages of an old non–archival volume; even better results can be obtained by a skilled photographer. It can often be more appealing to copy and enlarge only the key passage in a document since viewers are not likely to be enthused enough to read many lines of difficult handwriting. The selective use of photographic panels or murals is also effective. All copies of documents and photographs should clearly be labelled as such and identified by the full citation and size of the original.

Once the logistical factors of the exhibition have been defined, planners can turn their attention to content. Choices here revolve around three factors: appropriateness for the proposed audience, the availability of suitable records, photographs and objects, and the exhibitor's knowledge, skill and imagination.

This exhibit case would be more suitable if it had a solid pedestal base and more depth to allow materials to be seen from all sides. Courtesy — State Library of NSW.

Table Two   Some Ideas for Archival Exhibitions

About Archives Work:

General
- Archival activities from acquisition to research use
- What are archives?

Achievements
- Ways archives sources or staff saved money, time for host organisation or community
- New facilities, programmes, equipment, publications
- Anniversaries and commemorations

Acquisitions
- Recent acquisitions (after processing)
- Depositing papers (what is involved)
- Types of records sought (documents, photographs, ephemera)

Arrangement and Description
- Detective work identifying forgeries, estrays, unsigned materials, facsimiles
- Sources and process of research on provenance and administrative history
- Unusual Records

Conservation
- A document before, during and after conservation
- Hazards of metal fasteners, sticky tape
- Types of damage and their causes
- Preservation microfilming
- How to handle various types of records

Reference
- Copyright in archives (manuscript, artworks, photographs)
- Protecting confidentiality and privacy
- We'd like to know ... (examples of research inquiries)
- Effects of theft/vandalism
- Sources or how to's on popular research topics (tracing your family, dating your home, railways, gold, convicts)
- We helped ... (books, theses, TV programmes produced from records in the archives)

About the Community
- Yesterday and today (photos,problems of life or business, events in the news)
- Holidays (records describing or depicting)
- Commemorations (royal visits, jubilees, centenaries)
- Local 'firsts'
- Landmarks and localities
- Leading businesses, industries, public or charitable agencies
- Local personalities
- Pioneers and their families

Some ideas for exhibition topics or themes are listed in Table Two.

Identifying material suitable for exhibition can be facilitated by keeping exhibition potential in mind as records are appraised, arranged and described or used in the reading room. Staff members with these archival responsibilities are often a fruitful source of ideas and knowledge, and exhibition planners in search of ideas and material should make a beeline for them. In fact, it is highly desirable for archives staff to work closely with public information officers and exhibit designers as a team to produce educational materials and exhibitions. In this way the expert knowledge of all is pooled and the resulting project will generate internal enthusiasm and pride.

Correspondingly, the occasion of an exhibition can provide opportunities for direct communication between the archives and the managers and administrators of its host organisation. Often the direction to prepare an exhibition for an important anniversary or event comes from above. The easiest course is to rush around, prepare the exhibition and present the finished product for applause. But, in so doing, the archivist has missed a valuable chance to acquaint his/her supervisors with the work and resources of the archives. Build upon the initial interest which inspired the directive by discussing exhibition ideas and content with management representatives at key points. Better yet, encourage management to assign a staff member to work with the exhibition team. The exposure to archives resources and the communication developed during the project is an investment that will yield long term benefits.

Exhibition Guidelines

Exhibition planning and design is a specialised field with a rich literature of its own which archivists are urged to consult. The sources indicated in the *Further Reading* suggestions are recommended as a good starting point. A detailed explanation of the steps and considerations required for planning an exhibition is well beyond the scope of this chapter, but it is possible to offer readers a concise list of guidelines and insights which they may find useful in the development of exhibitions for archives. A selection of these tips are embodied in Table Three.

A staff team works to mount a major exhibition. Courtesy — State Library of NSW.

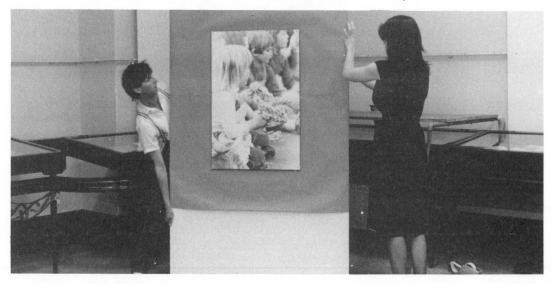

Exhibition layout can be a challenging and exacting task. Supplies for constructing exhibits are expensive, and it is important to measure dimensions and arrange materials accurately to minimise wasteful errors. Be sure to allow space for labels, text blocks, and for the supports or 'case furniture' that will hold the

Table Three   Tips for Exhibition Planners

Overall	• Exhibition area should be supervised and secure.
	• Base tone and contents of exhibitions on your own institution and holdings.
	• Do a limited number of exhibitions well; change them every few months.
	• Use few but a variety of record types and objects per exhibit.
	• Plan activities such as lectures and workshops to promote or complement the exhibit.
	• Design to achieve general impact of message on viewer within 45 seconds
	• Plan height limits within comfortable viewing range (1.1m – 1.7m).
Conservation	• Don't leave originals on exhibit longer than one month.
	• Keep lights separate from display case interior.
	• Use low ultraviolet fluorescent lamps or special bulb shields.
	• Monitor humidity inside cases and correct as needed.
	• Provide suitable acid–free mountings and supports for records and volumes.
	• Use facsimile copies if conservation or security is in doubt
Display Techniques	• Exhibits should be three–dimensional; avoid the "printed page" look.
	• Keep the exhibition simple and uncluttered.
	• Group material in some order with a feature or focus.
	• Use colour and texture to enhance, not overwhelm.
	• Place materials on different levels and planes within the case.
	• Use mounts to group small items so they don't get "lost."
	• Use coloured film overlays to point out key passages of text.
	• Seek design help from museums, galleries and design professionals.
Equipment	• Cases must be secure, i.e. have sturdy, unusual fastenings.
	• Use a few cases of varied, but related style.
	• Cases should provide easy access for changing exhibits.
	• Choose cases that are versatile or permit viewing from all sides.
Labels and Text	• Labels and text should encourage viewers to study materials.
	• Language should be clear, simple and brief.
	• Don't over label; this can detract from the overall effect.
	• Identify items on exhibit with proper citations.
	• Use appropriate type styles and sizes for easy reading.
	• Display transcripts with manuscript items.
Materials	• If possible, select records with graphic appeal and which are easy to understand; single sided, one page pieces are ideal.
	• Borrow appropriate objects or costumes, rather than acquire them.
	• Be sure all reproductions are top quality and labelled as such.

records safely in position. Many designers prefer to do an inexpensive paper and cardboard model of the exhibition, using
copies of the records pasted on sheets cut to size. Mounting the
test exhibitions into the case allows the preparer to assess the
overall effect and recheck all measurements before cutting into
the expensive matte board, fabric or Perspex/Plexiglas.

Exhibit planning also includes 'accessories' such as slide
shows, videos, posters, or catalogues, that extend the impact of
the exhibit over a longer term. For small exhibits, only a simple
publicity poster is really worthwhile. Catalogues, in particular,
are companions to an exhibit, but cannot substitute for it. Their
main value lies in allowing the exhibit preparers room for more
explanation and scholarly discussion than the exhibit panels
permit. Videos and coffee-table publications are generally
reserved for more complex exhibits with substantial funding, as
high-quality productions can be quite expensive. Slide shows
are within reach of most archives and provide a means of sharing
the exhibit with wider and more dispersed audiences. Producing
a synchronised cassette with music and narrative to accompany
well-composed slides adds a professional touch.

As the exhibit nears the final stages of preparation, arrangements for its promotion should be well underway. All new
exhibits, however modest, should be announced in appropriate
media outlets. The types and extent of publicity will naturally
reflect the magnitude and importance of the exhibit and its proposed audience. A single case exhibit in the reading room might

*This flexible case can easily accom-
modate three-dimensional objects
as well as records and
photographs.*

*An inexpensive, attractive exhibit
catalogue provides more detailed
information about the exhibit
theme.*

be announced with a poster in the foyer and a short piece in the archives newsletter. Having an opening for the exhibit provides an occasion to invite persons to the archives. Even the small exhibit mentioned above could be 'opened' with tea and biscuits on a day when the reading room is likely to be crowded.

Whatever the scope of your exhibit programme, the archives and its staff will benefit most from a balanced approach that is thoroughly in tune with the institution's aims and resources. The community, too, will be enriched from the additional opportunity to explore the archival sources of its heritage and grow in its appreciation of the valuable and important work of archives.

PUBLIC RELATIONS

Designing a programme of archival services without paying specific attention to *public relations* is like planning a party without inviting the guests. Regular communication with client groups is as important as any of the purely 'archival' activities, maybe even more so since our work is so heavily dependent upon the cooperation of depositors and users. Client relations, PR or publicity, as this work is variously termed, is a positive consciousness that should initially infuse one's work and then later be formalised into publicity, interviews, speeches, and other outreach activities.

It is important to build client–centred thinking into archival work with policies and procedures. A checklist of steps to complete during acquisition should include acknowledging each gift and placing the donor's name on the archives' mailing list. The reference staff could give departing researchers a self–mailing form soliciting their ideas for improvement. Visitors and researchers should be included when invitations are sent out for workshops or exhibits. Staff members, whether speaking to groups or meeting individuals, should always have a supply of basic brochures about the archives. While it is not appropriate to hand out leaflets in the street, one never knows when a casual contact might spark genuine interest which should be followed up.

Managing the Mailing List

The heart of any programme of client relations is a well managed mailing list. Direct communication with client groups, including the media, through the mail is a capability all archives must have; however, it is one that can lead to wasteful expense if it is not carefully monitored. Developing a mailing list begins by identifying those individuals and groups with whom the archives has a need to communicate. A comprehensive list might include the following recipients:

- Government officials and agencies responsible for or interested in heritage

A special invitation encourages participation in archives activities.

- Members of the governing or advisory board
- Depositors, actual and potential
- Managers and administrators of other branches of the host organisation
- Volunteers
- Members of your organisation or associated Friends groups
- Media representatives or personalities
- Recent visitors, researchers and participants in archives workshops or functions
- Professional associations of archivists, historians, museum curators, conservators, librarians and records managers
- Appropriate groups such as libraries, historical societies, history teachers, university schools or departments of history
- Sponsors, actual and potential, including corporations, businesses, charitable trusts, granting bodies

Occasionally there may be a special promotion, such as the sale of a publication, where a more general audience is sought. Rather than inflate the mailing for this occasion, consider using a marketing service that specialises in direct mail or approaching a publications distribution company.

Since postage can be a considerable expense, organise the mailing list to permit access to selected categories of addresses. This can be done manually by creating separate sets of master labels or colour-coded cards. A computer system can be invaluable because of its capacity to select, retrieve and print out the desired addresses on labels. For example, in advertising a local workshop, it might be useful to organise the system to select only those addresses with postcodes within reasonable travelling distance of the archives. The expense of large mailings can also be reduced by pre-sorting for bulk mail handling. Consult Australia Post for advice and incorporate their requirements into the planning of promotional material.

Once the list has been established, it must be maintained accurately. The culling and updating should be done regularly by archives staff or volunteers. If the list is large, it may pay to employ a firm which manages all aspects of mailing services.

Publicity

Publicity is getting a message across to an audience in an accurate, well-presented and timely manner. There are two basic ways of communicating with an audience: the direct method, which utilises the mail or a specialised distribution system and the indirect approach which works through an intermediary, usually a radio, television or newspaper journalist.

With the direct approach, the archivist, singly or working with an in-house publicist, prepares and packages the message which is then sent directly to known recipients. This method has several advantages. The archivist knows that the message sent is exactly

A well-written, one page press release announces a new acquisition.
Courtesy — State Library of NSW.

New South Wales Government

State Library of New South Wales

Macquarie Street
Sydney, N.S.W. 2000

MEDIA RELEASE

1986/2

Our reference:

Your reference:

Telephone (02) 230 1414

Telex: 12 1150

For Further Information

RECEIVED

1 8 FEB 1986

Sydney, 17 February 1986

SYDNEY OF THE 1920's
REVEALED AT THE STATE LIBRARY

Magnificent panoramic views of Sydney in the 1920's and rare domestic interior scenes of the same period, just acquired by the State Library of NSW, will be on display from 1 March to 6 April in the Library's vestibule as part of the activities for Senior Citizens' Week.

Sweeping views of the harbour foreshores, uncluttered by modern highrise; virgin scrub near Narrabeen Lagoon; Macquarie Street; St. Mary's Cathedral before its additions, and a serene Vaucluse Bay are among the images that will be on display.

"We are very excited about these Alan Row & Co. panoramas. They fill a gap in our holdings of this photographic firm's work as well as being superbly informative and marvellous to look at, instantly transporting you to a Sydney of a different era" said Paul Brunton, the State Library's Field Librarian.

The Library has chosen Senior Citizens' Week to launch a search for photographs of home interiors of the 1920's, 1930's and 1940's, as well as photographs of life during the Great Depression, as such documentation is urgently needed for the Mitchell Library's research collection. Many senior citizens may have such photographs at home without realizing how important they are in the documentary record of Australian life.

The Library is hoping that those with such photographs will contact the Field Librarian, Paul Brunton, and offer them to the Library for permanent preservation.

Interviews available: Paul Brunton, Field Librarian. Panoramas available for filming.

For futher information contact: Anne Wilson, Publicity Officer. Tel. (02) 230 1515 (w)
969 7224 (h)

what has been designed and that the timing suits the programmes' needs. He/she has also selected the recipients as persons or agencies worth cultivating.

However, there are also disadvantages to direct contact. The archives may not have the resources to produce materials to a professional standard or to bear the expense of regular mailing to a wide audience. Errors in timing can also result from lack of marketing experience or knowledge of competing activities.

Working through the media, the archivist is able to minimise costs, obtain wider coverage and deliver more professionally packaged messages, but not without certain risks. The message and the timing may undergo changes to meet media programming demands. Each media team attempts to package and present the 'best' material from what is available at any given time. The competition among news and feature items for space or air time is heightened by the additional pressures of deadlines, audience ratings, and those all–important sponsorship dollars. Thus working within the dynamic environment of media requires archival publicists to be both flexible and persistent in their efforts to exploit media resources.

Perhaps the best idea is to plan publicity efforts that combine self–distributed information with selected media exposure, relying more on the former than the latter. Using this approach, one can always be assured that the message will reach a primary audience and may be magnified and multiplied if media coverage is obtained.

Whatever approach you use, one of the best ways to increase the chances of success in obtaining appropriate publicity is to cultivate good relationships with writers, editors and programme–makers, both in–house and outside, who work in the field. Journalists are greedy for interesting material, and most archives hold plenty of it. It is a matter of matching these interests and people on a regular basis. Including appropriate media representatives and publicists in the archives mailing list will ensure that they are reliably informed of approaching activities and invited to special events. In addition, ideas and visual materials for feature stories about the archives and its collections should be provided to reporters with cultural or historical interests and responsibilities. Researchers, volunteers and staff members may also be canvassed for ideas and encouraged to give interviews regarding their work or knowledge. Earlier in this chapter, we discussed ideas for exhibitions, many of which will provide suitable topics for news items, feature articles or documentaries.

Whatever the topic, care should be taken to ensure that all materials provided to journalists and editors are accurate, concise, well–written and presented in an interesting way. Beginning the piece with an arresting opener, closely followed by the who, what, where, why and when information is a well–accepted formula. Be sure to include a name and telephone number of the person to contact for more information.

Help with publicity initiatives may be more available and forthcoming than you think. Many people with publicity skills and experience are willing to help a worthy cause. Retired members of the media and public relations community have a wealth of experience and contacts and may welcome the opportunity to use them on your behalf. Keep in mind, however, that help is just that. The archives must always accept its responsibility to provide the resources to get the work done.

Publicity is an art which calls for several levels of effort. All archives, large and small, must keep their clients informed about the archives' work and activities. This basic effort involves placing 'Publicity' on the agenda for major planning meetings. Staff can then identify recent accomplishments that should be

Archival treasures make interesting feature articles.

reported and develop a calendar of coming events. Responsibility for preparing these items and the dates of completion should also be established and monitored. Initially these reports may be placed in the reading room and sent to selected archival and historical journals on a quarterly or half–yearly basis. This information forms a base which the archivist can use to prepare and distribute an authoritative annual report to the archives' primary clientele. As the publicity programme grows, archives staff or volunteers can expand on the core material by preparing brief articles describing research projects, notable visitors, accomplishments or materials from the collections for inclusion in a newsletter.

The second level of publicity involves designing special publicity for specific activities or events sponsored by the archives. Although these are also announced and reported as part of the basic publicity programme, they usually require specialised promotion tailored to the needs of each occasion. The effort required to produce customised publicity can be minimised by including the category 'Publicity' in a checklist for planning special programmes and activities.

Attention can then be given in a systematic way to designing the message to be delivered, defining the audience to receive it, identifying the methods most appropriate and to establishing the timeframes, personnel and services needed.

Up to this point, the emphasis has been on preparing publicity materials for distribution, either directly or indirectly through the media, and on establishing and maintaining a good rapport with professional communicators. But we must not overlook the most important public relations assets of all — you and your staff. Opportunities to promote the archives present themselves many times daily in formal and informal ways, within and outside of the workplace. The key to success in this area is to exhibit a genuinely helpful and positive attitude in all interpersonal dealings, be they with staff, archives clients, or the public at large. Professional expertise, shared with courtesy and good humour, contributes to a pleasant working environment and clearly conveys the message that archives are rewarding as well as worthwhile enterprises.

As a natural extension of this outward–looking mentality, set aside time in the work week to call on or meet with persons or groups whom you wish to cultivate. There is a danger here, particularly if you have an outgoing personality, of spending too much time on outreach to the detriment of less exciting but equally important archival tasks. Your time and energy, like your collections, must be preserved as well as made available for access and use.

Inevitably, and delightfully, these contacts will lead to invitations to speak before groups or be interviewed on radio or television programmes. Anticipating such eventualities, you would be wise to learn a bit about public speaking. Take some slides of the archives and select materials from the collections to accompany your talk; these will add dimensions and increase the impact of your enthusiastic words. Remember too, you need not bear the weight of public appearances unaided. Look to members of your staff and to long–time researchers and volunteers for candidates with the potential to share the limelight.

Publicity for the archives is a challenging task requiring flexibility, tact, persistence and a sense of humour. The archival publicist must also temper his/her enthusiasm and skills for promotion. Creating too much demand without the resources to handle the response can overwhelm or threaten the existence of the very materials and programmes he/she hopes to strengthen. However, properly managed, a regular and balanced programme of publicity can be an invaluable asset for any archives.

PUBLICATIONS

Publications are among the best known and most popular user education programmes and are valuable tools for communicating information about the archives, its holdings and services. Also their impact is longer term and more easily measured than other forms of user education. However, publications also represent a considerable investment of resources. Much time and energy, usually of senior staff, go into their preparation; and production costs can be substantial, particularly if multiple colours and illustrations are used. So, our advice is the same as with other user education efforts — proceed with caution and build on established strengths. This message cannot be over emphasised

Basic brochures explain the archives' purpose, location, holdings, hours and conditions of access.

because unsuccessful publications are an expensive embarrassment which will occupy the shelves for a long, long time.

The term 'publication' can be used to describe a wide variety of productions, ranging from a single A-4 page to an elaborately illustrated book. The characteristic common to all is that they convey information to users of archival records and services in a form that is consistent and that can be kept and referred to as needed.

Basic Publishing

Every archives will find it needs publications to help it accomplish its work in three major areas: repository services, reference, and educational activities. Repository services such as depositing or transferring records into the archives can be facilitated by developing manual–style booklets for clients which explain the procedures and documents needed to accomplish these tasks. Such publications, used in conjunction with personal contact and special training programmes, foster good working relationships with donors and depositors who regularly transfer their modern records to the archives under a disposal schedule or continuing agreement.

In reference work, publications can make existing services more effective in a number of ways. For example, a free brochure providing brief answers to those frequently asked questions about the archives purpose, location, holdings, services, hours and conditions of access can be distributed widely. Similarly, how–to information sheets on using the finding aids, requesting records or ordering copies can help researchers learn procedures more quickly and confidently. Descriptive inventories to individual collections can be produced in multiple copies and distributed to libraries and other archives with related research interests. This practice helps to promote the use of the archives collections more widely and enables out–of–area researchers to determine whether or not a research trip will be fruitful and make better informed requests through the mail.

Checklists outlining the steps and sources for popular research topics such as family or local history are also valuable, as are sheets referring researchers to other institutions whose holdings complement those of the archives. All of these publications are simple and effective ways to inform users and help to minimise the strain on resources caused by having to prepare individual responses to repetitive inquiries.

Additional Publications

It is through regular and selective publishing that the archives establishes its wider reputation as a research institution. New additions to the publications 'family' should reflect and reinforce the natural growth of the archives programme rather than be products of momentary inspiration. The archives may begin by

publishing an overall guide to its holdings which abstracts basic
information from the descriptive inventories of individual collections and presents it in a summarised form. A basis for the guide
may be established by compiling the individual collection reports
which the archives may have submitted to journals or to national
guides such as the *Guide to Manuscript Collections Relating to
Australia*. Such comprehensive work may be further complemented by developing guides to sources suitable for major
types of research such as family, local or business history.
Specialised guides, however, should be undertaken with caution,
as records are often useful for a number of fields, and a good
index to the comprehensive guide can serve these research
interests just as well at less expense.

Many archives find it beneficial to combine their publicity and
publishing initiatives in a newsletter which announces and
reports archives activities to the community. The newsletter need
not be elaborate, a single typed sheet with a distinctive heading
will serve. It is more important to concentrate on producing
accurate, well-written articles and to distribute the newsletter at
regular quarterly or half-yearly intervals. Categories for articles
may include newly processed collections, programme achievements, interesting documents or photographs, a calendar of
upcoming events, special projects and activities, research in progress, notable visitors and staff news.

*Well-designed newsletters attract
readers and reflect well upon the
archives.*

The archives will also produce occasional publications which
encourage clients and members of the community to become
involved in educational activities sponsored by the archives. Individual brochures and leaflets are issued to promote exhibits,
workshops, classes and special events such as open days. These
pieces serve both as announcements and as invitations to prospective participants to pre-register for the occasion.

The need for a basic or additional publication is easy to identify. Staff members liaising with depositors can report issues or
problems which crop up in the course of their work. Reference
staff can keep track of frequently asked questions and of common research problems and topics. A list of these can then
become the basis for ideas for training sessions and workshops,
as well as for publications. Having selected those questions and
problems which would be effectively handled with a publication,
the archivist can then concentrate on the specific information to
be conveyed and the best way to present it. To save effort and
money, issues or topics that are related may be grouped into a
single publication, provided that the proposed combinations are
compatible and the information will not require frequent
changes. It is wasteful to put volatile information into a publication which might otherwise have a long life. All publications
should be assigned a unique number which embodies their date
of production. This number should be altered when the piece is

revised, but not if it is simply reprinted. Two copies of each publication should be set aside as part of your own programme's archives.

Good Design: A Wise Investment

Each publication, regardless of how modest, should be designed to attract readers. Appropriate, readable type faces, combined with simple graphics and a pleasing balance between text and white space, will enhance the message you wish to convey. Coloured inks can also be effective, but these should be used selectively with the advice of an experienced designer to avoid costly mistakes. It is a good idea to think of each of your published pieces, including your letterhead, as family members which share a visual identity. Standard page sizes, typefaces and cover formats will help establish continuity of image and still allow each item to have individual distinction. Hiring a professional designer to create the basic design framework is a worthwhile investment.

A Note about Souvenir Publishing

Many cultural institutions, archives among them, offer a selection of souvenir items for sale to researchers and visitors to promote the institution and raise funds. Souvenir publications include postal and greeting cards, notepaper, frameable prints and posters which reproduce graphic items from the collections. More complex examples are diaries or calendars, exhibit catalogues and sets of facsimile documents. Souvenir objects, such as carrybags, tea towels, ties, scarves and insignia jewellery are less common in archives than in museums, but some larger

Reproductions of posters, maps and photographs make nice souvenirs and generate income and publicity.

ARCHIVES OFFICE POSTCARDS 10¢

institutions do have shops, often operated by volunteers or members of a 'friends' group, which offer a range of such items. This type of publishing is truly an option rather than a necessity. It is expensive because many items fail to meet costs, and it can expose the archives programme to criticism from those who view souvenir items as trivial gimmicks. Opportunities for the production of souvenir items are frequent, but all should be scrutinised carefully to identify pitfalls and unfavourable consequences. As a general rule, such projects should be undertaken and financed by sources outside the archives and should not be endorsed or condoned by the archives unless they meet stringent quality standards. This policy avoids most of the problems, such as high expense and unsold stock, which can arise with souvenir publishing.

Large Scale Publishing

Publications in this category are usually undertaken by archives with comprehensive, well-established programmes or by a group of co-operating institutions, often working in conjunction with a professional publisher. Examples include publishing the full text of collections of diaries, letters, literary manuscripts or other personal papers, of business/corporate records, or of re-publishing runs of rare journals, gazettes and newspapers.

Illustrated publications such as exhibit catalogues and those which feature collections of historic photographs or of documentary art may also be considered.

A number of searching questions must be answered before undertaking such projects.

- Is there a genuine need for the publication?
- Will all the records be published or only a selection? If the latter, what criteria will be used to select those to be included?
- Will the publication be hard copy or microform?
- What will be the market for the publication?
- How will the initial costs of preparing the records for publication and distribution be met?
- Does the archives have the resources, both financial and human, to produce and market a quality product?

Unfortunately, the answers to these questions are usually discouraging to self-publishers, but worthwhile projects may still be realised. The answer lies in shifting the initiative – and the financial burden of producing the publication to resources outside the archives. Two main possibilities should be investigated. First, the material the archives seeks to publish may be part of a larger body of documentation held by several institutions. This is particularly true with collections of rare journals, gazettes and newspapers. By joining forces with other libraries and archives, the project may be able to attract special funding and produce a more authoritative and significant work than if it were undertaken by a single institution.

Second, the archives should approach established scholars and publishers who specialise in documentary works. These experienced professionals will investigate the proposed project and make recommendations regarding its feasibility. Keep in mind that working with professional publishers requires flexibility and an understanding of the realities of a competitive trade. These outsiders are, in essence, no different from other researchers working on publication projects. The archives is only the source of the raw material; and, beyond the normal obligations to protect materials from loss, damage or legal infringement, it will have no control over or responsibility for the quality of the product.

An exception to this situation is one in which the archives develops a formal partnership with a publisher to jointly produce a work. In such cases, the archives staff may be responsible for some or all of the work of preparing the records for publication. Often the publisher will have his/her own compiler or editor or both working on the project with the archives. Again, each partner will view the project from a different perspective, and a successful working relationship will involve compromises, most often in favour of the partner paying the bills.

Whatever level of publication you choose for your archives, the effort should be one that supports the work of the archives as a whole and is reflective of the quality you wish to have associated with your institution.

CLASSES, SEMINARS AND WORKSHOPS

For many archivists the term 'user education' is synonymous with classes, seminars and workshops. Indeed, these activities are among the most rewarding of all user education programmes for they are usually enjoyed by both staff and participants and measurably increase awareness of the archives within the larger community. These 'training' activities also benefit the archives in less obvious ways. Staff members involved in teaching gain confidence and renewed enthusiasm for their work when they see that it is interesting to others. Slide shows and videos produced as training aids may be adapted for wider audiences. Teaching research methods often leads to more effective reference procedures and improved finding aids, and many useful publications have their origins in handouts for workshops.

In-House Training

As with other user education programmes, teaching activities should directly support and facilitate the use of archival holding and services before developing a wider community service orientation. Acquisition and reference come to mind as natural areas where regular training sessions can improve the delivery of services. The purpose of the training would be to inform new staff

and agency representatives of their responsibilities in such areas as:
- Conducting records surveys for disposal.
- Developing disposal schedules.
- Donating records to the archives.
- Transferring records to the repository.
- Requesting records or information from the archives.

An understanding of the nature of the archives' work, its procedures and documentation can contribute greatly to the smooth operation of these important functions where clients interact directly with the archives staff.

Volunteers are another important audience for in-house training. A general introduction to the purpose and overall operation of the archives programme is as important for prospective volunteers as it is for new staff, and an orientation session could profitably include individuals from both groups. It is, however, important for instructors to remember that volunteers do not have the same accountability as paid staff and to understand that all training sessions which include volunteers must explain and maintain that distinction in a tactful and friendly way. Overall, there is a benefit in training staff and volunteers together as both groups then have a better understanding of the working relationship they will enjoy in future. Some examples of training sessions which could be suitable for volunteers include:
- Replacing fasteners, refoldering records.
- Flattening and cleaning documents.
- Encapsulating materials.
- Indexing.
- Assisting reference staff.
- Photocopying.
- Preparing Special Lists.
- Conducting tours for visitors.
- Giving talks about the archives.
- Writing newsletter articles.

Volunteers are an important asset for the archives and should be well-informed about the programme and its operations. More information about recruiting and managing volunteers will be presented later in this chapter.

Educating the Public

As a complement to and extension of in-house training, the archives should also develop educational activities for 'outsiders', whether they be members of the public or individuals from a specialised client group. As mentioned earlier, few people have had any opportunity to learn about archives work or original records in the normal course of growing up; therefore, it is in the archives' own interest to plan programmes to bridge this gap of experience and to minimise it in the future. Naturally, the type

Staff members and volunteers prepare to guide visitors through a special exhibition. Courtesy — State Library of NSW.

and content of educational offerings will vary according to the purpose of your archives, its scope and its clientele; smaller institutions may work informally while large ones may have a calendar full of scheduled events. The main point is that an appropriate level of outreach is necessary so that the archives can develop a base of community support from which to grow.

Mini-classes

The first priority of archival educators must be to convert first-time users into confident, competent researchers as quickly and as pleasingly as possible. While this process always requires the archivist to spend some individual time with researchers, the amount of that time and the extent of information conveyed can be modified by using group instruction and self-teaching aids. A number of archives have instituted programmes of mini-classes, half-hour sessions conducted at a regular time or when the need arises, to inform readers. The sessions can be conducted at a table in the reading room so that participants can familiarise themselves with the finding aids and facilities. Most classes combine talks and exercises to present basic information on the following topics:

- Introduction to the Reading Room.
- Using archival sources. General and various types such as newspapers and photographs.

- Research techniques and/or sources for popular fields such as family history.

After a few presentations, the staff will know what works best and can develop basic outlines and handouts for regular use. Instructors can include researchers and volunteers, as well as staff, to provide a variety of viewpoints and expertise. In this way the classes can reflect the needs of the users and build upon the strengths of the staff and collections.

An individualised alternative or supplement to the mini-classes is to develop an audio cassette programme which orients newcomers to the reading room. Modelled on the museum 'self tour' of exhibits, this instructional aid employs a portable cassette player with headphones and takes the new reader to numbered sites in the reading room. The tape then explains the sources and how to use them, incorporating tasks for the researcher to do to improve his/her understanding before moving on.

Seminars and Workshops

Extending beyond the immediate need to orient and instruct researchers and staff, the archives can also benefit from sponsoring workshops and seminars that provide more thorough coverage of archival subjects. In a pure sense, seminars differ from workshops in that they are usually directed discussions of issues and ideas whereas workshops are practical hands-on occasions where participants develop skills and techniques or solve problems. Both of these programmes are most effective with groups of up to twenty people.

Possible topics for workshops and seminars are as varied as the range of materials within the archives multiplied by the interests of the intended audience. In other words, the choice is vast. However, first ventures should be designed to explore established strengths, both of the collections and of available expertise. A modest half or full day programme, executed with confidence, will provide a base of success and enthusiasm on which to expand and diversify. Table Four outlines a basic programme which begins with mini-classes and evolves into workshops and seminars on popular themes. It also gives tips on scheduling, promotion and administration which are at least as important to the success of the effort as having a good topic.

Conferences

Conferences are more comprehensive undertakings than seminars and workshops both in content and in numbers. A programme is usually organised around a theme featuring one or more large general or plenary sessions followed by smaller, more focused presentations which may be concurrent as well as sequential to allow participants more choices.

Conferences can generate great interest within the community. Courtesy — State Library of NSW.

Table Four   Basic Classes, Workshop

	Subject	Administration	Promotion
Mini-Classes • Specific how-tos for beginning researchers	Intro. to research process • Using the finding aids • Proper handling of documents • Basic categories of sources and where they are located (documents, maps, news-papers, etc.	• Appoint staff committee to develop a presentation that can be given by several members of staff • Work class into regular workday schedule • Charge no fee • Hold weekly or bi-weekly at regular time 20–30 minutes	• List in basic brochure about the archives • Post announcement on sign board in reception area • Announce in research areas just before class begins
Workshops/Seminars • Specialised instruction focus-ing on specific topics or research problems • In-depth perspec-tives and dis-cussion of selected subject areas	• Researching historic sites, family or community history • Identification and care of historical papers, photo-graphs, graphic materials • Basic Conservation • Research on specialist topics (transport, churches, gold, convicts, WWI) • Indexing original records or contemporary sources (newspapers, school magazines) • Significant historical issues and themes	• Plan presentations, demon-strations and how-to activi-ties by staff and/or invited speakers • Prepare handouts • Charge a reasonable regis-tration fee • Pre-register participants • Have refreshments • Limit enrolment to 15–25 • Hold quarterly half- or full-day sessions (Saturday for optimum attendance	• Mail programme brochure to archival researchers, his-torical societies, libraries, high school social studies departments, and other appropriate audiences • Send public service announcements to media • Post on sign board and have in reception area • Pass information by word-of-mouth from readers and staff

A show of local hospitality is an important complement to a good programme, and the larger audience may include out-of-town participants who will need food and accommodation. Special tours, social events and/or entertainments add zest and contribute to the overall quality of experience. However, all of these ingredients – content, venue, and hospitality – must be measured and combined carefully to ensure a balanced result. Too much or too little of any one of them can spoil the overall effect.

Planning a successful conference can involve a considerable commitment of time. The effort is manageable if the work is shared, and good delegation skills are essential for conference coordinators. Most meetings involve planning in two main areas – programme content and local arrangements – and it is helpful to select a responsible person to coordinate each of these. Table Five provides a schedule and checklist of activities for basic conference planning. For more detailed information consult the suggestions for *Further Reading* at the end of the chapter.

Conference planners must also decide in advance whether or not to publish the proceedings and make the necessary arrange-ments with authors and printers. Several cautions are worthy of

note. Editing verbal presentations into written form is difficult, as is working with multiple authors; persistence and skill are needed to produce proceedings in a timely manner. Conference papers also vary considerably in quality so it may be best to encourage selected authors to publish in a refereed journal, noting that the paper was first presented at the conference. In this way, the work is published, the conference credited and someone else does the editing work.

Giving a group of new researchers a short introduction to the archives can reduce repetitive questions.

Activities for Students

Students are among the most important client groups, particularly for school and local community archives. In the writer's view, all students above age sixteen should have some exposure to the riches of contemporary and original sources as part of their general education. Otherwise, a critical, perhaps unique, opportunity to acquaint them with archives and archival work is lost and the level of community ignorance perpetuated. Few archives are able to cope with mass onslaughts of researchers, particularly of inexperienced ones as students generally are; nor should they be expected to do so. After all, research is an individual or, at most, a small group activity; and there are ways, other than on-site visits, to have students interact with original sources.

Duplicates, facsimiles and, in some cases, originals of archival materials can be loaned or taken to libraries and classrooms where students can examine them and learn to evaluate evidence or pursue a line of research appropriate for their age and level of experience. Local and family history projects provide excellent laboratories for both exploring and for creating documentary

Table Five Basic Conference Planning Checklist

5-6 months in advance	1)	Meet with colleagues and collaborators to discuss the general theme and scope of the conference and solicit ideas for prospective sessions, topics and speakers.
	2)	Check calendars of upcoming events and set a tentative date.
	3)	Reserve meeting facilities; book caterers.
	4)	Meet again with fellow planners to finalise session topics and speakers. Have an alternate for each prospective speaker in case the first choice is unavailable. Decide whether or not to publish conference papers.
	5)	Invite the speakers:

- Telephone each speaker to explain the purposes of the conference, the general topic you would like him or her to cover, and the date, time and place of the meeting. Indicate whether there will be an honorarium or reimbursement for travel/expenses. At the very least, speakers should be given complimentary registration, meals, and parking.
- Send each speaker a letter confirming the invitation and discussing the topics. Have speakers return a form in which they indicate their exact titles (i.e., how they would like to be listed on the programme), give brief descriptions of their presentations and agree to publishing/ typing arrangements.

	6)	Send announcements of the event to calendar sections of all appropriate journals and newsletters.
	7)	Start a file for each session and event on the agenda. Include correspondence, biographical information about the speakers, session outline forms, and notes on special logistical requirements (e.g., extra chairs, audiovisual equipment, microphones, transportation).
3 months in advance	8)	Prepare a programme flyer:

- Prepare programme copy and artwork.
- Get in touch with speakers for any information not yet received.
- Ask how long the printer will take to produce finished copies.
- Send the text to the printer so the programme is in the mail no less than two months before the conference date.
- Prepare the mailing list and labels while the programme is at the printer.

2 months in advance	9)	Mail programme flyer.
1 month in advance	10)	Confirm arrangements with speakers.
	11)	Confirm arrangements for meeting facilities and coordinate final plans for meals, receptions, tours or other conference events.
	12)	Visit the meeting site and assign rooms for the conference sessions. Make arrangements to rent audiovisual equipment as needed.
The week before	13)	Complete the preparation and duplication of handouts, and assemble registration packets, final check of all arrangements.
1-2 days before	14)	Be prepared to transport speakers to and from meeting site and/or accommodation, if needed, and give them a tour of your facility.
During conference	15)	Introduce — or arrange for another participant to introduce — speakers at the sessions. Thank speakers personally for their participation.
Shortly after (no more than a month)	16)	Send speakers a thank-you letter, and mail speakers and participants an evaluation form
	17)	Collect evaluation forms and prepare report assessing the strengths and weaknesses of the meeting.
Within 6 months	18)	Edit/publish selected conference papers (optional).

Note: These lead-time estimates are based on the requirements for a substantial metropolitan meeting and may be scaled up or down for other levels of conferences.

sources. Whatever the proposed project, archivists must recognise that their responsibility is to encourage and support the educational effort, not to design or conduct it; the latter is the domain of the professional educator. Supporting and encouraging activities can include:

1) Developing policies, plans and procedures which
   a) establish and nurture an appropriate level and scope of interaction between the archives and the education system and
   b) facilitate the use of archival sources and services by educators and students.
2) Giving presentations to groups of educators to make them aware of the archives and its holdings and
   a) identify materials related to course curricula;
   b) explain the terms under which materials can be made available and
   c) suggest ways teachers and students can use source materials.
3) Collaborating with educators to give workshops on the use of archival materials in teaching.
4) Working with educators to
   a) identify local structures, sites, events, or individuals for which there is sufficient documentation in the archives to do a local history research project.
   b) design projects to document community life on a continuing basis combining photography, oral history and archival research.

Facsimile documents and posters provide intriguing learning opportunities for students.

The policy and planning work is particularly important because it establishes a framework for an ongoing relationship and enables the archives to respond selectively and appropriately to requests for student activities without being overwhelmed.

Some questions that archival policy makers should ask include:

a) At what grade level should students
    • be introduced to primary sources in a classroom setting?
    • become involved with individual research projects using archival resources
    • be permitted to do research at the archives and under what conditions?
b) What types of experiences are appropriate for the archives to provide for students and how should they be managed? What facilities and staff would be required?
c) How will the products of student work, particularly those of high quality, be used?

The answers to these questions will provide a sound basis for discussion with educators and enable you to determine a level of involvement in student activities that is suitable for your programme and resources. Remember, there is no requirement for the archives to cater to every interest group or demand. It is better to do a few things well.

Follow–up Activities

Any learning experience is beneficial in itself and rewarding for the individual who undertakes it, but the result can be even more significant and worthwhile if it is seen as a lasting contribution to be shared and appreciated by others. Students, or anyone for that matter, including volunteers and staff, will invest more time and effort into their work if they know it will be used and enjoyed. For this reason, archival educators should incorporate plans for the use of archival projects into the programme design. The type and extent of promotion and use will vary with the nature of the project, but the suggestions given in Table Six are a good starting point.

Instructional programmes be they in–house training, workshops/seminars, conferences or activities for students all have one thing in common: they involve people with archives and expose them to the fascination of archival work. The benefits of such involvement are multiple and diverse, ranging from increased staff knowledge and confidence to new recruits for the volunteer workforce; from an index to a series of previously inaccessible records to a major work of local or family history; from a gift of a single photograph to a host of new collections or substantial gifts of funds. Of all the educational programmes, these which implant lasting knowledge and skill through involvement ultimately have the most lasting impact and continue to generate benefits in ever widening circles.

Table Six   Follow–up Activities

Type of Project	Ideas for Promotion and Use
Students bring archival materials from home to share with class	• Prepare a series of selected items for small exhibits within the school, local library or archives. • Work with local newspaper or TV station to feature the historic photograph, object or document of the week.
Documenting a local building or community landmark	• Prepare a small exhibit of documents, photographs and/or objects for an appropriate community setting. • Produce a facsimile package of documentary sources for study by future students.
Listing local landmarks and/or historic structures/sites	• Prepare a series of walking tours based upon project research. • Work with local television stations to produce a 'heritage commercial' or background slides for station breaks.
Local or family history research papers	• Give prizes for outstanding papers. • Publish or arrange publication of individual or collections of significant work • Encourage researchers to give presentations based on their work to local historical or community groups.

COMMUNITY SUPPORT SYSTEMS

'He who has a thousand friends has not a friend to spare' is the opening line of a famous couplet by Ali Ben Abu Taleb, and one that archivists are well advised to take to heart.[1] While it is true that ongoing, responsible enterprises must plan their programmes within the bounds of the recurrent financial support they receive from their own budgetary authorities, a gift of special funding and assistance from sources in the outside community is always welcomed and appreciated. The ability to attract and utilise extra equipment, services, personnel and funding is an acquired skill and one which can, with practice, become an important asset for a developing archives. However, before hitting the solicitation trail, you must do your homework and adhere to a few basic rules.

1)   Outside support must always be considered as an extra. It should not be viewed as a requirement for the success of any venture.

---

[1] The full couplet reads: 'He who has a thousand friends has not a friend to spare and he who has one enemy will meet him everywhere.'

Corporate sponsors 'adopt' a three-dimensional record and pay for its conservation. Courtesy — State Library of NSW.

2) Outside support should only be sought for specific projects of limited duration. Few benefactors are willing to give to general ongoing programmes, and they prefer to see the results and the gratitude quickly, certainly within the same budget year.

3) Develop and maintain a 'Wish List' of defined projects, items or areas where special funding or help can be used to maximum effect. The list should describe the commitment required in terms of time, equipment, services and funds and should outline the benefits the gift will bring to prospective benefactors and to the archives.

4) Before seeking outside support, determine your objectives, themes or messages and requirements (conservation for instance) which the project must meet. Flexibility and room for compromise should be an integral part of project planning, but these are the points you must explain and adhere to in negotiations with prospective donors.

5) Prospective donors, whether of time, money, equipment, facilities or services, all hope to gain some benefit meaningful to them. Altruism is a nice idea in the abstract, but in the real world, donors want to realise some clear benefit for their help. Your job is to find out what they want and build it into the project proposal.

6) Philanthropy is a very competitive business. Most donors have limited funds and many requests for them. You must find out what their funding cycle is and get your request in early to ensure consideration. The proposal must be well-prepared, succinct and specific (as explained in point 3).

7) Develop and maintain a 'Hit List' of funding and support 'prospects'. See that key representatives of these groups/

agencies are on the mailing list to receive the archives newsletter, calendar of activities, and invitations to special events such as exhibit openings.

8)   Seek a variety of types of support. Money is only one among many possibilities. The archives may benefit equally from a special piece of equipment, a gift of flowers or refreshments, the use of a meeting or conference venue, free publicity or a complimentary brochure. Services which could be donated include graphic design, typesetting, printing, photocopying, word processing, audio or video recording, consultancy (automation, exhibits, fund–raising), photography, music, compere or public speaking duties and interviewing.

9)   Allow plenty of time for the donor to deliver his/her gift. Many businesses are willing to contribute equipment, facilities or services during their slack periods. If you allow donors to set their own schedule, you will improve your chances of success.

10) If at first you don't succeed, don't be discouraged. Seek advice on how you can improve your proposal and/or its timing in the future and identify other sources of support. Potential donors who cannot help you themselves may be prepared to suggest other prospects and may even offer to use their influence to help you on your way.

11) Donors or contributors who have given once are fertile ground for additional aid. However, you must proceed with caution as you do not want to over exploit your friends. On the other hand, those who have helped you in the past may want to continue the special relationship and may be offended if they are not asked to do so.

12) Show your appreciation in ways which are both appropriate to your institution and meaningful to your benefactors.

13) Managing community support and participation well is a demanding task. Designate a capable senior person to manage/handle this important work.

Exploring sources of support within the archives' area of service is a gradual process. Most archivists begin by asking for specific help or funding for a well–defined project or activity such as refreshments for an exhibit opening, folders for a seminar or workshop or guides for an open day tour. The most difficult part of getting started is making that first appeal. Once you have asked once and been successful, the task gets easier, and your credibility as a 'worthy cause' grows. Offers of assistance may even come spontaneously. Attendees at a workshop seeking further involvement with archival sources may offer themselves as prospective volunteers. Community businesses may volunteer their services, facilities and/or equipment for future projects, particularly if they see their competitors gaining valuable publicity for similar contributions. Once the ball is rolling, it will gain momentum, and it will be necessary to establish regular and formal structures to manage the process to the archives' best advantage. If your archives is part of a larger organisation, there may already be programmes or personnel in existence to handle these tasks for you. Many educational institutions, for example, have strong, well-organised alumni groups and may also operate a trust fund or foundation to receive grants, gifts and/or income generated by educational and special activities. Research institutions, particularly universities, have development offices or special corporations which seek and manage funds for the benefit of the institution. Your first step then is to investigate the potential use of any of these existing structures for the benefit of the archives. Tapping these important resources can begin with a meeting to explain your programme and present a 'shopping list' of your needs. You need not feel that you are an indigent seeking a handout; rather you are offering these experts another vehicle for attracting support from potential benefactors.

Many archives will not have access to established mechanisms for receiving and managing community support and will need to set up their own programmes. Several possibilities come immediately to mind, among them a volunteer programme, a friends group and special funding vehicles such as endowments or trusts. These three may be separate entities or they may be combined under the overall umbrella of a community relations programme. The task is not an easy one and will require considerable time and effort from senior staff to accomplish.

Volunteers

A frequent first step is to develop a volunteer programme to coordinate gifts of personal services to the archives. Volunteer labour, though freely given, is not without cost to the archives programme. The orderly recruitment, training, scheduling and supervision of volunteers is essential;and this work should be a significant job duty for a responsible staff member. Volunteer help must be viewed realistically. Volunteers are not a substitute for paid staff, and they must not be used by the organisation to avoid its responsibility to provide the archives with reasonable resources. Furthermore, volunteers do not have the same accountability as paid staff and solving problems such as low productivity, poor quality of work and absenteeism must depend almost exclusively on persuasion and tact. The quality of work by volunteers is directly dependent upon there being clear policies, procedures and standards for each type of work. Many problems can be minimised, if not avoided, by setting up reasonable standards of qualification, attendance and performance for volunteers. The status of volunteers should be a distinction which must be earned and maintained. Therefore it is important for the archives to formulate policies and guidelines for recruiting, managing and terminating persons volunteering to work on its behalf. Some matters to address in these documents include:

- An application process.
- A description of the extent of commitment expected from volunteers,· including training, standards of performance and attendance.
- Descriptions of the types of work available for volunteers.
- A system for establishing accountability for volunteers, including procedures for evaluating work performance, for assessing suggestions of suitable projects and duties and for resolving problems and disputes.
- A clear understanding that all products, resources and funds generated by volunteer labour are the property of the archives to be managed and administered according to its requirements.
- An objective and tactful process for terminating volunteers.
- An advisory committee composed of staff, volunteers, and managers to assist with the management of the volunteer programme, including evaluating ideas for new projects and duties.
- Working with volunteers can be very rewarding, both in terms of productivity and in the development of management and interpersonal skills. Particularly in a small archives where one archivist may be responsible for everything, a *corps* of volunteers can be an essential resource, supplying not only labour but insights, ideas, community contacts and feedback.

Volunteers often operate shops which sell postcards, posters and other reproductions from the collections.

Friends Groups

Given nurturing and good management enthusiastic volunteers may organise, evolve into or lead the effort to develop formal bodies known generically as *'friends' groups*. While volunteer programmes operate within the archives programme and are directly accountable to it, friends groups are separate entities whose purpose is to rally and focus community support for the archives. Because they are independent, friends groups can engage in activities that the archives may not be able to undertake, such as raising and retaining money and political lobbying to promote archival causes. On the other hand, friends groups can be a powerful platform vulnerable to domination by those seeking to change the policies and/or programmes, even the personnel, of the archives; therefore, every care must be taken when the organisation of a friends group for the archives is proposed. Several measures can help to ensure that the friends groups stays friendly to the archives.

1)   Archives staff should work closely with friends group organisers to:

Friends group lectures and special events attract members and publicity. Courtesy — State Library of NSW.

a) embed goals and purposes that fully serve the archives within the basic organisational documents;

b) limit the terms of service of office bearers and ensure a ratio of new to continuing members in each executive.

2) Archives staff should be encouraged to become active members of the friends group, but should avoid a disproportionate representation, particularly as office bearers.

3) The archives' administration should be welcoming and supportive of the friends group, but mindful of the limits required to maintain the group's independent position. For example, would provision of office space and/or administrative support for the friends compromise their legal status?

4) The archives should maintain regular official communication with the friends group, both to inform them of activities and needs and to acknowledge and report on the use of their contributions. Individual members of the friends should be added to the archives mailing list.

5) Show special appreciation for your friends group by having some 'friends only' occasions.

A well-managed, effective friends group is a great asset to its beneficiary as the extensive literature in the subject attests. Some of the more popular achievements of friends groups include:

• fundraising for new facilities, renovations and additions
• purchases of major or specialised equipment
• development and/or operation of programmes for volunteers
• sponsorship of publications, exhibits, seminars/workshops and special events (films, tours, lectures, parties).

Friends groups provide a direct means for people of many backgrounds to share their enthusiasm and appreciation for archives and to contribute tangibly to its growth.

Funding arrangements

Funding for educational activities is a complex area and could well occupy a chapter of its own. Part of the complexity lies in weighing the dollars and cents cost associated with such activities against difficult to measure benefits such as community awareness, appreciation and cultural enrichment. Responsible planners must always develop budgets for their work and keep good records of their expenditures. Educational work requires a heavy investment of staff time, and this cost should be monitored. Estimates should include internal expenses such as mileage, photocopying, postage and equipment maintenance. A carefully devised budget based upon a reasoned estimate of costs will enable planners to make a realistic assessment of their funding needs.

Meeting the costs of educational activities can be done in various ways. A portion of recurrent funds should be set aside for this work but supplementary sources should be explored as well.

Fees

Some of the costs of educational activities may be recovered by charging reasonable fees or by asking for donations from those who participate in them. Fees are particularly appropriate for publications, workshops/seminars, conferences and other activities which offer services above and beyond the normal level. Setting a fee for an event is complex and requires one to consider a number of factors including the actual costs per participant, what the market will bear, what related institutions are charging and your community service obligations.

Institutions that have income from fees and the sale of publications may wish to establish a special account or fund to support educational activities. Again, this is a specialist area and will require expert advice. While the existence of a special fund does enable the programme to be more flexible and responsive to unforeseen opportunities, it also has definite disadvantages. Special funds imply that educational activities should pay their own way, which is not often the case. It is also hard to define 'educational' since many such activities are natural extensions of normal archival services. Finally, budget officers and accountants may be concerned about regulating the fund so that it is used responsibly.

Special Funding

Educational activities are usually well–defined and limited in duration, and, as such, are ideal candidates for special funding from a granting agency, foundation or private/corporate benefactor. While the practice of seeking special funding is not widespread among archival agencies in Australia, it is an area of increasing interest and a few tips on how to go about it are presented in Table Seven.

Friends groups may sponsor a variety of educational and fund raising activities in support of the archives.

Table Seven   Hints for Obtaining Special Funding

A.   Overall Strategies

1) Find out as much as possible about government and private sources for special funding and the kinds of projects they support. *Philanthropic Trusts in Australia,* cited in the Further Reading, is a basic guide.
2) Most agencies will have application guidelines and timetables. Study these and plan ahead; many funding bodies take six months or more to review and process requests.
3) Assemble your local resources. Some agencies favour proposals which demonstrate evidence of community support which they can then augment or match.
4) Be sure that the amount of money you are seeking is worth the effort you are making to acquire it. It may take the same investment to obtain a thousand dollars as it does ten-thousand.
5) Don't be discouraged if you don't succeed on your first try. Fund raising is competitive and increasingly sophisticated. Ask why you were turned down; insights and advice will help you prepare a stronger application for resubmission or for application to another source.

B.   The Funding Proposal
Competitive funding proposals must

1) Reflect a realistic assessment of the needs and interests of a defined audience.
2) Demonstrate substantial and/or lasting benefits to significant and/or representative groups.
3) Have realistic goals, realisable within the time frame specified by the funding source (usually one to three years).
4) Show awareness and consideration of what other institutions are doing/have done to avoid duplication and build on existing strengths.
5) Present evidence of good research and careful planning of programme design and implementation.
6) Indicate the involvement of qualified staff and consultants. Experienced personnel who are known to be capable performers add weight to any proposal.
7) Include a realistic and authoritative budget and timetable for completing the project.
8) Explain how the project can, or will, be able to serve a variety of needs or be adapted to produce multiple benefits. For example, a proposal for an exhibit could include plans for a book on the theme and/or documentary on its production.

Although the above suggestions were developed for writing proposals for outside funding, they are just as valid for preparing requests for support from internal sources. All financial analysts, regardless of setting, will be impressed with a well-researched request.

Documentation and Evaluation

No chapter on user education would be complete without a brief discussion of reporting and evaluation procedures. After all, if education and greater awareness of archives are our goals, we must document our efforts and try to measure our progress towards achieving them. It is also useful to have accurate records and reports to identify projects worth repeating or expanding, to devise future plans and budgets and to highlight both successes and mistakes.

Sometimes it is difficult to rally the energy and/or reserve the time for post–programme assessment. One way to ensure that proper reviews are conducted is to build reporting and evaluation mechanisms into the programme schedule when it is first planned. The process should be divided into phases which follow the project as it progresses.

Table Eight provides an example.

Table Eight   Steps for Documentation and Evaluation

Before	• Design the evaluation methods and procedures.
	• Set up a file to receive records documenting the major stages of the project.
During	• Add key documents to the project file, beginning with plans, schedules, budgets and continuing with correspondence, press releases, receipts and programmes.
	• Distribute evaluation forms to participants, both attendees and staff, and establish a reliable method for ensuring a good return.
Immediately After	• Meet with project staff.
	• Complete the project documentation file.
	• Analyse the evaluation forms.
	• Prepare a report on the project or event which includes
	• a description of the project (purpose, background, steps or phases to completion).
	• a list of project costs, including staff time, copying, supplies and administrative support, as well as items which required a direct payment.
	• an assessment of the projects strengths and shortcomings under such headings as scheduling, publicity, programme content, local arrangements, audience reaction, results.
	• A summary for future planners. Should the project be repeated, expanded or abandoned? Record suggestions and insights you consider essential.
	• File the report and project documentation so that it can be readily retrieved.

Good documentation and evaluation systems are important for the continued success of all archival programmes. Without them planners lack objective information on which to base future decisions and the means to determine whether or not their efforts have been worthwhile. And it is that last word *worthwhile* which evokes a parting thought. We who labour in and with archives know our work is worthwhile, but unless we employ effective means for communicating this knowledge to others, particularly to our managers and major client groups, we will be undervalued, even ignored. Involving yourself in user education and public relations activities is one way you can share and reaffirm your enthusiasm for archives. Don't miss the opportunity; begin now.

A commemorative photograph of a workshop group makes a thoughtful souvenir.

FURTHER READING

Association of Australian Philanthropic Trusts, *Philanthropic Trusts in Australia.* Fourth Edition. Hawthorne, VIC: Australian Council for Educational Research Limited, 1983.

Casterline, Gail F. *Archives and Manuscripts : Exhibits.* Chicago, IL: Society of American Archivists, 1980.

Eutick, Mal L. 'On the display of archives,' *Archives and Manuscripts* 12/1 (May, 1984): 17–23.

Freivogel, Elsie F. 'Educational programs: outreach as an administrative function.' *American Archivist* 41/2 (April, 1978): 147–153.

American Association for State and Local History (AASLH). *Technical Leaflets.* Nashville, TN: AASLH, various dates. Some relevant numbers and titles include: No.34 Walker, J.J.Jr., Publishing in the historical society (April 1966); No.39 Derby, C.S.,

Reaching your public: the historical society newsletter (January, 1967); No.42 Smith A.L., Producing the slide show for your historical society (June, 1967); No.43 Richman, I., A guide to planning local history institutes (August, 1967); No.45 Gignilliat, M., Reaching your public through the newspaper (April, 1968); No.62 Alderson W.T., Securing grant support: effective planning and preparation (December, 1972); No.124 Adams, G.D., Working effectively with the press: a guide for historical societies (February, 1980).

Eastman Kodak Company. *Planning and Producing Slide Programs.* S-30. Rochester, NY: Eastman Kodak Company, 1978.

Pardo, Thomas C. *Basic Archival Workshops: A Handbook for the Workshop Organiser.* Chicago, IL: Society of American Archivists, 1962.

Pederson, Ann E. and Gail F. Casterline, *Archives and Manuscripts: Public Programs.* Chicago, IL: Society of American Archivists, 1982.

Australian Government Publishing Service (AGPS). *Style Manual for Authors, Editors and Printers.* Third Edition. Canberra: AGPS, 1978.

Watson, C.S. and M. Richards, *Friends of the Library Resource File.* Melbourne: Library Association of Australia (Victorian Branch) September, 1981.

Gwyn, Ann, Anne McArthur and Karen Turlow, 'Friends of the Library', *College and Research Libraries* (July, 1975): 272-282.

GLOSSARY

Clive Smith

Access

The granting of permission to:
1) use the reference facilities of an *archives* institution;
2) examine and study individual *archives* and *records* or collections held by an *archives*;
3) extract information from *archives* and *records* for research or publication.

Access to archives may be restricted or withheld to prevent physical damage to original records or to protect confidential information.

Access Policy

The official statement issued by the authorities managing an archives setting out which records and archives are available for *access* and under what conditions. It should be in writing, and should be available to users and potential users.

Accession

(n.) A group of records or archives from the same source taken into archival custody at the same time.

(v.) The process of formally accepting and recording the receipt of records into archival custody.

The aim of accessioning is to get incoming material under basic control as quickly as possible, to prevent its being confused or mixed with other material in custody.

Accession number

The unique number which permanently identifies each *accession*, or part thereof.

Acidity

That quality in paper which causes its chemical degradation to the point that it becomes discoloured and brittle and will ultimately fall apart. Usually expressed as pH value.

Acquisition policy
An official statement issued by the authorities managing the archives which identifies the kinds of materials the archives will collect or acquire and the conditions or terms which affect the acquisition or collection of such materials.

It is a basic document for the guidance of archives staff, organisations and persons interested in depositing their papers.

Active records
Those records which are required for the day–to–day functioning of an *agency*.

Administrative change
Change made to the organisational structure of an *agency*, or to the allocation of the functions administered by one or more agencies. Such changes are, or may be, reflected in the agency's record–keeping systems.

Administrative history
That part of a *finding aid* which describes:
1) the history of an *agency* or a group of related agencies, its/ their organisational structure and functional responsibilities, or
2) the highlights of the life and career of a person or family. The administrative history of a person is also known as a *biographical note*.

Administrative value see **Archival value**

Agency
A government body, business, organisation or institution that creates or manages its own records in the course of its business or activities. In the case of large organisations or institutions, subordinate parts such as departments or sections may be regarded as separate agencies.

Aperture card see **Micrographics**

Appraisal
1) The process of determining which *records* are to be retained as *archives*, and which will be destroyed.
2) The monetary valuation of gifts of records.

Archival quality/standard
Term generally used to designate records media (paper, microfilm) and related supplies (inks, ribbons, fasteners) as suitable materials for creating permanent records or archives. Such materials must be stable and free of acid or other chemical contaminates. In addition, archival standard microfilm/microfiche must be exposed and processed to meet standards of technical quality.

Archival value
The values, both *evidential* and/or *informational* which justify the indefinite or permanent retention of records as archives:

Evidential Value. The value for providing evidence of the origins, structure, functions, policies, and operations of the agency or person that created the records. The three major categories of records having evidential value are those that:

1) have continuing *administrative, legal* or *fiscal* value for the body or individual which created them, or for any subsequent bodies;

2) record details which may serve to protect the civic, legal, property or other right of individuals or the community at large;

3) reflect the historical evolution of the creating body, its structures, functions, policies, decisions and significant operations; or which reflect the evolution of the individual's career, interests, or activities.

Administrative Value. The value for the conduct of current and future administrative business.

Fiscal Value. The value for the conduct of current financial or fiscal business.

Legal Value. The value for the conduct of current and future legal business.

Informational Value. The value for reference or research deriving from the information the records contain, as distinct from their *evidential value.* Records and archives often contain information which has reference or research uses not envisaged by their creators.

Historical Value

1) The value arising from exceptional age, and/or connection with some historical event or person.

2) A synonym for *archival value,* in the sense that 'historical' encompasses other kinds of values.

Archives

1) Those records which are no longer required for current use but have been selected for permanent preservation because of their evidential or informational value.

2) The place (building/room/storage area) where archival material is kept. See also *Repository.*

3) An organisation (or part of an organisation) whose main function is to select and make archival records available for use. There are two main types:

Collecting Archives: An organisation which has as its principal function the collection of the records of a variety of organisations, families and individuals. Collecting archives are often referred to as manuscript libraries or manuscript repositories.

In-house Archives: That part of an institution or organisation maintained for the purpose of keeping the archival records of that institution or organisation. An in-house archives usually restricts its collecting to material generated by its parent institution or organisation or by other closely associated bodies or people.

Archives box

A standard sized storage container made of cardboard (which may be acid–free) held together without the use of glues or staples.

Archives programme

A specific ongoing plan or operation to manage an archival collection or to identify archival material and arrange its transfer to an appropriate archival repository.

Archivist

A person professionally responsible for the administration or management of archives.

Arrangement

The process of putting archives and records into order in accordance with accepted archival principles, particularly those of *provenance* and *original order*. If there is no original order, the archivist may impose an order which presents the records objectively and facilitates their use.

Artefact

Objects, not being records, retained because of their informational value or because of their relationship with the records or archives.

Automated data processing (ADP)

The use of an electronic device (such as a computer) for processing information, including storing and manipulating the information (also called Electronic Data Processing (EDP)).

Biographical note see **Administrative history**

Cellulose nitrate film

A flexible support or base used for negatives and cine film from c.1890 to c.1950. It is extremely unstable, self–destructive and represents a major fire hazard as it is highly flammable. Nitrate based film records should be sent to the National Film and Sound Archive for copying.

Collecting policy see **Acquisition policy**

Collections see **Holdings**

COM (Computer output microfilm) see **Micrographics**

Conservation

The physical aspects and processes of preservation of original archival materials.

Preventative Conservation: Those measures taken in order to prevent or delay future degradation of collections, e.g. the provision of environmentally sound and secure storage, the installation of warning devices, the withdrawal, restriction or copying of fragile items.

Restorative Conservation: Those measures taken to repair or restore damaged or deteriorated archival (and other) material to its original condition. In doing this, it is important that the evidential value of the original be retained, and consequently repairs are usually reversible and visible.

Conservator

A person professionally responsible for the physical preservation of archival (and other) materials.

Copyright

The exclusive right, granted by law, of the creator of a work (or his/her assignees or employers) to make or dispose of copies of and otherwise to control the use of a literary, dramatic, musical, artistic or other work. Ownership of copyright in a work does not necessarily pass with ownership of the work itself. The laws relating to copyright are complex and require specialist legal advice.

Creator

The person or agency which creates or brings into existence *documents* and *records*.

Cull

The removal of selected *documents* from a *series* because they lack *archival value*. Also referred to as weeding or stripping.

Custody

The responsibility for the care of records, archives or other material, based on their physical possession. Custody does not always include legal ownership, or the right to control *access* to records.

Deaccession

The process of removing material from the care and custody of an archives, either because the material has been reappraised and found to be unsuitable for the archives' collections, or because the legal owner has requested its return, or because it has been agreed to transfer it to another repository. Deaccessioning is a serious matter which requires careful consideration and documentation. See *Accession*.

Deacidification

The process of eliminating *acidity* in documents and other materials, or reducing the acidity to a more acceptable level.

Dehumidify

The process of reducing the *relative humidity* in the atmosphere. See *Humidity, Relative humidity*.

Description

The process of recording information about the nature and content of the records in archival custody. The description identifies such features as *provenance, arrangement, format* and *contents*, and presents them in a standardised form. See *Arrangement*.

Disaster plan

A document which sets out the measures to be taken to minimise the risks and effects of disasters such a fire, flood, or earthquake, etc. and to recover, save and secure the vital records should such a disaster occur. It is part of *preventative conservation*.

Disposal

1) The final decision concerning the fate of records, i.e. destruction or transfer to archives.

2) A programme of activities to facilitate the *orderly* transfer of *intermediate* and *inactive* records from current office space into low cost or archival storage. It includes surveys, scheduling and records destruction.

Disposal schedule

A systematic listing of records created by an organisation which plans the life of these records from the time of their creation to their disposal.

A disposal schedule lists:

- the records *series* created by the agency;
- the *retention period* for each series;
- the *disposal sentence* for each series, specifying whether the records are to be retained as archives or destroyed;
- the *custody* arrangements for each series, specifying when the records are to be transferred to *intermediate storage* and/or to archives.

Documentary value see Archival value — *Evidential Value*

Documentation

1) The organisation and processing of written *descriptions* of records and archives for the information of users, resulting in *finding aids*.

2) In relation to *machine-readable records:* The organised series of descriptive documents which explain the operating system and software necessary to maintain and use data contained in machine-readable form.

3) The policies, procedures, forms and reports which provide evidence of the programmes, functions, work activities and commitments of an organisation.

Documentation programme

A programme of regular activities designed to identify, re-record, and possibly create records or information for inclusion in the archives' collections.

Document

The smallest complete unit of record material which is accumulated to form a *file*, i.e. a letter, photograph, report.

Donation

A voluntary deposit of records, involving the transfer of legal ownership as well as *custody* to the archives.

Donor

A person or organisation who has donated records to the archives.

Electronic data processing (EDP) see Automatic data processing

Encapsulation

The process of encasing a document in a polyester envelope, the edges of which are then sealed. The aim is to provide support for a fragile document which needs to remain visible.

Ephemera

Items, usually printed or manufactured in quantity for a specific event or activity, which are intended neither to survive the topicality of that event or activity nor to survive as original records, but which may be retained for their information or as graphic specimens.

Estray

A record or document which has been alienated from the possession of its legitimate custodian.

Facsimile

A reproduction of a document or item, that is similar in appearance to, but not necessarily of the same size as, the original.

File

An organised unit of *documents*, accumulated during current use and kept together because they dealt with the same subject, activity or transaction.

Film–based records see **Non–textual records**

Financial value see **Archival value** — *Fiscal Value*

Finding aids

1) The descriptive media, published and unpublished, created by an archival repository, to establish physical or administrative and intellectual control over records and other holdings. Basic finding aids include guides (general or repository and subject or topical), descriptive inventories, accession registers, card catalogues, special lists, shelf and box lists, indexes, and, for machine–readable records, software documentation.

2) The registers, indexes, and filing system guides produced by the organisation or person who created the records, usually referred to as 'control records' or 'contemporaneous finding aids'.

Fiscal value see **Archival value**

Format

1) The physical medium in which information is recorded or carried, e.g. paper files, computer printout, photographs, microfilm, machine–readable records, plans, cards, volumes, etc.

2) A selection of descriptive elements set out in a prescribed manner and sequence so that the resulting description will be standardised for all types of records.

Historical value see **Archival value**

Holdings

The whole of the records and archival materials in the custody of an archives.

Humidification

The process of adding moisture to the atmosphere, usually to correct an excessively dry environment, or to reduce brittleness in paper. See also *Humidity, Relative humidity*.

Humidity

The concentration of moisture in the atmosphere. See *Relative humidity*.

Inactive records

Those records no longer required for the conduct of business and which may therefore be transferred to archival custody or destroyed. See *Disposal*.

Informational value see **Archival value**

Intellectual control

The control established over the informational content of records and archives resulting from ascertaining and document-ing their provenance, and from the processes of *arrangement* and *description*.

Intermediate records

Those records that are required so infrequently in the conduct of current business that they can be transferred from offices to sep-arate storage areas. Sometimes referred to as 'non-current records' or 'semi-current records'. See *Disposal*.

Intermediate storage

A low-cost, warehouse-style repository or storage area where *semi-current* or *intermediate records* are housed and referenced pending their ultimate destruction or transfer to archives.

Item

1) The standard component of a *series* (i.e. a file in a series of files; a volume in a series of volumes; etc.)

2) A component in an *accession* of sufficient size or importance to warrant individual listing in documentation describing the contents of the accession.

3) Sometimes the term is also used as equivalent to *document*.

Legal value see **Archival value**

Location index

A *finding aid* listing every *accession* or *series* and giving its location in the *repository*. Where *items* within an accession or series are stored in different locations (because of their size or format or for some other reason), they should be separately listed in the location index.

Machine readable records

Those records created and maintained in such a way that the information they contain is inaccessible without the aid of the appropriate machine, e.g. sound recordings (both discs and tapes), video recordings, and computer tapes and discs.

Magnetic tape

A storage medium consisting of a polyester base and a metallic coating on which data is stored by selective magnetisation of the surface of the coating.

Manuscript library/repository see **Archives**

Memorabilia see **Artefacts**

Microclimate

The environment (temperature, *relative humidity* and air move-ment) contained within a confined space, such as inside an archives box or display case.

Microfiche see **Micrographics**

Microfilm see **Micrographics**

Microfilm jacket see **Micrographics**
Microforms see **Micrographics**
Micrographics

The use of photographic processes to produce reduced size images (usually too small to be read without magnification) of textual or graphic material on high resolution fine grain film stock. Formats more commonly produced are:

Aperture Cards: Cards containing an aperture or window in which is inserted a single frame of *microfilm,* usually used for mounting images of maps and plans. The cards allow the recording of information about each individual image and also allow images to be used independently of each other.

COM (Computer Output Microforms): Computer output produced directly as *microfilm* or *microfiche* without the need for a paper printout.

Microfiche: A flexible transparent sheet of film containing a number of images sequentially arranged in rows and columns.

Microfilm: A film in roll form, usually 16mm or 35mm in width.

Microfilm jacket: A transparent holder into which individual strips of *microfilm,* usually 16mm, can be inserted.

Nitrate film see **Cellulose nitrate film**
Non–current records see **Intermediate records**
Non–textual records

Items that are of a pictorial or graphic nature, as opposed to written or textual, e.g. photographs, films, illustrations, diagrams, plans, etc.

Optical disc

A specially coated disc onto which information is recorded in analogue or digital form by a laser. The information can be retrieved by having a laser read the disc and the result decoded by a microprocessor into sounds or images.

Original order

The order in which *records* and *archives* were kept when in active use. The principle of original order requires that the original order be preserved or reconstructed, unless it is absolutely clear that there was no original order and that the records had been accumulated haphazardly.

Physical control

The control established over the physical aspects (such as *format,* quantity and location) of the individual records in an *accession* or *series.*

Preservation see **Conservation**
Preventative conservation see **Conservation**
Primary value see **Evidential value**
Privacy

The right of a living person to be secure from the unauthorised disclosure of or access to information of a private or confidential nature about himself/herself or his/her immediate family contained in records and archives.

Provenance
1) The office or person of origin of records, i.e. the entity which created or accumulated and used the records in the conduct of business or personal life.
2) The chain of custody which reflects the office(s) or person(s) that created, received or accumulated and used the records in the conduct of business or in the course of personal life. Identifying and documenting the provenance of records is an essential part of establishing their authenticity and integrity as evidence.
3) In archival theory, the principle of provenance requires that the archives of an organisation or person not be mixed or combined with the archives of another.

Public programs see **User education**

Records
Documents, containing data or information of any kind and in any form, created or received by an organisation or person for use in the course of business and subsequently kept as evidence of such business.

Records centre see **Repository**

Records management
The area of general administrative management concerned with the design and operation of programmes to achieve economy and efficiency in the creation, distribution, organisation, maintenance, retrieval, use, protection and *disposal* of all types of records.

Records manager
A person professionally responsible for records management programmes.

Reference
The range of activities involved in providing information about or from records and archives, e.g. making records and archives available for *access* and providing copies or reproductions of records and archives.

Register
(n.) A log or list of brief descriptions of matters or things (accessions, letters sent or received, actions taken) usually in a single sequence (chronological or numerical) which serves as a *finding aid* to the matters or things listed.
(v.) The process of formally recording information in a register.

Registry
Literally, an office responsible for maintaining one or more *registers*. Commonly used to denote the sub-unit responsible for the creation, control and maintenance in files of the active and semi-current records of an organisation.

Relative humidity
The ratio, expressed as a percentage, of the amount of water-vapour present in the atmosphere to the amount required to saturate it at the same temperature. Relative humidity varies with temperature.

Repository

The building or room, or part thereof, set aside for the storage of archives and/or intermediate records. Archival repositories are often constructed to meet specific environmental standards designed to ensure the longevity of the records.

Reprography

The full range of processes used to replicate or copy documents by optical or photographic means. Reprography includes photocopying, photoduplication, microphotography, photography and the family of printing processes.

Restoration see **Conservation**

Restorative conservation see **Conservation**

Restriction see **Access**

Retention period

The period of time, usually based on an estimate of the frequency of current and future use, and taking into account statutory and regulatory provisions, that records need to be retained before their final *disposal.* Sometimes used to indicate the length of time records are to be retained in offices before being transferred to *intermediate storage.*

Secondary value see **Archival value** — *Informational Value*

Semi-current records see **Intermediate Records**

Series

Those records or archives having the same *provenance* which belong together because:

- they are part of a discernible filing system (alphabetical, numerical, chronological, or a combination of these),
- they have been kept together because they result from the same activity, or
- they are of similar formats and relate to a particular function.

Survey

1) An examination of archival records to ascertain their *provenance, original order* and *inter-relationships* prior to commencing full *arrangement* and *description* processes.

2) An examination of *active* or *intermediate* records noting briefly their nature, systems of arrangement, date ranges, quantities, function, physical condition, reference activity and rates of accumulation. This information is used to develop disposal schedules, plan conservation, or project space requirements, among other uses.

User Education

The education and training of actual and potential users of archives in matters such as the availability of material and services, the use of finding aids, the use and interpretation of archives, and the value and importance of archives and archival work.

Vital records

Those records which are essential for the ongoing business of an agency, and without which the agency could not continue to function effectively. The identification and protection of such records is a primary object of *records management* and *disaster planning.*

ABOUT
THE AUTHORS

GUNNEL BELLVIKEN
Co–author of Chapter *Getting Organised*. BA Upsala University,
Archives Science Course Stockholm University, Diploma in
Information Management — Archives Administration University
of NSW. Currently Archives Documentation Officer with the
Council of the City of Sydney. Previously worked as an Archivist
for the City Archives of Vasteras, Sweden and also briefly for the
National Archives, Sweden, the Royal Technical Academy,
Stockholm, Sweden and the Archives of the University of NSW.
Assisted the Secretary with ASA membership records
1985–1987.

PAUL BRUNTON
Member of the Editorial Board and co–author of Chapters
Accessioning and *Arrangement and Description*. BA University
of Sydney, Diploma in Librarianship University of NSW. Currently
Manuscripts Librarian, Mitchell Library, State Library of NSW.
Book Reviews Editor of *Archives and Manuscripts*, 1983–1987.
Contributor to several publications on archives and ASA Confer-
ence Proceedings. Council member of the ASA for three terms
and former Convenor of its Sydney Branch.

AVERIL CONDREN
Author of Appendix on *Indexing,* and of the *Index*. BA(Hons)
from London and MA(Hons) from Sydney University; PCE London, Diploma Information Management — Archives Administration University of NSW. Currently enrolled for PhD on the
history and theory of archives. Beit Scholar; first winner of
Metcalfe Medallion (1985). Foundation archivist Abbotsleigh
School; also currently archivist for Community Research

Archives University of NSW. Formerly archival consultant for ARGC project at La Trobe University; freelance researcher; sometime visiting lecturer, University of NSW. Various papers published in international symposia and journals, in the fields of the history of ideas, literary criticism and archival studies. Several published indexes. Ongoing research (additional to PhD) computer based analysis of seventeenth century political bibliography.

SANDRA HINCHEY

Co-author of Chapter *Access and Reference Services*. BA in history and sociology and Diploma in Archives Administration University of NSW. Currently employed as the Archivist of the State Bank of Victoria. Formerly held the positions of Research Officer in the Archives/Records Management Section of the Reserve Bank of Australia and Archives Officer for the Council of the City of Sydney. An active member of ASA Inc. participating in seminars and workshops held by the Sydney and Melbourne Branches of the ASA Inc and Honorary Treasurer for the 1985–1987 Biennium.

SIGRID McCAUSLAND

Member of the Editorial Board and co-author of chapters *Finding Aids* and *Access and Reference Services*. BA(Hons) in history Australian National University, Diploma in Information Management — Archives Administration University of NSW, enrolled in the Master in Archives Administration programme. Experience includes several years in Australian Archives, ACT Regional Office, followed by two years in the Manuscripts Section of the Mitchell Library, State Library of NSW. Currently Tutor, School of Librarianship, University of NSW, teaching archives administration. ASA Council Member (1983–85), Convenor, Sydney Branch 1984–85. Involved in organising Keeping Archives workshops in country areas of NSW 1986–.

KATHLEEN OAKES

Member of the Editorial Board and co-author of Chapter *Finding Aids*. BA(Hons) University of Sydney. Diploma in Archives Administration, University of NSW. Currently Assistant to the Pro-Vice-Chancellor, University of NSW. Previously Assistant Archivist, University of NSW; Archivist, CBC Bank, Sydney and Archives Clerk, Australian Archives, Canberra. Co-author of *Women in Australian Society 1901–1945 A Guide to Archival Material relating to women in Australian Archives (1977)*. Author of reviews in *Archives and Manuscripts*. Former Secretary ASA Sydney Branch. Vice-President ASA 1985–1987, with responsibility for educational matters.

ANN PEDERSON

Editor-in-Chief and author of Chapters *User Education and Public Relations* and *Documentation Programmes*. BA(cum laude) in history from Ohio Wesleyan University, MA(research) in history from Georgia State University, PhD in Archives Administration (in progress) from the University of NSW. Currently Lecturer in Archives Administration and Records Management, School of Librarianship, University of NSW. Former Director of Archives Division, Georgia Department of Archives and History. Co-author of *Archives and Manuscripts: Public Programs* for the Society of American Archivists. Author of articles and reviews in *Georgia Archive*. Former editor of *Georgia Archive*, now *Provenance*, and director/writer of several multi-media productions about or using archival resources. Guest lecturer for Modern Archives Institute, National Archives and Records Administration (US) and Georgia Archives Institute (US).

MICHAEL PIGGOTT

Author of Chapter *Conservation*. BEc(Hons) Monash University, Diploma in Librarianship Canberra College of Advanced Education and Bachelor of Letters, Australian National University. At present researching T.R. Schellenberg's visit to Australia in 1954 as a thesis topic for the Master in Archives Administration from the University of NSW. Senior Curator, Written Records Section, Australian War Memorial. Former positions include Librarian, Manuscripts Section, National Library of Australia. Author of various articles, book reviews and guides on several subjects, notably sources for military history. Co-author of *Commonwealth Government Information* to be published in 1987. Secretary/Treasurer ASA Canberra Branch 1977–1978, Convenor 1979–1980, Member of ASA Fifth Biennial Conference Committee, 1985.

BARBARA REED

Author of the Chapter *Acquisition and Appraisal*. MA(Hons) University of Melbourne, BA(Hons) University of Sydney, Diploma in Archives Administration University of NSW, ARMA, ALAA. Since 1985 a consultant archivist and records manager in Sydney. Previous experience with Australian Archives, Central Office and ACT Regional Office in Canberra and in the Records Management Section of the University of Melbourne. Contributor of articles and book reviews to *Records Management Quarterly* and *Archives and Manuscripts*. Secretary of the ASA Canberra Branch 1980–81, member of ASA Council and Technology Contact Pearson 1983–1985 and Secretary ASA 1985–1987.

DAVID ROBERTS

Author of Chapter *Use of Computers and Micrographics*. BA University of Sydney and Diploma in Archives Administration University of NSW. Presently the archivist in charge of machine-readable records in the NSW Regional Office of the Australian Archives. Prior to this he worked primarily with audio-visual records. An active member of the ASA, having served as Convenor of the Sydney Branch, and author of a number of articles and reviews on audio-visual and machine-readable records.

TIM ROBINSON

Member of the Editorial Board, and co-author of Chapters *Accessioning* and *Arrangement and Description*. BA(Hons), specialising in Australian history Macquarie University, Diploma in Information Management — Archives Administration University of NSW. Currently College Archivist, Sydney College of Advanced Education. Previous positions include Archives Systems Officer, Council of City of Sydney Archives and Archivist, Society of Australian Genealogists. Former Convenor ASA Sydney Branch, ASA Council Member 1985–1987. Involved in ASA Sydney Branch's Keeping Archives Workshop Programme, part of the NSW Bicentennial Council's Conservation on the Move Project.

ANNE–MARIE SCHWIRTLICH

Author of Chapter *Introducing Archives and the Archival Profession* and co-author of Chapter *Getting Organised*. BA(Hons) Macquarie University, Diploma in Information Management — Archives Administration, University of NSW. Undertaking Master in Archives Administration from the University of NSW. Presently Assistant Director, Personal Archives and Special Projects in the ACT Regional Office of Australian Archives. Previously held several positions within Australian Archives, NSW Regional Office. Author of articles in *Archives and Manuscripts* and contributor to ASA workshop proceedings. Co-editor of *Our Heritage: A Directory to Archives and Manuscripts Repositories in Australia* (1983). An active member of the ASA in Sydney and Canberra. Secretary ASA 1983–1985.

CLIVE SMITH

Author of *Glossary*. BA(Asian Studies) Australian National University, Master of Archives Administration (in progress) from the University of NSW. Currently Senior Archivist, Westpac Banking Corporation, Sydney. Formerly with Australian Archives, Canberra, in various positions including Archivist, Survey and Disposal, ACT Regional Office, and Senior Project Officer, Disposal (Procedures and Standards), Central Office. Contributor to series of articles on 'Archives and Administrative Change: Some Methods and Approaches' by P.J. Scott in *Archives and Manuscripts*. Treasurer, ASA Inc. 1981–1983, President 1985–1987.

INDEX

Averil Condren

INTRODUCTION TO THE INDEX

Basic considerations:

When constructing the INDEX I kept in mind that *KEEPING ARCHIVES* is intended for a non-professional as well as a professional audience. This has led to the following strategies:–

1) A number of non-technical terms have been used as leads to the technical terms with which they are cross-referenced.

2) A second index to figures, i.e. to BOXES and TABLES, has been included. This is supplementary to the main subject index (all the entries will be found in the main index under the appropriate subject heading). It is intended only as a quick access tool to the summarised information and the facsimile documents or forms, which the figures present.

3) Because the CONTENTS present the main topical divisions, and serve as a form of index to chapters, these main divisions were generally **not used** as index terms. Thus there is no main entry for 'finding aids'. Instead the reader will find entries for 'bridging aids', 'descriptive inventories', etc. thus providing quicker access to specific types of finding aids.

Technical considerations:

1) The number of cross-references has been kept to the bare minimum. All archival activity is related and systematic, and comprehensive cross-referencing would have overloaded the index. As a corollary to this decision, some entries have been inserted twice under the subject headings where both provide an appropriate entry.

2) Photographic illustrations have not been indexed. Since there are a great many of them, and in most cases they are so closely tied to the text, a separate entry would have been superfluous.

3) All PROPER NAMES of persons or institutions are in capitals; all other entries are in lower case.

4) Subject entries have been standardised; synonyms have been cross-referenced.

5) Alphabetical order is word-by-word.

GENERAL INDEX

INDEX TO TABLES, BOXES, APPENDICES, ETC.